CROSSROADS ARE FOR MEETING

Crossroads Are For Meeting

Essays on the Mission and Common Life
of the Church in a Global Society

Edited by
Philip Turner and Frank Sugeno

Sewanee
S·P·C·K / U·S·A   1986

ISBN: 0-933667-01-9

LCCCN: 85-50770

To Edward A. Bayne

This book is dedicated to Mr. Edward A. Bayne, a layman whose life and work epitomize the global awareness on which life—for Christians as for other citizens of the world—depends in these latter days of the twentieth century. His professional career, spanning several decades and covering vast areas of the world's geography, found its center in Rome, where for a quarter century he was active in St. Paul's Church and in the fledgling Anglican Centre.

His sense of history and his vision for the future mission of the Church resulted in the idea of the Pan-Anglican Symposium on the Theology of Mission. As a member of the Episcopal Church's Standing Commission on World Mission, he saw the value of setting time apart for representatives from around the world to conduct a serious discussion of the theological grounds for the Church's mission in a postcolonial era. And as an active churchman in the diocese of Connecticut, he proposed to its Committee on World Mission that the symposium be a part of the diocese's two hundredth anniversary celebration. When both bodies and the 1982 General Convention agreed to sponsor the event, it seemed natural to invite the Scottish Episcopal Church to be a cosponsor. Bishop Alastair Haggart, the Primus, assumed major leadership in convening the gathering, bringing his strong experience with the Anglican Consultative Council.

Special recognition must go to the Board of the Church Missions Publishing Company in Connecticut for its willingness to commit substantial funding to the project. Major additional support was provided by the Episcopal Church Foundation and the Standing Commission on World Mission and by several individuals.

The Right Reverend Arthur E. Walmsley

Bishop of Connecticut and Chairman
of the Pan-Anglican Symposium

Contents

The Nature of Christian Mission

Mission and the Common Life of the Church

Foreword

I welcome this collection of essays written by Anglican authors from many different churches of our Communion. All the authors, writing from very different standpoints, have enabled us to share with them their special concerns, whether it be mission and liturgy, mission and culture, or mission and liberation theology. Professors Turner and Sugeno have written a very helpful introduction to the symposium.

The conclusions reinforce the four major elements of mission that were identified by the Anglican Consultative Council in Nigeria as:

1. To proclaim the good news of the Kingdom
2. To teach, baptize, and nurture the new believers
3. To respond to human needs by loving service
4. To labor for justice within and among nations

These essays are forthright and demanding, yet at the same time they are deeply reflective and theological. The authors have skillfully described to us just how far we have moved away from the limitations and dependency of the colonial era. Yet we still have to discover what the Spirit is calling our Church to become in this new interdependent world. Mission is now becoming increasingly ecumenical; and as these essays reveal, there are already in existence a whole new range of Anglican initiatives that we need to understand better and share more fully.

At the Lambeth Conference in 1988, we shall have to immerse ourselves in the consideration of a vast range of needs, dilemmas, and priorities. These writers will help us greatly to begin to focus our minds, and to see some of the pressing issues of our time from the widest Anglican perspective.

I gladly commend their work for prayerful study and discussion throughout the Anglican Communion.

The Archbishop of Canterbury
*The Most Reverend and Right
Honorable Robert Runcie*

Acknowledgments

Mr. David Andrews

The Reverend John S. Barton

Eileen Brady

Mr. J. Revell Carr and the staff of Mystic Seaport

Miss Peggy Chisholm

Church Missions Publishing Co.

Mrs. Ann Cooke

The Reverend Douglas T. Cooke

The Right Reverend A. Donald Davies

Mr. Don Keck DuPree

The Episcopal Church Foundation

Mrs. Beverly Fawcett

Sister Rosemarie Franklin, M.M.

The Reverend Canon James R. Gundrum

Mrs. Ann Gushee and the staff of Trinity College

The Very Reverend Stephen H. Gushee

The Most Reverend and Mrs. Alastair I. M. Haggart

Mrs. Carman St. John Hunter

Mr. Constancio de Jesus

Mr. Jerry Kelly

Ms. Rosa Lindahl

The Reverend Molly O. Louden

Mr. and Mrs. Clifford Mallory

Mr. D. Barry Menuez

Mr. John Christopher Pell

Mr. Frederick L. Redpath

The Reverend Francis Roberge, Sister Marcella, and the staff of
    Holy Family Retreat House

Mrs. Linda Ross

Dr. Anne Rowthorn

Dr. Timothy F. Sedgwick

The TypeWorks

Mrs. Roberta C. Walmsley

Mrs. Christine Wheeler

Preface

While SPCK is well known as a publishing house in England, and although publishing is not presently on our agenda in the United States, we offer this volume as a contribution to the ongoing debate about mission in the Anglican Communion. The diversity of views expressed reflect some of the many stances taken by Anglicans as we explore our understanding of our global task in response to our Lord's Great Commission.

The positions taken by the authors of the papers in this symposium are their own and do not necessarily reflect those of the Board of Trustees or staff of SPCK/USA. Nevertheless, each stimulates and challenges in a different manner. In a rapidly changing world the Church is called to respond afresh to a breadth of circumstances, and our contributors have certainly done that. For their hard work and seminal thinking, we express our gratitude.

Finally, I would like to thank Doctors Philip Turner and Frank Sugeno for their work in editing this volume, and Mr. Frederic C. Beil III for preparing it for publication. As the 1988 Lambeth Conference of Bishops approaches, may the content of this book play a small part in stimulating their thinking, discussions, and prayers.

The Reverend W. Richard Kew
Executive Director, SPCK/USA
Sewanee, Tennessee
November 14, 1985
Feast of the consecration of Samuel Seabury,
first American bishop, 1784.

Mr. Christopher Templeton
Mr. John M. Templeton
Mr. Thomas S. Tisdale, Jr.
The Reverend Canon Samuel Van Culin
The Reverend Clifford S. Waller
Mr. Tom G. Watson
The Right Reverend David Young

THE REVEREND W. RICHARD KEW, EXECUTIVE DIRECTOR
MRS. KAREN CRIPPEN, ADMINISTRATIVE ASSISTANT

Introduction

At the invitation of the Right Reverend Arthur E. Walmsley, bishop of Connecticut, and the Most Reverend Alastair I. M. Haggart, primus of Scotland, a number of Anglicans from Africa, Asia, Latin America, North America, Oceania, and the United Kingdom gathered in Hartford, Connecticut, from September 1 through September 10, 1984, to participate in a symposium on the mission of the Church. The symposium was held as a part of the celebrations marking the two hundredth anniversary of the consecration of Bishop Samuel Seabury, the first bishop of an Anglican diocese located outside the British Isles.

The consecration of Bishop Seabury by the bishops of the Scottish Episcopal Church marked one of the first and most important events in the history of the Anglican Communion. Because the growth of this communion has played such an important role in the modern expansion of Christianity, a conference designed to bring to light the various views of mission now prevalent within it seemed an appropriate way to honor Bishop Seabury's memory.

A symposium on the mission of the Church also seemed a way to help the Anglican Communion prepare for the next Lambeth Conference of Bishops to be held in 1988. At that conference the nature of the Church's mission will be one of the most significant issues. There are a host of voices calling for mission to be given a more important place in the life of the Church. Many believe that the predominantly pastoral model of the Church that Anglicans inherit from their establishmentarian roots needs now to be balanced by a model of the Church that is shaped more by a concern for the Church's mission.

History has thrown a question at the entire Anglican Communion—a question that thrusts all its member churches out of the nest and forces them to ask how they ought to understand themselves. More particularly, what place ought mission to play in that self-understanding? There are a number of answers being given to this question. The essays collected here will not end the debate that has begun, but they do make clear most of the issues involved.

Clearly, the nature of the Church's mission is an ecumenical concern. To argue or behave otherwise is to encourage factionalism and confessional rivalry. By sponsoring a "Pan Anglican" symposium, it was not the intention of anyone to encourage partisanship. It was the belief of the architects of the symposium, however, that each Christian throughout the world comes from a particular tradition that exerts a powerful influence upon them. Further, the designers of the conference believed that each Christian tradition has particular gifts to offer a uniting Church and that each has certain aspects of both belief and practice that hinder common life and witness. It is well to be aware of the strengths and weaknesses of one's own tradition. In the hope of gaining such self-knowledge and so clearing the way for an effective Anglican contribution to the mission of the whole Church, the symposium was planned and brought together.

In order to focus discussion and promote fruitful debate, each person invited to the symposium was asked, prior to arrival, to consider four questions:

1. What is the mission of Christ's Church?
2. How is the Church in the particular setting about which you are writing related to the social order?
3. How might the common life of the Church in your area be formed so as more effectively to carry out its mission?
4. From the perspective of the Church in your area (nation, region, culture), in what ways are the Anglican heritage and the Anglican Communion a help or a hindrance to mission?

A number of members of the symposium were asked also to prepare papers focusing on one or more of these questions and to make their work available to the other participants as a basis for discussion and debate. These papers are contained in this volume.

If these essays are to be rightly understood, one ought to note first of all that they are the work of authors who represent not only different churches and cultures but also different vocations within the Church. Some are lay and others clerical. Some are professional theologians and some are bishops or executive officers. By design, this collection is not the work of professional missiologists. Its purpose is not to bring together the opinions of those whose business it is to think, teach, or write about the mission of the Church. Its purpose is to make available representative positions from within the Anglican Communion and to bring to light points of both unity and diversity, convergence and divergence. The aim of these essays is not to further an academic debate, but to further a crucial discussion that is going on at all levels of the life of the Church.

The simple fact that these essays are the product of people of such diverse background and calling means that they should be read as a text or picture of the times—as a representation of a spectrum of opinion. If they are looked at in this way, they will help us locate where at present the Anglican Communion is in its thinking about the mission of the Church.

As commentators on these essays, we have presented them here in a particular order. The sequence we have chosen represents, however, only one choice out of many possible ones. The essays were not written to be presented in a particular order. Each reader is in consequence invited to arrange or rearrange them as he or she sees fit. Each arrangement will represent another interpretation or another way of listening to the discussion.

No matter how one may choose to order and interpret these essays, however, one thing will stand out. The Anglican Communion has come to a crossroads and must ask in which way God wants it to walk. It must ask how it is to understand itself in relation to God's mission.

These essays reveal a moment of crisis—a point of judgment and decision that cannot be avoided. It is best to let the authors here assembled describe in their own words how they see the crisis, but as editors we can say that it has been in the making for a number of years.

The issues with which these essays deal, first began to present themselves at the time of the Enlightenment. It was then that the unique place of Christianity in world history was first challenged in the West. It was then that Westerners began to look at religion in an historical way and to regard it as yet another human phenomenon to be studied by means of science.

The imperialistic expansion of Europe from the sixteenth through the nineteenth centuries only made the questions more pressing. Colonial history had the ironic effect of bringing into question the centrality of both European civilization and religion. As more was known about other cultures and other religions, a triumphalist view of the Church became more and more difficult to defend. Religious and moral relativism became more and more powerful opponents of the exclusivist claims the Christian Church had for centuries made.

The social revolutions of the twentieth century and the collapse of the old European empires have added another element to the crisis. It is increasingly obvious that fewer and fewer people enjoy more and more of the world's wealth. Christians from the churches spawned in the wake of colonial expansion now throw back to their brothers and sisters to the North and West questions about the moral and social implications of Christian belief that demand an answer with just as much urgency as the question spawned by the encounter of Christianity with other world religions.

Historical developments like these have placed all Christian churches at a cross in the road wherein they must ask once more about the nature of their mission upon earth. It is this question that these essays seek to answer.

Anglicanism always has been shaped more by a book of common prayer than by a doctrinal confession or a clerical hierarchy. Dr. Micks, professor of biblical and historical theology at Virginia Theological Seminary in the United States, rightly assumes that if one wishes to identify the mainstream of Anglican thinking about the mission of the Church one would be wise to study first the forms of public worship now in use. In her essay, "Mission and Prayer," she concentrates her efforts on the *Book of Common Prayer* as it has evolved and been revised in the Episcopal Church, U.S.A.

On the basis of an analysis of what the Daily Offices, the rites of the Holy Eucharist, the calendar, and the catechism say about the mission of the Church, Dr. Micks concludes that the concept of mission that now obtains in the Episcopal Church is not single but "multiple." The bulk of the papers that follow suggest a similar conclusion about Anglican churches in other parts of the world, but Dr. Micks's analysis of public worship offers an empirical method for the validation of this conclusion and an indication that diversity of vision and belief about an issue even as fundamental as the nature of the mission of the Church need not be a cause of disunity. If multiplicity can be contained in public worship, it can be contained in all dimensions of the life of the Church.

This conclusion warrants some emphasis because, despite an Anglican tendency to contain rather than eliminate diversity, Anglican forms of public worship have not always reflected such diversity in respect to the nature of the Church's mission. Thus, as Dr. Micks points out, there are two prayers for mission in the American *Book of Common Prayer* of 1892. These prayers are the "Prayer for All Sorts and Conditions of Men" and the special collect "For Missions." The first of these dates from the eighteenth century and reflects England's colonial expansion. The second dates from the nineteenth century and reflects America's own colonial ambitions.

The "Prayer for All Sorts and Conditions of Men" asks that "God's ways be known upon earth and his saving health [salvation] among all nations." The special collect for missions asks that God "bring the nations into [His] fold and add the heathen to [His] inheritance." The collect asks further that God "accomplish the number of [His] elect." The social and political motivation behind these prayers (the first concerning the mission of the Church to appear in Anglican forms of public worship) may well have been colonialism, but in both cases the mission of the Church is understood as a matter of evangelism and Christian instruction—as a task of making God's salvation and God's ways as revealed in Christ known. There is no diversity of opinion about this matter reflected in either of the prayers.

The revision of the *Book of Common Prayer* that appeared in 1928 did, however, add a diverse note. In the 1928 book, this new collect appears:

> Almighty God, our heavenly Father, guide, we beseech thee, the Nations of the world into the way of justice and truth, and establish among them that peace which is the fruit of righteousness, that they may become the Kingdom of our Lord and Saviour Jesus Christ.

In commenting on the meaning of this prayer, Dr. Micks says that "It suggests that God's mission has as much to do with justice and peace among nations as with 'Christianity'." She goes on to say that "It opens the door to new thinking about the relationship between religious pluralism and Jesus Christ." Dr. Micks suggests, in short, that a different view of mission is, in the 1928 book, contained alongside the more traditional one. According to this more recent view, the mission of the Church includes a struggle for justice within and among nations. Further, the mission of the Church may require dialogue about the nature of God and salvation rather than bringing to others power and knowledge to which they otherwise have no access.

In noting this development, Dr. Micks puts her finger on a view of mission that is by no means limited to American Episcopalians. Mission as evangelism or mission as service and dialogue are competing views that appear again and again throughout the essays collected here. Diversity of opinion about the nature of the Church's mission is by no means limited to American Episcopalians.

The division of opinion hinted at in the 1928 *Book of Common Prayer* appears clearly in the new book approved in 1979. A striking thing about the new book, however, is not simply the diversity of views it contains but also the vastly increased importance it gives to the theme of mission. As Dr. Micks says, "Whereas in 1928 advances in liturgical attention to mission were minimal, by 1979 an explosion had occurred." The new book reflects not only changes in our understanding of mission, but also changes in the importance assigned to it.

The movement of Anglicanism from being identical with the Church of England to being a global communion of churches has forced upon it an issue that was not a part of its original heritage. In considering its relation to its environing culture, the established church of a "Christian Nation" does not have to think over much about what it means to be "sent." Churches that exist in a religiously and culturally diverse environment and that have in large measure been spawned by the colonial expansion of a single nation do.

Given its increasing importance in the way the Church understands itself, it is vital to ask what specifically the new and multiple concept of mission is. In her review of the prayers connected with the Daily Offices, Dr. Micks notes that in the required versicles and responses the traditional emphasis on proclamation and instruction remains. In the six collects concerning mission that are now made available for use at morning and evening prayer, however, new themes begin to appear. Thus in the collects to be used in the morning, emphasis is placed on the mission given each person in his or her daily life and work. The collects imply that this work is carried out in the power of the Spirit of God and that through the same Spirit the whole Church is given power to reach out in love.

In the three collects provided for evening prayer the theme of loving service and fellowship predominates. Taken together, the collects for mission used in the morning and evening depict mission as a Spirit impelled, reaching out in love on the part of both individuals in their life and work and by an entire community of faith. The purpose of this reaching out is so that all people will love God and one another. As Dr. Micks says:

> Taken together, these six prayers . . . reflect an understanding of mission as centrally the work of God the Spirit, working through every Christian for the sake of all women and men on this planet. They invite us to recognize the Holy Spirit as "the chief actor in the historic mission of the Christian church," and also to recognize the enormous diversity of those who are "missionaries of the Holy Spirit." Indeed they call us to recognize the fact that the mission of the Spirit begins, continues, and ends in loving.

Mission is a Spirit impelled, reaching out in love. What specifically, however, is implied by this love? Dr. Micks's analysis of the Eucharist, calendar, and catechism shows that more emphasis is given to love expressed as service than to love expressed as proclamation.

The six forms provided for the Prayers of the People are all, according to the introductory rubric, to be offered for "The Universal Church, its members and its mission. . . ." Nonetheless, only form 5 mentions mission directly. In form 5 the congregation is invited to pray "For the mission of the Church, that in faithful witness it may preach the Gospel to the ends of the earth."

In the other five forms of intercession, the word mission does not appear. Dr. Micks notes, however, that a strong emphasis on peace and justice does. She concludes her analysis by saying:

> The cumulative effect of these appointed intercessions for "The Universal Church and its mission" weights the definition of mission on the side of ministry to the suffering. Preaching the Gospel to the ends of the earth is construed primarily in terms of loving outreach to human need.

The demand to preach the Gospel remains but the primary vehicle, for this proclamation appears to be loving service. The centrality of service, however, is an emphasis only. The catechism makes clear that the means of mission are indeed multiple. It insists that the mission of the Church is directed to all people and that its purpose is to restore the unity of all people with God and each other. The catechism insists also that each Christian is called to participate in the mission of the Church in a variety of ways: through prayer, worship, proclamation, the promotion of peace and justice and love.

Dr. Micks's essay is a useful starting point because it brings to light the fundamental tension in current Anglican thinking about the mission of the Church. Is mission to be thought of as proclamation with a view toward conversion or is it to be understood as loving service and dialogue designed to restore the unity of all people with God and one another?

Another essay that brings to light basic elements in current Anglican thinking is that of the Right Reverend Doctor David M. Gitari—"The Mission of the Church in East Africa." His essay is based upon a reading of what the New Testament has to say about the mission of the Church and is for our purposes instructive because it shows that the way in which Holy Scripture is interpreted and exposited is, like public worship, a good way to identify current opinion.

Bishop Gitari, representing the Church of the Province of Kenya, comes from a church with a strong evangelical tradition— a church that has in its past history understood mission as proclamation with a view toward conversion. Basing his argument on an interpretation of the New Testament rather than upon liturgy, Bishop Gitari defends an extended and more complex view of mission. In this respect, his essay is similar to that of Dr. Micks.

Bishop Gitari begins with the premise that mission first of all must be understood as God's. God "sends" Jesus to do His work and the Church is called and sent to participate in that work. The view that mission belongs first to God rather than to the Church is one shared by all the authors represented in this collection. This belief is, in consequence, a point of convergence in the midst of diversity and as such provides a basis upon which discussion and perhaps wider agreement can take place.

What then is involved in the mission that belongs first to God? Mission includes all that God sends Jesus to do. It, therefore, involves not only evangelism but also teaching, healing, and reconciling, and a responsibility to seek a transformed social order. In Bishop Gitari's words: "The mission of the Church then is to continue with the mission of Jesus in the world. Our mission to the world is to evangelize, witness, heal, feed the hungry, clothe the naked, challenge the injustices of this world, and bring about reconciliation in the troubled world." The project that Bishop Gitari undertakes is to show what the wider view of mission he advocates implies for the life of his own church. He clearly invites people from other churches to undertake the same sort of exercise.

One aspect of the position Bishop Gitari advocates warrants special attention. We are speaking of the suggestion contained throughout his article that the Church is to be a leaven within society. Bishop Gitari presupposes that the Church ought to be related to the wider society of which it is a part as a friendly adversary—a sort of social watchdog. Thus, he thinks of the Anglican heritage, in spite of the fact that in many ways it is foreign to the ways of East African peoples, as an asset because it has given the Church a place in national affairs. Despite the fact that the Church of the Province of Kenya is not established and even though Bishop Gitari apparently does not favor an established church, still he sees the heritage of establishment as a help rather than a hindrance.

In taking this position, Bishop Gitari presents a view of mission that clearly distinguishes the life of the Church from the life of society as a whole but does not at the same time manifest a sectarian mentality. His view of what is often called the social mission of the Church seems to be that the Church is called upon to be salt and light in the midst of society rather than a city set on a hill—a community both distinct and separate from the society that surrounds it. In taking this position, Bishop Gitari espouses another common theme that runs throughout these essays. Most Anglicans are no longer establishmentarian, but neither are they sectarian. In carrying out the mission of the Church they look for a more dialectical view of the relation between church and society than either establishmentarianism or sectarianism will allow.

Dr. Micks and Bishop Gitari both plead for an expanded view of mission. Lady Oppenheimer, a member of the Doctrinal Commission, Church of England, enters a cautionary note. In her essay, "Mission, Morals, and Folk Religion," she expresses a concern that if mission is made to include everything, it may in effect become nothing. She is, as a result, led to adopt the view that mission is a word that properly should be used to refer specifically to the duty of the Church to "spread the Gospel."

Lady Oppenheimer's essay is important because it asks about the impediments to spreading the Gospel among a people who once were Christian but who are now at best only marginally so. She asks about the mission of an established church in a secular society.

It is the juxtaposition of secularity and establishment that poses the issue of mission for the Church of England. In addressing what it might mean for an established church to "spread the Gospel" in a secular society, Lady Oppenheimer focuses her attention on three social facts that in her view hinder the British people from accepting the Christian message. These three facts are "polarization," "secularization," and "establishment." By "polarization" she refers to the tendency in both church and society to dismiss people with whom one disagrees and by so doing view them as hostile strangers rather than as friends who, in trying to work out solutions to common problems, may disagree.

The polarization of factions within the Church of England and within British society, she believes, hinders both the proclamation and the acceptance of the Christian message. Love, she insists, demands forgiveness, tolerance, and even delight in others. Her argument is that if the Church is not itself a community of love, its message of love can neither be spoken with power nor heard in faith. She makes the important point that "spreading the

Gospel" implies that the common life of the Church display in some way the Gospel it proclaims.

In her discussion of secularization and establishment, she focuses not on the practical aspects of Christian living but upon certain intellectual impediments to belief. If the Church is to spread the Gospel, it must take account of the secular mind. The secular point of view places a heavy emphasis both on equality and moral autonomy. To assert as many Christians do that God moves us about like so many pieces in a chess game is both false and offensive. All things in this world do not seem ordered for the best, and a view of providence that suggests that they are is not only suspect but off-putting. Lady Oppenheimer suggests, therefore, that if the Church of England wishes to "spread the Gospel" it should emphasize a doctrine of grace rather than providence. It should stress that God is with us always in love and mercy even if God does not intervene constantly so as to make this the best of all possible worlds or to bring about in all circumstances situations of which He approves.

The hindrance to mission that she sees in the Church's established position is that people belong without commitment. Most people are devotees not of Christianity but of a moralistic folk religion. Moralistic folk religion has as part of it the mechanical view of providence just mentioned. God rewards the good and punishes the bad. In combination, moralism and a distorted view of divine providence obscure the true nature of the Christian Gospel and so make it difficult both to spread and believe. Lady Oppenheimer's answer to the distortion of Christian belief is what she calls "a dose of deism." She argues for a theology that displays a God who is present with us in grace and mercy, but not as a puppeteer who moves our lives about at will.

Lady Oppenheimer pleads for a national church that seeks to spread the Gospel, but in a way that includes rather than excludes people. She wants a church of the nation that spreads the Gospel in a way that does not offend the best insights of the secular mind. Her essay makes clear that acceptance of the Christian message can be hindered not only by intolerance and narrowness, but also by an unconvincing presentation of Christian belief. There are genuine hindrances to belief, and these must be addressed by something more than unreflective fideism.

Lady Oppenheimer's essay is a plea for a Christian apologetic that is convincing and moving to the secular mind, and as such it displays a long-standing aspect of Anglican theology. The need for a convincing apologetic theology is one that might be easily overlooked in a time when so much attention is focused on religious experience, commitment, and the practical aspects of Christian service. Lady Oppenheimer's essay serves to remind the Church that it cannot give attention to mission and at the same time ignore the very real objections to belief that people have. We believe Lady Oppenheimer would agree that the objections present may be quite different in London than they are in Calcutta. The implication of her essay is that in both cases, indeed in all cases, objections must be taken seriously and addressed if the Church is indeed "to spread the Gospel."

In each of the previous essays the general assumption has been made that we can and ought to speak of the Church having a mission. Everyone knows, however, that the word "mission" has about it many negative connotations. The next two essays, one by the Reverend Pritam B. Santram, who is general secretary of the Church of North India Synod, and one by John S. Pobee, associate director of the Program for Theological Education of the World Council of Churches, contribute to our understanding of why the notion of a Christian mission is so problematic. Pritam Santram's essay even suggests that we look for another word to use when speaking of the work the Church is sent to do.

Father Santram's essay, "Mission of the Church in the Indian Context," suggests that it might be better to speak of "faithfulness" or "obedience" than to talk of the mission of the Church. He notes that "mission" is not really a New Testament word. Its use does not have behind it unambiguous biblical authority. What we need, he says, is a term that will express the idea of mission as "the overflow of the Christ experience."

What factors lead Father Santram in this direction? He notes that the words "missionary" and "mission" bring to the minds of Indians images and ideas from the colonial past and that it is difficult for the churches in India "to dissociate these words from their past colonial images and concepts so as to arrive at a contemporary and Indian understanding of 'missionary' and 'mission'." These words bring to mind such things as mission compounds, foreign funds, and foreign imperialism. In the past, mission was understood as a form of conquest in which conversion meant defeat—the replacement of one religion and culture by another. This view of mission bred a sense of inferiority, dependency, and resentment.

Father Santram in consequence searches for another way to

speak of what the Church in the Indian context is sent to do. He notes that there are images other than conquest by means of which one can speak of the work of the Church. One can picture Christian belief, life, and witness as a "completion" or "fulfillment" of the work of God everywhere. One can think also of the relation of Christians to people of other beliefs as a form of "dialogue" through which all learn to discern the witness of the Spirit of God that is present everywhere.

Only with these images in mind is Father Santram willing to speak of mission, and in doing so he insists that mission belongs to God. It is to be understood as God reaching out to us in the place where we live and in the culture by which we have been formed. What Father Santram means by God reaching out is captured most fully in the following paragraph:

> What is described as *missio Dei . . .* is not just a redemptive movement from God to the human family in a vacuum. It is a movement of God's self-giving, liberating power to the human race in the totality of life. It is oriented to particular historical situations and needs. And in the fullness of time it reaches out to the human family in a decisive way in "flesh" (John 1:14) completely identified with and relevant to a particular given historical, national, religious, and cultural context of the first-century Palestine.

The paradigmatic example of God reaching out is to be found in Christ. In Christ we see that God makes Himself known to us where we are. God's mission is incarnational and so implies that we struggle to see how God now reaches out to us in our own particular context.

Father Santram suggests at one point that this contextualization of God's mission implies that the claims made about Christ's uniqueness may need to be reexamined. He believes that reformed Hinduism, with its emphasis on tolerance and inclusiveness, is forcing this issue on Indian Christians.

Whatever the case may be, God's mission in the Indian context requires that in faithfulness, obedience, and the overflow of what Father Santram once calls "the Christ experience," Indian Christians look seriously at both their socioeconomic context and at their religious and cultural context. In respect to the first, God's reaching out implies for Christians that they struggle along with all people of good will to right the many injustices of Indian society. In respect to the second, God's reaching out implies not a conflict with other religions but with sin. What God asks is not conquest and conversion but "dialogue" so that people of all faiths can together struggle against the forces of evil and for a just and peaceful society.

Father Santram seeks to recast the understanding the churches of India have of the work they are sent to do. He does so because he believes the understanding of mission out of which the churches were born has in many ways been discredited. Professor John S. Pobee's essay, "Mission, Paternalism, and the Peter Pan Syndrome," suggests that similar things need to be said in respect to the churches in Africa. He notes that the missionary efforts of the last century created dependency. The legacy of this history is a continuing paternalism on the part of the church of the North and a continuing childhood (the Peter Pan Syndrome) on the part of the churches of the South.

The dependency created by European domination of the African churches—a domination that included all aspects of the life of the Church from the disposition of money to theology and liturgy—was made more severe by the "missionary doctrine of the *tabula rasa*." This doctrine held "that there was nothing in the non-European cultures on which Christian faith and mission could build." The doctrine said in effect that "outside the North Atlantic civilization there is no salvation."

Discussion of the nature of the mission of the church in Africa can be understood only in relation to this history of domination and dependency. The reaction of African Christians to this history is diverse. Some see Christianity as a new religion that requires Africans to jettison their traditional religion and much of their traditional culture. Some support a reverse position—that "Christianity should be Africanized, not Africa Christianized."

Like Father Santram and most of the other authors represented here, Professor Pobee supports a more incarnational approach. He believes that the mission of the church in Africa should be understood by use of the Greek word *skenosis*, which means "to pitch a tent." The mission of the Church in Africa is, in short, to make a home and place of worship for Christ.

What is required if Christianity is to become incarnational and so take up residence in Africa? The Church as a whole must realize that Africa must make Christianity its own and must do so in its own way. As Professor Pobee says:

> The rise of African theology . . . is not only a reminder that the eternal, nonnegotiable Word of God can and should enter into dialogue with the African context, body, heart, and soul, but also that the formulation of the theological agenda by the North Atlantic . . . is not the last word on the subject.

The mission of the church in Africa is to take up residence and speak with a Christian voice that is in all respects African. Professor Pobee next asks how helpful his own Anglican heritage is in this venture, and the answer he gives is mixed. On the one hand, Anglicanism has remained foreign to Africa. On the other, it has exerted great influence and continues to do so. The influence is of a both positive and negative sort. Its negative influence stems from the continuing power of missionary societies and from a clericalism that stifles the life of the Church and distorts its self-understanding. The positive influence stems from Anglicanism's openness and from its attempts to permeate the social order. These remarks by Professor Pobee reflect the views of most of the essays collected below. The Anglican view of mission tends to center on the doctrine of the Incarnation. It stresses openness to other cultures and religions, and it places emphasis on trying to permeate and transform both social order and culture.

The dominant theological position represented in the essays discussed thus far is clear. The Incarnation of God in Christ and the universal presence of the Holy Spirit rather than human sin and the atoning power of the Cross receive greatest emphasis. In consequence, mission is understood as following Christ where He already has gone, as presence, service, and dialogue rather than as being sent to a place Christ has not been; to proclaim a message not yet known; and to convert people to a radically new way of believing and acting.

As might be expected, there are a number of Anglicans who do not wish to posit a universal presence of the Spirit of Christ like that assumed by the dominant position and who wish to give greater emphasis not only to the centrality but also to the uniqueness of the person and work of Christ. For these people, evangelization plays a more important part in their conception of mission.

The two essays that follow Professor Pobee's represent the majority rather than the minority opinion. They, in fact, focus even more heavily on mission as service and dialogue. The Reverend Doctor Kortright Davis, associate professor of theology at Howard University Divinity School in the United States, and the Reverend Doctor Jaci C. Maraschin, professor of Ecumenical Studies in Brazil, raise a new question in their essays. The question concerns the place of the Church in God's mission. Both Doctor Davis and Doctor Maraschin assign the Church a "privileged place," but the place assigned it is, nonetheless, less central than that presupposed in the essays we have reviewed to this point.

In his essay, "Can Mission and Church Be Integrated?", Doctor Davis poses the question in a wonderfully direct manner.

> Now, if we recognize that the Church is one of our basic social institutions and that it is expected, and permitted, to perform in a certain way, what about the mission with which it is associated? Is it identical with the Church, or is it to be acknowledged as being quite distinct in essence and expectation?

Doctor Davis is concerned that the conservative nature of ecclesiastical institutions, particularly Anglican ones, may in fact disqualify the Church from being a suitable agent for the mission of God.

It is easy to miss the significance of the question Doctor Davis presses upon us. By speaking of *missio Dei* rather than of the mission of the Church, it becomes an open question as to whether it is right to speak of the Church having a mission. Perhaps God has other agents in mind for carrying out His purposes?

Doctor Davis sets out to answer the question by asking first what God's mission is and then by asking how we ought to understand the Church in relation to that mission.

The mission of God, Doctor Davis believes, is not identical with proselytism and church growth. God's mission is His persistent activity, which is directed toward reconciling all people to Himself and to one another. His mission is to establish His "Kingdom." God's mission, accordingly, is to the whole world. It is an attempt to bring the world into a kingdom of love, justice, and peace that is ruled by God and that includes all people.

Mission must then be understood from the perspective of the future—from the point of view of God's completed work. If looked at in this way, God's mission can be seen most clearly in what is new and surprising in history. In particular, it can be seen in those historical forces that bring liberation to the poor and oppressed and that create justice and peace among nations.

If, then, we are to understand God's mission, we must make an interpretation of the history of our times in the light of the Kingdom it is God's purpose to establish. If we make such an interpretation, it will become plain that the Church often hinders rather than helps God in His mission. It also becomes apparent that many people who are not yet Christians and many who are no longer so may well be active participants in God's work. Thus, in asking about our relation to God's mission we must look beyond the Church and on occasion away from it. We are called first to judge all people, Christian or otherwise, on the basis of whether their actions are or are not Christ-like.

Doctor Davis moves to open God's mission to all people and in
so doing once more places emphasis on service and dialogue.
Nevertheless, he believes firmly that the Church occupies a special place before God. Its apostolic calling can make it particularly
sensitive to human suffering, and its vision of the Kingdom can
give it a special ability to see God at work. It also seems to be
special in "the compelling witness to the risen Christ in the faith
of the whole Church, the transforming power of the whole Gospel, the nature of the hope of the poor in Christ, the relentless
surge of deep joy for those who seek to realize God's reconciling
and healing love."

It may be closer to what Doctor Davis argues to say not that the
Church does but that it can occupy a special place in God's mission. The key as to whether the Church does or does not occupy
this position lies in the nature of its life as a sacrament of the Good
News of God's Kingdom.

The secret of integrating the Church into God's mission is to see
that mission both in relation to the Church and to human society
in general. If the Church realizes that in all cases the mission of
God is concerned with "the otherness of ourselves," it will seek to
be faithful and so be a special sign of the Kingdom of God. Doctor
Davis means simply that in both church and world God seeks
always to make us new; and, thus, God's mission is to those who are
Christian, to those who are not, and to those who are no longer so.

Doctor Davis spends considerable time describing a church
that takes seriously the fact that God's mission is always to "the
otherness of ourselves." In doing so he places yet another issue
before us—namely, the relation of the forms and quality of the
common life of the Church to God's mission. It is this question
that comes to the fore in the several essays we have placed toward
the end of this collection. We have seen that the interpretation we
give to the nature of God's mission will determine what we understand the Church is called upon to say and do and how we
understand it is called to say and do it. It now appears that our
understanding of mission may determine what we think the common life of the Church is to be like and how it is to be organized.

Before turning our attention to this question, however, Doctor
Maraschin's essay "Toward a Latin American Understanding of
Mission," deserves particularly close attention. He makes an even
more definite distinction between church and mission. He believes it is the mission of theology in Latin America to give an
interpretation of what it means to be of "service to men." It is this

task that has been undertaken by liberation theology. This task is not the only one that theology has, but it is the right one for the time and place in which Doctor Maraschin lives.

In undertaking an interpretation of what it is to be "of service to men," theology in Latin America must set itself free "from the enormous burden usually required of theologians—namely, the discussion of all questions raised through the long history of the Church." Theology must give itself in service as the times require and so become a kind of "thinking in the way" that seeks to understand reality as now it is.

For theologians working in Latin America, the tools available for such a project are the social sciences on the one hand and the Bible on the other. Use of these tools will reveal the ideological basis of current theology and so make possible a more accurate depiction of reality. Doctor Maraschin's point is that social science serves within Latin America to expose current social, economic, and political structures; and that the Bible, by giving insight into God's historical purposes, provides a way of seeing the underlying reality of the present and so also a way of grasping the way in which our moral and political efforts ought to be directed. In short, the Bible provides a knowledge of what God is up to in history, and this knowledge allows us to understand the moral significance of the social reality brought to light by social analysis.

What then is the nature of God's mission and what relation does the Church have to that mission? The mission of God is human salvation, and that salvation is defined most fully by Jesus' use of Isaiah 61:1–2 and 58:6 to describe the mission given Him by God. According to Luke 4:18–21, the mission of Jesus and so of God is to preach good news to the poor, to preach deliverance to the captives, the recovery of sight to the blind, to set at liberty those who are oppressed, and to proclaim the acceptable year of the Lord.

God's mission is in the first instance political. It is a mission of liberation that brings freedom from injustice and sin. Even sin, however, is understood in large measure as referring to unjust social structures. If sin is first a sociopolitical reality, clearly redemption from sin must in large measure be sociopolitical as well.

Jesus makes known and undertakes to be of service to God in accomplishing His mission. Further, as Jesus is sent by God, so the Church is sent by Jesus in the same way and for the same purpose. For this reason, the Church is "a privileged place for mission."

The Church enjoys a privileged place, but only in a limited sense. Mission is defined as "a service to the liberation of man," and this liberation is first of all political. As a result, everyone—be they Christian or not—who works toward this liberation, shares in God's mission and they do so in the same way as do Christians.

The privileged place of the Church, therefore, does not mean that Christians are God's only agents of mission or that they are always His most important ones. The privileged place of the Church rests upon its calling and the knowledge provided in Christ of God's historical purposes. This calling and insight can be denied or understood inadequately, and so the Church's privileged place rests in God's intent for the Church rather than upon the historical reality of its common life. Within history, the Church may be blind and disobedient and so God may find His servants in other places.

The relation between God's mission and God's Church depends in history upon the extent to which the Church sees the reality of what God is doing and undertakes to be of service to God and so also "of service to men."

The next essay is that of the Reverend Canon Doctor Alan Chan, professor of theology, Chung Chi College, Chinese University of Hong Kong. In "Mission Theology: A Hong Kong Chinese Understanding," he well summarizes the various views of the mission of the Church that have emerged thus far. In addition, Canon Chan's work introduces the succeeding essays that focus not so much upon the definition of the Church's mission as upon the relation of that mission to the forms of the Church's common life. Canon Chan notes at the outset that despite a plethora of views about the mission of the Church, there are still a number of missiological insights that are now shared by people who stand nonetheless for widely divergent positions. These insights are that the mission of the Church belongs to the whole Church and is not the special preserve of mission agencies; that mission is not a one-way flow from West to East or from North to South, but a calling given to all churches; and that mission is not a synonym for evangelism. These convergencies are accompanied, however, by divergencies; and Canon Chan's summary of these several views of mission is so lucid and thorough that it deserves special attention. He says:

> Mission could mean evangelization and the planting of the Church among the yet unreached; it could mean the venture of witnessing to Jesus Christ in the time between His first and second coming with the aim of gathering people to be the children of the Kingdom so that

they could escape the coming destruction; it could mean the transformation of the latent church, in its hiddenness under the forms of paganism, Judaism, humanism, etc. . . . into its manifestation; it could mean participation in God's mission to gather up all things in Christ and to set up signs of the shalom of God in this world. Or it could even go so far as to mean the calling of the people of God into God's happenings that take place everywhere, inside or outside the institutional churches or missionary agencies, to the point and in the sense that God can "create a body of Christ with honest politicians for saints, seekers after truth as priests, writers and artists and film-makers as preachers, and flower-children, civil rights marchers and crackpot advocates of total disarmament and world government as martyrs."

Most of the essays presented here fit more in the second half of this paragraph than in the first. Canon Chan, however, makes an observation and presses a question that forces us to take seriously the entire range of opinion and ask if there is perhaps not truth to be found throughout the spectrum. He notes that there are two emphases revealed in his survey of mission theology. One is vertical and the other is horizontal. One focuses on God's saving action in the lives of individuals and the other on human relations in the world.

Canon Chan believes that some relation must be made between these two emphases. The question is, What sort? Most attempts still leave us with a fairly pietistic view of evangelism or with the unsatisfactory view that if one is doing social work they are thereby doing evangelism as well. Canon Chan suggests that the ideas of Raymond Fong, developed during his work as an industrial missioner in Hong Kong, provide a satisfactory way ahead. The essence of Fong's idea is that a distinction must be made between the sinner and the sinned against. The Gospel must offer both forgiveness and power to resist those forces that sin against others. Christians should join with others in small groups to resist the forces that sin against others. In joining with others in this struggle, Christians will come face to face with personal sin.

The first evangelistic task of Christians in these small groups is then to call everyone to repentance. This means to call those who sin against others to stop and for those who are sinned against to stop feeling such self-contempt. God always hears the pleas of the poor for justice, and He responds by calling everyone to be His disciple. He calls everyone into a community that follows His ways. Following in the way is more basic than belief. It allows for common life even where there is diversity of religious belief.

Canon Chan believes Fong's idea of mission to have appeal because (1) it is useful in more than an urban industrial complex, (2) it takes into account both sin and those sinned against and unites two vital concerns, (3) it gives a full picture of human nature and the nature of human social relations, and (4) it allows for Christians to cooperate with those who do not believe as they do.

With these views concerning the nature of the mission of the Church in mind, Canon Chan turns his attention to two aspects of the social context in which the mission of the church in Hong Kong China is carried out. One is the importance of Chinese identity to the Chinese in general and to the Hong Kong Chinese in particular. The other is the problems posed by the nature of urban society for the Church as it is now constituted. In respect to the first issue, Canon Chan believes that the ideas of mission that he defends allow people to become Christian without feeling they must give up being Chinese. In respect to the second, he believes his ideas suggest forms of church life that are more appropriate for urban life than those that now exist. His point is that if it is to carry out its mission the Church must adapt its institutional forms to fit the context in which it finds itself. The common life of the Church and the institutional forms it takes are to be assessed on the basis of how well they serve the purposes of God's mission. By implication, the Anglican heritage of establishment, tolerance, and hierarchy is to be judged on the basis of this standard as well.

It is just this theme that dominates the four essays we have placed next. The Right Reverend Colin Buchanan, bishop of Aston, understands that it is the mission of the Church to "bring all things under the rule of Christ." In his essay, "Mission and Establishment," he discusses how the established position of the Church of England now hinders rather than helps mission. It carries with it a legacy that holds back a church that ought to see itself on a pilgrimage rather than as settled. That legacy includes countless historical monuments that must be maintained, large sums of inherited money that inhibit present giving, a folk religion that distorts the true nature of Christian belief and practice, state control that inhibits the church's independence, a clericalism that stifles the ministry and service of the entire church, and forms of governance that are inadequate to present circumstances.

Establishment is more of an impediment to mission that a servant of mission, and that this is so becomes apparent at three particular points. The first is, as a state church, the Church of England has been slow to recognize that England itself is a place for mission. Establishment has encouraged the church to think of mission as something done for others.

The second point at which the disadvantage of establishment can be seen is that, as the established church, the Church of England has sought to address the entire nation. Because of the increasingly secular nature of the times, in speaking in this way the church appears both presumptious and paternalistic.

The third point at which establishment inhibits mission is this: Establishment abolishes both the Church and the world to which the Church believes itself sent. This last point is the most important one that Bishop Buchanan makes. He insists that boundaries must be drawn between a pilgrim church and the world through which it travels. Establishment wipes out the boundaries and so dissolves a necessary distinction. Bishop Buchanan makes his point with some force. He says:

> There is a people of God, expressed in local congregations but united in a catholic fellowship; and they are separate from the world in principle, and have a message for the world and a mission to the world. Establishment not only abolishes the Church; by the same action it abolishes the world. It is no accident that the 1662 Prayer Book, of a nation assumed in that age to be wholly conformist and "C of E," has no concept of mission at all. Let the boundaries be drawn too tightly or too loosely (and mistakes can certainly be made), and there may be problems. But let no boundaries be drawn, and there is catastrophe.

How does Bishop Buchanan suggest we draw the line between church and society so that the form of the Church truly serves its mission? He gives us but a hint of the direction he thinks the Church of England ought to be moving. He places heavy emphasis on small congregations of baptized Christians who see their baptism as a commissioning for mission and who are trained to carry out that mission. He designs a far less clerical church and one that has shed the trappings of establishment so that it travels light.

Bishop Buchanan implies the need for a revolution in the form, order, and self-understanding of the Church of England if it is in fact to serve mission. The Most Reverend Paul A. Reeves of New Zealand proposes a different sort of revolution, but a revolution nonetheless. In his essay, "Mission and Church Identity," he suggests that there is a need within the church in New Zealand for a revolution in the nature of episcopacy and the ministry and that, within the entire Anglican Communion, there is need for a new relation to authority.

The issues that confront the church in New Zealand do not stem from establishment but from the colonial past. The basic issues listed by Archbishop Reeves are the disposal of wealth, racial strife, pluralism of culture, authority, and isolation. All of these issues, he believes, are focused in the present conflict within the Church of New Zealand concerning episcopacy, the ministry, and the locus of authority within the Anglican Communion. Each dispute serves to make apparent the necessary relation between the mission of the Church and its form and order.

The issue concerning episcopacy arises out of the recent establishment in New Zealand of the bishopric of Aotearoa. The bishopric of Aotearoa is the first in the history of the Anglican Communion to have no relation to a geographical area. The bishop of Aotearoa functions not as the bishop of a place but as bishop to a people (the Maori), who are scattered throughout the several dioceses of New Zealand. The bishopric was established to minister to the particular needs of the Maori and to represent more adequately their point of view.

The archbishop of New Zealand states the justification for such a development in Anglican polity in this way: "In my estimation, democracy safeguards the rights of individuals but does not safeguard the rights of a group, especially if it is a minority. Maori language, Maori institutions, and Maori values are group possessions that have been denied real substance." Archbishop Reeves is more than aware that the institution of this ethnic bishopric may have wide-ranging implications throughout the Anglican Communion. He notes in particular its importance for American Indians and for French Canadians. As editors who come from a country made up of immigrant groups from various national and cultural backgrounds, we could extend the archbishop's list considerably. Our extension would, however, only serve to underline the significance of this development. It would not settle the issue that Archbishop Reeves mentions—namely, that the development in polity that he describes might promote divisions within the Church rather than serve its mission.

Archbishop Reeves views the development as full of promise and argues that the establishment of the bishopric of Aotearoa serves the necessary function of promoting both unity and diversity within the Church. It is not, therefore, a hindrance but a help to mission. It helps the Church become the sort of unified yet mixed community it is called under God to be.

The next issue Archbishop Reeves addresses is one that has

appeared already in a number of these essays. Does the parish-based model of ministry, with its emphasis on worship and pastoral care, serve in effect to eclipse a model of ministry, both lay and ordained, which is formed by mission? The recent report of the Mission Strategy and Advisory Group (MISAG) of the Anglican Consultative Council raised just this question on behalf of the entire Anglican Communion when it asked if, throughout the member churches, a pastoral model of the Church did not overshadow in a harmful way a missionary model. The emphasis on pastoral ministry rather than mission, which both Archbishop Reeves and the MISAG report note, is in all likelihood an aspect of the inheritance of establishment. Whatever its source may be, however, Archbishop Reeves makes it clear that it hinders mission in New Zealand by working against the evolution of forms of ministry that better serve this purpose. He concludes with this rather stark observation: "Quite obviously a system of licensing clergy, which presupposes parish ministry and little else, no longer fits our evolving situation."

The evolving situation in which the Church carries out its mission in New Zealand demands new forms of ministry and church order. Because of its isolation, the Church of New Zealand needs both help and support. It particularly needs the blessing of other churches within the Anglican Communion. This fact raises, for Archbishop Reeves, the question of authority within the Anglican Communion. Archbishop Reeves is particularly concerned with the place of the Archbishop of Canterbury. Will this office be used to help in the evolution of diversity within unity so that the mission of the Church will be better served, or will it be used to hinder developments that Archbishop Reeves believes must come about if the Church in New Zealand and in other parts of the world is to carry out the mission on which it has been sent?

Before proceeding to the final papers in this collection, we should pause to note an important distinction between the proposals of Bishop Buchanan and those of Archbishop Reeves. Bishop Buchanan seems to want a form and order that will preserve the boundary between the Church and the world. Archbishop Reeves wants a form and order that will allow the Church to carry out its mission by becoming a part of the soil, by adapting its order to present social conditions. Behind these differing emphases lie differing notions of mission. One stresses the need for proclamation, conversion, and amendment of life; and the other, the need for service and dialogue. The themes Dr. Micks identifies in her essay on liturgy and mission have proven to be critical variables not only in respect to the mission of the Church, but also in respect to the form and order of the Church.

In the next essay, "The Mission of Christ in Urban America," the Right Reverend A. Theodore Eastman continues to probe the relation between the mission of the Church and the nature of its common life and order. The focus of his investigation is his own, largely urban diocese. He begins by saying that the mission of the Church can best be understood not so much as being sent but as faithful following of Christ, who leads the Church where He wishes it to go.

The question Bishop Eastman must answer is where Christ leads in the city. Taking his lead from one of the collects for mission mentioned by Dr. Micks, he discusses mission under five headings: reconciliation, comprehensiveness, diversity, urgency, and restraint. In each dimension he finds that promise is accompanied by the possibility of conflict. How so?

Christ's call to the Church to follow Him as reconciler provides the first case in point. Bishop Eastman mentions the significant number of small groups now working in urban centers to bring peace in one or another area of social tension. Groups concerned with the arms race and with poverty are prime examples.

Bishop Eastman sees enormous potential in such groups. They provide forms of common life that can aid the Church in following Christ's lead. Nevertheless, they can also exacerbate the very tensions they are meant to overcome. There can and will be honest disagreements between people working even for the same goals. Thus, for example, those who choose to represent the cause of the poor against what they perceive to be unresponsive systems and structures may well clash with those who are working for the same ends by trying to change those systems and structures from within.

Bishop Eastman is thus lead to ask, "How can these two aspects of Christian social concern keep in touch with one another to serve the common good and to create an atmosphere of peace?" He elsewhere pleads for openness and tolerance, but he leaves the reader with a question rather than an answer.

A similar question hovers about the elements of mission Bishop Eastman identifies as comprehensiveness and diversity. In the city Christ calls the Church to take in all sorts and conditions of people (comprehensiveness) and give opportunity for their many gifts to be expressed (diversity). The potential riches of a faithful urban church are enormous. Nevertheless, can such a church, with its comprehensive diversity, hold together? How much heterogeneity can a community stand and still claim to be a community? Once again, Bishop Eastman issues the Church an invitation. Once again he poses a question and once again he makes it apparent that the answer to the question he poses is far from clear.

As might be expected, Bishop Eastman, in discussing the urgency and restraint called for in following Christ in the city, leaves us with a similar tension. Thus, Christ calls urgently for the Church to come to the help of the poor of the city. Obedience to the call, however, requires restraint in the midst of urgency. How shall help be given and how received? Finding answers to such questions requires thought and consideration as well as fervor and determination.

Following Christ in the city faces us with opportunity and with perplexity at every turn. How well is the Episcopal Church of the diocese of Maryland, with its establishmentarian Anglican heritage, equipped to follow? Bishop Eastman, like so many of the authors collected here, gives a mixed report. The Anglican heritage stresses diversity and tolerance, and these are of enormous importance in an urban environment; but the very diversity upon which Anglicans pride themselves can serve to prevent the Church from speaking and acting with "unity, certainty, and strength."

Furthermore, the Anglican heritage brings with it a certain class consciousness. The detriments of this tradition are obvious. Its strength is that it places a number of Episcopalians in a position where they could do enormous good, and it opens the possibility for an apologetic to the most sophisticated elements of American society. Both these things are possibilities for good; but neither, Bishop Eastman believes, have been much realized.

Bishop Eastman gives a mixed report on two other elements of Anglican tradition—Anglican polity and the *Book of Common Prayer*. Both serve to draw people to the Episcopal Church, and Anglican polity encourages wide participation in the common life of the Church. Despite these strengths, however, Bishop Eastman's final statement about the effectiveness of the Episcopal Church in mission is sobering. He concludes, "We do poorly in assisting people to convert from paganism or secular atheism to faith in Jesus Christ."

Bishop Eastman's report on how well the present forms of the common life and order of his church serve mission is mixed. He points in the end more to possibilities for mission than to actual achievements. The same thing must be said about the analysis of mission in the Anglican Church of Canada. This is given by the Most Reverend Edward W. Scott.

In "The Mission of the Church and the Culture of a Nation" Archbishop Scott's view of the mission of the Church catches up the various themes that have emerged in these essays and gives some attention to each of them. His major focus of attention, however, is the relation between the Anglican Church of Canada and its surrounding culture. He concludes, like Bishop Eastman, that though the potential for mission is great, the Anglican Church of Canada has over identified with its cultural surroundings and so forfeited much of its chance to be a missionary force.

In Canada the church must carry out its mission in an urban, industrial, and technological society. The question is, once more, how well the Anglican Church of Canada is equipped to do so.

Archbishop Scott believes the Anglican heritage provides many strengths for mission. As is common, he mentions liturgy, tolerance, and a view of authority that encourages liberty and creativity. Nevertheless, he is concerned that the establishmentarian heritage of the Anglican Church in all its forms proves more and more to be a serious obstacle to mission. In the case of the Anglican Church of Canada, it has encouraged too close an identification between church and culture.

Archbishop Scott's concern is similar to that of Bishop Buchanan. He notes that the Anglican Church tends to become "a noncritical part of the social fabric." It tends to become "a social institution rather than a community of faith." It tends also to identify with the middle and upper classes of society.

Because of this part of its heritage, the Anglican Church of Canada has proved to be more concerned with its own survival than with the mission with which it has been entrusted. Archbishop Scott notes these liabilities of the heritage of his church and searches for a way ahead. He argues that three things are needed if the Anglican Church of Canada is to become a missionary church. The first is a new sense of the reality and power of God present in the life of the Church. The second is a strong ecumenical approach to mission that involves a full sharing of resources. The third is a renewal of parish life that involves a change in the way in which the local congregation thinks of itself and a change in the way the Church thinks of its ordained ministry. Archbishop Scott, like Bishop Buchanan, suggests that baptism incorporates all Christians into a community that has a mission. The identity of the Church lies then in baptism rather than in a particular form of church order. Archbishop Scott calls for each parish within the Anglican Church of Canada to see itself as a missionary cell and to understand that its common life and the form of its ministry ought to equip it for carrying out the mission God has given it.

We have placed at the end of this collection two essays that illustrate what a fearful and difficult task participation in God's mission can be. The Reverend Clement H. Janda, general secretary of the Sudan Council of Churches, in his essay, "The Mission of the Church in an Islamic Country," shows what is involved in participating in the mission of the Church in a country divided by tribal, racial, and religious strife; and the Right Reverend Adrián D. Cáceres, bishop of Ecuador, in his essay, "The Anglican Communion in Latin America," traces the implications of being a missionary church amidst the social turmoil that now characterizes life in Latin America.

Father Janda describes for us the life of a country whose social fabric is being torn asunder by conflicting tribal, racial, and religious groups. The mission of the Church in such circumstances is to promote unity and to seek reconciliation. Father Janda notes the power of the Christian message to promote unity. He points to both the belief that we are all creatures of one God and to the reconciling power of Christ's Cross. The Christian doctrines of both creation and redemption promote the unity his country so desperately needs.

Nevertheless, the witness of the Church to unity and reconciliation, both through what it says and does, is made in the midst of horrendous circumstances. Tribal rivalry, religious war, and a displacement of both indigenous and foreign peoples that has turned thousands of people into refugees, set the scene for the mission of the Church in the Southern Sudan.

Father Janda describes the circumstances that surround the Church in the Sudan in measured tones, but it is not difficult to see that obedience on the part of the Church to its mission of unity will certainly lead to both suffering and martyrdom.

Bishop Cáceres' essay leads us to make a similar connection. At the outset, he makes this statement about mission.

> If God is at the heart of the world and is the Lord of the world, Christ came to the center of the world and from that center there calls His disciples to fulfill the mission with Him and to form the communion of the citizens of the Kingdom. The Church and its people should carry this job out within the same demands that Christ, the Great Missionary had, and within the same framework that He laid out for this action.

More than any other essay in this collection, that of Bishop Cáceres makes a direct connection between mission and the way of the Cross. The Church cannot "carry this job out" and at the same time avoid the Cross. The mission of Christ and the Church is rooted in love, service, the Incarnation, and the presence of the Spirit of God; but Bishop Cáceres adds to this familiar list the words "passion" and "discipline." Thus he says, "Love is engendered out of suffering; salvation out of crucifixion; the apostolate out of martyrdom."

The way of mission leads in the way Christ walked and so to suffering and death. For this reason, the way of mission is also the way of discipline. In Bishop Cáceres' words: "If mission is to 'make disciples,' the discipleship is a quality of following the 'discipline'—that is, the . . . teaching of the Teacher." That teaching, Bishop Cáceres reminds us, is that "He who wants to follow me, must take his cross and follow me."

To carry out its mission, the Church must walk in the way of the Cross. Obedience leads toward Golgotha, and Bishop Cáceres' essay makes plain why, in his particular circumstances, this is so. Latin America, the bishop reminds his readers, is a continent in which most people live with "hunger, chronic sickness, ignorance, illiteracy, impoverishment, injustice." They are pauperized by an unjust system of international commerce, and they are denied fundamental human rights by governments that practice both tyranny and torture.

The Church in Latin America carries out its mission in the midst of a "mortgaged" people. To speak and act in the name of Christ will in these circumstances lead toward a suffering witness. There is no other way.

Bishop Cáceres concludes by pointing to the tremendous potential of the Anglican Communion to be a constructive force in the circumstances he describes. Of this communion, he says:

> Its influence is great, its prestige is enormous. . . . As a church, it is the pioneer of ecumenicism with its Lambeth Quadrilateral; and it is receptive to what is happening in other churches. It has respect for the historic churches; a loyalty to man as man, and to the constituted public order; a sensitivity to the social problems and sufferings of man; a zeal for evangelization and pastoral care; a concern for mission; a sacramental and historic catholicity, with evangelical reform; an awareness of interdependence in Christ's Body; an incarnate and contextualized liturgy; a loyalty to the Church without dogmatic pressures; and a democratic polity in its laws and structures. Above all, it has humility, simplicity, and an adaptability, with a desire to

walk with the people, and within the people, without distinction of race, class, ideology, or politics, nor even religious belief.

Bishop Cáceres senses the potential of the Anglican presence in Latin America, but he juxtaposes this potential with its actual history—one that manifests not the way of the Cross, but the way of colonialism and private enterprise. It's presence remains then only a potential and one, at that, which is buried by a murky history.

Bishop Cáceres' essay is particularly useful because it makes so clear the crossroads at which the Anglican Communion stands. Either it becomes a missionary and ecumenical force or it will walk the way of the young man who went away sorrowing because he had great possessions. It seems to us that Bishop Cáceres' essay poses most graphically the deepest issue presented by these collected essays. The Anglican Communion does stand at a crossroads that lies between its establishmentarian origins and the way of mission and ecumenism on which all the churches throughout the world are being led. Which way the Anglican Communion will choose to walk is a decision that will not be taken by the writers of essays, but by the member churches in and through their common life. If they choose, however, to follow Christ on His mission into the world, they will have to give the nature of Christ's mission the sort of serious attention reflected in these essays.

In this summary we have sought to highlight the issues concerning the nature of the mission of the Church that these authors present to the member churches of the Anglican Communion. We have sought both to present the main lines of argument of each essay and to suggest some of the interconnections between them. No summary can possibly do justice to the rich nature of the material these essays contain. Inadequate as any summary may be, however, certain issues have arisen that demand immediate attention. We list the most important of these as a conclusion to this introductory essay in the hope that they will be taken up with the seriousness they deserve.

First, it is a common view that every church is called upon to take part in God's mission. This recognition results in a cry for all the member churches to shift the emphasis in their self-understanding so as to give mission a more prominent place. A shift of this sort requires changes both in polity and in the way local congregations form and order their common life. In particular, a greater emphasis on mission requires less clericalism and more emphasis upon the many ministries and vocations to be found in each congregation.

In fact, baptism emerges from these essays as the defining feature of the Christian congregation. It is baptism that all share, and it is baptism that draws each and every Christian and each and every congregation into God's mission.

The question is how God's mission is to be understood. We have noted that these essays favor a view of mission that centers on service and dialogue. As Father Santram and Bishop Eastman note, if mission is first dialogue and service, we perhaps ought to speak less of mission and more of following Christ where He leads. The Incarnation and the universal presence of the Spirit are the doctrines most cited in support of this opinion. A particular view of the relation between church and society also accompanies this conception—namely, that the Church ought to permeate society and transform it from inside out. Church order and common life ought to serve this purpose.

There is a less common view, more often implied than directly stated, which is also present in the collection and which was articulated with considerable force in the replies given to these papers during the course of the symposium itself. According to this view, mission involves first witness with a view to conversion and amendment of life. Accordingly, it is vital to speak of the Church having a mission—of the Church being sent into the world to make known a truth the world does not know. The doctrines most often cited in support of this view are the fall and the atoning work of Christ. The picture of church and society displayed highlights the difference between the pilgrim band of the Church and the world through which it travels. The Church plays a more central part in mission than it is given in the dominant position. Since the witness of the Church is necessary if people are to be saved from sin, its role in God's mission is not so much privileged as it is essential.

The differing significance these two views attach to the role of the Church in God's mission is accompanied by a difference in emphasis placed upon what Alan Chan calls the vertical and horizontal emphasis of mission theology. The dominant view places most emphasis upon the horizontal dimension—on human relations within the world. The less-dominant view places more emphasis on the vertical dimension—on God's saving actions in the lives of individuals both through and within the fellowship of the Church.

These are differences in emphasis only. They do not necessarily represent irreconcilable views. They do, nonetheless, reflect differing views of the nature of the Kingdom it is God's mission to establish. The dominant view locates that Kingdom first in historical realizations of peace and justice. The less-dominant view has a more inward focus. Within history, it locates the signs of the Kingdom first in the human heart, and in transformed individual and corporate life within the Church.

The two emphases that we have identified often are seen as irreconcilable. Our belief, however, is that each emphasis needs the other. The way forward, we think, is suggested by Bishop Cáceres, who connects love, the Incarnation, service, and the presence of the Spirit on the one hand with the passion of the Cross and discipline on the other. It is the Anglican way to include rather than exclude; and in respect to the doctrinal issues identified here, our way we believe will be to find once again the connection between the Incarnation of God in Christ and the death of Christ upon the Cross. It will also be our way to unite in the practice of the Christian life and so in our participation in God's mission a passionate longing for the presence of God and a burning desire for communion with all God's people.

These essays present to the Anglican Communion the questions being addressed to it by God at an important crossroads in its history. We commend them to the churches of the Anglican Communion and to all Christians in the hope that they receive the attention they deserve and in the hope that they provoke a response that will lead us more deeply into the mission upon which all Christians have been sent.

Philip Turner
Frank E. Sugeno

CROSSROADS ARE FOR MEETING

The Nature of Christian Mission

Mission and Prayer

Doctor Marianne H. Micks

When Samuel Seabury traveled from Connecticut to Pennsylvania in the fall of 1789, he carried with him a notebook of liturgical jottings. On the cover he had inscribed the words "Occasional Prayers and Offices."[1] At that Philadelphia Convention, Seabury constituted fifty percent of the House of Bishops. The other half was Bishop William White. The third American bishop was home, sick.

Seabury had been consecrated five years earlier in Aberdeen, Scotland, on November 14, 1784, by bishops of the Scottish church. He came to Philadelphia strongly influenced liturgically by the eucharistic consecration prayer he had encountered in Scotland. Fortunately, we don't have to worry about scholarly debates over the doctrine of the Eucharist in the first American prayer book. We are concerned, rather, with its theology of mission.

This whole essay will, in fact, focus on the theology of mission explicit or implicit in the four American versions of the *Book of Common Prayer*. Those successive books show a growth, a deepening, and a broadening of understanding of the Church's mission. By looking at the nature of that development of doctrine through the past two centuries, we will be in a better position to draw a trajectory into the twenty-first century.

Underlying this essay in historical and constructive theology is the familiar maxim, *lex orandi, lex credendi*. I am convinced that there is a reciprocal relationship between liturgy and theology. Worship both expresses and shapes doctrine; and doctrine, in turn, influences worship. The Latin tag, *lex orandi, lex credendi*, is perhaps most familiar to us from its use early in this century, in the Modernist controversy, by such Roman Catholics as George

5

Tyrrell. In more recent times the principle is pivotal in Pope Pius XII's encyclical, *Mediator Dei*. There the imperative "Let the law of prayer establish the law of belief" is balanced by its corollary, "The law of our faith must establish the law of our prayer."[2]

An Anglican, however, is entirely justified in claiming the authority of Richard Hooker for using the prayer book as the basis for exploring doctrine. And the practice goes back at least to Augustine of Hippo. In the fifth century, his disciple, Prosper of Aquitaine, argued for allowing the law of prayer to establish the law of belief with specific reference to the intercessions in the Eucharist, in words that anticipate conclusions we will come to in this essay:

> For when the presidents of the holy congregations perform their duties, they plead the cause of the human race before the divine clemency and, joined by the sighs of the whole church, they beg and pray that grace may be given to unbelievers.[3]

At a symposium commemorating Samuel Seabury, it would be pleasant to claim that his farsighted missionary vision is stamped on the pages of the first American *Book of Common Prayer*. It is not. Indeed, his chief concerns in the revision debates, as reflected in the surviving documents, appear to have been about the article in the Apostles' Creed, "He descended into Hell"; the inclusion of the Athanasian Creed as an option; and the placement of the rubric about what prayers could be omitted when the Litany was read in Morning Prayer. In the opinion of the American liturgical scholar, Marion Hatchett, to cite one voice, Seabury resisted the proposed book of 1786 (on which the 1789 book was based) not out of conviction but out of his desire to placate some "reactionary Connecticut churchmen."[4] On the other hand, even while he is protecting a conservative image back home, Seabury is said to be presenting some revisions of a "Latitudinarian type" in Philadelphia. Such revisions were incorporated in that notebook he brought with him to Philadelphia—revisions that found their way primarily into the "Occasional Prayers and Thanksgivings" at the end of the 1789 book.

The strongest expression of a sense of mission in the first American prayer book comes, however, in Morning Prayer. The Daily Offices were the work of a committee of laity and clergy from the House of Deputies, not of the bishops. The prayer in which it occurs is from the 1662 English book, only slightly revised. It is "A Prayer for all Conditions of Men":

O God, the creator and preserver of all mankind, we humbly be-seech thee for all sorts and conditions of men, that thou wouldst be pleased to make thy ways known unto them, thy saving health unto all nations.

The petition that God will make his ways known to everyone, to all nations, comes directly from Psalm 67:2. The original author of the prayer is uncertain. Among the seventeenth-century nomi-nees are Peter Gunning, bishop of Chichester and Ely; Robert Sanderson; and Edward Reynolds. Far more important than his-torical uncertainty about authorship is the content of the interces-sion. Massey Shepherd, the liturgical scholar, claims that this prayer marks the first time any concern for mission found its way into the Anglican liturgy. He goes on to say that "it doubtless reflects the development of English colonial expansion in the sev-enteenth century."[5] One might well add that it also reflects the Psalmist's concern with all nations and peoples, the kind of bibli-cal universalism also found in Second Isaiah. The imperative for mission is deep-rooted in Scripture.

A little over a century after the first American prayer book was issued, a revised version reached the pews. In this, the 1892 prayer book, mission received added emphasis by the inclusion of a new prayer bearing the heading "For Missions." If the 1789 book caught the flavor of England's seventeenth-century colonial expansion, this one reflects America's nineteenth-century co-lonialism. As the major historian of missions, Kenneth Scott Latourette, aptly described it, the nineteenth century was "The Great Century of Expansion."

Although it is meet and right that we deplore and repent of some of the confusion between Christianity and colonialism in those decades, we need not belittle the thousands of Christians from Western nations who listened to Christ's command, "Go ye into all the world . . ."—and who obeyed. For example, Reginald Heber's familiar missionary hymn, written in 1819, makes us wince today. It is rightly disappearing from revised hymnals. We can no longer sing, "From Greenland's icy mountains to India's coral strand," because of the blatant sense of cultural superiority in such lines as:

Can we whose souls are lighted
With wisdom from on high,
Can we to men benighted
The lamp of life deny?

Blindness, sin—yes. But vision and grace, also:

Salvation, O salvation!
The joyful sound proclaim,
Till each remotest nation
Has learnt Messiah's name.

The same mission prayer in the 1892 revision also was adapted for inclusion in the 1928 book. It is even more prominent now in the 1979 book because it is a part of daily Morning Prayer. The prayer also has found its way into many other Anglican books. The original author was George Edward Lynch Cotton, missionary bishop of Calcutta from 1858 to 1866. He drew together scriptural quotations from Acts, Ephesians, Second Isaiah, and Joel. In the 1892 book his prayer read:

> O God, who has made of one blood all nations of men for to dwell on the face of the whole earth, and didst send thy blessed Son to preach peace to them that are far off and to them that are nigh; Grant that all men everywhere may seek after thee and find thee. Bring the nations into thy fold, and add the heathen to thine inheritance. And we pray thee shortly to accomplish the number of thine elect, and to hasten thy kingdom; through the same Jesus Christ our Lord.[6]

It is noteworthy that the prayer was placed immediately after the prayer "For the Unity of God's People."

The 1928 prayer book removed the phrase "and add the heathen to thine inheritance" from its revision of Cotton's prayer; but (rather curiously) added another prayer for missions, which gives God thanks "for opening heathen lands" to the light of His truth. This additional prayer, written originally by William Reed Huntington for an 1886 book of prayers, expresses a strong sense of urgency about spreading the Gospel; but it also sounds a triumphalist note. It thanks God that the Church is now planted "in all the earth." It beseeches God "that with lively faith we may labor abundantly to make known to all men thy blessed gift of eternal life."

The 1928 book also added another collect, newly written by Edward Lambe Parsons, bishop of California, and included in the same section of prayers and thanksgivings following the Daily Offices. It bore the heading "For the Family of Nations." And so it stretched our notion of mission beyond that of converting "the heathen." For God's justice and truth and peace were here of central concern, recognized as hallmarks of the Kingdom:

> Almighty God, our heavenly Father, guide, we beseech thee, the Nations of the world into the way of justice and truth, and establish among them that peace which is the fruit of righteousness, that they may become the Kingdom of our Lord and Saviour Jesus Christ.

Although this prayer does not bear the label of a prayer for mission, either in the original or in its adapted form as a prayer in the 1979 book for international peace, it expresses a major dimension of contemporary theology of mission, one to which we shall return in our final section. It suggests that God's mission has as much to do with justice and peace among nations as with "Christianity." It opens the door to new thinking about the relationship between religious pluralism and Jesus Christ.

Whereas in 1928 advances in liturgical attention to mission were minimal, by 1979 an explosion had occurred. During the prolonged and often painful period of "trial usage," which accompanied this most recent revision of the American book, a series of Prayer Book Studies was issued. In a 1970 study of the Daily Office, the Liturgical Commission included this plaintive paragraph:

> A proposal that there should be a daily stated prayer for the mission of the Church proved in experimental use to encounter difficulties. Any single collect seemed both monotonous and inadequate to represent *the multiple concept of mission which now obtains.* Accordingly, a further versicle and response have been added in the words of Psalm 67:2, familiar from use in the *Deus misereatur.*[7]

"The multiple concept of mission which now obtains" remains, however, an apt description of the theology of mission expressed in the present American *Book of Common Prayer* authorized nine years later. The most concentrated and perhaps the most powerful expression of that new sense of mission is articulated in "The Great Vigil of Easter" and in the closely related service of Holy Baptism.

In both liturgies all the people of God are invited to renew their baptismal vows. Every Christian is asked, "Will you proclaim by word and example the Good News of God in Christ?" Every Christian is invited to answer, "I will with God's help." In the same dialogue all Christians are asked whether they will strive for justice and peace among all people, and respect the dignity of every human being. Their pledge to do so with God's help underlines the inclusive both/and nature of today's theology of mission. Mission encompasses both evangelism and social action, to use inherited labels. It is everyone's responsibility.

Mission theology also comes to explicit expression in the book in four other chief contexts—in the Daily Offices, in the Eucharist, in the calendar, and in the catechism. We will look at each in turn.

First, the imperative of mission is underlined in at least two places in the Daily Office, morning and evening. In the suffrages of morning and evening prayer, the versicle and response from Psalm 67:2 cited above receives regular use:

V. Let your way be known upon earth;
R. Your saving health among all nations.

Thus the scriptural parallelism alluded to in that 1662 prayer for all sorts and conditions of humanity is retained in daily prayer in this revision of the late twentieth century, even though that intercessory prayer itself (in an inadequately adapted form) is relegated to the end of the book.

Second, the rubrics demand further prayer for mission each morning and each evening: "Then, unless the Eucharist or a form of general intercession is to follow, one of these prayers for mission is added." Three choices are given both morning and evening. All are rich in theological content. Altogether they reflect the multiple concept of mission currently present in the American Episcopal Church.

In Morning Prayer the options are a prayer "for all members of the Church in their vocation and ministry"; a modernized version of Bishop Cotton's 1892 prayer, "O God you have made of one blood . . ."; and a tough-sinewed collect focused on the Cross. In Evening Prayer, following the identical rubric directing that "one of these prayers for mission" be used, three different emphases appear. Worshipers are invited to pray for global obedience to God, for people who are suffering, or for companionship in the Spirit. The six-sided theology of mission implicit in these prayers has burst the bonds of geography. No longer do we define mission as stretching from Greenland to India. Instead it stretches from the hard wood of the Cross to those who "work, or watch, or weep this night."

We need to take a closer look at each of these six prayers designated as prayers for mission. They constitute a remarkable collection of old and new. They invite a thorough rethinking of what we mean by mission in 1984 and beyond.

The first spotlights Christian ministry, lay and ordained. We ask that all members of the Church in their vocation and ministry may truly serve God. This is an ancient prayer going back to the Gregorian Sacramentary.[8] It has had a place in our books of common prayer since 1549. In the American book of 1979 it appears also among the Good Friday and the Ember Day collects. The work of God's Holy Spirit is explicitly mentioned.

The second and third collects for Morning Prayer also focus attention on the work of God's Holy Spirit. In words familiar from the books of Joel and Acts, we pray that God's Spirit may be poured out on all flesh. We also pray that we may be so clothed in His Spirit that we may reach forth our hands in love to those who do not know Jesus Christ. This prayer was written by Charles Henry Brent, bishop of the Philippines from 1901 to 1918.

In two of the three evening prayers for mission, God the Spirit is not named. Rather the word common to the petitions in all three is "love":

> Let the whole earth also worship you, all nations obey you, all tongues confess and bless you, and men and women everywhere love you and serve you in peace.

These words are from a prayer written by Eric Milner-White, first published in 1933.

> Tend the sick, Lord Christ; give rest to the weary, bless the dying, soothe the suffering, pity the afflicted, shield the joyous, and all for your love's sake.

These words come from Saint Augustine of Hippo, through the office of Compline.

> Send forth upon us the Spirit of love, that in companionship with one another your abounding grace may increase among us.

This prayer goes back to the Gelasian Sacramentary.

Taken together, these six prayers—any two of which are mandated for daily use—reflect an understanding of mission as centrally the work of God the Spirit, working through every Christian for the sake of all women and men on this planet. They invite us to recognize the Holy Spirit as "the chief actor in the historic mission of the Christian Church"[9] and also to recognize the enormous diversity of those who are "missionaries of the Holy Spirit."[10] Indeed they call us to recognize the fact that the mission of the Spirit begins, continues, and ends in loving.

The next major liturgical context in which prayer for mission finds mandatory use is, of course, the Eucharist. The rubric introducing the prayers of the people specifies: "Prayer is offered with intercession for The Universal Church, its members and its mission. . . ." Following the principle of flexibility, which is basic to the 1979 book, any of six forms of intercession may be used. Somewhat surprisingly, the word "mission" itself occurs in only one of them. In Form V, the deacon or other leader bids the people to pray "For the mission of the Church, that in faithful witness it may preach the Gospel to the ends of the earth." They respond, "Kyrie eleison" or "Lord, have mercy." The two succeeding petitions are for those who do not yet believe or who have lost their faith, and for the peace of the world.

Although the word "mission" does not occur in the five other forms, a strong emphasis on justice and peace does. Form I prays for the peace of the world and the unity of all people. Form II bids prayer for peace and for the well-being of all people—and then for the poor, the sick, the hungry, the oppressed, and those in prison. The other alternative forms do not add any new motifs, but they intensify the impression that the Church is enormously concerned for all people in their daily life and work. The Church prays for "the victims of hunger, fear, injustice, and oppression." It prays for "all who work for justice, freedom, and peace." The cumulative effect of these appointed intercessions for "The Universal Church and its mission" weights the definition of mission on the side of ministry to the suffering. Preaching the Gospel to the ends of the earth is construed primarily in terms of loving outreach to human need.

Another place in the eucharistic liturgy where a theology of mission is necessarily evident is in the dismissal. How are we sent out? The 1979 American book provides the deacon with four alternatives, none of them very explicit about that mission but all of them charged with energy: "Let us go forth in the name of Christ"; "Go in peace to love and serve the Lord"; "Let us go forth into the world, rejoicing in the power of the Spirit"; "Let us bless the Lord."

Equally a part of the dynamic of the sending forth are the words of the preceding thanksgiving. The more traditional form speaks of "doing all such good works as thou hast prepared for us to walk in." The most contemporary form heightens the missionary thrust:

> And now, Father, send us out
> to do the work you have given us to do,
> to love and serve you
> as faithful witnesses of Christ our Lord.

What the eucharistic liturgy is now hammering into the consciousness and the unconsciousness of believers, if one may speak in those terms, is a sense that all of us are sent forth to do something. How each one of us may translate that mission in terms of his or her own personal witness and service, service and witness, will doubtless vary greatly. But the eucharistic liturgy, through its intercessions, suggests that justice and peace have high priority on the agenda. And the thanksgivings prior to the dismissals add an exciting dimension of individual tasks in mission, each with a name attached. Perhaps the crucial question is not "What is mission?", but rather, "What is my mission?"

Challenging and yet at the same time supporting this individualist formulation of the question is the theology of mission incorporated into the new calendar of the church year, which became part of the American book in 1979. That is the third context in which mission comes to new prominence. We are newly encouraged to commemorate a sequence of "lesser feasts and fasts," which holds before us heroes of the faith whose lives can tell us more about what mission has meant and still means. Sadly, all those who are now cited by name and also designated "missionary" in that calendar are male. As a feminist, I must observe that that may be one of the reasons why our mission is only (at best) half effective in today's world.

Eleven men bearing the label "missionary" have, nevertheless, entered the newly fattened and enriched calendar. Some of them raise vexing questions about hagiography for those of us who were brought up on the historical critical method. We do not know very much about many of them. Yet we are now invited to remember, in chronological order, Gregory the Illuminator, Patrick of Ireland, Willibrond of Utrecht, Boniface of Mainz, and Cyril and Methodius, missionaries to the Slavs. All of these lived and worked between the fourth and the ninth centuries.

For some reason we then jump to the eighteenth century, to Thomas Bray. Thereafter we American Episcopalians are asked to remember three nineteenth-century missionaries—and one who lived on into the twentieth. Frankly, in spite of being trained as an historical theologian, with numerous courses in church history, the only names on this list that I have ever heard of were Gregory, Patrick, Boniface, Cyril, and Methodius; and they were only given a passing nod. I take this as pointing to a serious weakness in our missiology. We do not know the names of most of the Christians who have pioneered in mission through the centuries, much less their theological reflections on their experience.

Nevertheless, the biographies of these eleven men, limited as our knowledge of them is, further stretch our concept of what mission is. A missionary is an educator. A missionary is a translator. A missionary has a bias in behalf of the indigenous and oppressed people in any land. A missionary is called into inter-faith dialogue. We will illustrate these assertions from the lives of those five persons commemorated in the calendar who lived during or after the lifetime of Samuel Seabury.[11]

First, Thomas Bray, founder of the Society for Promoting Christian Knowledge as well as of the Society for the Propagation of the Gospel. When he visited the colony of Maryland in 1699, Bray expressed great concern for the education of clergy, lay persons, and children in the American church. He not only founded many schools in the colony, but also established thirty-nine lending libraries. His biographer notes that he was an advocate of prison reform and that he also developed and sustained interest in the plight of native Americans and blacks.

Henry Martyn, an English missionary in India and Persia, is remembered for translating the New Testament and the prayer book into Hindi and Persian. He also is said to have organized schools and to have engaged in theological discussions with learned Muslims in Iran, who helped him correct his translations. Unfortunately, this gifted linguist died in 1812, at the age of thirty-nine, before he had time to fulfill his dream of translating the New Testament also into Arabic.

In the next generation, Jackson Kemper and his younger contemporary, George Augustus Selwyn, reflect similar interest. Kemper, "the first missionary bishop in the United States," is remembered not only for establishing missions in the frontier regions of what is now called the Midwest, but also for founding two colleges and our Wisconsin seminary, Nashotah House. He also wanted the Church to pay more attention to the Indians and to translate the liturgy into Indian languages. He apparently joined in worship with the Oneida people, since he wrote about their reverence and obedience "to that Great Spirit in whose hands are the issues of life." Similarly, Selwyn, "first missionary bishop of New Zealand," learned the Maori language and is said to have been beloved by the Maori people.

Finally, Channing Moore Williams, a native of Richmond, Virginia, and a graduate of the Virginia Theological Seminary, went to Japan in 1859. He was chosen missionary bishop for China and Japan in 1866. He founded a divinity school, which is now St. Paul's University in Tokyo. He translated parts of the prayer book into Japanese. He helped form the Nippon Sei Ko Kwai. He returned to the United States in 1908, after almost fifty years' work in Japan.

Such consistent attention to education and to translation on the part of the missionaries who are included in the Proper for the Lesser Feasts demonstrates once again, I think, that Anglicans are a People of the Book twice over. We believe it to be imperative both that the Word of the Lord be proclaimed and that the Name of the Lord be worshiped in a language "understanded of the people." Although this part of the calendar is authorized for optional use only, many parishes, and certainly many seminaries, use it regularly. When one of these missionaries is remembered at the Eucharist, the Proper Preface designated is almost always either that for an Apostle or that for Pentecost. Thus we have further evidence that the theology of mission informing the 1979 American *Book of Common Prayer* is centered around a people sent forth "to preach the Gospel and to teach all nations,"[12] in the power of the Holy Spirit who unites "peoples of many tongues in the confession of one faith."[13]

The fourth and final context in which the American prayer book addresses the subject of mission comes at the end of the greatly expanded book, in a catechism called "An Outline of the Faith." In fact there are four questions and answers on the subject in the text, in the section headed "The Church." Each of the four traditional notes or marks of the Church is examined. The note of apostolicity evokes this answer:

> A. The Church is apostolic, because it continues in the teaching and fellowship of the apostles and is sent to carry out Christ's mission to all people.

Appropriately enough, the next three questions ask what the mission of the Church is, how the Church pursues its mission, and through whom. The answers are clear and straightforward, yet they add a new theological note not sounded in the material we have so far listened to.

> Q. What is the mission of the Church?
> A. The mission of the Church is to restore all people to unity with God and each other in Christ.

The use of the term "to restore" sounds strangely backward-looking, as if our goal were a return to some imagined Eden. It raises a question in my mind about its relation to an authentically biblical eschatology. Is it consistent with the forward thrust of Scripture, with the dynamic offered by its horizon of the future? Yet the underlying idea is certainly Pauline. One suspects that the authors of the catechism are thinking of the ministry of reconciliation as Paul speaks of it, for example, in II Corinthians 5.

Q. How does the Church pursue its mission?
A. The Church pursues its mission as it prays and worships, proclaims the Gospel, and promotes justice, peace, and love.

The threefold form of this answer is notable. The sharp recognition that the Church at prayer is the Church in mission is theologically important. I think it suggests a helpful way to think about the polar tension in much current discussion of mission as to whether it is primarily proclaiming the Gospel or primarily working for justice, peace, and love. To this issue we will also return in the final section.

The last question and answer in this section underline once again the fact that all baptized persons are sent on mission, a fundamental emphasis of this 1979 book throughout:

Q. Through whom does the Church carry out its mission?
A. The Church carries out its mission through the ministry of all its members.

We need now to turn to two questions posed by the architects of this symposium that so far have been addressed only very obliquely. It has undoubtedly been apparent that I write as a member of the Episcopal Church in the United States; but it has not necessarily been apparent how that church is related to the social order, nor how I think the common life of the Church in my area might be formed so as to carry out our mission more effectively. I must speak more concretely and more personally.

The seminary in which I teach theology, the seminary from which Channing Moore Williams was graduated in 1855, is situated on a hill across the Potomac River from Washington, D.C. If I climb the tower of our classroom building, I can see the Washington Monument in my nation's capital. My thinking about mission must be rooted in this geography even as it must abandon the notion of mission as rooted in distant lands with exotic flora and fauna—the kind of territory described in another outmoded mission hymn:

Remember all the people
  Who live in far off lands,
In strange and lonely cities
  Or roam the desert sands. . . .
Some work in sultry forests
  Where apes swing to and fro.

Instead, the people I need to remember are the thousands and thousands of "government workers," women and men who clog our highways during every morning and evening "rush hour"; and the hundreds and hundreds of hungry and homeless men and women who walk the streets of that same city. They are people of every known faith and of none. Washington, D.C., is surely one of the most pluralistic societies in the world. As Donald Coggan remarked in a lecture called "Beginning at Jerusalem," if you cannot witness in your hometown, it is vain to think that change of place will make you an effective witness.[14]

My thinking about mission must also be affected by this time, 1984. It is a year in which the citizens of this nation will elect a president—the fortieth since Seabury's days. I risk this political note in order to share with you two quite conflicting personal reactions to the social order of which I am a part.

The first was born out of my experience last summer when I spent almost a month at the World Council of Churches Assembly in Vancouver, where I was a member of the worship committee. Our worship was blessed by the Holy Spirit, but my personal discovery of feeling *persona non grata* simply because of my nationality was deeply painful. I don't believe that I am personally responsible for people starving in East Africa or for missile bases in Europe, or that the Episcopal Church is. But I and we must acknowledge our share in our corporate identity in this society, and in the patent fact of what is rightly called "structural sin." As we think and talk about mission, we need to think and talk about sin.

The second and conflicting reaction bounces right out of the editorial columns of my daily *Washington Post*. Since this is an election year, "Religion" is in the news; and the news makes any theologian shudder. The religion in question is what Robert Bellah properly called "American Civil Religion." Two news stories from this spring will illustrate its character.

In March 1984 the Supreme Court of this nation rendered a decision that a small city in the smallest of our fifty states might exhibit a Christmas Nativity scene on public property without violating our constitutional separation of church and state. A crèche is now considered a secular display. In this same month the Congress assembled in "my home town," as it were, is hotly engaged in debate over prayer in the public schools, something banned by our Supreme Court. The President's advocacy of "letting God back into our schools" led one columnist to call him "Theologian-in-Chief" and to describe his religion in these terms:

> Just exactly what this religion is is hard to tell since it obviously entails something like twice-a-year church attendance. It is, though,

vaguely Protestant; supportive of the military; stands in amicable partnership with the government; favors America over all other nations; has a special affinity for the Republican Party and envisions a heaven that, like the American Express gold card, requires a certain minimum income for admission.[15]

In the midst of this social order one is tempted to argue that the chief task of mission here is what Gustavo Gutierrez called the task of denunciation—denunciation of this "civil religion," which is so contrary to the Gospel of Jesus Christ but which, alas, can sound even "vaguely Protestant" to a journalist.

In this place and at this time, and against the background of the theology of mission described in the last section of this essay, I choose, instead, to focus briefly now on three issues that I believe to be critical for our understanding of what God is sending us to do. I have already introduced most of them, at least indirectly: How do we preach Jesus Christ in a pluralistic society? How does our mission as Anglicans relate to the mission of the universal Church? How do we best balance evangelism with social action in our understanding of mission? These are all complicated questions. I hope merely to sharpen them, not to answer them.

American theologians John Cobb and Tom Driver, among others, are calling openly for a rethinking of the centrality of Jesus Christ in a pluralistic age. They find it difficult to believe that loving or honest or thoughtful people today can any longer claim that a first-century Palestinian Jew is the "flaming center" of world history, the single "fulcrum of the future."[16] They urge us to adopt a more modest vision. They call us to affirm the insights of other world religions and to enter into dialogue with their believers.

Cobb, in fact, in a lecture entitled "God and Buddhism," goes beyond the Christological question. He asks us to rethink our doctrine of God as well:

> What the encounter with Buddhism encourages us to do is to re-open the question of what it means to be ultimate. It may be that the biblical God is ultimate in some respects and not in others, and that the effort to treat God as ultimate in all respects destroyed the fundamental biblical vision.[17]

He goes so far as to assert that "the Christian God is not the answer to the Buddhist question." Even more relevant to our current topic is his eschatological comment toward the end of the same lecture:

> The Christian's attention should not be on what has happened but on what will or can happen. Of course, her or his perceptions are

shaped by the past and are sharpened by repeated return to their sources of nourishment. But our judgments about how to order the life of the church and society should not be derived from how this was done in the first century. They should be derived instead from our anticipation of how they will be ordered in whatever we can understand to be the hoped for and fulfilling future, that which counts for us as the Kingdom of God.[18]

In the same vein, Driver punches holes in our traditional complacencies. He begins a chapter in a recent Christological study[19] with a diagram he saw when he was a student in seminary—one that I frequently use in my own classes still. The figure is an hourglass on its side. It illustrates Hans Conzelmann's interpretation of the theology of Luke–Acts. All history flows toward the neck of the hourglass—toward Jerusalem, toward the Cross. After Easter all history flows out from that turning point, that center— toward Rome and the ends of the earth. This paradigm, Driver says, just won't do in 1984. We need other maps of reality, maps that can encompass more of the globe and more of the human story in all of its rich diversity.

On this critical issue, I am currently a reverent agnostic. I agree with Donald Coggan that we need to enter into deeper dialogue with other world religions, taking the stance of humble learners.[20] That stance was well illustrated in the lives of the five missionary heroes we reviewed earlier. For example, more than a century ago Henry Martyn was open to learning from Islamic scholars. In my own experience I have had a Muslim friend who clearly knew God better than I do and who taught me much about practicing God's presence. At the same time, I call the Gospel of John the "Word of God." Is there no other name than that of Jesus which is the Way, the Truth, and the Life?

The second issue does not leave me in the same uncomfortable position. I am an ardent "ecumaniac," completely convinced that any effective mission in the future, anywhere in the world, must be the witness of the universal Church. That conviction was signaled earlier when I noted that the prayer for mission in the 1892 prayer book appropriately followed the prayer "For the Unity of God's People."

No one that I know of has spoken more persuasively on this issue in recent years than the American ecumenist Paul A. Crow, Jr., in his brief book *Christian Unity: Matrix for Mission.* Crow is refreshingly open about the fact that the so-called Christian countries of the Western world are today mission countries. "We, too," he writes, "are a church in a hostile 'non-Christian' environment.

The church is everywhere in a missionary situation, far more critically than many are willing to admit; and unity is essential for our witness."[21] I thoroughly agree.

A central chapter of Crow's book explores the theme of unity and mission around what he calls "four characteristics of a truly missionary life"—proclamation, presence, service, and Eucharist.[22] The chapter shares my central thesis that prayer and mission are deeply interconnected. Crow's discussion of "presence" includes moving stories of people who have undertaken "the adventure of going to live with others in the world in the name of Christ." He interprets John 1:14a as "a mandate for incarnational evangelism." Unless the love of the one Lord radiates from our presence in the world, proclamation is to no avail.

In order for our presence to radiate love, we must know the presence of Christ in our lives. Crow admits that the idea of mission and evangelism as Eucharist may seem strange to some, but he argues convincingly (if all too briefly) that "a missionary presence is the fruit of participation in the Lord's Supper." He supports my earlier observations about the Eucharist when he writes: "The communion table is the matrix of mission, the place where the church and world intersect in the presence of Christ, the place from which Christians are sent forth to serve and to love."[23] He therefore calls us all to share one bread and one cup of the Lord to empower us for service to the needs of a suffering world.

Although I am convinced that full eucharistic sharing is essential to more effective mission, and although I am therefore excited about our growing ecumenical convergence in that direction, reflected in the Lima document, I do not think that membership in the Anglican Communion is in any way a detriment to mission. For one thing, the Anglican ethos forestalls an either/or mentality, such as one that would vote for evangelism against service in defining mission, or vice versa. The both/and of Anglicanism as I understand it is far from a flabby fence-sitting. It encourages us all, to adapt Hooker's words, to deem it not impossible that we may err. But equally it opens us to use a wide-angle lens as we inspect and interpret reality.

In what I take to be the spirit of Anglicanism, then, I turn to the final question that I want to address, that of the tension between service and evangelism in world mission. A recent study entitled *Contemporary Theologies of Mission* has put the question starkly: "Is eternal separation from God more disastrous than going to bed hungry?"[24] The authors of this survey think that it is. As evangelical Christians, they opt for what they call a "classical" definition of mission, one which they equate with "discipling." Their theology of mission is based, they claim, on the whole of Scripture. It appears to me to be based almost exclusively on Matthew 28:19.

In spite of the fact that I disagree with their either/or conclusions, the authors present an intriguing typology for thinking about contemporary missiology. They identify four different schools of thought, four "campgrounds" that they label evangelical, Roman Catholic, "conciliar," and "liberationist." The so-called conciliar theory is that of the World Council of Churches. The so-called liberationist theory is that, primarily, of Latin American theologians. In their conclusion, however, they reduce these four positions to two. "On the one side are the evangelical and official Roman Catholic theologies of mission. On the other side are the conciliar and liberationist theologies of mission."[25] (I'm sure that this line-up would amuse Richard Hooker, who found himself caught between the millstones of Papists and Puritans.)

Far more constructive, in my judgment, is the discussion of the same issue by David Bosch in his *Witness to the World* (1980). He sees a creative tension between evangelical theology and liberation theology, akin to the tension between the Church and the world. And he likens *kerygma* and *diakonia* to the two blades of a pair of scissors that operate in unison, held together by *koinonia*.[26] Bosch's position is closely akin to that taken in my prayer book catechism: "The Church pursues its mission as it prays and worships, proclaims the Gospel, and promotes justice, peace, and love."

In conclusion, therefore, it seems to me that the eucharistic fellowship of the ecumenical Church and the individual spiritual lives of its missionaries, who are all of its baptized members, form the only matrix for carrying out God's mission. It is a mission that He alone initiates, incarnates in the world, and sends forth in the power of His Holy Spirit.

NOTES

1. Marion J. Hatchett, *The Making of the First American Book of Common Prayer, 1776–1789* (Seabury Press, 1982), p. 108.
2. As cited by Geoffrey Wainwright, *Doxology: The Praise of God in Worship, Doctrine, and Life* (Oxford University Press, 1980), p. 222. Wainwright's whole treatment of systematic theology revolves around this principle.
3. *Ibid.*, p. 225.
4. Marion J. Hatchett, *op. cit.*, p. 2.
5. *The Oxford American Prayer Book Commentary* (Oxford University Press, 1950), pp. 18–19.
6. *Alterations and Additions in the Book of Common Prayer . . .* (Printed for the General Convention, 1892), p. 30.
7. *The Daily Office: Prayer Book Studies 22* (The Church Hymnal Corporation, 1970), p. 23. Emphasis added. Historians both of liturgy and of mission theology will always bemoan the fact that no record exists of the discussions underlying that paragraph.
8. For the historical facts in this section, I am indebted to Marion J. Hatchett, *Commentary on the American Prayer Book* (Seabury Press, 1981).
9. John V. Taylor, *The Go-Between God* (Oxford University Press, 1972), p. 3.
10. *Ibid.*, p. 38.
11. In this section my historical facts are dependent on *Lesser Feasts and Fasts* (Church Hymnal Corporation, 1980), *loc. cit.*
12. Proper Preface for Apostles, *Book of Common Prayer*, p. 381.
13. Proper Preface for Pentecost, *Book of Common Prayer*, p. 380.
14. Donald Coggan, *Mission to the World* (Hodder & Stoughton, 1982), p. 39.
15. Richard Cohen, *Washington Post* (March 12, 1984), p. A19.
16. See Carl E. Braaten, *The Flaming Center: A Theology of the Christian Mission* (Fortress Press, 1977). Braaten is a helpful interpreter both of recent eschatological thought and of liberation theology.
17. David Tracy and John B. Cobb, Jr., *Talking About God: Doing Theology in the Context of Modern Pluralism* (Seabury Press, 1983), p. 67.
18. *Ibid.*, p. 87.
19. Tom F. Driver, *Christ in a Changing World* (Crossroad, 1981), p. 57.
20. Donald Coggan, *op. cit.*, p. 29.
21. Paul A. Crow, Jr., *Christian Unity: Matrix for Mission* (Friendship Press, 1982), p. 44.
22. *Ibid.*, p. 59.
23. *Ibid.*, p. 58.
24. Arthur F. Glasser and Donald A. McGavran, *Contemporary Theologies of Mission* (Baker Book House, 1983), p. 237.
25. *Ibid.*, p. 233.
26. David J. Bosch, *Witness to the World* (John Knox Press, 1980), p. 227.

BIBLIOGRAPHY

The Alterations and Additions in the Book of Common Prayer of the Protestant Episcopal Church in the United States of America. Adopted by the General Convention in the Years 1886, 1889, and 1892. Boston: Printed for the Convention, 1892.

Bosch, David J. *Witness to the World: The Christian Mission in Theological Perspective.* Atlanta: John Knox Press, 1980. Bosch is at the University of South Africa, Pretoria.

Braaten, Carl E. *The Flaming Center: A Theology of the Christian Mission.* Philadelphia: Fortress Press, 1977.

Coggan, Donald. *Mission to the World: The Chavasse Memorial Lectures, 1981.* London: Hodder & Stoughton, 1982.

Crow, Paul A., Jr. *Christian Unity: Matrix for Mission.* New York: Friendship Press, 1982.

The Daily Office: Prayer Book Studies 22. New York: The Church Hymnal Corporation, 1970.

Driver, Tom F. *Christ in a Changing World: Toward an Ethical Christology.* New York: Crossroad Publishing Company, 1981.

Glasser, Arthur F., and Donald A. McGavran. *Contemporary Theologies of Mission.* Grand Rapids, Michigan: Baker Book House, 1983.

Hatchett, Marion J. *Commentary on the American Prayer Book.* New York: The Seabury Press, 1981.

————. *The Making of the First American Book of Common Prayer 1776–1789.* New York: The Seabury Press, 1982.

The Proper for the Lesser Feasts and Fasts, Together With the Fixed Holy Days. 3rd ed. New York: The Church Hymnal Corporation, 1980.

Shepherd, Massey Hamilton, Jr. *The Oxford American Prayer Book Commentary.* New York: Oxford University Press, 1950.

Taylor, John V. *The Go-Between God: The Holy Spirit and the Christian Mission.* New York: Oxford University Press, 1972.

Tracy, David, and John B. Cobb, Jr. *Talking About God: Doing Theology in the Context of Modern Pluralism.* New York: The Seabury Press, 1983.

Wainwright, Geoffrey. *Doxology: The Praise of God in Worship, Doctrine, and Life.* New York: Oxford University Press, 1980.

The Mission of the Church in East Africa

The Right Reverend Doctor David M. Gitari

THE MISSION OF CHRIST'S CHURCH

Introduction

Most Christian literature on mission has continued to use "mission," "witness," and "evangelism" interchangeably; and an important dictionary of Christian theology regards "evangelism" as synonymous with the word "mission." But the word "mission" is a much more comprehensive word, embracing everything that God sends His people in the world to do. He sends them to evangelize, but this is only one aspect of the mission. Whereas "evangelism" is included in the word "mission," the word "evangelism" is inadequate to express the meaning of the word "mission." Similarly the words "witness" and "service" do not in themselves exhaust the meaning of the word "mission," for witness and service do not summarize all that God sends His people into the world to do.

The God of the Bible Is a Sending God

The mission of the Church to the world arises primarily out of the nature of God Himself and not necessarily the nature of the Church. One aspect of the nature of God is love. It was C. H. Dodd who said, "to say that 'God is Love' implies that all his activity is loving activity." One of the activities of the living God of the Bible is to send. Because God is love, He is always "reaching out after others in self-giving service."

God sent forth Abraham from his country, commanding him to go to the unknown land of Canaan, and promised to make him a great nation (Genesis 12:1–13). He sent Moses to liberate His politically, socially, and economically oppressed people in Egypt (Exodus 3:10). Later He sent a succession of prophets with messages of warning and promises. After the Babylonian captivity, God sent the remnant of the captives back to the land to reconstruct the national life. And finally, when the time was fully come, God sent forth His Son to the world. As John Stott has put it, "The primal mission is God's, for it is he who sent his prophets, his son, his spirit. Of these missions, the mission of the son is central, for it was the culmination of the ministry of the prophets, and it embraced within itself as its climax the sending of the spirit. And now the Son sends as he himself was sent."

As the Father Has Sent Me, Even so I Send You

The Great Commission according to John's Gospel is simply "As the Father has sent me, even so I send you" (John 20:21b). We have already stated that the mission of the Church embraces everything that God sends His people in the world to do. The Son was sent by the Father to the world, and now He sends us to continue with the work that the Father had sent Him to do. Our understanding of "mission," then, must begin by investigating what Jesus considered His mission in the world to be or rather His understanding of what His Father had sent Him to do. This investigation is an important clue to our understanding of "mission" because Jesus, according to the fourth Gospel, is saying that whatever His Father had sent him to do, in turn, He now sends His disciples to continue.

Jesus' Mission According to Matthew. "And Jesus went about all cities and villages, teaching in their synagogues and preaching the gospel of the Kingdom, and healing every disease and every infirmity" (Matthew 9:35). According to this verse, Matthew sees the ministry of Jesus as threefold: teaching, preaching, and healing. The teaching ministry of Jesus (*didachē)* was primarily the ethical instructions as in the Sermon on the Mount, whereas the preaching ministry (*kerygma*) was the proclamation of the Good News of the Kingdom to the nonbelieving world. The content of the Gospel that Jesus preached was the Kingdom of God. His healing ministry included exorcism as well as healing "every kind of disease and infirmity." There is a sense in which the threefold ministries cannot be separated, for the good tidings of the Kingdom are not only experienced in the actual proclamation but also in the teaching and healing ministries.

In the following chapter, Matthew reports the calling of the twelve disciples and their being sent to "the lost sheep of Israel." Jesus sends them to go ahead of Him to various villages and cities, and uses the following commissioning words: "Preach as you go, saying, 'The Kingdom of Heaven is at hand.' Heal the sick, raise the dead, cleanse lepers, cast out demons" (10:7–8). After resurrection and before ascension, the risen Lord tells His disciples:

> Go therefore and make disciples of all nations, baptizing them in the name of the Father and of the son and of the Holy Spirit, teaching them to observe all that I have commanded you; and lo, I am with you always, to the close of the age (*Matthew 28:19–20*).

The task of the Church is to make disciples of all nations, to baptize them, and to teach them to obey everything that Christ has commanded. This often-quoted verse containing the Great Commission has made the mission of the Church in certain circles to be seen exclusively as a preaching, converting, and teaching mission. Although the cumulative emphasis of the Great Commission is preaching, witnessing, and making disciples, the disciples must be taught "to observe all that I have commanded you." Matthew gives a summary of commandments by quoting the greatest commandment:

> You shall love the Lord your God with all your heart, and with all your soul, and with all your mind. This is the great and first commandment. And a second is like it, you shall love your neighbour as yourself (*Matthew 22:37–38*).

The Great Commission must be taken with the Great Commandment. As John Stott has said:

> The Great Commission neither explains, nor exhausts, nor supersedes the Great Commandment. What it does is to add to the requirement of neighbour-love and neighbour-service a new and urgent Christian dimension. If we truly love our neighbour we shall without doubt share with him the good news of Jesus. . . . Equally, however, if we truly love our neighbour we shall not stop with evangelism. Our neighbour is neither a bodyless soul that we should love only his soul nor a soulless body that we should care for its welfare alone, nor even a body-soul isolated from society. God created man, who is my neighbour, a body-soul-in-community. Therefore if we love our neighbour as God made him, we must inevitably be concerned for his total welfare, the good of his soul, his body, his community. Moreover it is this vision of man as a social being, as well as a psychosomatic being, which obliges us to add a political dimension to our social concern.

To be sent by Jesus to the world means going to make disciples as well as teaching them to observe all that He has commanded us. Those things include the rendering of service to mankind. It is to respond in loving service to the needs of our neighbor. Mission then embraces "the church's double vocation of service to be the salt of the earth and the light of the world. For Christ sends his people into the earth to be its salt and sends his people into the world to be its light" (Matthew 5:13–16).

Jesus' Mission According to Mark. According to Mark, the Kingdom motif is the keynote of Jesus' ministry. Soon after John the Baptist was arrested, Mark reported: "Jesus came into Galilee, preaching the Gospel of God and saying, "The time is fulfilled, and the Kingdom of God is at hand, repent and believe in the Gospel" (Mark 1:14–15). The writer of the first Gospel follows through on this announcement by presenting the full range of Jesus' activity, which defines the meaning of the Kingdom of God. Mark is virtually saying that "God's reign is here, or at least is so near at hand that already the signs of its activity are manifest; and men must make some response to the claims which it lays upon them."

The Kingdom of God is first demonstrated by the miracles— particularly in exorcism—performed by Jesus. When the scribes accused Him of being possessed by Beelzebub and to be the prince of demons because of casting them out, Jesus answered: "If a Kingdom is divided against itself, that Kingdom cannot stand" (Mark 3:24). Jesus makes clear that the issue here is not civil war within the kingdom of satan, but rather a war of aggression against Him. The miracles are, as it were, enacted proclamation that the Kingdom of God has come and that the kingdom of satan has been successfully invaded. "In his exousia of Jesus, one encounters the saving power of the kingdom, the very 'Gospel of God.' "

As Donald Senior and Carroll Stuhlmueller have indicated, "the compassionate face of Yahweh the King and his saving intent is also revealed by Jesus' provocative association with outcasts and marginal people." Jesus has table fellowship with tax collectors and sinners (Mark 2:14–17), and associates with women, children, and even lepers.

Mark also takes into account the prophetic dimension of the mission of Jesus. The conflict between Jesus and the authorities begins almost immediately in the Gospel story as Jesus directly challenges the scribes and Pharisees on issues of Sabbath law and fasting (Mark 2:23–28), dietary laws, and divorce (Mark 10:2–12). "Jesus' prophetic challenge to wrong priorities and insincere piety comes to a dramatic climax in the cleansing of the temple" (Mark

11:15–18). According to Mark, the mission of Jesus is to inaugurate the Kingdom of God. The arrival of the Kingdom provokes an unavoidable crisis—it challenges men to draw near to the Kingdom of God, and their response to it is shown by their attitude to Jesus Himself. "For it is in the person and deeds of Jesus that God's reign has actively begun, that the assult against evil, physical and spiritual, has been launched."

The Gospel According to St. Mark has been called a "mission book." "Not only does Mission have a firm place in Mark's Gospel, but it comes to the fore in precisely those texts and themes that are at the center of the evangelist's concern. Mark invites the Church to take up the powerful redemptive mission of Jesus—a mission that embraced Jews and Gentiles. But this Mission will be genuine only when the community (and the societal status quo) has been transformed by a servant Jesus and his cross."

Jesus' Mission According to St. Luke. Donald Senior and Carroll Stuhlmueller have observed that "the very fact that Luke binds together the story of the early community and the story of Jesus' life indicates that one of his major purposes was to show the relationship between the Mission of Jesus and the Mission of the church." Indeed Luke's two volumes, the Gospel and the Acts of the Apostles, may be the clearest presentation of the Church's universal mission in all the New Testament.

Luke concludes the story of the birth of Jesus by telling the reader how Jesus grew: "And Jesus increased in Wisdom and in stature and in favor with God and man" (Luke 2:52). This verse summarizes the four essential aspects of human growth: wisdom, stature, favor with God, and favor with man. Put in another way, a child requires:

1. Mental growth, which includes the need to observe, remember, integrate, analyze, and make wise decisions;
2. Physical growth, which includes the physical needs, such as food, shelter, exercise, and a healthy physical environment;
3. Spiritual growth, which is the need to develop, nurture, and maintain a vertical relationship with our Creator; and
4. Social growth, which is the need to develop, nurture, and maintain horizontal relationships with individuals, our neighbors, and different communities and groups of people.

The pattern of the growth of Jesus should be the model for our growth. Just as Jesus was able to grow mentally, physically, spiritually, and socially, we should also grow in all four aspects. Indeed the mission of the Church to the world is to facilitate the four-dimensional growth of God's people.

Luke tells us that Jesus, at the beginning of His ministry, entered the synagogue on a Sabbath day in His home village and read a passage from the Book of the Prophet Isaiah: "The spirit of the Lord is upon me, because he has anointed me to preach the good news to the poor. He has sent me to proclaim release to the captives and the recovering of sight to the blind, to set at liberty those who are oppressed, to proclaim the acceptable year of the Lord" (Luke 4:18–19). This passage summarizes the program of Jesus' mission to the world. He has come to proclaim the Good News to the poor—those who are economically disadvantaged. He has come to release the captives—those who are socially and politically disinherited. He has come to heal the blind, which includes bringing hope to those who are physically disinherited. He has come to set at liberty those who are morally and spiritually disinherited.

The program of the mission of Jesus gives special attention to those on the periphery—the poor, the captives, the blind, and the oppressed. These are the recipients of Jesus' Spirit-filled ministry. He befriends and shares table fellowship with tax collectors and sinners (Luke 5:27–32; 15:1–2). Jesus, according to Luke, is also interested in outsiders, such as the Gentile centurion (7:1–10), and in Samaritans, and has a special interest in women.

The mission program enunciated in the commission text of Luke 24:44–49 is carried out by the Apostles and the community in the Acts of the Apostles. "The scope, the structure, and the content of Acts are dominated by the question of universal mission. The Kingdom Ministry of Jesus, which reached a climax in Jerusalem with His death, resurrection, and triumphant return to the father, will be continued through the guidance of the risen Christ and the power of the spirit in the community's own history." Luke also observes the reluctance of the Jerusalem church to reach the Gentiles and the dawning consciousness of Peter and the Twelve about the acceptance of the Gentiles. The conversion of Saul, the persecutor of the Church, and his mission to the Gentile world demonstrates the evangelist's conviction of the universal mission of the Church.

The mission of the Church then is to continue with the mission of Jesus in the world. Our mission to the world is to evangelize, witness, heal, feed the hungry, clothe the naked, challenge the injustices of this world, and bring about reconciliation in the troubled world.

TOWARD A MORE EFFECTIVE MISSION OF THE CHURCH
IN EASTERN AFRICA

Evangelism

Though most of the countries in Eastern and Central Africa have a
large Christian population, the evangelistic task of the Church has
not yet been completed. Of the eleven countries under consideration—Ethiopia, Somalia, Kenya, Uganda, Tanzania, Zaire, Mal-
awi, Zambia, Zimbabwe, Mozambique, and Angola—three have
a Christian population of less than 50 percent of the total population: Tanzania (44 percent), Mozambique (38.9 percent), and
Somalia (0.1 percent). Somalia, Ethiopia, and Tanzania have a
relatively large Muslim population; and throughout the region
there are pockets of people who still cling to the African traditional religion and have not yet heard the Gospel of Jesus Christ.

Primary evangelism in this region has been done by missionaries from Europe and the United States of America. Time, however, has come for the Church in Africa to start sending its own
missionaries to the unreached parts of the earth. The Anglican
Church in Kenya has been invited to send missionaries to Zaire to
help in equipping pastors and evangelists in their mission. There
is also no reason why the vigorous Church of Uganda should not
send missionaries to Tanzania and neighboring Sudan, where the
Christian population is only 9.1 percent. To evangelize effectively
among those who still follow the African traditional religion, the
potential evangelists must be trained in cross-cultural evangelism.
They must not repeat the mistake of early missionaries who condemned the African culture as un-Christian and virtually wanted
their converts to adopt European customs and behavior. As the
Lausanne Covenant observes: "The Gospel does not presuppose
the superiority of any culture to another, but evaluates all cultures
according to its criteria of truth and righteousness, and insists on
moral absolutes in every culture. Missions have all too frequently
exported with the Gospel an alien culture, and churches have
sometimes been in bondage to culture rather than to the scripture." The African missionaries must not repeat similar mistakes,
but must "humbly seek to empty themselves of all but their personal authenticity in order to become the servants of others."

The older churches may join in this partnership by giving financial support where necessary. The Episcopal diocese of Southern Virginia has entered into partnership with the diocese of Mt.
Kenya East in sending missionaries to the Anglican diocese of

32 David M. Gitari

Bukavu in Zaire. The diocese of Mt. Kenya East will provide personnel, and the diocese of Southern Virginia will give financial support. This partnership will initially be for a period of three years (1985–1987).

One of the greatest challenges facing the Church in this region is the resurgence of Islam. Millions of dollars from the oil-rich Muslim countries of the Middle East are being spent to build mosques in every important town or village in various places. In some cases the Muslim teachers are trying to win people by showing the superiority of Islam over Christianity, often by distorting the Christian Gospel. Some Muslims claim to offer "one God and many wives," unlike Christianity, which offers "three Gods and one wife!"

Christian evangelists in a Muslim context must seek to understand the teaching of Islam. Aggressive evangelism, including open-air crusades, cannot make any impact among Muslims. It is much more effective to follow the method of "dialogue," which presupposes a willingness to listen sensitively in order to understand. Such understanding of Islam will help the evangelist to avoid the pitfalls that make many Muslims switch off before they have had the opportunity of hearing the truth about Christianity.

Competition among churches in evangelism has many times hindered effective outreach. Because of its political stability and religious freedom, Kenya has been a fertile soil for evangelism. Some of the overseas sects, especially from the United States of America, which were late during the "Scramble for Africa," are now invading the country during this eleventh hour with a hope of extending their ecclesiastical empire. They come with sophisticated electronics and thousands of dollars to lure Christians from historic churches. Such evangelism does not do justice to the mission of the Church. In a country where 73 percent of the total population is Christian, new missionaries coming from overseas should come to help the existing churches in fulfilling their missionary task instead of coming to "steal flock" from the existing churches. Such missionaries would be more helpful if they were to go "where Christ has not been already named."

The evangelistic task is further hindered by multiplicity of breakaway churches and sects. The Registrar of Societies in Kenya receives several applications for registration of new churches each month. Between 1973 and 1979, ninety-one new indigenous churches were registered in Kenya, some bearing such names as: Truth in Leadership of Spirit Church of God, Power of Jesus

Around the World Church, Church of Peace in Africa, Gospel of Jesus Christ Around the World, Chosen Church of the Holy Spirit, Apostles Christian Church of Africa, The Holiness Salvation Church of God, Church of Mercy of Jesus Christ. Most of these churches arise because of personality clashes. Some of the people who feel they should lead and are not elected to positions of leadership start their own sects and usually get some followers. Some independent churches have their background in a genuine concern that Christianity as presented by foreign missionaries distorted the truth of the Gospel on cultural and political issues. As Jomo Kenyatta once said, when the white men came "we had the land and they had the Bible. Now we have the Bible and they have the land."

Inspite of these negative forces, it is generally accepted that the Church is growing faster in Kenya than probably any other part of the world. I have witnessed this in my own diocese, where thousands of people are turning to Christ. We are beginning an average of two congregations each month; and as a bishop, I have the task of confirming about six thousand candidates each year. In one parish a few years ago, I confirmed a record of 895 candidates on a Thursday afternoon. After confirming four hundred candidates, we had to break for a cup of tea. This fast growth is evident in various other parts of Kenya.

Teaching Ministry

The teaching ministry of the Church is crucial in enabling the Church in Africa to fulfill its mission. In Kenya and Uganda the Church has many "preachers" but few teachers. Many people, including the laity, have no problem in confronting unbelievers with the Good News of Jesus Christ and in persuading them to accept Christ as their personal savior. But a relatively small number of these "preachers" have the ability and the knowledge required to help the new believers to understand the implications of becoming Christians. Hence we have many preachers but few teachers. Consequently there are many believers who have remained undernourished. Some Pentecostal sects are known to have invaded villages and proclaimed the Gospel. Many people accept the message and are baptized. The evangelists then move on to new areas leaving no one behind to teach the new believers. Anxious to be taught, the new believers invite Anglican pastors to come to teach them more about Jesus; and before very long, they all become Anglicans as they are impressed by the stability, better organization, and, above all, the teaching ministry of the Anglican Church.

To be effective in its teaching mission, the Church in Africa requires well-trained clergy. The greatest temptation today is that even with the Anglican Church, some bishops, on account of the great demand for ordained ministers, are hastening to ordain people with virtually no theological or pastoral training. Whereas less-educated people have a role to play in the mission of the Church, the Church would be at a great disadvantage without well-educated Christian leaders. St. Paul, the best educated person among the Apostles, made greater impact on the mission of the early Church than those who had been with Jesus during His lifetime. His writings continue to inspire the Church throughout its history. Equipping the clergy for the ministry must then be given a rightful place in Africa. To this end, the existing theological colleges—such as St. Paul's United Theological College in Limuru and Bishop Tucker College in Mukono, Uganda—should give the kind of theological education that will enable the clergy to serve various sectors of East African society with dedication and confidence. The graduates of these colleges should be capable of proclaiming with authority the Gospel in schools, colleges, and city pulpits, and should be capable of exercising an effective, prophetic ministry.

Overseas partners should consider giving financial support to these colleges, allowing them to start post-graduate programs so that East African theological students should not need to leave their home countries to go to do post-graduate courses overseas, but should do these studies within the context of the church they will serve. Theological education, whether in colleges or Bible schools, should be done in such a way that students are not only taught theology but are also introduced to other aspects of the mission of the Church. This is why the diocese of Mt. Kenya East has established St. Andrews Institute for Mission and Evangelism, which is "the theological and development resource center" for the Church. Thirty theological students are currently attending a three-year theological course in preparation for ordained ministry while at the same time shorter courses in community health and rural development are being offered to other persons. The candidates for ordination are not being trained in isolation. They mingle freely with people from all walks of life who come to attend short development courses.

Since we started theological education by extension in 1978, we have found many lay persons anxious to learn more about the Bible and Christian doctrine. The T.E.E. program aims at taking "theology" where people are. During the last two years, two tutors have been trying to start one class in each of our 260 congregations. As it is virtually impossible for two people to meet such a demand, the tutors have tried to train at least one facilitator from each congregation who can teach the other people. We have a long way to go before we can achieve our target, but we are deeply impressed by the desire of many lay people to learn more about Jesus Christ.

There is great need for cooperation in theological education in Kenya. St. Paul's United Theological College is one important symbol of cooperation among churches. Originally founded by the Anglican Church, the college is now jointly owned by the Church of the Province of Kenya, the Presbyterian Church of East Africa, the Methodist Church of Kenya, and the Kenya Reformed Church. In recent years, however, a number of evangelical theological schools have mushroomed in and around the city of Nairobi without any coordination. Such schools include Daystar International, Nairobi Evangelical Graduate School of Theology, Nairobi International School of Theology, Eastern Bible College, Scott Theological College, and East African Bible School. These schools are funded from external sources.

Healing and Reconciling Ministry

The pioneering missionaries played a leading role in the healing ministry of the Church. They built hospitals and dispensaries, and some of them were well-qualified medical doctors. At one time some politicians in Kenya wanted the government to take over all church hospitals. The government was reluctant, as 40 percent of the medical work in Kenya is done by churches, and the expenses of taking them over and running them would have been prohibitive. The government, therefore, has continued to urge churches to be partners in the healing ministry.

At the time of independence most of the African countries pledged to fight against disease, poverty, and ignorance. The battle seems to have been lost in all three areas. The continent of Africa is said to be poorer now than twenty years ago. More than 100 million people are threatened with starvation. Diseases, which have long been eradicated in some other parts of the world, continue to bring death to millions of people in Africa. Five million children in Africa are said to die each year before they reach

the age of five because of diarrhea. Others die of such immuniza-
ble diseases as measles and whooping cough.

The World Health Organization has told the Third World countries that the battle against disease cannot be won if these countries wait until they have a sufficient number of doctors trained in
the traditional Western way. Even after five years of university
training, the doctors tend to stay in cities instead of moving to the
rural areas where the need is greatest. The World Health Organization has recommended a crash program of training community
health workers for two months, who then go back to their respective villages to pioneer in primary health care. Following this
advice, the diocese of Mt. Kenya East has already trained 170
community health workers, who are doing commendable work in
rural villages. Their training is narrowed to the five most common
diseases, and they are taught how to prevent them. Some of them
are also involved in family planning programs. We are also urging
pastors, evangelists, and lay readers to use the pulpit to remove
ignorance from our people. For instance UNICEF has recently
found a simple formula to treat diarrhea. As soon as diarrhea
begins, the child can be given a mixture of sugar and salt in clean
water and in appropriate proportions until diarrhea stops. This
simple formula can be communicated to mothers from church
pulpits and can help to arrest this killer of African children.

In order to bring about community health in Africa, churches
need to join hands with governments and all other agencies and,
as far as possible, work together in cooperation. The churches
should also play their role in tackling the problem of hunger,
which poses a great threat to the social and political stability of
African nations. The Church cannot just evangelize; indeed she
cannot effectively evangelize hungry people. "An empty stomach
has no ears," to quote an African saying.

The Church and Social Transformation
Many Christians in Africa and in other parts of the world have
accepted social service as part of their mission to the world. They
will quickly respond to financial appeals for famine relief, earth-
quake victims, casualties of civil wars, and epidemic diseases.
They will support with a clear conscience all philanthropic and
humanitarian activities and will gladly identify themselves with
the Good Samaritan and all that he stands for. The same Christians will find it difficult to be involved in social action that may
mean political and economic activity aimed at transforming the

structures of the society that are by and large responsible for most human suffering.

St. John records the story of the man who was ill for thirty-eight years and could not get anyone to help him to get into the pool of Bethesda. The society was so selfish that this helpless man had no one to help him get to the pool at the right time. Jesus not only healed this man but also commanded him to break the Sabbath: "Rise, take your bed and walk" (John 5:8). The more I read this story the more I am convinced that the writer wants his readers to know Jesus is not only interested in healing the sick, but also in challenging the structures of the society that are responsible for human suffering. The authorities were more concerned about observing the Sabbath and maintaining the status quo than seeing a man who was sick for thirty-eight years receive health. Jesus deliberately asked this man to challenge this inhuman society by an act of defiance of its rule. God had provided the stirred-up pool of water for the healing of this man. But the social structures were such that the society, with all its selfishness and useless piety, would not give this man a chance to be healed. Jesus was convinced that what needed stirring up was the social pool of a stagnant, selfish Jewish society for the holistic healing of men. There are many sick men, women, and children in the Third World who die daily, not because treatment is unavailable, but simply because no one cares to extend health facilities to them.

It is well and good to provide soup to famine-stricken, nomadic people. It is even more important to find out the cause of hunger and seek ways and means of solving the problem. The Kenya government has often said it has sufficient food in its stores to feed all Kenyans. But many people in Kenya are suffering from a food shortage. One of the basic problems is poor channels of food distribution and attempts by middlemen to gain as much profit as possible when demand is high and supply low. Many poor people have often queued in shops for some items that have become scarce because a few selfish men have smuggled the goods across the border and consequently have enriched themselves at the expense of the powerless. Sometimes bad planning is responsible for hunger in some of the African countries.

The Church in Africa must address itself not only to hunger, malnutrition, disease, poverty, and ignorance, but must also struggle for a just society. Most of the countries have accepted the human rights as contained in the United Nations Declaration of 1948, but these rights are not always enjoyed by the citizens of these countries. The churches should take initiative in teaching people about their basic human rights so that they can take a stand when they are denied their rights. In order to exercise their prophetic ministry, church leaders must make a serious effort to understand political issues in their respective countries and help other citizens form an intelligent public opinion. Church leaders should, as far as possible, avoid being too closely associated with the powers-that-be, but should be in a position to give them support whenever they uphold standards of justice and righteousness that God requires; and they should be prepared to criticize them fearlessly when they depart from the standard of justice that God requires from those to whom He has given authority to rule.

The great disadvantage of the Church getting "too hand-in-glove" with the state is that the Church ceases to be "the salt of the earth." If the Church is favored by the state, there is always the temptation to remain silent when it should speak out. The opposite danger is for the Church to withdraw too radically from the world. This also prevents it from becoming the salt of the earth. A Christian community that is cut off from the rest of society and that is living an enclosed life of its own cannot be effective and may become paralyzed or perish altogether. Christians should not be mere obedient spectators, but active participants in the social and political welfare of their nations. Those who have the right to elect leaders and to influence the welfare of their nation should take full advantage of their privileges. There are, however, some governments that do not tolerate criticism and they will be quick to silence the voice of prophets. In such cases Christian leaders must be united in exercising their prophetic ministry and be willing to suffer together rather than leave a lone prophet to suffer alone. In countries where Christians have the opportunity to exercise their prophetic ministry, they should do it fearlessly. "Otherwise they will have only themselves to blame when totalitarian governments take over, such as Idi Amin's regime in Uganda."

One of the main dilemmas of many Christians in Africa is whether a Christian should participate in armed struggle for political and economic independence. Many of our Western brethren condemned armed struggles in Mozambique, Angola, and Zimbabwe, and continue to condemn freedom fighters in Namibia and South Africa. There was an outcry in the West when the World Council of Churches initiated the "program to combat racism" in the early 1970's. The same Western brethren would not have seen anything wrong in Christians taking up arms to fight against Hitler during World War II. Many of our Western brethren will see violence when the oppressed people take up arms to liberate themselves, but they do not see the violence when the black people suffer in the hands of the white racists in South Africa.

It is because the system in South Africa is already violent that some of the Christians believe they have the duty to be involved in the liberation struggle. To make it worse, "the institutionalized violence" is supported by certain aspects of the Church in the name of preserving Christian civilization. Of course the shedding of blood should be avoided as much as possible. But if all peaceful methods of bringing justice in an injust system fail, then institutionalized violence may be confronted by armed struggle. Because of its racist policy of apartheid, South Africa is moving toward a regrettable, bloody confrontation. This can be avoided if this country, which claims to be a Christian nation, changes its racist policies to conform with the Gospel of Jesus Christ. The Dutch Reformed Church, which gives the government its "theological" blueprint, must change its attitude and adopt the stand of some of its theologians who no longer believe "apartheid policy" has a sound biblical base.

ANGLICAN HERITAGE AND THE MISSION OF THE CHURCH

In the former British colonies the Anglican Church was a favored church by the colonizers. To some extent this proved to be a disadvantage during the struggle for independence. This disadvantage is no longer an issue, especially as leadership of the Church is now in the hands of the local people. In some countries, however, the Anglican Church still enjoys certain privileges. In Kenya, the Anglican archbishop is always invited to represent Protestants in saying prayers during the opening of Parliament and other important national festivals. The Anglican Church has the sole right of appointing chaplains to the armed forces. In this privileged position the Church, under the right and able leadership, can make great impact in the society.

The 1662 prayer book, which is still in use in Kenya, is a hindrance in the mission of the Church. There is great urgency for an alternate prayer book based on African cultural heritage. The African people are usually joyful people. The alternate liturgy should give room for a truly African, joyful worship.

The African Church has not fully made use of the good cultural concepts in its life. For instance, the concept of "community." African culture believes that man is not truly man in isolation. As Professor Mbiti has said: "I am because we are / And because we are / therefore I am." We have made the mistake of adopting Western individualism instead of enriching the Christian faith with our understanding of the solidarity of the individuals within the community.

Our Anglican heritage has also been a hindrance in dealing with some of the pastoral problems that confront the Church in Africa. Polygamy is at the top of the list of such problems. As early as 1862, Bishop John Colenso, the first bishop of Natal, wrote to the Archbishop of Canterbury expressing his conviction on this issue: "The conviction has deepened within me more and more that the common practice of requiring a man, who may have more than one wife at the time of his conversion, to put away all but one before he can receive Christian baptism, is unwarranted by scriptures, unsanctioned by apostolic example and authority, condemned by common reason and sense of right, and altogether unjustifiable." Yet the 1888 Lambeth Conference resolved: "It is the opinion of this conference that persons living in polygamy be not admitted to Baptism, but that they be kept under Christian instruction until such a time they shall be in a position to accept the Law of Christ." Since 1888, the Church in Africa has excluded polygamists from enjoying Christian sacraments, although in some provinces polygamists are baptized but cannot be confirmed and are excluded from receiving Holy Communion. Some of them regularly attend church and patiently wait until God "frees them" from the state of polygamy so as to benefit from the sacraments of the Church.

After several years of studying the problem of polygamy, the Church of the Province of Kenya has recently adopted a new regulation on polygamy:

CHURCH AND POLYGAMY

The Church of the Province of Kenya is convinced that monogamy is God's plan for marriage and that is the ideal relationship for the expression of love between a husband and wife. Nevertheless this teaching is not easily understood in many Kenyan cultures in which polygamy is widely practised and is socially acceptable. While it teaches monogamy, the Church must be pastorally sensitive to the widespread existence of polygamy.

(a) *People Who Were Polygamists Before Becoming Christians*

That a person who becomes a polygamist before becoming a Christian shall on accepting the gospel be baptised with his believing wives and children on condition that he shall not take any other wives. The Bishop may confirm such a polygamist, his wives and children after further instructions in the Christian faith. That person who has contracted a polygamous marriage before or after baptism should not in any way be required or compelled to put away any of his wives as a condition of being admitted or re-admitted to the Holy Communion.

(b) *People Who Become Polygamists While Already Christians*

A Christian who becomes a polygamist deprives himself of the privileges of participation in Holy Communion, standing as sponsor in baptism and in holding office as a member of a church committee or parish council. Also that in keeping with the teaching of St. Paul, no polygamist should hold office as a Bishop, Priest, or deacon or lay-reader. The Bishop shall have the discretion to re-admit a polygamist to the full privileges of lay church membership after due consideration of the following circumstances with regard to each individual case.

(i) The lapse of a notable time.

(ii) The polygamist's repentance for his faults in breaking the vows which he made at his marriage.

(iii) The acceptability of such re-admission in the eyes of the local church.

(iv) Special factors operating in an individual case which made it hard for the polygamists to resist to take a second wife.

CONCLUSION

To conclude this essay, allow me to quote from one of the recent documents prepared for the Sixth Anglican Consultative Council meeting held in Nigeria in July 1984.

There is a growing consensus that the Church's mission in some way involves proclamation, the common life of the Church, and the Church's relation to society as a whole. The mission of the church involves speaking, being and doing. We can say that mission involves making known the truth about God revealed in Christ through what Christians say, through what they are and through what they do. Speaking, being and doing are all aspects of the Church's proclamation. Each must in some way be present if the word spoken and the deeds done are to have power. Thus if the church only speaks of God but does not live a common life that shows forth the nature of God's life, her words will seem empty. If the church cares only for its own members and shows no compassion for human suffering and no outrage at human injustice, the love she proclaims and displays will appear shallow or selfish. If on the other hand the church only does good works and seeks justice, she will fail to speak of God and so fail to make known the one in whose name she has been sent.

"As the Father has sent me, so I send you."

BIBLIOGRAPHY

Anglican Consultative Council. *Giving Mission Its Proper Place*. London: A.C.C., 1984.

Barrett, David B. *The World Christian Encyclopedia: A Comparative Survey of Churches and Religions in the Modern World, A.D. 1900 to 2000*. Oxford: Oxford University Press, 1982.

Gitari, D. M. "Church and Polygamy," in *Transformation: An International Dialogue on Evangelical Social Ethics*, vol. I (January–March 1984).

National Christian Council of Kenya. *A Christian View of Politics in Kenya: Love, Peace, and Unity*. Nairobi, Kenya: Uzima Press, 1983.

Provincial Board of Theological Education. *Let the Church Be the Church*. Nairobi, Kenya: Uzima Press, 1984.

Sine, Tom, ed. *The Church in Response to Human Need*. Monrovia, California: Missions Advanced Research and Communication Center, 1983.

Stott, J. R. W. *Christian Mission in the Modern World*. London: Church Pastoral Aid Society, 1975.

Tuma, Tom and Phares, Mutibwa, eds. *A Century of Christianity in Uganda, 1877–1977*. Kampala, Uganda: Church of Uganda, 1978.

Mission, Morals, and Folk Religion

Helen Oppenheimer

What Is the Mission of Christ's Church?

The Oxford Dictionary defines "mission" as "a sending or being sent to perform some function or service." The Analytical Concordance to the Revised Standard Version of the New Testament gives only three instances where the Greek is translated by the noun "mission," but more than a hundred instances of the verb *apostello* ("I send"), from Herod, who sent and killed the innocents,[1] to the Father, who sent his Son.[2]

The mission of Christ's Church, then, is whatever it is sent by its Master to do. "Mission" is not to be shrunk to mean "evangelism" only; and that part of mission that is evangelism is itself not to be shrunk to mean simply preaching the Gospel across the seas. We know that "all churches are in a missionary situation."[3] The task of every church is to testify by word and deed to the sovereignty of God.[4] So understood, "mission" is a most comprehensive word meaning practically everything, or maybe everything except worship when we turn toward God for refreshment and restoration before being sent outward again.

So the idea of mission expands to mean whatever we do in God's name: and here our problems begin. To talk to our "task of mission"[5] is almost to say our "task of task." We have to inquire: How can we talk about mission as such? It is proclaiming the Gospel, it is social concern, it is helping one another, it is studying theology. It is not some distinct enterprise we can concentrate upon and try to do better. When I read some enthusiastic accounts of the all-embracing mission of Christ's Church, I am reminded of that famous character in one of Molière's plays who was impressed to realize that he had been talking prose all his life. But if he had, then prose is simply language. And if all we do is mission, then mission is simply Christian activity and has no special theology of its own.

If the meaning of mission is neither to be expanded to general busyness nor shrunk to proselytizing, what is it? We may try to strike a balance between the vaguely general and the narrowly particular by saying that mission is spreading the Gospel. This way of putting it positively invites us to keep in touch, both with general and fundamental theology, and with particular and definite policies. On the one hand we have to consider what is this Gospel we are sent to spread; and, on the other hand, how we are to set about spreading it.

This is a way of limiting the notion of mission so that it is not just a way of talking about our whole Christian activity while giving the impression of being more specific. But I think it carries with it the corollary that mission is not an end in itself. Spreading is for gathering. If the gatherers only gather in order to spread again, the whole exercise, though self-perpetuating, is pointless. Somewhere we must come to rest in a Christian life to be lived, not simply communicated. We shall never know what our mission truly is unless we know what mission is for, and mission is not just for more mission. So the question "What is the mission of Christ's Church?" requires an answer to the question "What is the Gospel?", not because they are really the same question but because the one depends upon the other.

Once this has been sorted out, we can see that a theologian (almost by definition) can best contribute to our task of understanding our Christian mission and making it effective by attending to the theological question "What is the Gospel?" rather than to the practical questions about strategy and tactics. This indeed is where I would hope to have something to say.

The formulation, however, is too simple, for two reasons. First, if the theologian is a moral theologian; the question "What is the Gospel?" will arise in the form "What is the Christian life?" So it cannot be separated from questions about how people may be encouraged to lead the Christian life. And, in fact, moral theology is not a category on its own. However hard philosophers may try to segregate "is" and "ought," Christian theology as doctrine cannot really be separated from Christian theology as ethics. The way we are to live is to be a response to what we believe about the nature of God. Whether we use the terminology of the Kingdom or of being "in Christ," we are talking both theology and morality. So the theory that is to back our mission, the theory that the theologian's task is to interpret, cannot stay theoretical.

Second, the question "What is the Gospel?" can hardly be answered "neat." The most basic statement of what the Gospel is, if it is to be comprehensible to a particular society, must be in terms of what that society understands already. So again, the theological questions, although distinct from the questions about communication, are not separable from them.

So must I as a theologian be my own sociologist? Perhaps it is good enough if I know that I need sociologists and that I am not one; and better still if I know that whatever I try to say I cannot step clean out of my own setting, which a sociologist might study. My thoughts must be about my own world and are bound to be conditioned by it.

Three Selected Problems

Rather than enter into the strategy and tactics of Christian mission, I should like to offer some theological support for the practical task. I will select three obvious aspects of the English setting—polarization, secularization, and establishment—and indicate in each case something that seems to be going wrong and that needs theological attention as foundation for Christian mission. With the first of these it is the polarization itself that is wrong. Secularization and establishment are more neutral, and, indeed, I believe that establishment on balance is good; but all is not entirely well. What I should like to say is the same under each heading—that hasty ethical assumptions are making it unnecessarily hard to see what the Christian Gospel really is. In each case, of course, this is only a small part of the whole problem. The three aspects are selected out of the whole picture, and a limited slice of each will be looked at; but if this much could be seen more clearly, we might be on a better footing for commending and practicing our faith.

Polarization. The application to polarization is the simplest and the most obvious, but as urgent as any problem we have. Not so much violent emnity but a kind of indifferent antagonism besets public life in general and haunts Christian attempts to take the whole of human existence seriously. C. S. Lewis' Screwtape pointed out long ago that, but for the work of the devil, the high and low parties in the Church of England might have become "a perfect hotbed of charity and humility."[6] Today the deadening hostility has shifted from "high" versus "low" to "traditional" versus "radical." What could be a life-enhancing difference of emphasis seems to straddle a watershed. On the one hand stand the ancient dogmas and ways of worship; on the other stands modernity tending toward humanism. The people across the ridge are hardly seen as real human beings; and the best of "ours" and the worst of "the others" are relentlessly seen as typical. The "trendies" are strongest on social concern; but when they seem to upset all the old certainties, including moral standards, they make compassion look like a bandwagon that some people wish would roll away. Meanwhile some of the "diehards" in their rectitude seem to have so little imagination about where the shoe pinches for other people that they hide their own need and their own human fears and miseries behind too impenetrable a mask.

So slogans become war cries, and gloomy analyses turn out to be self-fulfilling. It is tempting for those theologians who are not inclined to rush into the political fray to hold their peace and think about something else. But somehow real Christian love has got to be brought back into the picture. "Equality" and "liberty" are having every ounce of goodness squeezed out of them, but somehow "fraternity" is getting lost.

Is that just another watchword, generating another set of platitudes to be overworked by some and ignored by others? We cannot avoid platitudes; in fact, we need them. But how can we put them to work without making them into war cries, deafening rather than encouraging? At least we can try to offer our platitudes with courtesy, to look at them in the round rather than from only one angle, to keep giving them a rest and a change. To say that critical affection is what we need in both church and nation is, of course, a platitude; but it is what we need, and it could be a help to say so. Criticism without affection is destructive; affection without criticism is complacent. There is a world of difference between anger and crossness. We are told that the Lord wept over Jerusalem.[7]

If it is a good platitude that we most need for overcoming the polarization that besets us both in church and nation, then where does "a mistaken view of Christian ethics" come in? Nobody is going to object to the obvious statement that disagreeable polarization comes from a failure of love. There may not be much inspiration, but there is no evident error to correct.

In fact I have already begun to try to edge away from platitude toward something more controversial by specifying not simply "love" but "affection" as what we need. I believe that there is a false understanding of Christian ethics, indeed of Christian theology, which is being a real stumbling block to Christian mission.

There is a prevalent idea that Christian love is something imper-
sonal and generalized, that it has nothing to do with delight in
somebody's existence but simply with willing somebody's good.
No wonder then that we signally fail to delight in the existence of
those on the other side of the political fence.

It is frequently said as a comfort to people who are finding their
fellows hard to love that, at any rate, there is no Christian obligation to like one another. I am convinced, and have argued at
length elsewhere,[8] that this is a profoundly unsatisfactory way of
understanding what love is meant to be.

We shall never learn to love our neighbors, let alone to have an
"option for the poor," unless we can somehow learn to like other
people, to let their doings and their troubles matter to us, to mind
about what happens to them with warmth, not merely undertake
their betterment with dutiful coolness. The Lord ate and drank
with the most assorted people. If He had not enjoyed their company and they His, He would hardly have been welcome in their
midst.

This is no trivial matter. It is a matter of what we think a human
person is and how people are to be valued. The doctrine that there
is no need to like offers us a dismal picture of life in the Kingdom.
It may be suggested that it is only too clear that our likes and
dislikes are not in our own control, so they cannot be part of our
duty. I have suggested

> . . . that love is not obviously in our control either, in fact that there
> is something paradoxical about its being commanded. We may well
> discover that it is no more difficult after all to try to like than to try to
> love. People do learn to like things. We talk about acquired tastes.
> When people refuse even to try to like garlic, we call them faddy.
> When they are sure they cannot like people, we call them prejudiced.
>
> There is a way of meeting the world with a readiness to be pleased
> which is at least as much within our power as behaving as if we were
> pleased when we are not. Loving is not really any more within our
> own capacity than liking is.[9]

That is the main point here. We cannot keep any of God's com-
mands in our own strength. We shall always need Augustine's
prayer "Give what thou commandest" before we can truly say
"Command what thou wilt."[10] The effort that is asked of us is
much more like a hopeful direction of our attention than a vain
prodding of our wills.[11]

Of course there is a great deal more to be said if "liking" in its
apparent triviality and one-sidedness is to be set up as an essential
part of Christian love. I am convinced that the argument is impor-

tant, but this is not the place to pursue it further. Here let me seize on the point that to allow love to be compatible with dislike is hardly the way to overcome polarizations in church or nation. People who have such a limited understanding of love will never learn to attend to one another as God's children. Our mission needs to be grounded on a more constructive way of looking at Christian ethics, and to affirm this is a matter of theology. So we are pointed back from our practical situation to the question "What is the Gospel?"

Secularization. The most prominent feature of the practical situation in Western society is, of course, secularization. Instead of trying to analyze our condition sociologially, let me take hold of one aspect of it as an ethical and theological problem, leading once again to inquiry about the content of the Gospel.

It is another slogan-turned-war-cry to say that mankind has "come of age." It is certainly a platitude to assert that all over the world human societies are showing the symptoms, welcome or unwelcome, of healthy adolescence: a passionate affirmation of autonomy; an impatience with authority, especially when imposed from outside; an energy and self-assurance that promise great things; and a lack of caution that frightens the orderly. It is a steadying thought that this frame of mind is not brand new. Wordsworth hailed with affection the "Glad Hearts! without reproach or blot," who do not ask whether the eye of duty is upon them but

> who in love and truth
> Where no misgiving is, rely
> Upon the genial sense of youth.[12]

Of course secularization creates difficulties for Christian mission, but I do not think what we need is a grand attack upon worldliness and the "permissive society." It is doubtful whether human beings are trying any less hard to be good than they ever were, although they may see goodness in a somewhat different light. What is quite clear is that in some parts of the world, including England, they are worshiping God a good deal less; and it is more to our present purpose to consider this fact. How is it related to the present emphasis upon moral autonomy and independence?

Another misleading shortcut opens up here, and hasty criticisms push themselves into the argument. It is an easy oversimplification to say that modern man is a rebel, turning his back on God, withholding the duty he ought to realize that he owes, defiantly eating the fruit of the tree of knowledge of good and evil and needing to be taught obedience. To see what is going wrong we need to go a longer way round than that.

What modern men and women have discovered afresh is that our human autonomy, our moral and political self-rule, is a good thing. Autonomy means that we have a need to make our own mistakes and find our own way, to discover for ourselves what is worthwhile, and not always take our values automatically from other people. The hierarchical view of life has gone. We do not believe that the world is supposed to be organized in permanent pyramids, with people inexorably slotted into their proper stations, from which it will not please God to call them up higher or pull them down lower. It is equality now that seems as obvious as hierarchy once seemed; but a corollary of this is that a good deal that once used to pass for the worship of God on high has become suspect too. It has come to look like ignoble self-abasement before a powerful ruler who has been presumed to be wise because in any case we have had to submit to Him.

Loyal Christians can see that true worship is certainly not like this, and may be tempted hastily to blame autonomy and equality. It needs to be reasserted that to believe in the equality of God's people before their heavenly Father is potentially at least as "religious" as to believe that we should order ourselves lowly and reverently to our betters. It is not right to misuse the idea of becoming as little children to keep us infantile. We can be more hopeful that, in the words of the Epistle to the Ephesians, we may attain "to mature manhood, to the measure of the stature of the fullness of Christ."[13] It is not in loss of hierarchy that I am identifying mistaken assumptions about the nature of Christian ethics. It is much better that we should worship God for His goodness, not for His stark power. But in a way we have not taken this development far enough. We still have a tendency to assume that since, by definition, God always knows best, His goodness must take the form of a moment-by-moment apportionment of heavenly favor. The new-found understanding of human rights is at one with the old-style submission to divine right in assuming that God's power means a Providence that guides the universe on a very tight rein.

Moralism is profoundly human. Its most endearing shape is an intense belief in fairness. But that belief can lead us to take short-cuts, instead of wrestling like Job with the implications of an unfair world created by a good God. The old shortcut was to deny the unfairness; the new one denies the good God.

The sufferings of the world have always been obvious. If God is good and everything that happens is His will but a great deal that happens is very unpleasant, something is wrong somewhere. Before we "came of age" and began to appreciate moral autonomy, we could simply assume that God was right and we were wrong about what constituted fairness. Once upon a time it was much easier than it is now to assume that everything that is wrong is somehow wrong with us. So when things went badly one could be sure that "these things are sent to try us." Pain and suffering were good for our souls. Untimely death was a delivery out of the miseries of this sinful world. Everything was really for the best, and trust was the best virtue. For this kind of "moralism," trust is trust in Providence.

People, however, who have come to understand that democracy is not mob rule, that might may not be right, and that to defy authority is not always rebellion, are not going to continue straightforwardly in lowly subservience to an almightly but unseen king. When Providence fails to back our moral endeavors, when the actual course of events is by all human standards not "for the best" at all but positively disastrous, what this seems to show is not the sinful folly of our human impatience but the impossibility that God is good. But if God is, then we know He is good. It seems to follow that there cannot be a God. So atheism takes a moral slant.

It is hardly possible to overrate the extent to which this appreciation of the ancient problem of evil is both the result of secularization and then, in turn, the cause of more secularization. It only remains for the pious to assure us that evil is not the problem at all, but sin, for faith to take on an almost malign aspect. How dare we seem to say that God is quite happy about cancer so long as people are kind to one another? This resentment of undeserved suffering, not moral laxity, is the acute difficulty confronting our mission today. Mission is not just urging lazy and worldly people to be more "committed." It is convincing people of integrity that there is any sense in talking about a God who claims our commitment. At least we are no longer allowed to say, "The fool hath said in his heart, there is no God."[14] The onus is on us as believers to give reason for the faith that is in us,[15] to vindicate ourselves and the God we worship as not, after all, heartless about human misery.

So once again we are pushed by moral considerations to look

urgently at the content of our belief. I think it will be necessary to sit much more loosely to believe in providence than Christians have been wont to do, and to consider more closely what we mean by grace. To anticipate the conclusion: far from belittling grace, I should like to try to understand it, not as an external force that pushes things about for our edification, but as an internal influence.[16] It is both cruel and implausible to say that everything that happens is God's will. What we can say as Christians is that God enters into everything that happens, that He is to be found in the world and in ourselves.

Establishment. Before enlarging upon this way of understanding the Gospel, let me come to the third conspicuous aspect of the English setting—establishment. Here I will be more selective than ever, to lead up to what I most want to say. But first let me explain that by "establishment" I mean the fact that the Church of England is historically the Church *of England;* that, for both good and ill, church and nation are linked by law and custom and sentiment. The advantages and disadvantages of our situation have been much canvassed lately. As far as the political question of establishment versus disestablishment is concerned, for myself I go along with the conservative conclusions, lightened by ecumenism, recently expressed by the Archibishop of York.[17] He clarifies the discussion[18] by distinguishing at the outset between "establishment" in its "limited, technical meaning," and "the Establishment" in its more modern pejorative sense as "an omnibus term for the real or imagined élite at the centre of English society." He denies that nowadays the Church is actually part of "the Establishment" in this second sense; and goes on to face squarely and, I believe, meet, the objections that are being made to "establishment" in the technical and historical sense. Whatever the outcome, what we need most for the sake of the well-being of the Church and its mission to the whole of society is surely, once again, critical affection.

For some Christians, however, their affection for the Church as it is is sternly tested by its tendency to encourage mere belonging without definite commitment. Our establishment has cushioned us for centuries, and now we are at risk of being identified with the church in Laodicea: "Because you are lukewarm, and neither cold nor hot, I will spew you out of my mouth. For you say, I am rich, I have prospered, and I need nothing; not knowing that you are wretched, pitiable, poor, blind, and naked."[19]

It is easy to see the Church of England that way—easy but

superficial. Of course there is a problem, but I do not believe that either the more gloomy diagnoses nor the more drastic cures proposed have entirely understood the case. The symptom that is causing most concern goes by the name of "folk religion," a phenomenon that infuriates the orthodox and baffles the tidy-minded.

The regular complaint about "folk religion" in England is not that the true faith cannot be grounded in a substratum of something less specific, nor that the true faith may not take different characteristic forms in different cultures. What is causing a good deal of clerical indignation is the worry that the nation at large is letting itself be taken in by a substitute for the true faith. The worry is not simply imaginary, but it is one-sided.

What is "folk religion"? For good and ill, it is the kind of religion that is indigenous in whatever society we are talking about. It is the fertility rite, the tribal dance and the local shrine, the harvest festival and the Christmas crib. It is calling on the name of the Lord in a crisis. It is weddings and funerals and the tending of graves. It is as it were homemade "do-it-yourself" piety, evolved over centuries, resilient, even obstinate, but inclined to be inarticulate and untheological. It can be vigorous and primitive or it can resemble the line of seaweed on a beach when the tide is going out. It is a people's own style of religion that anthropologists could study, a complex of customs and maybe superstitions that may not seem to make logical sense but are deeply rooted in common esteem. English folk religion is English first and religious second. This does not mean that it is insincere, but that, like charity, it is apt to "begin at home" whether or not it ends there. It does not draw a clear line between love of country and love of God. It is inclined to look on enthusiasm as "a very horrid thing."

A potentially quite acrimonious argument is developing between those church people who think that "folk religion" is a good basis to build on and those who look on it as a deplorably soft option. Some have a vision of "the Lord's people at the Lord's service on the Lord's Day" and would count it betrayal to settle for anything less. Others are beginning to urge attractively that "folk religion" has validity in its own right and that "commitment" is a special vocation.[20]

To speak for myself, I must affirm that I have no sympathy with the legalists and rigorists here and find it horrifying when Christians cast themselves in the role of Elder Brother.[21] Yet on the other hand, are some of us putting ourselves in the position of sending food parcels to the prodigal in the far country, encouraging him to think there is no need to come home at all? The rigorist misses the point of God's mercy, but the liberal misses the point the other way when he has no sympathy at all for the laborers in the vineyard who have to bear the burden and the heat of the day.[22]

Of course it is discouraging for pastors with a vision of God's people answering His call and dedicating themselves to His service to find the Christian faith being looked on as a sort of branch of patriotism and good citizenship. It is natural for clergy to feel, not just that they themselves are being "used," but that God Himself is being "used" just to impart "that little bit extra" to a rite of passage, by people who at ordinary times in their lives simply do not care. No wonder disapproval tips into resentment, and would-be prophecy expresses itself simply as nagging. The result is unedifying. Human beings are not inclined to respond to nagging, and English human beings know in their bones that it is not a good thing to wear their hearts on their sleeves. So when more commitment is urged upon them, they are embarrassed, not responsive. Worse, when more commitment is demanded of them as the price of the welcome they thought they could expect for themselves and their children, they simply go politely away, sheep who really are lost because they no longer want to be in the fold. They will not argue or give reasons or ask for anything; they will simply melt away. But it is part of the meaning of establishment that they do still belong and very likely still call themselves Christian and "C of E." Neither to write them off on the one hand nor to speak merely soothing words to them on the other seems to be in accord with the Spirit of Christ. Haunted by the demand for perfection,[23] we are at a loss how to apply it to people who seem somehow to have been inoculated against real commitment by small doses of Bible teaching so that they cannot catch a live faith.

A small suggestion, which sounds merely tactical but is not without theological bearings, is that the word "commitment" itself is overworked. It seems to belong to a particular style of mission, not the Gospel itself. It is liable to antagonize as much as it encourages because it gives the appearance of an onslaught on people's integrity. It is not just laziness that makes some good but not pious people draw back from it, so much as a distaste for "showing off," for praying on street corners and "making a fuss." The demand for commitment is apt to come in such a way as to provide a fine excuse for not praying anywhere at all.

Where "commitment" is seen as an encouragement, it may encourage people to think that their Christianity is somehow their own doing. Of course that is extremely far from being what is intended. We are to commit ourselves into God's hands. "Justification by commitment" ought to be the same as justification by faith. But even if it is, claiming to be committed sounds very like claiming to be actually faithful. It is all too easy to imagine that we have somehow put God in our debt.

We do need a word to do the work that "commitment" is being pressed to do. I would suggest that "practice" would be a useful alternative. If perfection really is our goal, it is not commitment that "makes perfect" but practice. A practicing Christian is as definite and energetic an idea as a committed Christian, without the smug overtones. A beginner practicing on a musical instrument can make some horrible sounds, not at all agreeable at first. A lot of practice is needed to make heavenly music. A children's concert is delightful to proud parents, but hardly to connoisseurs. What we are promised is that one day we can be good enough to tune our harps for God's own pleasure; and God is the proudest of parents and the most exacting of connoisseurs. Meantime we may well suppose that a Christian minister can better be compared with the conductor of a band than with a swimming instructor wondering whether to induce shivering bathers to jump in by wheedling or pushing.

That was a digression. I set out to comment, not on commitment, but on the lack of commitment that goes by the name of "folk religion" in a country with an established church that is taken for granted. What is this "lack" that worries pastors so much, this hole that our mission is supposed to fill? It cannot simply be a lack of congregations on Sundays. The absence of any felt need or obligation to go to church is a symptom of whatever is really lacking, not the trouble itself; or we should have to say that church attendance is the be-all and end-all of the Christian life. Do we want to say even that worship is the whole point of the Christian life? That would make nonsense of the "inasmuch" parable[24] and of the story of the Good Samaritan.[25] What is lacking then? Why do we still want to say more to people than simply the Fatherhood of God and the brotherhood of man?

Now I have reached what I most want to say, and it will turn out to consist of theology. The reason we seem not to be able to locate a gap in many people's lives, which we can as it were plug with the Christian Gospel, is that the gap is being closed up, with the best intentions, by a way of thinking best called "moralism." English folk religion is weak on theology, but it is apt to be strong on morality. People who would never think of looking up the Epistle to the Hebrews have no doubt in their minds that if God exists it is His job to be "the rewarder of those who seek him."[26] Inarticulate, untheological religion seems to be "all about" reward and punishment. If mercy comes in, it comes in as a letting of people off from punishment. If trust comes in, it is trust that sooner or later there will be a reward. If God is a Father, He is a Father who is most interested in His children behaving properly. At the end of the day He will come home and spank us, but we hope He will not forget our pocket money.

Of course this is a caricature. In fact it is a caricature, not of a total error, but of a caricature. Moralism is not simply false but a distorted description of something true. The God we worship is concerned with our behavior, and there is a great deal about reward and punishment in the Gospels. But, once again, what has happened is that the belief in a just God, which Christianity inherits from Israel, has joined forces with the assumption that God's providence guides the universe on a very tight rein;[27] and these two assumptions combined in ordinary English religion have more or less squeezed out the most fundamental Christian faith in a God who does not abolish evil but endures and overcomes it.

The results of this distortion are serious. They can amount to an unhappy combination of complacency, insensitivity, and ingratitude. None of these is necessarily culpable. They all spring from a lack of imagination and misunderstanding; but we need to see how we are to be able to say anything prophetic or persuasive.

The complacency is precisely pharisaical. It is good people, exponents of a great tradition, who become complacent. It is quite fashionable now to rehabilitate the Pharisees and point out that Christians have maligned them. Yet they seem to have been the Lord's most recalcitrant opponents—a particularly clear example of the principle that the worst is the corruption of the best. If God is just and what happens is His will, then our prosperity is ordained by God and good for everyone. That is the argument of the upright man who serves God and sees good days, and it is a natural, not a perverse, argument. The trouble is that it has a terrible vulnerability.

The upright man may easily and almost innocently become blind to the sufferings of other people. He knows they are not his fault; he knows he has done his duty as he was brought up to do it; he knows that God is just. So surely some of the suffering he hears about must be mythical, and quite a lot of it must be the victims' own fault. Moralism and belief in Providence combine to screen the woes of the world. So to the complacency of a latter-day Pharisee is added the insensitivity of a latter-day Job's comforter.

When the woes of the world take the particular shape—not of a social problem but of the misery of a friend—the protective screen collapses. But what is there to say? Suddenly it has become clear that some victims really are victims and are not to blame for their own troubles. Job is not a sinner, but what can his comforters offer him? They would truly like to help, but it is hard for them to clear their minds of the conviction that really everything that happens must be all for the good. "These things are sent to try us." "God knows best."

When the suffering is still nearer home, it becomes only too clear that much religious comfort is insensitive. The message of Providence is bitter and insulting to people who know that the agony they are going through, physical or mental, is disastrous not holy, destructive not inspiringly tragic. The folk religion that has assured them that God will always look after them has evidently let them down. The alternatives seem to be either disillusionment or an obstinate and cruel reaffirmation of God's inscrutable love. Maybe one can submit to His will and hope for better days, but this is not a God to whom one can keep offering up grateful thanks. Really one would rather have as little to do with Him as possible.

A Distortion to Correct

I think there is a fairer way to understand English folk religion than either to tolerate it as adequate or to condemn it as lazy. It is time to pick up again the indications I have been trying to give that (in the setting from which I come) there are ethical and theological misunderstandings at the root of our troubles. A distorted Gospel is mistaken for an established orthodoxy; secularization feeds upon it; and polarization is intensified. In the light of all of this, what can our mission be?

When John Robinson's *Honest to God*[28] came out, a Sunday paper hailed it with the headline "Our image of God must go." The book itself, of course, was attacking not our fundamental belief but an oversimplification. What I am trying to say is that the oversimplification of our Christian faith, which now "must go," is the easygoing belief in Providence that is making the Gospel look like a story for children, and is incapacitating us, either for facing our own troubles or for looking after other persons in theirs. We need to stop preaching the false gospel: "Only be good" or "Only have faith, and God will here and now wipe every tear from your eyes." And, more particularly, we need to stop preaching the false doctrine that is no gospel at all: "Because you can trust your heavenly Father, everything that happens to you is His will." If these assumptions could die, something stronger might rise again and we might come nearer to finding out what our mission really is.

I tried to express this some time ago by suggesting that Christians ought to go through a stage of being more deistic.[29] Let me define deism as the theory, often used by thoroughgoing Christians as a bogey, that God made the world and then left it to its own devices. Of course deism cannot be adequate; but it could be a wholesome corrective to a false picture of a God who adjusts every detail of the world from minute to minute. A dose of deism need not be defeatist but might prove beneficial.

Professor Michael Langford, in a book that in fact is a defense of Providence, not an attack on it, strongly recommends that a Christian

> avoid saying "It's God's will," when some terrible event occurs, such as the accidental death of a child. . . . Clarity would be much better served by insisting that many things happen that are not God's will, whether it be moral fault, which results from the autonomy of man, or calamity, which results from the autonomy of nature.[30]

Likewise Professor Ronald Preston insists that

> we cannot assume that God operates directly on the human scene in the way that the Old Testament thought he did. . . . Not everything that happens can be presumed to be directly God's will, still less as focussed on his chosen people.[31]

Writing particularly impressively of the dreadful disaster at Aberfan, Dr. W. H. Vanstone in *Love's Endeavor Love's Expense* insists that "something went wrong." This was not the will of God.

> Our preaching on the Sunday after the tragedy was not of a God who, from the top of the mountain, caused or permitted, for His own inscrutable reasons, its disruption and descent; but of One Who received, at the foot of the mountain, its appalling impact, and Who, at the extremity of endeavor, will find yet new resource to restore and to redeem.[32]

This is miles from deism, and I have quoted it here as an anticipation, to show the way we are heading. But to appreciate it we need first to explore further the world in which many of our contemporaries are living, a world from which God seems to be absent in spite of all the promises we were brought up to believe. I am arguing that we need to be just deistic enough to inhabit that world, to breathe its cold air and find out that Christian faith is hardier than we thought and can stand the frost.

It is Providence to which I am urging that we should sit more loosely—not because we can lay down rules about what God may or must do, but because we have some evidence in our experience about what He does or does not do. We can think of His possible activity as a kind of spectrum with miracle at one end (amazing interventions in the course of nature), Providence in the middle (day-to-day control over events), and grace at the other end (influence upon human minds and souls). Philosophers have found difficulties in all these, and it often seems a reasonable compromise to affirm grace and Providence but draw the line at miracle. I am arguing that of the three, Providence is the most dubious. It would be faithless to rule it out, but our mission would be strengthened not weakened if we gave the idea a rest, or rather, if we were deistic enough to acknowledge that Providence really is a sort of miracle.

In general, we believe that our Creator stands back from the material world, He lets it run according to its laws, He gives it the independence to be a reliable context for the development of human life. Having said that, we may add that down the centuries we have some evidence that this is not the whole story. There have been marvels that have witnessed—not compulsively but illuminatingly—to God's concern for His creation.

To believe that God will bend the course of events for our sakes is to believe in miracles. To pray for a fine day or for rain or for an illness to be cured is not to ask for something God can easily grant if we can only attract His attention, so that if it fails to happen we must conclude that it was against His will. Of course, if we believe in God at all, we come into His presence with all our hopes and fears and tell Him what we really mind about, and sometimes we cry out desperately for a miracle; but we ought not to think that there is a workaday force, short of miracle, called Providence, into which we can plug our lives if we only know how. Yet too much everyday Christian teaching encourages us to believe just that.

At this point both skeptics on the one hand and people of real faith on the other will round upon the deistic Christian in reasonable indignation. It is too obvious that this minimizing of Providence is just a way of trying to cover up a pitiful lack of faith. Is it not just an excuse for an inability to walk with God? A skeptic believes that there is no God with whom we could walk; a trustful Christian believes that we could experience His Providence quite easily if we would only put our faith in His power, like the centurion with the sick servant[33] or the Syro-Phoenician woman.[34] Do we or do we not believe that not a sparrow falls without our Father?[35] The believer reminds us that the Gospels are full of simple trust; but the skeptic reminds us that sparrows fall every day, and human beings too who are supposed to be of much more value.

Here we reach the limits of deism and must go beyond it in one direction or the other. We must either abandon faith or affirm a fuller faith. Unless we can say that God does act in the world, there is very little sense in continuing to talk about God. But if we have learned from deism, what we shall go on to affirm is that God's mighty acts in the world are nothing like day-to-day tinkering to keep things going, but are clustered in a significant pattern. The Gospel in a nutshell is that something of total importance happened at a particular date in the midst of human history. It cannot, I believe, be expressed without the idea of Incarnation— the assertion that God entered into the world He had made in the life of one particular human being. The more distinctly we see the point of affirming that "God was in Christ," the less we need to look for everyday providences.[36]

It is experience, not theology, that tells us that the world is harsh and that there is no simple way to trace divine purpose in it. But we have inherited a tradition from people who were totally convinced that they did recognize divine purpose, first in the life of a people and then concentrated in the life of one man. These people have not seemed to be talking nonsense and have witnessed to the impact of certain events upon them in which they have been convinced they have found the authoritative love of God. We still find that nature is indifferent and mankind a mixture of good and evil, but we have been given reason to believe that behind it all there is a Power who has not abandoned us but takes full responsibility. We say that He came into the world to save us from our sins, but first we need to say that He came to claim the right to create a world like this at all.

If these ideas makes sense to us, we can locate God's Providence in the life, death, and resurrection of Jesus Christ, considered as the pledge that He is both willing and able to be the focus of our faith. A great deal more painstaking consideration would be needed to show that these ideas do make sense and are true. This is where Christian mission must engage in biblical scholarship. The present point is that Providence and miracle are here amalgamated in the one expectation that mighty works would indeed cluster around the person of the incarnate Lord. So the message of the centurion and of the Syro-Phoenician woman and of blind Bartimaeus and all the others is not "Have faith like they did and the twentieth century will be strewn with miracles too," but "What did these people see? What must be the truth about this man who had such an impact?" If, on all the evidence of the impression He made and makes still, we believe that God was in His life, we can believe more easily that wonders as it were went off around Him like fireworks. "The blind received their sight and the lame walk, lepers are cleansed and the deaf hear, and the dead are raised up, and the poor have good news preached to them."[37] The whole effect is one of celebration, not of administration. Preachers have wondered why when healing a deaf man he should "sigh" as he said "Ephphatha, be opened."[38] Perhaps one can fancifully find an appropriateness in such a sigh, to mitigate the euphoria of supposing that this is how the world is for Christians. Marvels may be a clue that "a greater than Solomon is here,"[39] a foretaste of fulfillment to some; but meanwhile they are "a drop in the bucket" compared with the remaining troubles of the world, not a lesson in the daily dealings of God with mankind.

What Is the Gospel?

The Good News for the twentieth century cannot just be about some popular excitement in the first. If the Gospel says, "Have faith and all will go well," it has forgotten the Lord's journey to Jerusalem and what happened when He got there. The cup did not pass away, and the Passion story, not long-ago healings, is the ground of our hopes in the troubles of today.

What our mission is about is the Cross and the Resurrection. They belong together. Taken together, they are the pledge of something more sustaining than the desperate conviction that whatever happens has to be the will of God. They are the pledge that He is present in whatever does happen, however disastrous.

Julian of Norwich is famous for saying, "All manner of thing shall be well"; and, out of context, many people find this hard to believe. She is more encouraging when she spells out the message she has had: "He did not say: You will not be troubled, you will not be belabored, you will not be disquieted; but he said: You will not be overcome . . . for he loves us and delights in us."[40]

Julian's message to her fellow Christians is based on her vision of the Cross. We may take the death of Jesus as a fact: the question is, who this was who died, and what came of it? The Cross is Good News because of the Resurrection, and the Resurrection is Good News because of the Cross. They elucidate each other. The story of Christ who suffered and died is incomplete unless first He really suffered and died, and second He really is vindicated as Christ.

In the world we know, where things often go badly, our best hope is based on the worst moment in the story, the Cry of Dereliction. If we can say that God was in Christ, when Christ undergoes the human experience of the absence of God, then even that experience is not without the real presence of God.[41] But unless something more did truly happen "on the third day," we have no reason to say that God was in Christ; the Cry of Dereliction is simply a cry of dereliction. Unless the point of our mission is that the best is raised out of the worst, we shall get lost—either in despondency, or in the euphoria of shortcuts, or in the dead end of moralism.

The Report of the Church of England's Partners in Mission consultation *To a Rebellious House?* has on its cover a ring of jolly little people dancing round a cross. I do not think it is just a debating point to insist that unless there is something more serious than that at the heart of everything we might as well say to our contemporaries "Let us eat and drink, for tomorrow we die." The children's game of "Ring-a-ring of roses" ends with "all fall down."

If "the Lord is risen" is the point of our mission, we can reclaim the faith that whatever happens, He is there. Those Christians to whom the idea of "the sacrament of the present moment" means a great deal do not have to pin their faith to a providence that pushes the furniture of the world about. They can allow that a great deal that happens is contrary to God's will and feel the greater awe at the thought that there, where the trouble is, is where He will consent to come.

We shall have to exercise more self-restraint than some Christian preachers do in telling people to be grateful for the joys of life as direct gifts of God—a kind of gratitude that makes some people, excluded from those joys, feel excluded from God's love too. That is where we ought to be more deistic in our teaching. But if we can manage this restraint, we can hope for the reward of being less forlornly deistic, even a little bit pantheistic, in finding God wherever we may happen to be. He is not a God who sits up on high watching and judging. If He could be on a cross, He can enter into whatever we mind about and not preach to us that it is just what we needed. Surely Hamlet is wrong that there is "a special providence" in the fall of a sparrow,[42] and the fancy of John Keats is more in the spirit of the New Testament: "If a Sparrow come before my Window I take part in its existence and pick about the Gravel".[43] The Christian hope is that God Himself takes part in our existence. I am encouraged that this line of approach may be both sound and relevant to our purpose by a sentence in our background material: "African spokesmen often see the relationship of God to human society holistically—God is present in all we do and are—and charge in contrast that Westerners frequently compartmentalize their individual relationships with the divine, recognizing the immanence of God only in the inexplicable."[44]

Gratitude

It might seem as though Christians who sit loose to the idea of Providence would fall short in thanksgiving. They will not feel at ease with the hymn that says, "All this day thy hand has led me." Am I advocating a presentation of the Christian faith that is disastrously impoverished? On the contrary, I am attempting to direct our attention toward where our riches really are; and find myself helped here by our Anglican tradition. The General Thanksgiving in the *Book of Common Prayer* blesses God "for our creation, preservation, and all the blessings of this life; but above all, for [His] inestimable love in the redemption of the world by our Lord Jesus Christ; for the means of grace, and for the hope of glory." The thanksgiving is general, but it is not vague or abstract. It fastens upon what we believe are the facts of our faith.

It starts with creation—not the mythical forming of the first man out of clay, but God's responsibility for the whole universe. As commentary on it, may I quote the seventeenth-century writer Thomas Traherne:

> Your Enjoyment of the World is never right, till every Morning you awake in Heaven: see your self in your fathers Palace: and look upon the Skies and the Earth and the Air, as Celestial Joys. . . . You never Enjoy the World aright, till the Sea it floweth in your Veins, till you are Clothed with the Heavens, and Crowned with the Stars: and

Perceiv your self to be the Sole Heir of the whole world: and more then so, becaus Men are in it who are every one Sole Heirs, as well as you.[45]

On its own this almost mystical appreciation of the natural order could be heartless, if it were not based on the belief "above all" that the Creator entered into His world to live in it, suffer in it, and redeem it. In writing about mission, I have slid rather gently over the question of sin, not, of course, because I think it unimportant or outdated, but because so many attempts to use it as a "way in" for the Gospel feed the moralism of our society rather than overcome it. Repentance is not a hurdle to be jumped in order to qualify for salvation; it is a response to something seen, which calls out our gratitude.

What I want to stress now in conclusion is the offer of "the means of grace and the hope of glory" as alternatives to moralism. What is hindering us from the building up of a Christian way of life that will attract and not repel is the assumption that God is primarily a lawgiver and that what I must do to be saved is conform, obey, and be grateful for everything as His inscrutable will. This way of thinking is simply no foundation for a recognizable Christianity. It falls apart into priggishness or disillusionment, to the accompaniment of recrimination. The hope that moral exhortation will do the trick and make sinners into saints is not very promising. It is not much help to keep on telling the prodigal to come home. At least we can make a start by fattening the calf in readiness to welcome him.

What is wrong with folk religion, what is wrong with our secularized and polarized everyday life from a Christian point of view, is not wickedness but a kind of undernourishment. People know that belief is asked of them, but have lost touch with the Cross and the Resurrection as the ground of belief. They are trying to be grateful in the wrong direction and not finding what there is to be grateful for.

What we have to offer them are ways of keeping in touch, "means of grace," pledges of God's presence. God is perfectly capable of being present unannounced, but there are places where we believe He has undertaken to be. Anglicanism, Catholic and Reformed, has traditionally found sustenance both in the Eucharist, where we give thanks over material things and use them as channels of grace, and in the Scriptures, which claim our careful and honest attention. We must never think that we have God taped. We cannot predict, still less stipulate, what we shall find if we look.

Our mission is to invite and to nourish, to feed people's energy and goodwill, not to give them orders. Many people at the moment are finding themselves confronted by the demand to take more interest in the rest of God's world, to cultivate our common life rather than the state of our separate souls, to look at the way other people have to live and take more part with them. The question is not what is prohibited or permitted but what needs to be done or not done in the face of the crucified and risen Lord. God's will is to be put into effect, not just endured; and sometimes we can be "means of grace" to one another.

As for the "hope of glory," the Gospel is not complete without it. Christ lived and died and we believe He rose; and the world goes on. Unless we believe that His rising is a pledge of our own, we might as well admit its irrelevance to our troubled world. But if the God of Abraham, Isaac, and Jacob is truly not the God of the dead but of the living,[46] if all we are told about the infinite value of every human being is not just talk, then there is something more in store for us that we cannot yet imagine. We have foretastes of it when we delight in one another's company. Some of us hope that artistic creation gives another kind of foretaste. Some people, to whom the presence of God is more immediate than for most of us, seem to have real glimpses of heaven. Their mission is to include us in what they have found; ours is to join with them and encourage rather than exhort other people to join in with us.

NOTES

1. Matthew 2:16.
2. John 4:14.
3. *Mission in Global Perspective*, p. 8.
4. *Ibid.*, p. 14.
5. *To a Rebellious House?* Report of the Church of England's Partners in Mission Consultation 1981, paragraph 91.
6. *The Screwtape Letters*, end of Letter 16.
7. Luke 19:41.
8. *The Hope of Happiness*, SCM 1983, Chapter 14.
9. *Ibid.*, p. 125–126.
10. *Confessions*, X, 29.
11. *The Hope of Happiness*, p. 126.
12. "Ode to Duty."
13. Ephesians 4:13 ff. RSV.
14. Psalm 14:1.
15. 1 Peter 3:15.

16. See Oman, *Grace and Personality* (Cambridge University Press, 1917; Fontana, 1960).
17. John Habgood, *Church and Nation in a Secular Age*, DLT 1983, Chapter 6.
18. *Ibid.*, pp. 94–95.
19. Revelation 3:16–17.
20. For example, Denis Shaw, *Church Times* (November 11, 1983) and Clifford Longley, *Times* (December 19, 1983).
21. Luke 15:25–32.
22. Matthew 20:12.
23. See John Wesley, *A Plain Account of Christian Perfection*; and Bernard Häring, *Christian Maturity* (Burns and Oates, 1967), part III.
24. Matthew 25:31–46.
25. Luke 10:33–37.
26. Hebrews 11:6.
27. See Häring, p. 11.
28. SCM Press, 1963.
29. *Incarnation and Immanence*, Hodders, 1973.
30. Michael Langford, *Providence*, pp. 88–89.
31. *Church and Society in the Late Twentieth Century*, p. 105.
32. Pages 64–65.
33. Matthew 8:5–13; Luke 7:2–10.
34. Mark 7:25–30.
35. Matthew 10:29.
36. See *Incarnation and Immanence*, Chapter IV.
37. Matthew 11:5.
38. Mark 7:34.
39. Matthew 12:42.
40. *Showings*, Chapter 68.
41. *The Hope of Happiness*, pp. 183–184.
42. Act V, Scene II.
43. Letter to Benjamin Bailey, Saturday, November 22, 1817.
44. Page 5.
45. *Centuries*, 28 and 29.
46. Mark 12:26–27.

Mission of the Church in the Indian Context

The Reverend Pritam B. Santram

POPULAR NOTIONS ABOUT MISSION

In India, "missionary" and "mission" are maligned words. "Missionary" and "mission" belong to a period of about four hundred years of Western missionary activity that began in the sixteenth century and coincided with the Western colonialism and dominance in India. "In fact," as Englebert Zeitler, a Roman Catholic scholar in India, puts it, "Mission and colonial expansion grew together and afterwards died together."[1] The words "missionary" and "mission" bring to the minds of people in India images, models, and ideas from that colonial past; and it is a hard job for the churches in India to dissociate these words from their past colonial images and concepts so as to arrive at a contemporary and Indian understanding of "missionary" and "mission." Here are some of the images, models, and ideas associated with the words "mission" and "missionary": institutional buildings, mission compounds, foreign funds, and foreign control.

It is not necessary to dwell for too long on the popular conceptions or misconceptions about Christian mission and missionary to recognize that in India these words are associated with alien concepts and models of Christian service. It would, however, be necessary to examine whether "mission" is the necessary term and mode of Christian obedience in India, or to cleanse it of the embellishments it has gathered during the Western colonial era.

MISSION IN THE PAST

The present understanding of the Church's mission as well as the patterns of missionary work in India are mainly a result of the Western missionary enterprise of the past four hundred years or so.

Along with the spread of the Gospel and establishment of strong churches, there was also an awakening of the Indian nation as a whole, and a renewal and revival of the traditional religions. There was also a sharpening of political consciousness and national identity. Struggle for national independence grew stronger.

In 1947 the British rule in India came to an end and India gained its independence. From then on, the situation began to change radically and rapidly, and the churches were thinking about the "Church's role in nation-building." The number of foreign missionaries began to decrease. The "churches" took the place of "missions" and have now fully assumed the responsibility for mission and evangelism.

One very important aspect of the history of the churches in India during the period of Western missions, particularly during the nineteenth and twentieth centuries, is the quest for unity motivated primarily by the mission-concern, or more precisely, by the evangelistic-concern. This came out powerfully at the famous international conference of missionaries held at Tranquebar in 1919. The statement issued by this conference puts it this way:

> We believe that the challenge of the present hour calls us to mourn our past divisions and turn to our Lord Jesus Christ to seek in Him the unity of the body expressed in one visible Church. We face together the titanic task of the winning of India for Christ—one fifth of the human race. Yet confronted by such an overwhelming responsibility, we find ourselves rendered weak and relatively impotent by our unhappy divisions—divisions for which we were not responsible, and which have been, as it were, imposed upon us from without.

This close relationship between mission and the quest for unity of the Church is vital in the life of the churches in India. There are certain features and consequences of the Western missionary activity of the past three centuries in India that must be noted.

Religion as Mission Frontier

The ultimate goal of all missionary societies from the West was to spread the knowledge and message of Jesus Christ among those whom they considered "heathen" or "non-Christians" or "people of other faiths" in such a way that they might be "converted" to faith in Jesus Christ and join the Church. To put it bluntly, the frontier of their mission was the religion of other people. It was assumed that all the evils in the Indian society—poverty, disease, superstition, ignorance, illiteracy, immorality—were a consequence of the religious beliefs of the people. It was, therefore, concluded that the traditional religions of the Indian people were inadequate, if not false, and that these should be replaced by what they believed to be a more adequate and superior religion—that is, Christianity.

They all aimed at a conversion of the people of other faiths in the hope that some day the whole nation would be Christianized. This hope was expressed in the popular slogan: "Winning of India for Christ."

The underlying concept of Christian mission here was that of mission as conquest for Christ. Other religions, which were thought to be inadequate, were to be replaced by Christianity, and their adherents were to be conquered for Christ through the preaching of the Gospel and through the sharing of Christ's love in service to others, especially to the poor, the sick, and the oppressed. It was not only in the Salvation Army that military terminology was applied to Christian discipleship and evangelism. Terms like "missionary strategy," "defense of Christianity," "evangelistic thrust," "soul winner," and "Christian soldiers," which were quite common in missionary parlance, belonged to the "conquest" concept of mission. Some of these expressions, no doubt, have their roots in the New Testament in the concepts of the "Kingdom of God," lordship and kingship of Christ, and in the Pauline concept of battling against "principalities and powers" or of the Christian as a "soldier" loaded with a spiritual armory.

In such an approach to mission, increase in numbers of converts was important. The Western missionaries and the evangelistic minded among those converted to Christianity went all out to preach the Gospel to the people of other faiths and baptized those who accepted the Christian faith, thus adding more and more to the numbers of their denominational churches. As has been pointed out above, this resulted in the establishment and growth of diverse Western types of denominational churches all over the country. As the religion of the indigenous people was the main frontier of mission, the converts soon developed their own identity as Christians and began to emerge as a distinct and somewhat "Western" community. This resulted in the hardening of the communal boundaries between the so-called Christian community, or the Church, and the other religious communities loosely described by Christians as "non-Christians." Baptism became "the waters that divide." Mutual alienation developed and in some cases led to mutual suspicion and hostility. As an increase in numbers in one religious community causes a decrease in the membership of another religious community, conversion to Christianity could no longer be regarded as a purely religious or spiritual matter. It became a religious or spiritual matter with social, economic, and political consequences in the Indian society and, consequently as such, a socioeconomic and political issue. Before going on to the next observation, we may add that the "conquest" and "replacement" concepts of mission were not the only ones that prompted Western missionary enterprise in India.

The nineteenth and twentieth centuries have been times of great reforms and of a renaissance of religions in India. Ancient scriptures, religious concepts, and practices were reinterpreted in the light of new knowledge and experience, particularly because of the impact of Christianity and Western domination. This brought to light the inner beauty and strength of the Indian religions and cultures. The Western missionary in India was faced not with a museum of dead or ornamental religions, but with a universe of living faiths that shaped the lives and destiny of millions of people. The divine truth in other religions was evident and was recognized. Christian mission was then seen not as a "conquest" of other religions but as a "completion" or "fulfillment" of other religions. The concept was drawn from Christ's words: "I have not come to abolish them but to fulfill them" (Matthew 5:17). In the preaching of the Gospel, Christ was seen as coming to the religions of India not to conquer or to replace them but to fulfill them and to bring them to completion in Himself. Thus J. N. Farquhar, in his famous book *The Crown of Hinduism* (1913), could say that in Christ "is focussed every ray of light which shines in Hinduism. He is the Crown of the faith of India."[2]

Then there followed a series of writings that indicate a marked development in the Indian Christian's understanding of and relation to other religions and their adherents and, therefore, a positive development in the concept of mission. For want of space we shall only mention here the titles of four that adequately suggest the main themes of these books.[3] They are Raymond Panikkar's *Unknown Christ of Hinduism* (1964), M. M. Thomas' *Acknowledged Christ of the Hindu Renaissance* (1970), Marcus Braybrooke's *Undiscovered Christ: A Review of Recent Developments in the Christian Approach to the Hindu* (1973), and J. S. Samartha's *Hindu Response to the Unbound Christ* (1974). These and other writings, mostly by Indian or Asian authors, reflect a radical shift from the "confrontation," "conquest," and "completion" concepts of mission to such concepts as "mission in dialogue" and "mission as discerning and witnessing to the 'inner working' of the Spirit everywhere."[4] As the churches in India come to terms with the contemporary sociopolitical, cultural, and economic realities of the country, they move toward a more comprehensive understanding of their missionary obligation.

Mission of Compassion and Service

Western missionaries had been appalled by the socioeconomic backwardness of the vast masses of the Indian people. They were moved by the problem of human suffering caused by ignorance, superstition, oppression of the poor and weak by the rich and powerful (often sanctioned or patronized by religion or tradition), disease, and illiteracy. Their love of Christ moved them to engage in a ministry of compassion. They began by serving the poor and needy, and selflessly labored to uplift the downtrodden and the outcasts of society. Such ministries of compassion have continued in diverse forms; but these have particularly developed in small and large medical and educational institutions and such other services as caring for widows, orphans, the aged, the handicapped, and the destitute. The unique contribution of the pioneering educational and medical institutions started by missionaries and now being carried on by the Indian churches to the general enlightenment and development of the Indian people has been widely recognized by the nation. In recent times the churches, while recognizing the need for ministries of compassion, have begun to give due attention to the basic causes of suffering. In recent years there has been greater emphasis on social action and development.

It may be noted that the ministries of compassion and the service institutions that developed from them are not unrelated to the mission of the Church as the pioneers understood it. In some cases these were seen as a preparation for evangelistic mission and in others as appropriate and necessary instruments of mission and evangelistic outreach.

The churches in India have inherited these missionary structures, patterns, and institutions; and it is these that tend to shape the concept of mission as well as the methods of "doing" mission in India.

Mission and Geographical Expansion of the Church

From the way the Western missionaries operated in India it appears that mission was understood by them as an activity that demanded a "movement" or a "going" or "sending" from one place to another. No doubt the ideas of movement, going, and sending are basic to mission (see Matthew 28:19; Luke 24:47; and John 17:18; 20:21). But in the past these seem to have been understood mainly in terms of a geographical movement and expansion—"you shall be my witnesses . . . to the end of the earth" (Acts 1:8). The missionary was one who was sent from one country to another, who extended the boundaries of the Church and spread the Gospel over an ever-widening area. Mission was exercised as a kind of a religious expansionism; and as this took place about the same time as the expansion and consolidation of the British rule in India, it was seen by the Indians as another form of Western colonialism.

Mission and Culture

In their enthusiam to convert the people of India to the Christian faith, Western missionaries were not only tempted to reject the indigenous religions but also the cultures of the Indian people. Alexander Duff, the first missionary of the Church of Scotland to India (1830–1860), who did pioneering work in the field of education in Calcutta, was criticized for his conviction to "unnaturalize Indians in their own country." Those who accepted the Gospel from Western missionaries were uprooted from their social and cultural moorings and found themselves planted in a new community with a different language, culture, and life-style; and gradually they succumbed to this alien culture.

There were, of course, exceptions. Roberto de Nobili, a young Jesuit missionary who arrived in South India (Madurai) in 1605, tried to identify himself completely with the Indian way of life and thinking. Brahmabandhab Upadyaya (1861–1907) of Bengal was a convert from the Brahmin caste. He maintained his roots in his own culture and thought. He did some pioneering work in what is now being described as Indian Christian theology, expounding the Christian doctrines in genuinely indigenous terminology and thought-forms. There were also other great Christians—V. Chakkarai (1880–1958), P. Chenchiah (1886–1959), P. D. Devanandan (1901–1962), Sadhu Sundar Singh (1889–1929), A. J. Appasamy (1891–1978), to name a few—who embodied in their life and thinking a genuinely indigenous Christianity. There are also certain parts of the country where the missionaries did not impose their Western ways or, rather, where even the Western missionaries themselves respected and adopted the local language and culture. In such places the churches are better rooted in the soil of the country than in other places. The relation between the Gospel,

Christian faith, and the local culture continues to be a burning issue in the Church in India and surfaces under such descriptions as "indigenization," "contextualization," and "inculturation" of the Gospel and the Church.

Mission and Dependency

Most missionary work in the past was backed by generous funds from the sponsors in the West. Those who became Christians were either themselves from the poor class or had to leave behind their wealth to the community or family from which they were converted. As they joined the new community of Christians they needed financial assistance for their survival. This was provided. When the congregations grew larger and were organized on the same patterns as those in the West, they needed resources to sustain the ministry and the structure. The ministries of compassion also required resources that could not easily be generated from the local congregations. Later, when the service institutions grew larger, more and more funds were needed for buildings, equipment, and workers. These needs were also met through the generosity and sacrificial giving of devout Christians in the West. For over a hundred years leadership and the control of resources remained with the founding fathers and their successors from the West, though some attempts were made by some missionary societies to devolve responsibility to Indian personnel. The vast majority of Christians of the mission-churches, particularly in the north, were mostly on the receiving end. The result was dependency.

Now that the number of foreign missionaries is diminishing fast, and with that, also the influx of foreign grants, the churches that have inherited the Western ecclesiastical structures and also the large medical, educational, and other service institutions that were being supported by foreign grants are passing through a very difficult time. Charity has caused dependency because the developmental aspect of mission had been neglected. Dependency is the legacy with which the churches in India will have to contend for many years to come.

THE INDIAN CONTEXT OF MISSION

Mission of the Church in India as represented by Western missionaries and their Indian associates (such as catechists, evangelists, and preachers) during the sixteenth to nineteenth centuries was largely a one-way traffic. It came from the West to India equipped with a ready-made message, resources, and personnel. It was for the Indian to respond to it or reject it. Two factors were not given sufficient consideration. First, the whole depth and diversity of centuries-old religions and cultures of those to whom the mission was directed. Second, the complexity of socioeconomic conditions and structures that kept a vast majority of the Indian people poor. Although the Gospel was preached to the masses who were believed to be in need of salvation, the aim of this evangelization was to draw the individual recipient of the Gospel into the believing community where personal salvation would be experienced and sustained.

The result of the neglect of these two factors was that those who believed in Christ and were received into the fellowship of the Church through baptism also made a complete break with their past religion and culture, and also developed a concern for personal salvation of the individual. This trend brought into being churches that until the twentieth century remained aloof from the multireligious ethos and other religious communities as well as from the real aspirations and struggles of the masses for a better, fuller life. This is not to say that there were no overseas missionaries or church leaders (as well as individual Indian Christians) who tried to relate the Gospel to other religions and to the socioeconomic and political realities that govern peoples' thinking and life in India. There were many such people, both Indians and foreigners, who have played a vital role in calling the churches to develop both a theology of other religions as well as of involvement in the sociopolitical processes—that is, to the dialogical and social dimension of mission in respect of other religions and society at large.

There can be no one-way mission nor a mission in a vacuum. If it is to be relevant and fruitful, mission must always be related to the context in which it is realized. In fact, M. M. Thomas, using A. G. Hogg's expression, describes mission as "challenging relevancy." What is described as *missio Dei* ("God's mission")— and there is general agreement that mission is God's, not of the Church—is not just a redemptive movement from God to the human family in a vacuum. It is a movement of God's self-giving, and of His liberating power to the human race in the totality of life. It is oriented to particular historical situations and needs. And in the fullness of time it reaches out to the human family in a decisive way in "flesh" (John 1:14), completely identified with and relevant to a particular given historical, national, religious, and cultural context of the first-century Palestine.

The context of *missio Dei* in India is quite complex and challenging. We briefly survey here a few of the features of this context.

Socioeconomic Context

Formerly, when in religious circles—especially in "missionary" circles—India was mentioned, the first thought that came to people's minds was religion or religions. India has had a reputation of being a country of many religions. But now "India" calls to mind the picture of "teeming millions" (almost 700 million people) and of all that goes on with overpopulation in a tropical climate. It is spoken of as a part of the Third World and as a developing country. If you set aside the religious aspect of the Indian population for awhile and look closely at the country, you see a hive of buzzing activity of the 700 million people. The skyline and the landscape of the forests, deserts, villages, towns, and cities have rapidly changed over the past thirty years. Modernization, industrialization, urbanization, development, growth in the GNP—all these and other things that go with progress are all here. Machines and computers are not only replacing manual labor and increasing production and efficiency, but also increasing unemployment. The country has seen five national plans for socioeconomic development from 1951 to 1979, and the sixth one is being implemented. This has resulted in a marked progress in the national economy from 1946 to 1979; with increases in the rate of growth from 1.2 to 3.5 percent for national income, 0.3 to 2.7 percent for agriculture, and 2.0 to 6.1 percent for manufacture and mining. This should suffice to indicate the direction in which the national economy has been moving. There has been a tremendous growth in technology, industry, and agriculture. With this there has also been a loosening of caste and tribal bonds and a marked progress toward national unity and integration. The country has also demonstrated its capability for development of nuclear power for peaceful purposes as well as for space exploration.

With regard to social justice, one may examine the socioeconomic achievements of the nation in the light of Articles 38 and 39 of the Constitution of India. According to these, the state shall strive to promote the welfare of the people by securing and protecting as effectively as it may a social order in which justice, economic and political, shall inform all institutions of the national life. The state shall, in particular, direct its policy toward securing: (a) that the citizens, men and women, equally, have the right to an adequate means of livelihood; (b) that the ownership and control of the material resources of the community are distributed as best subserve the common good; (c) that the operation of the economic system does not result in the concentration of wealth and means of production to the common detriment; (d) that there is an equal pay for equal work for men and women; (e) that the health and strength of workers, men and women, and the tender age of children are not abused, and that citizens are not forced by economic necessity to enter vocations unsuited to their age or strength; and (f) that childhood and youth are protected against exploitation and against moral and national abandonment.

The Five-Year Plans for socioeconomic development that were undertaken from 1951 onward aimed at achieving these goals and made some headway in these directions. The fourth Five-Year Plan (1969–1974) contained a statement of the objectives of "Social Justice and Equality." In order to ensure equitable distribution of the benefits of development and special care and betterment of the poor and weaker sections of society, it proposed to initiate the following measures: control of monopolies, tax and fiscal measures, local planning, development proposals for the weaker sections of the society—for example, the so-called "scheduled tribes," "scheduled castes," "landless labourers,"—employment and minimum wages, development of the *panchayat* ("local government") system, cooperatives, nationalization of banks, and the regulation of the economy. Special emphasis was laid on the removal of poverty (the *"Gharibi Hatao,"* that is, "Remove Poverty" slogan was popularized). The fifth Five-Year Plan particularly stated that "removal of poverty and attainment of self-reliance are the two major objectives." These goals, however, were frustrated on account of an increase in the population, the drought of 1972–1973, and the inflation of 1973–1975. The sixth Five-Year Plan (1980–1985) continues to press forward toward removal of poverty and socioeconomic inequalities. But the achievement is "far short of what we aimed at." But this is not all. Whatever progress there may have been, we are told that "over 350 million of our fellow citizens are living in poverty." There is also the serious problem of unemployment. The benefits of the increase in industrial and agricultural production do not reach the poor masses. The poor remain poor and powerless and are, therefore, exploited and oppressed by the rich and the powerful.

The socioeconomic situation is further vitiated, particularly by two other factors that need to be mentioned but cannot be analyzed here for want of space: illegal economy and corruption and the caste system. The first of these is symptomatic of a moral degeneration. "The cancer of corruption," says Metropolitan Geevarghese Osthathios of the Orthodox Syrian Church, India, "is eating up India's heart."[5] A well-known Indian economist who has had a lot to do with national planning says that

> the real disaster of the illegal economy is that it breeds corruption, it feeds corruption, and it makes the acceptance of corruption a part of the normal national and international way of life, leading to the shocking justification of corruption as "an international phenomenon."
>
> The gravest danger to our national, family and individual life is not simply poverty, inequality, unemployment, nor the known production excesses and lacks, but it is corruption in us that gives rise to the illegal economy, while the unreported/illegal economy in its turn strengthens and breeds corruption.[6]

The persistence of the illegal economy adds "to the inequality of the system whereby some become rich and richer at the expense of others who remain poor and become poorer."[7]

The second of the two factors vitiating the socioeconomic situation in India, namely the caste system, has its origin in the Hindu religion,[8] which is the religion of nearly 83 percent of the Indian people. According to this system, society is divided into four main castes or sections, which are determined by birth and are hierarchical in order. The highest of these is Brahman, the class of the priests and intellectual leaders. Then comes Ksatriya, the class of warriors and soldiers. The third is Vaisya, the class of tradesmen, financiers, and agriculturists. The last and the lowest is Sudra, the class of those whose lot is to do the so-called "menial" work and to serve the people of the other three castes. Some among these were regarded as untouchables. Even though untouchability has been abolished by law, the plight of those who belong to this caste (and its subcastes) and are described in a schedule of the Constitution of India (and are, therefore, commonly referred to as the "scheduled castes") is pitiable. They are often the most discriminated-against section of the Indian society, even though the Constitution of India guarantees certain privileges for them.

Quite apart from the pitiable condition of millions of people of the scheduled castes and scheduled tribes, the society is so structured that the control of the nation's wealth and resources continues to remain concentrated in the hands of a minority of about 15 percent of India's population, and the remaining 85 percent have to be content with the crumbs that fall from the rich man's table. It is not easy to decide whether the number of the poor is increasing or decreasing. But there is no denying the fact that over 350 million out of the population of about 700 million are living in poverty.

What does believing in and commitment to Christ mean in such a socioeconomic context in India today? This is a missiological question to which the churches in India are beginning to address themselves in diverse ways.

Religious and Cultural Context

As has been mentioned above, India is a land of many religions and cultures. This adds a very complex factor to any consideration of the mission of the Church in India. The religious factor, along with the geographical, racial, linguistic, and climatic factors, has produced a rich diversity of cultures over the five thousand years of the known history of India. The churches in India, therefore, find themselves placed in a multireligious and multicultural context.

The religion of the majority of the Indian people is Hinduism. It is generally agreed that Hinduism is not so much a single religion as a "league of religions" (Professor D. S. Sarma, in *What is Hinduism?*, p. 10). It is a designation that covers a great variety of beliefs, practices, and approaches to the ultimate reality that lies behind all that exists and gives meaning to life. Hinduism has emerged as a result of a mixing of the religious beliefs and cultures of the Aryans, who migrated to India around 2000 B.C., and the religions and cultures of the original inhabitants (the aboriginal and the Dravidian) of India. Although Hinduism has been responsible for a lot of beliefs and practices that are today seen to be cruel, oppressive, and dehumanizing—such as *Sati,* the practice of a Hindu widow being cremated on the funeral pile of her husband, which was abolished by the British in the nineteenth century; the caste system and untouchability of low-caste people; idolatry; superstition; fatalism—it has undergone renaissance and reform over the past three centuries. In recent years it has given birth to new religious movements that have tried to develop a new kind of spirituality to meet the needs of the modern world. Some of these movements are spreading out all over the world with a sense of mission.

Hinduism has generated a faith and spirituality that continues to inspire millions of people to live a meaningful life in every generation. It has dominated the thought, conduct, and cultures of most of the Indian people. In all its varied forms Hinduism is a living, dynamic religion. It has produced sages, saints, statesmen,

men and women of great intellectual and spiritual stature, and a nation that stands for nonviolence, peace, and justice. One of the greatest qualities that Hinduism has cultivated in the Indian people, particularly in the Hindu community, is tolerance. This quality enables the Hindu to be open to the truth wherever and in whatever form it may be manifest. It enables Hindus to adopt and assimilate what is true and good rather than reject or challenge it just because it is embodied in another religious community. This attitude is not very different to what is advocated in Philippians 4:8; "Whatever is true, whatever is honorable, whatever is just, whatever is pure, whatever is lovely, whatever is gracious, if there is any excellence, if there is anything worthy of praise, think about these things." Hinduism has no difficulty in including Jesus Christ among its pantheon and within the numerous incarnations (*avatara*) believed in and worshiped by Hindus. In fact, there is the whole phenomenon in India of "unbaptized Christians" to reckon with. These are those who believe in Christ as their Lord and worship Him and also testify to their commitment to Christ by word and actions, but they see no need to join the institutional Church through baptism. For Hindus, the problem with Christianity arises only when it makes exclusive claims to truth, salvation, spirituality, and ethics, or when it threatens to destroy or replace the Indian cultures and religions with some alien (Western) way of life. Ideas, therefore, such as the uniqueness of Christ and salvation through Jesus Christ alone, appear irrelevant and unnecessary to Hindus. They believe in "unity in diversity" and are able to accommodate almost any religious belief within the broad and flexible framework of Hinduism.

The religion of the next large community in India—that is, of the largest minority community of about 11.5 percent of the population—is Islam. This religion came to India over a thousand years ago. It has contributed to India a rich literature, art, culture, and architecture; a pure monotheistic faith; and a community with a strong sense of solidarity among its members. It is opposed to caste discrimination and idol worship. Culturally, it has developed its own ethos with a Middle Eastern cultural tinge. Like Christianity, Islam is missionary in character. Muslims in the past went all out to spread their religion, often with somewhat aggressive fervor. This sometimes leads to tension between the Muslim and Hindu communities. But generally, Hinduism and Islam coexist happily and contribute to the rich religious and cultural plurality of the Indian people.

The next largest minority community in India is the Christian community (about 2.6 percent of the population). It is better known as the "Christian community" rather than the "Church." We have already referred to the "foreignness" of mission and its general rejection of the rich religious and cultural traditions of India. The result was that those who became Christian were culturally uprooted, and the resulting churches tended to develop their organized life, thinking, liturgy, and modes of operation in forms that were somewhat alien to the Indian milieu. So marked was this foreignness that the Father of the Nation, Mahatma Gandhi, is said to have remarked that Indian Christians are "strangers in their own country and aliens in their own land." There are also the scars of denominational divisions on the Church in India. Both these elements have a bearing on the mission of Christ's Church in India.

The other religious communities—the Buddhists, Jains, Sikhs, Parsees (Zorastrians), Jews, and others—all numerically add up to about 3.1 percent of India's population. Although their membership is numerically small, they do not lack vitality. These, along with other religious groups, contribute to the rich diversity of the religious heritage of the Indian people.

When we consider the cultural aspect, we witness a great diversity of cultures shaped by the diverse climatic, religious, geographical, and linguistic factors. How do the expressions of Christian faith fit into this multicultural milieu? This is where the much discussed issue of the relation between the Gospel and culture becomes very important in India.

What does mission of Christ mean in such a multireligious and multicultural context of India? This is the crucial question with which the churches in India are grappling. The answers are varied and so are the models of "doing" mission.

MISSION TODAY: TRENDS IN THINKING
AND DOING OF MISSION

As the concepts and modes of "doing" mission are something the Indian churches have inherited from the West, the mission of the Church continues to be understood and carried out very much in the same way as it was being done in the past colonial, missionary era. Most Christians still share the same old missionary assumptions about the world and about the cultures of the Indian people. It is therefore not surprising that such assumptions and methods of mission also produce the same kinds of results—that is, hostility of other religious communities; denominational divisions; and a marginal increase in the numbers of such Christian communities that care for an individual's salvation but generally remain unconcerned about the wider society, social injustice, corruption, and exploitation of the poor and the weak by the rich. Metropolitan Paulos Mar Gregorios of the Orthodox Syrian Church in India reacting to such an approach to mission says:

> Our self-conscious emphasis on mission makes the Church an unbearable bore. . . . We Asian Christians seem to have been thoroughly brainwashed in this regard. We have acquired that dangerous missionary self-consciousness which leads to hypocrisy, sham and pride. We too have started bragging about the number of Asian missionaries sent out by the Asian Churches.[9]

On account, however, of rapid changes in the socioeconomic, political context and closer contact with the rich multicultural and multireligious milieu, the process of critical assessment, reflection, adaptation, and change has already begun. While a vast majority of Christians in India still continue to understand and engage in mission with the old assumptions and motivations and in the same old traditional way, a new thinking on mission and new ways of "doing" mission are already emerging. Like the Church and the nation, mission is in a state of transition. In what follows we briefly outline the areas in which this transition is taking place.

Use of the Term "Mission"

On account of its associations with the past colonial, missionary era, there is considerable difficulty about using, or rather excessively using, the term "mission" in relation to the Church's primary purpose or task in the Indian context. This is in spite of the fact that the churches in India are intensely aware of their missionary vocation and obligation, and the term "mission" is being increasingly used by the churches in India and abroad. In India this term carries a suggestion of religious and cultural aggression. It is not translatable in many of the Indian languages, and it is not strictly a biblical term.

Although the idea of a divine movement toward the world (and toward the whole creation) for its wholeness is central to the biblical revelation, the word "mission" as such occurs only three times in the English Revised Standard Version of the Bible:

1. Acts 12:25. The Greek word here is *diakonia*, meaning "service" or "ministry."
2. II Corinthians 11:12. "Boasted mission" or "vaunted mission" in NEB. Here the context decides the meaning.

3. Galatians 2:8. Here the Greek work is *apostolē*, meaning "apostleship" or "a sending."

The Greek word *apostolē* occurs only four times in the New Testament (Acts 1:25; Romans 1:5; I Corinthians 9:2; and Galatians 2:8); but it is translated as "mission" only once, in Galatians 2:8, where it comes closer to the connotation this word developed in the past missionary era.

In India the churches will need to purge the term "mission" of its past colonial connotation or will have to abandon its use in favor of some such term as "faithfulness" or "obedience" to Christ/Gospel or "discipleship" of Christ. Whatever term is employed, it should express the reality of the Church's relationship to Christ/God and to His redeeming work rather than suggest an attitude of aggression or attack on other people's religion or suggest an organization inspired and sustained by foreign ideas, interests, and funds. Here Englebert Zeitler's observation is noteworthy:

> Missions have become huge organizations in India involving annual budgets of crores and employing an army of full-time workers. And yet: Mission is essentially something that is very different; it is the overflow of the Christ experience in a community in which the Spirit of Jesus lives and which, therefore, urges those who have ever had this experience to share as the "Glad News" with those who have not experienced it as yet. Mission can, therefore, never exist without a deep concomitant life of *contemplation and prayer* which in India naturally will take Indian forms. . . .
>
> Much of the often bitter antagonism of non-Christian groups would disappear, if they would experience the Church as a spiritual community and not as a power structure that can dispose of an enormous amount of foreign money.[10]

We need a term which will express the idea of mission as the "overflow of the Christ experience."

Biblical and Theological Motivation

The Bible witnesses to a movement from God toward His creation for its wholeness and perfection. It is this divine movement that is the basis and motivation for the mission of the Church. The Church is constituted by this divine movement supremely revealed in Christ, and it participates in this movement for the wholeness of the world. Mission is God's; the Church participates in it.

Christian understanding of mission must be rooted in the biblical doctrine of creation—as also in that of redemption. This will save mission from becoming pietistic, parochial, and irrelevant.

The story of creation in the book of Genesis is a revelation of God's mission, *missio Dei*. God's Spirit moves over the chaos and darkness and brings about order and beauty (*kosmos*), endowing it with the potential for further development and growth toward perfection. God creates man and woman in His own image and commissions them as stewards of His creation with the blessing "Be fruitful and multiply, and fill the earth and subdue it" (Genesis 1:26–30). Men and women are included as stewards, participants, and instruments in the divine movement for the integrity and wholeness of God's creation.

God's mission is reflected in His choosing of Abraham and in His promise to Abraham; "By you all the families of the earth will bless themselves" (Genesis 12:1–3). It runs through the calling and sending of prophets and others like Nebuchadnezzar, king of Babylon (Jeremiah 25:9), and Cyrus, king of Persia (Isaiah 44:28; 45:1), who carry out His purposes. It is supremely embodied in Jesus Christ. In His message and life, God's Kingdom becomes a present reality. He is God's invitation to all people to turn to God in repentance and faith and to enter His Kingdom of love, justice, peace, and freedom. He views His mission in continuity with and fulfillment of the mission of the Old Testament prophets. He says:

> The spirit of the Lord is upon me, because he has annointed me to preach the good news to the poor. He has sent me to proclaim release to the captives and recovering of sight to the blind, to set at liberty those who are oppressed, to proclaim the acceptable year of the Lord (*Luke 4:18–19*).
>
> I must preach the good news of the kingdom of God . . . for I was sent for this purpose (*Luke 4:43*).
>
> I came that they may have life, and have it abundantly (*John 10:10*).

Early Christians saw in the message, life, death, and Resurrection of Jesus the breaking in of a new order and the promise of a "new creation" (II Corinthians 5:17), a "new man" (Ephesians 2:15).

Christ commissions his disciples to participate in His mission and to carry it forward into the whole world. He says:

> Go therefore and make disciples of all nations, baptising them in the name of the Father and of the Son and of the Holy Spirit, teaching them to observe all that I have commanded you (*Matthew 28:19–20*).
>
> You shall be my witnesses in Jerusalem and in all Judea and Samaria and to the end of the earth (*Acts 1:8*).
>
> As the Father has sent me, even so I send you (*John 20:21*).

The Church, therefore, as a body, and every Christian believer as a member of that body, is sent with a commission to be Christ's instrument of His mission. This commission and also the Christian believer's experience of liberation and fullness of life in Christ and the context in which the Church finds itself provide the motivation for mission.

Mission in Context

In the Indian context (developing country; overpopulation; unemployment; poverty; oppression and exploitation of the poor and weak by the rich; unjust social and economic structures; diversity of races, cultures, languages, and religions), the churches in India learn from the experience of churches in other parts of the world, especially from the churches in the African, Asian, and Latin American countries. While most of the Indian churches would agree with much that is contained in the statement called *Mission and Evangelism—An Ecumenical Affirmation,* issued by the Central Committee of the World Council of Churches in 1982, hardly any of the churches have yet worked out a statement affirming or clarifying their own perception of mission and mission priorities in the Indian context. The churches, however, are witnessing to the Gospel and are participating in Christ's mission in a variety of ways, some conventional and others more appropriate to the contemporary Indian situation.

Mission and Social Order. Conventional mission and evangelism continue in the sense of confronting individuals and groups with the message of the Gospel and deeds of compassion in such a way that those confronted or served may come to know Christ, believe in Him as their personal Lord and Savior, become His disciples, and may eventually become members of the visible Church through baptism. This approach is valid and necessary to some extent. The ultimate goal of mission must always be transformation of persons and society into the "new man" or new humanity in Christ. No change in social structures can create a just, sustainable, and participatory society unless the individuals who compose it also have undergone a *metanoia.* In the Indian setting, however, the churches are well aware of the need for social change and are engaging in various forms of social action.

In this, the traditional structures for mission—such as educational, medical, charitable, and other service institutions run by the churches—continue to have a vital place in the mission of the Church. Through such institutions, the Church comes into contact with masses of people (society) and expresses Christ's concern for the wholeness of the individual and the society at large.

These are also channels through which values derived from the Gospel are injected into society. The discomforting question these institutions have to ask is: Whom in the Indian society are they serving? Are these institutions serving the poor, the oppressed, the marginalized, or the oppressor and the exploiter? Are these instruments of radical change for justice and wholeness demanded by the Gospel, or are they promoting the status quo mentality?

Charity and Development. It is recognized by churches in India that while charity and relief programs meet particular immediate needs, these do not touch the causes that produce poverty and other calamities. Therefore, emphasis in mission has gradually shifted from charity and relief works to programs of development. These programs are located in areas of need among the weaker sections of society and they involve the "conscientizing" of people to their environment, organizing them for action, and helping them to help themselves till they are developed enough to decide for themselves and work for greater dignity and a fuller life. Such a ministry is seen as an integral part of the Church's mission, by which the Church penetrates society in obedience to the Gospel and prepares ground for social change.

Social Action. A new form of obedience to the Gospel finds expression in the struggles of what are called "action groups." They are inspired by Christ's concern for the liberation of the poor and the oppressed and to bear witness to the Church's solidarity with them. Groups of Christians engage in concentrated struggle for social justice along with the oppressed in a particular situation. Their ministry involves suffering and struggle with the oppressed for radical change in social structures. Almost all such "action groups" operate independently of the churches, and most of their members belong to other religions or nonreligious groups. This phenomenon needs to be studied from the standpoint of the Church's mission. While the securing of social justice for the poor and oppressed and the creation of a just and participatory society are Gospel imperatives, the action groups do not necessarily work toward a specific witness to Christ as the source of their motivation. Social action can produce balance of power or transfer of power from one section to another, but can it—without any reference to Christ—transform the liberated into the new humanity in Christ? Or, is social action to be viewed as a preparation for mission?

In the context of poverty and suffering of the masses in India due to oppressive social structures, the mission of the Church is to be a suffering and serving community in solidarity with the poor and the oppressed. It must be involved in the struggles of the oppressed and outcasts for human dignity and freedom. This the churches and individual Christians are trying to do.

Mission and Religious and Cultural Plurality. Reflecting on the missionary task of the Church in Asia, Choan-Seng Song says:

> Christian mission can no longer be conducted as if the world would eventually accommodate itself to Christianity. The assumption that spiritual forces other than that of Christianity would wane and decline and lose hold on millions of people on account of inherent weaknesses has proved to be false.[11]

We have earlier referred to the reformed character of the Indian religions and their capacity to inspire lofty ideals and lives of deep devotion to God and humanity. It is not other people's religion that the Church has to fight against but sin—sin in its subtle forms in human attitudes, behaviors, and in social structures. Churches in India can no longer consider other people's religions as a mission frontier. In an unpublished paper on "Evangelism in the Context of Other Religions," Russell Chandran writes:

> The boundary or frontier for the Christian mission is that between light and darkness, righteousness and wickedness, good and evil and not between Christianity as a religion and other religions. It is one of the mistaken developments in Christian history which made the missionary frontier identical with the frontier between Christianity formulated and organized in particular forms and other religions. Only Christ and no formulation of Christ can determine the frontier.[12]

Churches have to be a community in dialogue with people of other faiths, not in competition or conflict with them. It is a missionary task of the Church in India to reflect theologically on the reality of other living religions. Dialogue between Christianity and other religions goes on at various levels. This needs to be reinforced to find ways of working together against evil forces and of dealing with issues of justice and peace and human rights.

In relation to cultural plurality, the Church's mission is to make the Gospel and communal expressions of the Christian faith adapt diversely to the various cultural contexts. The cultures must also be judged by the Gospel and must be reformed by its light. Attempts have been made to "contextualize" or "indigenize" the Christian message and the communal expressions of the Christian faith. The process goes on very slowly.

In the midst of racial, linguistic, cultural, and religious diversity, the Church's mission is to work for unity not only of Christian denominations but also of all people. Already through ecumenical activities and movements for reunion of churches, the unifying mission has been promoted. The united churches also become uniting churches. They must continue to work toward developing a community in which differences of race, language, culture, class, and caste are transcended.

ANGLICAN COMMUNION AND THE MISSION OF THE CHURCH IN INDIA

Anglicanism came to India through the work of the chaplains of the Church of England and through the work of the Society for Promoting Christian Knowledge, the Church Missionary Society, and the Society for the Propagation of the Gospel. All these originated in Great Britain. Later, links were established with the Anglican Church of Canada, which supported the work of the Church in the Punjab (in north India). The Church of England in India continued until January 31, 1930. The Anglican dioceses in India, Burma, and Ceylon severed their legal connection with the Church of England in accordance with the Indian Church Measure (1927) and became an autonomous province of the Anglican Communion known as the "Church of India, Burma, and Ceylon" (CIBC). Later, after the bifurcation of India into Pakistan and India, it was known as the "Church of India, Pakistan, Burma, and Ceylon" (CIPBC). This autonomous Anglican province had its own dioceses spread over the three countries, with the bishop of Calcutta as its metropolitan. It was governed by its own constitution known as the "Constitution, Canons, and Rules of the Church of India, Burma, and Ceylon." The severance from administrative and ecclesiastical control of the Church of England and the formation of the autonomous province of the CIBC took place at a time when the churches in India were becoming increasingly aware of the sin of divisions in the churches and the need for Christian unity as a mission imperative in the multiracial, multilingual, multicultural, and multireligious context of India. A very important and forward-looking provision in the Constitution of CIBC was its Declaration No. 9:

> *Declaration 9. Of the Unity of the Church*
> It is the will of God that His Church should be one. That unity ought to be expressed, as it was in ancient days, by the unity of all the Christians of one place in one holy society. The regional Church of India, Pakistan, Burma and Ceylon ought thus to include all the

Christians of those countries. The prayer and effort of the Church of this Province will ever be directed towards this ideal, and it will seek to enter into union with any bodies of Christians in those countries which are not now in communion with it, provided always that by such union the inheritance of truth and grace which it has received with its Catholic Faith and Order be not impaired but rather established and strengthened.

And the Church of India, Pakistan, Burma and Ceylon further declares that it has the right to enter into any union with any other Church or Churches without loss of its identity on terms which this Church by resolution of the General Council has declared to be consistent with its principles.

This provision encouraged and undergirded bold ecumenical initiatives and enabled the Church to negotiate for union with other churches. In accordance with the provisions of the Constitution, all except one of the dioceses of the CIBC located in South India entered into a union with three other churches in the South that evolved into the Church of South India in 1947. The remaining dioceses of the CIPBC that were within the territories of India and Pakistan united in 1970 with five other churches—that is, some congregations of the Council of the Baptist Churches in Northern India, the Church of the Brethren in India, the Disciples of Christ, the Methodist Church (British and Australasian Conferences), and the United Church of Northern India—in accordance with the Constitution of the CIPBC. Out of this union evolved the Church of North India and the Church of Pakistan. By this union, the Anglican province known as the Church of India, Pakistan, Burma, and Ceylon ceased to exist in India and Pakistan. The Church of North India and the Church of Pakistan became legal and ecclesiastical successors of the CIPBC in India and Pakistan respectively. This merger of the Anglican dioceses into the Church of North India and the Church of Pakistan was a solid contribution of the Anglican Communion to the mission of the Church in India, even though it meant the end of Anglican provinces in these countries. Although the "Anglican Church" ceased to exist in India and Pakistan, the Anglican tradition continues to enrich the churches in India (and Pakistan) through the united churches into which it was merged. It is from the former Anglican province of the CIBC that the Church of South India, the Church of North India, the Church of Pakistan (and also the Church of Bangladesh) have received a rich heritage of liturgy; the three-fold ordained ministry of bishops, presbyters, and deacons, in which the episcopate is both historic (in historic continuity with the early Church, in "apostolic succession") and constitutional (the episcopal ministry is appointed and exercised in accordance with the constitution of the Church); the diocesan system of church government; an ethos in which the Church and the Sacraments of Baptism and the Lord's Supper have a central place; and a lot of other things that will determine the shape of the Church in future. The capacity of the Anglican Communion to hold together its commonly called "evangelical" and "catholic" wings and its openness to the ecumenical movement have contributed to the growing unity and integration of diverse traditions within the united churches in India and thereby to their strength for mission. The emphasis on the Church and the Sacraments and the historic episcopate in the Church of South India and the Church of North India and the full intercommunion relationship of these churches with other churches in the Anglican Communion continue to be a source of enrichment to these churches and open to them the possibility of ecumenical relationships with the Roman Catholic and Orthodox churches on the one hand and the commonly called reformed, evangelical, charismatic, Protestant churches on the other.

As episcopal churches inheriting the reformed traditions of the Western churches, the Church of South India and the Church of North India and the churches of the Anglican Communion can continue to enrich one another and support each other in the mission of Christ if appropriate structures can be developed for this purpose.

NOTES

1. Englebert Zeitler, "Mission Yesterday and Today: Lessons From Indian Church's History," in *Our Common Witness* (National Council of Churches in India and the Catholic Bishops' Conference of India, 1981), p. 13.
2. J. N. Farquhar, *The Crown of Hinduism* (London: Oxford University Press, 1913), p. 458.
3. Raymond Panikkar, *The Unknown Christ of Hinduism* (London: Darton, Longman and Todd, 1964). M. M. Thomas, *The Acknowledged Christ of the Hindu Renaissance* (Madras: The Christian Literature Society, 1970). Marcus Braybrooke, *The Undiscovered Christ: A Review of Recent Developments in the Christian Approach to the Hindu* (Madras: The Christian Literature Society, 1973). J. S. Samartha, *The Hindu Response to the Unbound Christ* (Madras: Christian Literature Society, 1974).
4. Christopher Duraisingh, "Mission Yesterday and Today: Reflections on Missiological Thinking in India," in *Our Common Witness* (CBCI and NCCI, 1981).

5. Geevarghese Osthathios, "Combat, Witness and Diakonia—Biblical Understanding," in *Our Common Witness* (NCCI and CBCI, 1981), p. 104.
6. Malcolm S. Adiseshiah, "Socio-economic Imperatives and the Christian Response," in *Christian Perspectives on Contemporary Indian Issues*, ed. Ram Singh (Madras: The Institute for Development Education, 1983), p. 42. This is also the source of most of the material in the section on "Socioeconomic Context."
7. *Ibid.*
8. The scriptural origin of the Hindu caste system is the text in *Rigveda* X, 90: "One fourth of the Supreme Being constitutes all beings, while three-fourths of Him are immortal and stand above. With the one-fourth below, He extended on all sides into the animate and the inanimate. . . . His face became the Brahman. His arms were made into the Ksatriya. His thighs became the Vaisya. From his feet the Sudra was born."
9. Cited by Christopher Duraisingh, "Mission Yesterday and Today," in *Our Common Witness* (CBCI and NCCI, 1981), p. 69, from Paulos Mar Gregorios, "The Cultivation of the Christian Life," in *South East Asia Journal of Theology* (April 1984).
10. E. Zeitler, *op. cit.*, pp. 35 ff.
11. Choan-Seng Song, *Christian Mission in Reconstruction*, p. ix.
12. Cited by C. Duraisingh, "Mission Yesterday and Today," in *Our Common Witness*, p. 68.

Mission, Paternalism, and the Peter Pan Syndrome

Professor John S. Pobee

For the past two thousand years, and more so since the late eighteenth and early nineteenth centuries, Christians, individually and severally, have engaged in mission because universality of the faith has been understood as the mission of faith. As it has turned out, there has been a one-way street of missionaries from the countries of the North to the countries of the South. Africa, south of the Saharah, except perhaps Ethiopia, has been evangelized principally from the North Atlantic. Anglicanism appeared in West Africa in the eighteenth century with the Society for the Propagation of the Gospel (S.P.G.) work in the Gold Coast by the Reverend Thomas Thompson and the Church Missionary Society (C.M.S.) work in Sierra Leone.[1] For reasons of the provenance of the historical missions to Africa, there is the tendency to call the churches of the North "mother churches" or "older churches" and the countries of the South "daughter" or "younger" churches. For all the historical veracity of the parent or age metaphor, it has tended to produce a Peter Pan syndrome. This needs to be examined from the angle of the churches of the North as well as from that of the churches of the South.

To start from the standpoint of the churches of the South, the churches tend to rely heavily on funds from the countries of the North. Of course, yes, the churches of the North are better endowed in resources than the churches of the South. But there is too much readiness to be dependent on the churches of the North for human and material resources. In this regard, I find it interesting and significant that in the same countries in the South, the so-called African Christian Independency is able to raise locally more funds than needed to be self-supporting. The historic churches appear to have yielded to the dependency syndrome. In liturgical matters African churches of the main-line churches appear reluctant, if not unwilling, to depart from the inherited orders of the worship. Some years ago, the present writer served as a member of the official Anglican delegation to Church Union negotiations in Ghana. From that position he was asked to be convener of the indigenization subcommittee of the liturgical subcommittee to draw up an indigenous form of morning worship. A draft was produced, which to my mind had taken seriously the Anglican High Church tradition, which had considerable appeal for Ghanaians who have a love for color, pomp, and circumstances. One dear old archdeacon of the Anglican Church said to me, "John, are you Canterbury to draw up an order of service for us?" There can be no better example of the Peter Pan syndrome. An order of service is an aid to communion with God. Therefore, a meaningful order should always relate to the cultural setting of the worshipers. That obviously was not the concern of the archdeacon.

The other side of the dependency syndrome is the paternalism that marks the relationship between the North and the South.[2] Today several mission agencies from North America are rushing into Africa with programs that perpetuate the dependency syndrome. Several former missionaries who have found a voice with mission agencies have become paternalistic godfathers to churches overseas. The tragedy is that they often do not realize that things change so fast that a year out of Africa makes one out of date. Mission agencies prefer the statements of missionaries in the so-called mission field to the considered judgments of the national church leaders. The tragedy is several of these missionaries have been accredited with vast knowledge of the local scene on the basis of assumed familiarity with an area, the nuances of which they often do not really know or understand. All of these are unfortunate ways of perpetuating paternalism and are basically not different from the following position of the Reverend Mister Adolphus Mann, nineteenth-century local secretary of the C.M.S. in Nigeria:

> The native mind wants a guide, a stimulus, a superintendance, and this is the very thing you go about to take away from him through the NATIVE CHURCH. There will be no more the wholesome influence of the whiteman's energy . . . the absolute independence of the NATIVE I dread. . . . When I am no admirer of the Native independence I am so from the best of feelings for the African man: that he may be largely profited, for more than time allowed, by a wise presidency of the whiteman.[3]

There can be no better example of paternalism.

Africa's Precious Sparkling Stone

Today Africans are saying that a relationship between North and South is desirable, indeed, necessary, in the body of Christ, which stretches over the whole globe. But paternalism and a dependency syndrome are neither marks of a healthy relationship nor the marks of a truly living church. It is being said that what is required in the inescapable joint-mission in obedience to Christ is the relationship of partners, not patrons; brothers and sisters in a common task, not benefactors and bosses; co-workers, not overseers; and respect for the integrity of each other. That is the significance of the moratorium debate that raged in mission circles in the mid-seventies.[4]

On the other hand, it is also important for the receiving churches to examine themselves carefully as to the maximum they too can put into the life of the Church both at home and abroad, however, scanty their resources. The Right Reverend John Orfeur Anglionby, the second bishop of the diocese of Accra (1927–1950), wrote some words that are instructive.

> The African has his contribution to make to the Catholic Church of Christ. His simple trustful faith, his quick response to the appeal of an enlightened conscience, his natural reverence are the material—and splendid material too—upon which can be built a nation Christian and Christlike. He is a precious stone which will one day sparkle in the crown of the King of Kings when He makes up the number of His jewels.[5]

One may raise questions here and there with regard to "enlightened conscience," which might be identified with the North Atlantic culture. But by and large this is a striking positive attitude to Africa at a time when Africa was regarded as "the darkest continent." Africa—indeed, the church of Africa—has a contribution to make; its natural stuff is not useless and should be allowed to come into the fullness of the household of God. The question is: Is one's good, good enough? No positive contribution is too small for the life and work of the Church of God on earth. It is in this regard that I see mission not as a one-way street from North to South, but as a two-way street from North to South and vice versa with crossroads and other linkages and connections.

Another illustration of the one-way street perception of mission was the practice of the missionary doctrine of the *tabula rasa* ("clean slate"), by which it was implied, if not alleged, that there was nothing in the non-European cultures on which Christian faith and mission could build. That missionary philosophy may be summarized as "outside the North Atlantic civilization there is no salvation." Christianity has been thoroughly "cultured," to use a botanical imagery, in the North; Christ had been made so much a European that he could not be recognized originally as a Jew. Needless to say, the *tabula rasa* doctrine and practice were a relatively modern version of the old Jewish stance that *extra Judaeas nulla salus est*—that is, outside the Jewish church-state there is no salvation.

The practice of the *tabula rasa*, like the Peter Pan syndrome, put the African churches and Christians in North Atlantic captivity.[6] Christian missions laid upon African Christians greater burdens than were really necessary (compare Acts 15:28). In our view the *tabula rasa* is a religious version of European ethnocentrism, by which African Christians played second fiddle to Western culture, Western patterns of life and interests. It was imperialistic uniformity.

The response to the missionary practice of *tabula rasa* is very divided, ranging widely. But for our purpose it is enough to take three positions. First is the support position represented by the late Joseph Amihere Essuah, Roman Catholic bishop of Kumasi and later of Sekondi, a Ghanaian of the Nzima tribe, who wrote:

> The mystery of the Blessed Trinity is a truth revealed by God but which is above our human understanding. This is a very important point which obliges us to throw way our traditional idea about God the Supreme Being. If we think we should keep our traditional ideas as a very important part of our culture, then it is not yet time for us to become Catholics and we should openly go out of the church.[7]

Essuah, Roman Catholic though he was, spoke for several others even on the Protestant and African-Christian independency side.

Second is the opposite position of the total rejection of the *tabula rasa*, often represented by the African nationalist politicians. The following quotation from Nkrumah's speech to the meeting of the Independent African States in Accra in 1958 is the best illustration: "The stage opens with the appearance of missionaries, anthropologists, traders, concessionaires, and administrators. While the missionaries with 'Christianity' implore the colonial subject to lay up 'treasures in heaven . . . ,' the traders, concessionaires acquire his mineral and land resources, destroy his arts, crafts and native industries." In other words, the missionary is accused of having been an accessory in the enslavement of Africans. But third is the position represented by P. K. Sarpong, also a Roman Catholic bishop from Kumasi, Ghana—that is, that for all the uniqueness of the Christ event, there is room for culturing of the Gospel in Africa, just like it was "cultured" in Europe. Indeed, the title of one of his publications is most expressive: "Christianity Should Be Africanised, Not Africa Christianised."[8]

The present writer by and large takes his stand with Sarpong.[9] For one thing the *tabula rasa* doctrine ignores the important fact that cultural, historical, and sociopolitical factors contribute to the shaping of witness in any and every given context, just like the development of European Christianity shows. As such, European missions were doing to Africans what they would not like done to them. For yet another thing, the result of the *tabula rasa* is inefficiency. Because of the foreignness of the European mold of theology, liturgy, and spirituality, the church life was not exactly at the wavelength of the African people of God, addressing their hopes and fears. Sarpong has commented as follows:

> It is evident that traditional Catholic worship is anything but religious worship to the genuine African! It is dull, uninspiring, almost without emotional appeal. The prayers are defective in one hundred and one ways. Composed with a Roman mentality, their structure, syntax and concepts are unintelligible to the African. What their words, even when translated into vernacular, are meant to convey is anybody's guess. They are composed without reference to the occasion. They are therefore at best meaningless, at worst, a waste of time.[10]

Sarpong goes on to suggest danced liturgy and processions; dialogic sermons (which is following the pattern of the proverbial African "palaver"); the inventive use of drums, gongs, xylophones. Similar developments need to take place in theology and so forth. Third, the *tabula rasa* is an ignoring, if not a denial, of the lesson of the Incarnation.

I part with Sarpong, however, on the point of terminology. "Africanisation" is unsatisfactory. Partly as a result of the usage in African political circles (compare ideas of African personality, negritude) it has tended to stop at administrative and judicial aspects of the institution. "As long as the term Africanisation has a thick overlay and dose of politics, there is the danger of political goals eclipsing religious goals" (Pobee, in his forthcoming book, *Skenosis: A Tabernacling of Christian Faith in Ghana*, chapter 4). Besides, given the vastness and diversity in Africa, "Africanisation" almost becomes too diffuse a concept to be given content. Therefore, I prefer the word *skenosis*, the "tabernacling" of Christian faith in Africa. Not only is it a biblical image (compare John 1:14), but it also emphasizes the eternal, nonnegotiable part—

namely, the word of God that needs to and must be given a temporary abode, a tent—which must be constantly checked by succeeding generations.

North Atlantic Captivity of Anglicanism

What has been said of the North Atlantic captivity of the Church
as a result of the missionary doctrine of the *tabula rasa* is equally
true of the Anglican situation. It is a truism that Anglicanism is
very English. Cranmer's excellent *Book of Common Prayer* is very
English. The statement of theology by Anglicans is also very English. The Anglican method of the *via media* is also very English.
Now the *Book of Common Prayer* is used in Africa and has been
translated into African languages, supposedly in the name of
translation and indigenization. The theologies of Thomas
Cranmer (1489–1556), Richard Hooker (1554–1600), John Frederick Denison Maurice (1805–1872), and Charles Gore
(1853–1932)—the giants of Anglican theological reflection—are
still indices of Anglican soundness even in Africa. But is the En-
glishness of the *Book of Common Prayer* translatable into another
culture? The rise of African theology and black theologies on the
continent of Africa is not only a reminder that the eternal, nonnegotiable Word of God can and should enter into dialogue with
the African context, body, heart, and soul, but also that the formulation of the theological agenda by the North Atlantic (Anglican and all) is not the last word on the subject. The formula-
tions of Cranmer, Hooker, Maurice, Gore, and others can and
should stand alongside the formulation of African theologies without any sense of betrayal of the true spirit of Anglicanism. If
Anglicanism is a communion, then there is room for other etches
into the mosaic of colors, spiritualities, and races. In my view that
is the meaning of the Anglican method of the *via media,* which
represents the willingness to affirm others across the board; and it
is a very positive method that makes for communion.

One comic tragedy relating to the one-way street perception of
mission is the heavy intellectualization of the faith and that in a
society that is predominantly nonliterate. The indices of faith are
heavily intellectual—affirmation of creeds, the language of which
is most strange even to theological students, let alone illiterates
who have not been exposed to Greek ideas and so forth. The
importance of the Word of God has been interpreted to mean long
and incoherent harangues and monologues called sermons
through which the most faithful feel lulled, obliged, and pressed

to sleep. The criteria for the selection of priests are highly academic and intellectual. There is a high premium on rationality. I have no doubt that rationality is part of bearing the *imago Dei*. What I question is the one-sided emphasis on rationality at the expense of maturity based on experience, humanness, the Spirit. The result is that several in the main-line churches find no real satisfaction with their churches, and consequently, deal in double insurance; they attend the services of the Anglican churches often for respectability, and they also attach themselves to African-Christian independency for healing and experience of the Spirit. Here is another plea for a holistic approach to mission. Mission must address the body and spirit needs of Africans. It is also already a plea for the use of Africans who can be on a net with their congregations for mission.

One of the ugly faces of mission has been the introduction of denominationalism, which already compounds the divisiveness of African societies brought on by the fact that the new nations are really congeries of loosely-knit tribes. The theological, doctrinal, historical, cultural, and emotional factors in the splintering of the main-line churches are not too evident or real on the African scene; at the best they are minimal with the denomination doing business as usual. I have no doubt that God has used the scandal of denominationalism to bless Africa. For "the faithful witness given by one Church in a particular place can be part of the rich and diverse witness of the whole Church."[11]

There is evidence galore that denominations have stood up for the dignity of humankind in rotten situations of violence, suffering, and injustice; they have even made "silent witness of solidarity and intercession." But such Christian witness is the next best; it is not full witness until the churches have made real the prayer of Christ that all may be one (John 17:11). The true goal of mission is not to create a denomination, but a people of God, a community reconciled to God and, therefore, to and with fellow human beings and the rest of creation. In the face of conflicting ideologies around the globe, the ecumenical reality needs to address the deepest and most fundamental questions about the relation between God and humanity, society and customs.

If for reasons of theology and credibility, denominationalism is untenable, that is not a plea for a hasty, ill-conceived ecumenical movement. One can be responsibly immersed in the ecumenical movement only if he or she knows his or her roots and bearings. The Anglican method expressed in the phrase *via media*—that is, the willingness to accept the paradoxes of life and each other across the board, as well as the Anglican principles of rootedness in the Bible, serious engagement with tradition, and probable reason—places Anglicans most admirably for fruitful dialogue across all religious traditions with a view to "summing up all things in Him, things in heaven and things on earth" (Ephesians 1:10). There is no security in being an Anglican; in Anglicanism there is "no continuing city, no abiding stay." Mission into Anglicanism is only a halfway tent to heaven, which is ecumenical, multi-racial and yet nonracial, multiconfessional and yet nonconfessional—in short, when persons realize themselves as created "in the image and likeness of God," a covenanted people of God cutting across class, race, creed, sex.

In this regard I wish to put a particular burden on the churches of the North—especially the Church of England, or the Episcopal Church of the United States of America and the Anglican Church of Canada. In most places Anglicans who are eminently placed to dialogue into mission have either not gone beyond ecumenical sloganeering and courtesy, or pulled out of negotiations at the eleventh hour. For example, in Ghana the diocese of Accra pulled out in about 1974, although they had made a tremendous impact on the Church Union discussion, even in matters of ministry.[12] Several reasons could be adduced, such as carnal concerns, false security in supposed Anglican Establishment, and so forth. For the moment I am interested in a powerful factor that relates to companions of the North. There is the fear in Africa that Anglican churches that move into union schemes in their context betray the Church of England and this in spite of the statements of Lambeth Conferences and Anglican Consultative Councils. The debacle of the Church of England–Methodist union scheme and other such schemes only served to give African-Anglican opponents of union the ammunition. If Canterbury and York have turned their backs on it, who are we in Africa to move out of step? Do we, by not uniting with others, fall out of communion with Canterbury, the mother church? My point is that since for good or for ill the primacy of Canterbury is taken seriously in Africa, ecumenical schemes in Africa will not move in the right direction until they begin to move in Britain. In the absence of Canterbury moving, it is important for the Anglican churches of the United States and Canada to move ahead into union with other denominations. That will be good confidence boosters for the African churches because they, like the African Anglican churches, are autonomous national churches. It will demonstrate that it is possible to be loyal to the Anglican Communion by realizing the prayer of Jesus that "all may be one." This is an urgent and vital task; for the churches of Africa cannot afford the luxury of denominationalism above all because they are in a stiff race with other faiths and ideologies for the hearts of human beings to be subjected to the kingship of Christ.

In the comments on the ecumenical task of mission, I have made specific references to the Anglican contribution. I wish to stay a little longer with the Anglican Communion as it relates to mission.

Mission Agencies

In the Anglican record much of mission has been the responsibility of missionary societies, principally the Society for the Propagation of the Gospel (S.P.G.), the Church Missionary Society (C.M.S.), the Universities Mission to Central Africa (U.M.C.A.), and some religious orders—for example, the Order of the Holy Paraclete (O.H.P.), the Holy Cross, among others. These societies and orders, though related to an Anglican church, were, nevertheless, not exactly agencies of the Anglican church; they were autonomous and independent. In the field these agencies have tended to act independently of the local church, taking their orders from Europe. In these ways mission has not been directed by the Church and in a sense has not been the responsibility of the Church, except for, perhaps, the collection taken somewhere in the church for mission overseas. The foregoing development involves a questionable ecclesiology and theology of mission. As one reflects on this situation, one has been forced to ask whether the Church of England and through that, other Anglican churches, ever in practice had a very sensitive mission sense? The protest of John Wesley is in part this issue. As for the S.P.G., it was more concerned with chaplaincies to the factories and plantations overseas. I say this in spite of the work of the S.P.G. among Mohawk Indians. Has the Anglican church really grown beyond chaplaincies to mission properly so-called?

Mission entrusted to societies has had another unfortunate consequence in the obfuscation of the sense of unity within the one denomination. Tanzania presents a very interesting picture. It was evangelized by the three missions: U.M.C.A., C.M.S., and the Bible Churchman's Missionary Society. This has developed into segregated uniformity. For sometimes an Anglican from the

U.M.C.A. tradition, on transfer to an area evangelized by C.M.S., prefers to join the Roman Catholics for worship than to join fellow Anglicans of the C.M.S. tradition. Similarly, those in C.M.S. tradition prefer to join Lutherans than to join Anglicans of U.M.C.A. tradition. Surely there is something wrong when an Anglican cannot worship with a fellow Anglican and a compatriot, all because of the mission traditions in which they stand. Is it not odd that intradenominational concerns should take precedence over membership of the Church of God? Surely ecclesiology is wrong when this happens. Has the time not come for the missionary agencies to come together in the Church?

Mission entrusted to mission agencies carries with it a third danger. In the words of C. R. Taber it has become evident that

> agencies structured like business corporations bring about, intentionally or not, many of the undesirable effects as the business concerns: there is a similar emphasis on "distribution and promotion of the (uniform) product"; similar tendency to bypass local agencies (the national Church) which are in the same "business"; and above all similar control over the process. There may be something at least potentially demonic about operating in this way that may forbid its being justified even in terms of real pragmatic advantages.[13]

These comments on the mission agencies are not designed to write off all that they have achieved. They are meant to point out unfortunate consequences or aspects of that style of operation in mission and to plead for working out appropriate methods for the interplay between available resources and the gospel imperatives. And at all costs mission is and must be seen to be the task of the whole Church, the whole covenanted people of God.

Clericalization of Mission

Let me now briefly address myself to the clericalization of mission. There has been in Africa and elsewhere a tendency to think and behave as if ordained persons are the real agents of mission, all others being addenda, so to speak. A brief review of the biblical picture should be instructive.

Jesus had twelve assistants and, as Luke would have us believe, another seventy (Luke 10:1ff.). There is no suggestion that the twelve were priests, though they were commissioned to go out and preach and to heal the sick. In Paul's letters we come across several functionaries, apostles, prophets, teachers, workers of miracles, healers, helpers, administrators, speakers in various kinds of tongues. It is not as if these stood in water-tight compartments—for apostles also were teachers and healers. As the deutero-Pauline letter to the Ephesians sees it, all these have the one goal of "the equipment of the saints for the work of ministry, for building up the body of Christ" (Ephesians 4:12f). Commissioned personnel are enablers of the whole people of God for the mission in the world. In Acts of the Apostles we hear of apostles, elders, prophets, and those who serve tables (Acts 6:1–6). Then in the pastoral epistles we read of bishop (1 Timothy 3:1–7), deacon (1 Timothy 3:8–13), and possibly widows.

From this quick review the conclusion is that there is no protoministry and the ministry is in a state of flux. Of course the apostles had a special place as "eyewitnesses and ministers of the word" (Luke 1:2), persons who on the basis of their own experience vouch for the veracity of the gospel claims. This same concern for veracity in part led to the canonization of some books of the Christians.[14] But even the earliest witnesses did not have a monopoly of evangelism and mission. While it is not possible to reproduce New Testament patterns, there is a clear lesson that the task of mission to the whole world is so vast and diverse that it cannot be the preserve or monopoly of any one group. Besides, today, there is a new development—healing that used to be exercised by church functionaries is today exercised by the hospitals. Until recently there has been almost a rigid separation between the church and healing. Today the lesson of African-Christian Independence is that persons of God should be able to cure in the name of God. In other words, structures of mission should not be seen in terms of positions and hierarchy, but of wholeness of ministries that bring wholeness to the people of God and through that, be a blessing to humanity in general. The cure in the name of Christ is a powerful witness to the reality of the kingship of Christ. My plea is for a holistic conception of the agencies of mission and for a meditation on the concept of "fellow worker" (Romans 16:3). This is no plea for disorder; some sort of order to integrate the entire "business" is necessary. But such select persons do not become thereby specialists in spiritual matters, superior to all others. The only head is Christ. How dare we presume that our young inexperienced boys and girls from college, whose only merit is that they have sat at the feet of a professor, are the best equipped to lead and lord it over the people of God? Let us recall also that mission is servanthood, one of the images used to state the content of the teaching done on mission (compare Acts 2:13; Philippians 2:7). The servant image exhorts the faithful to pursue a life-style of powerlessness, humility, total obedience to the will of God, which means selfless and self-sacrificing devotion to fellow human beings. The Church and the missionaries do not seek nor wield earthly power, nor impose their views on others. How that is different from the use of force or manipulation to spread the Word! These recommended qualities of the people of God should not be interpreted to mean a romanticizing of the ways and condition of the poor and the oppressed. For the gospel is a two-edged sword—attacking hypocrisy, greed, and insensitivity of the powerful on the one hand, and the lethargy and sense of hopelessness of the oppressed on the other hand. To say mission is servanthood is to say that poverty is the locus where the power of God and the glory of God can most powerfully and dramatically condemn and liberate human beings, be they poor or rich, marginalized or powerful. Mission is selfless and self-sacrificing service to human beings in the image and likeness of God. The burden of my argument is that when we consider mission as servanthood and in terms of structures of mission, we need to examine theologically, sociologically, empirically, and practically what it really means to exercise *episcope*.

In our Anglican tradition there is a concentration on the Eucharist. That creates the need for priests for the administration of the sacrament at least on a Sunday. The simple truth in Africa today is that several congregations will be lucky to see a priest once in three months. Consequently congregations are for months denied the most elementary pastoral and missionary needs of the Church. Further, in hostile political situations it is not always easy, even if possible, to have seminary training on the spot for those who will in the near future proclaim God's word, give sacraments, and so forth. It becomes all the more urgent for the churches to get away from the clericalization of mission and to diversify the concept of ministry. The numerous catechists who really are the front-line agents of mission need to be really integrated more fully into the church administration than hitherto. Of their work Bishop Aglionby wrote:

> The work which our catechists do is indispensable and their withdrawal from the field or any diminution in their numbers will be disastrous. . . . It is the Catechist who had to teach them to worship and to pray, and often it is only after years of patient teaching and the example of a Christian life lived among them that one by one lives are changed, souls are saved, a church built, a school is opened and the seeds of our holy religion are sown and fostered.[15]

What a fine tribute to them! They are the real heroes of the African church history. And yet they are not canonically recognized and are treated as errand boys for the clergy. They must be recognized and authorized, after careful selection and relevant instruction, to administer sacraments as well. I am pleading for the recognition of the catechists as an order alongside priests and deacons.

Again there is the issue of the ordination of women. They have been the backbone of the church in Africa, and yet church and society have marginalized them. Today there is a revolution in the sound relationship between the sexes and therefore there can no longer continue to be rule of the Church without them. Ecclesiastical polity has to bring in the women in their own right. To me the argument that the issue cannot be settled by one section of this church is an excuse for not moving on a moral issue of the dignity of men and women who bear the *imago Dei*. Is it the case that women are incapable of spiritual power, lofty aim, and driving force? Beyond all things, of course, Africa needs leaders of their own race in the church as in state. Africans must be challenged to do mission in their own region.

School and Hospitals—The Handmaids of Mission

From fairly early times the school and the hospital have been seen as handmaids of mission. So all missions have invested so much in the social services. Today churches are fighting hard to hold on to their institutions in the face of national governments claiming them for their own in the name of the welfare state. I have no doubt that at the time when colonial governments were just not interested in the education and welfare of the Africans, the missionaries did a good job establishing schools and hospitals. Today national governments are claiming schools, and it is their proper function to provide education. For taxes are collected *inter alia* to provide such amenities. So I am not too sure that I would want to fight over government takeover of schools today, though I affirm with Vatican II that "parents who have the first and inalienable duty and right to educate their children, should enjoy true freedom in their choice of schools."

If that should happen, however, I would want some guarantees. First, since education has an objective of preparing men and women to cope with life in its manifold form, missions and churches must insist on their right, as taxpayers, to religious studies. Second, committed teachers and practicing Christians should be encouraged to take such classes. Lousy and unconvincing teachers make religious studies meaningless. Churches must encourage the right people to apply for such positions. Third, churches should promote the drawing up of good syllabi. The rote learning of biblical passages and stories as the religious course is really not helpful. Life-based teaching of religion is ideal. We need a meaningful syllabus in a plural society, which is not just a study of the important component of Western civilization, but also an encouragement to faith and critical respect for other religions in the society, without which there can be no peace. Denominational schools should be alternative instruments of integration and reconciliation and never instruments to reinforce segregated loyalties.

Governments make noises about taking over mission hospitals. Good luck to them, if they have the resources and expertise. But churches must be ready to help and give the medical field a human face. In any case, modern scientific studies have shown that medicine can be the teamwork of the pastor and the medical doctor because some ailments are psychosomatic.

I am suggesting that sometimes missions may need to be content with being pioneers in the social services, preparing for the eventual takeover by the government whose proper duty it is to provide such amenities. I am, however, convinced that there are large segments of the social services that have not even begun to be implemented, such as education and treatment of the handicapped as well as vocational training of the persons with no disabilities in society. That is a whole field for missions to pioneer. In most African societies, spastics, morons, and other deformed or malformed persons are consigned to a life of emptiness, deprivation, shame, degradation, and hopelessness. Institutions are not doing enough for many who could be in some kind of vocation, rather than in the academic stream. A mission focus on such persons would help them realize themselves in the *imago Dei*. There is the whole area of vocational training, which has not been developed, especially when too many people are in blind-alley jobs from which they find no self-fulfillment.

Mission and the Search for Viable Political Institutions Today
The Ariadne thread running through the various aspects of mission is that the mission of the Church seeks to create a people of God whose "ideology" has the twin ideas—the *imago Dei* and the kingship of God. It is not fashionable to use the word "ideology" of the teaching of the Church. That is in part because ideology is often understood as a set of dogmas to be imposed by the govern-

ment, with force if necessary. That understanding of ideology has many an ugly face because of its exclusive basis for political action and organization of society. But I use it here in its proper sense—that is, as a set of ideas about what form the good society should take.[16] And the Christian mission has to relate to or engage other ideologies in the new states of Africa. The issues at stake in this engagement in nation-building are the right balance between authority and freedom, new social integration, new cultural orientation, formation of new human type, economic growth, and so forth. There is no opting out of this engagement because basic problems of life as well as factual disorientation lead human beings to look for ideology. And if the Church is to be taken seriously, she must engage in the quest for an ideology by which the state will be built. Indeed, she has a contribution to make.

All to often this dialogue is carried on as if it is only a choice between capitalism and socialism. Could it be that the people of God, the *tertium genus*—that is, a third race, a new culture—have an alternative ideology to offer? One is reminded of the fable of a heavily loaded camel being asked by its owner: "Would you prefer to go up-hill or down-hill?" Whereupon the camel replied: "Is the road across the plain closed?" I do not believe in Africa we are between the devil of plutocracy and the deep blue sea of socialism. The choice is not between "right" and "left," as the issue is often put; rather it is a choice between fascism, which destroys the basic structures of liberal government—such structures as independent judiciary, legal means for the change of government, free press, trade unions controlled by party bosses—on the one hand, and liberalism on the other hand. What we shall search for is a plurality of moral authorities that can ensure freedom. The Christian mission has a chance to help chart "the road across the plain." And only then can the Church find the peace and quiet for the mission to make real the kingship of God.

NOTES

1. See T. Thompson, *An Account of Two Missionary Voyages by Appointment of the S.P.G.* (1758); S. Neill, *Christian Missions* (1964); C. P. Groves, *The Planting of Christianity in Africa* (1948); and G. Hewitt, *The Problems of Success . . .* (1971).
2. See P. Hetherington, *British Paternalism and Africa* (1978); and M. A. C. Warren, *The Missionary Movement From Britain in Modern History* (1965) and *Social History and Christian Mission* (1967).
3. A. Mann to H. Wright, February 24, 1875; CMS CA 2/03(d).
4. See J. Gatu, Address to Mission Festival at Milwaukee (1971); and J.

S. Pobee, "Moratorium Revisited," in *Ghana Bulletin of Theology*, vol. 4, no. 9 (1975), pp. 57–67.
5. J. O. Anglionby, *Golden Shore*, no. 7 (January 1927), p. 182.
6. See J. S. Pobee, "The Church in Western Africa," in C. R. Taber, ed., *The Church in Africa, 1977* (1977); and *Towards an African Theology* (1979).
7. J. A. Essuah, "Bishop Essuah Speaks to Catholics," in *Standard: National Catholic Weekly*," vol. 39, no. 14 (April 3–10, 1977), p. 3.
8. P. K. Sarpong, "Christianity Should Be Africanised, Not Africa Christianised," in *African Ecclesiastical Review*, vol. 17, no. 6 (1975).
9. J. S. Pobee, *Towards an African Theology* (1979).
10. P. K. Sarpong, "African Religion and Catholic Worship," in *Standard: National Catholic Weekly*, vol. 39, no. 15 (April 10–17, 1977), p. 5.
11. World Council of Churches, *Common Witness* (no date), p. 23.
12. Ghana Church Union Committee, *Proposals for Church Union in Ghana* (1973).
13. C. R. Taber, "Contextualization," in W. Shenk, ed., *Exploring Church Growth* (1983), p. 128.
14. See H. E. Turner, *The Pattern of Christian Truth* (1954); and H. von Campenhausen, *The Formation of the Christian Bible* (1972).
15. J. O. Aglionby, *Golden Shore*, no. 2 (January 1945), p. 22.
16. See K. Wiredu, *Philosophy and an African Culture* (1980), p. 52; and J. Verkuyl, *Contemporary Missiology* (1978), pp. 373–404.

BIBLIOGRAPHY

Aagaard, J. *Mission, Konfession, Kirche, Die Problematik Ihrer Integration in (a) Jahrhundet in Deutschland*. 2 vols. Lind: Gleering, 1967.
Aglionby, J. O. *Golden Shore*, no. 7. January 1927.
———. *Golden Shore*, no. 2. January 1945.
Bertram, G. ἔθνος, etc., in *Theologisches Wörterbuch zum Neuen Testament*, vol. II. Stuttgart: Kohlhammer, 1935. English translation "ethnos etc.," in *Theological Dictionary of the New Testament*. Grand Rapids, Mich.: William B. Eerdmans, 1964, pp. 364–369.
Bonhoeffer, D. *Letters and Papers From Prison*. London: S.C.M., 1967.
Bosch, D. J. "The Structure of Mission: An Exposition of Matthew 28: 16–20." In *Exploring Church Growth*, edited by W. Shenk, pp. 218–248. 1983.
Crampton, E. P. *Christianity in Northern Nigeria*. London: G. Chapman, 1963.
Desai, R. *Christianity as Seen by Africans*. Denver: A. Swallow, 1962.
Essuah, J. A. "Bishop Essuah Speaks to Catholics," in *Standard: National Catholic Weekly*, vol. 39, no. 14 (April 3–10, 1977).
Freire, P. *Pedagogy of the Oppressed*. New York: Seabury, 1974.
Gatu, J. Address to Mission Festival at Milwaukee, U.S.A., 1971.
Gensichen, H. *Glaube für die Welt*. Gütersloh: Gerd Mohn, 1971.
Ghana Church Union Committee. *Proposals for Church Union in Ghana: The Inauguration and Constitution of the United Church*. Accra: Ghana Church Union Committee, 1973.
Groves, C. P. *The Planting of Christianity in Africa*. London: Lutterworth, 1948.

Hahn, F. *Mission in the New Testament*. London: S.C.M., 1963.
———. "Der Sendungsauftrag des Auferstandenen: Matthäus 28, 16-20," in *Fides Pro Mundi Vita*. Ed., Theo Sundermier. *Missionstheologie Heute Hans-Werner Gensichen zum 65. Geburtstag*. Gütersloh: Gerd Mohn, 1980.
Hastings, A. *Wiriyamu*. London: Search Press, 1974.
Hetherington, P. *British Paternalism and Africa*. London: F. Cass, 1978.
Hewitt, G. *The Problems of Success: A History of the Church Missionary Society, 1910–1942*. Vol. 1. London: S.C.M., 1971.
Hooker, H. *Jesus and the Servant*. London: S.P.C.K., 1959.
Jeremias, J. *Servant of God*. London: S.C.M., 1965.
Kimble, D. *A Political History of Ghana, 1850–1926*. Oxford: Clarendon, 1963.
Ladd, G. C. *Jesus and the Kingdom*. London: S.P.C.K., 1966.
Lampe, G. W. *The Seal of the Spirit*. London: Longmans, 1936.
Lundstrom, G. *The Kingdom of God in the Teaching of Jesus*. Edinburgh: Oliver & Boyd, 1963.
Matthey, J. "The Great Commission According to Matthew." *International Review of Mission*, no. 274 (April 1980).
Moule, D. F. D. *The Meaning of Hope*. London: Highway Press, 1953.
Neill, S. *Christian Missions*. Harmondsworth: Penguin, 1964.
Nkrumah, K. Speech at the Conference of Independent African States. Accra: April 15, 1953.
Orchard, R. K. *The Ghana Assembly of the International Missionary Council, 1957–58*. London: Edinburgh Publishing Press, 1958.
Padilla, R. "The Unity of the Church and the Homogeneous Unit Principle," in Shenk, *Exploring Church Growth* (1983), pp. 285-303.
Pobee, J. S. "Moratorium Revisited," in *Ghana Bulletin of Theology*, vol. 4, no. 9 (1975).
———. "The Church in Western Africa," in C. R. Taber, ed., *The Church in Africa, 1977*. South Pasadena: William Carey Library, 1977.
———. *Towards an African Theology*. Nashville: Abingdon, 1979.
———. "The People of God and the Peoples," pp. 181–190 in Shenk, *Exploring Church Growth*, 1983.
———. *Persecution and Martyrdom in the Theology of St. Paul*. Sheffield: Society of New Testament Studies, 1985.
———. *Skenosis—The Tabernacling of Christian Faith in Africa* (no date).
Rengstorf, K. 1964 ἀποστέλλω 135–165 etc. in TDNT I.
———. 1965 διδάσκω etc. in *TDNT* II Eerdman.
Saayman, W. A. "The Case of South Africa: Practice, Context and Ideology," in Shenk, *Exploring Church Growth*, 1983.
Samuel, V. K., and Sugden, C. *Christian Mission in the Eighties—A Third World Perspective*. Bangalore: Partners in Mission—Asia, 1981.
Sarpong, P. K. "Christianity Should Be Africanised, Not Africa Christianised," in *African Ecclesiastical Review*, vol. 17, no.6 (1975).
———. "African Religion and Catholic Worship," in *Standard: National Catholic Weekly*, vol. 39, no. 15 (April 10–17, 1977).
Sithole, N. *African Nationalism*. London: Oxford University Press, 1959.
Shenk, W., ed. *Exploring Church Growth*. Grand Rapids, Mich.: Eerdmans, 1983.
Taber, C. R. "Contextualization," pp. 117–131 in Shenk, *op. cit.*

Taylor, J. V. *For All the World: The Christian Mission in the Modern Age.* London: Hodder and Stoughton, 1966.

Thompson, T. *An Account of Two Missionary Voyages by Appointment of the S.P.G.* London: S.P.G., 1758.

Trilling, W. *Das wahre Israel, Studien zur Theologie des Matthäusevangelium.* München: Kosel, 1964.

Turner, H. E. *The Pattern of Christian Truth.* London: Mowbrays, 1954.

Verkuyl, J. *Contemporary Missiology: An Introduction.* Grand Rapids: W. Eerdmans, 1978.

von Campenhausen, H. *The Formation of the Christian Bible.* London: A & C Black, 1972.

Warren, H. A. C. *The Missionary Movement From Britain in Modern History.* London: S.C.M., 1965.

———. *Social History and Christian Mission.* London: S.C.M., 1967.

Wiredu, K. *Philosophy and an African Culture.* Cambridge: Cambridge University Press, 1980.

World Council of Churches. *Common Witness: A Study Document of the Joint Working Group of the Roman Catholic and the World Council of Churches.* Geneva: W.C.C., n.d.

Yoder, J. H. "Social Shape of the Gospel," pp. 277–284 in Shenk, *op. cit.,* 1983.

Can Mission and Church Be Integrated?

The Reverend Doctor Kortright Davis

How probable is it that a citizen of Poland, or of Tibet, will one day be elected prime minister of the Commonwealth of the Bahamas? Or how feasible is it to expect that a young citizen of Brazil, or of Angola, could ever accede to the British throne? Some probabilities are plainly unthinkable. The institutions that we establish for the effective ordering of our social and political ethos are so fixed and firmly rooted in specific orbits that the possibilities for orbital shifts are generally regarded as remote. By and large, we human beings are creatures of habit, and we normally prefer things to remain as they are and to function in their predesignated and accustomed way. Now, if we recognize that the Church is one of our basic social institutions and that it is expected, and permitted, to perform in a certain way, what about the mission with which it is associated? Is it identical with the Church, or is it to be acknowledged as being quite distinct in essence and expectation? Is mission to be regarded as institutional as well, or is it to be understood as functioning in an entirely different orbit? Can there be mission without the Church? Or can the Church function authentically without mission? Which is unthinkable without which? Are they integral to each other, or is it the endless Christian task to work toward the full integration of both? What are the implications of regarding them as separate, and what are the consequences of treating them as identical? These are our present concerns. Let us first reflect on what mission means.

The Meaning of Mission
Our understanding of the word itself suggests that "mission" has something to do with "sending." It always involves movement, and it is chiefly an activity between persons. Normally we think of it as having four aspects—first, the sender; second, the person

sent; third, that which is to be done by the person who is sent; fourth, the effects of what has been done. It is possible to speak of a "personal mission" in the sense that an individual sets a special task or goal for himself or herself, but perhaps in such cases the concept of mission is incomplete. One could seriously argue that a so-called self-imposed mission was only a manner of speaking about one's own ambitions and aspirations or, even, a symptom of a dual personality. Be that as it may, we simply wish to posit at this time that mission involves a sender and a person sent with something to do. This multiple aspect of mission dominates the true meaning of the prophetic tradition in the Old Testament and also gives to ancient Hebrew religion a unique feature far beyond the reach of its contemporaries. The great figure of Moses, which throws its bright beams of light back to a Babylonian old man, points us to these words: "So Abram went, as the Lord had told him; and Lot went with him. Abram was seventy-five years old when he departed from Haran" (Genesis 12:4). Those bright beams also enable us to find two cousins at the river Jordan arguing about who should be baptized by whom, and then the eventual words from a third party: "This is my beloved Son, with whom I am well pleased" (Matthew 3:17).

So the God of the Old Testament is One who sends, and the covenant relationship that is understood to be in effect between Himself and His chosen people of Israel seems to carry with it all the time the component for mission. This missionary component does not appear to be locked into the institutionally arranged order of things; it comes to the fore in strange and unexpected ways, so much so that there are times when the officers of the covenant ritual, the priests, seem unable to determine whether a mission is authentic or not. The prophets always seemed to be standing outside of the institutional framework, while at the same time calling for a return to the original relationship that the covenant produced. No wonder then that Jesus of Nazareth is recognized as an outsider by His own people and eventually disposed of as such a person. Nevertheless, His claim was that His mission was not to destroy any of the religious tradition but simply to fulfill it. We must notice that He is never credited with the notion that fulfillment meant either institutional reform or expansion, but only radical shifts in relationships and perspectives. The Great Commission of Matthew 28, therefore, takes place on top of a mountain, reminiscent of Moses. The question of authority for mission is not in doubt; it belongs to the same God who is the

Lord of Creation; the teaching and the baptizing must be done in the name of that God whose presence is assured.

We must notice how the first generations of Christians chose to carry out their missionary task in faithful response to the Lord's commission. First, they proclaimed the Easter *kerygma* and called on their hearers to repent and be converted. Second, they developed small and manageable communities of believers—they encouraged the growth of household "churches." Third, they used current means of communications and produced kerygmatic literature to aid their missionary task—out of this we have our lasting treasure in the New Testament. Fourth, they were not afraid to give their lives for what they were proclaiming with their lips. Christian martyrdom was a most effective missionary tool. We need only recall the connection implied in the Acts of the Apostles between the stoning of Stephen and the conversion of Saul of Tarsus. All of this was the missionary strategy of the early Church.

The meaning of mission continues to be a debate of enormous proportions in Christian circles today. What is the Christian attitude to non-Christians? What does mission mean in relation to peace and justice? What is the missionary task toward other Christians? What is the relationship between mission and growth? All of these are questions that concern every Christian; and, indeed, the non–Roman Catholic world has in these last decades been actively engaged in dialogue and action to discover, and to demonstrate, what is the authentic meaning of the Great Commission of Jesus in the light of contemporary realities.

How should we proceed to understand what mission truly is? There is a real need to find some way of conceiving and proclaiming what is the most appropriate response to the Gospel, and an earnest attempt to address it will surely help our cause in the living and active integration of mission and church. For the Gospel is about forgiveness and freedom; it is about life in all its fullness; it is about faith and food for the whole person in the whole world. The Gospel says that God is Bread, and Jesus speaks of himself as the Bread of life. The foundations of the Gospel are characterized by a religion of mercy and compassion, and Christians today can speak with boldness about the grace of God that has been experienced in the world in general and in the Church in particular. There is a very real sense in which we are to acknowledge by faith that world history and salvation history are identical, for the God who creates is always the God who saves.

Ion Bria rightly suggests that mission must be understood as an actualization of "God's economy in the midst of the world, by a community which is by its nature a 'sign' of that economy."[1] What does this mean for mission as we are to understand it? It means surely that mission is central to Christian theology since it springs out of the very character of God, a God who sends. Mission is itself an aspect of the doctrine of God rather than an aspect of either the doctrine of the world or of the Church. The mission is always God's mission; and at best the Church merely participates in it—it neither defines nor performs it because it is essentially God's activity. True mission can neither originate with the Church nor can it point to the Church.

A number of considerations flow from this. First, the basis of mission is the self-disclosure of the solidary love of God in creation, redemption, and fulfillment. This trinitarian disclosure of God as Father, Son, and Spirit means, secondly, that God's mission is cosmic in scope. Third, William Frazier is on the right track when he suggests that the purpose of mission is to discover the purpose of mission.[2] Fourth, we begin to see what mission is not. For example, it is defined by origin rather than by objective. It is neither church extension nor proselytism, but God's actualization of reconciliation on a worldwide scale. It is not a retreat from secularization, for in Christ it is demonstrated that God takes the world very seriously. It is not primarily concerned with conversion and individual salvation, but with the redemption of the whole world. True mission arises out of an acknowledgment of responsible dependency upon God rather than out of radical allegiance to a particular aspect of the movement called church. True mission then is a sign, a sign of witness that God's Kingdom has already been established as a present reality in the world.

The witness of the Church is a sign of the Kingdom, and that witness is expressed in proclamation, fellowship, and service. But mission is more than that. It is truly an exegesis of history in the light of the Kingdom of God, and it is carried out by a changing Church in an ever-changing world. Thus we are led to concur with the claim of a large body of Christians who in 1980 declared that

> Mission that is conscious of the kingdom will be concerned for liberation, not oppression; justice, not exploitation; fullness, not deprivation; freedom, not slavery; health, not disease; life, not death. No matter how the poor may be identified, this mission is for them.[3]

In any attempt we make to understand and respond to the mission of God, we need to take very seriously the following words of

Bonhoeffer: "There is no relation to men without a relation to God, and no relation to God without a relation to men, and it is only our relation to Jesus Christ which provides the basis for our relation to men and God."[4] Our relation to men and God in Jesus Christ is experienced chiefly (but not only) through the Church, and we need to discuss the nature of the Church before we suggest the modes of integration of mission and church.

The Nature of the Church

A casual acquaintance with the Bible provides anyone with the stark realization that the Church is a most difficult community to define. The concept of church in the Old Testament hovers continuously within the tension of the exclusivist perceptions of the Jews as the people of God, God's elect, the קהל ("Qahal"), and the unconditional sovereignty of God in calling whomever He wills to serve Him. So, for example, Cyrus of Persia is accorded the same title that Israel, or Jacob, or a prophet enjoys: Cyrus is the servant of Yahweh. How unthinkable in ordinary Jewish terms! Again, God's salvation is not only for His elect (as far as ethnicity is concerned); His salvation is to extend to the ends of the earth, and the Jews are to be a "light to the nations." Where are the boundaries of the Church in such situations, and what are its true frontiers?

In the New Testament we find a different type of tension in operation, not so much between Jewish and non-Jewish considerations, as in Acts, Galatians, or Romans, but rather between the proclamation of the Kingdom of God by Jesus and the proclamation of the Gospel of Jesus Christ by the apostolic Church. Jesus preaches the Kingdom, while Paul preaches Jesus. So the proclaimer becomes the proclaimed, and those who accept the Gospel by baptism are said to have put on Christ. Collectively they are called saints; or they are referred to as "the Body of Christ"; or some other image is used. Seldom, if ever, is the Church defined, or referred to, in institutional terms; hardly is it mentioned in terms of status or organizational arrangement—never a settled establishment. The missionary dynamic of the apostolic generation of Christians is undoubtedly the reason for this, but the difficult question remains about how exactly is the Church to be defined. Our most authentic clue seems to lie in the direction of understanding the meaning of church in the Bible, and thereafter, in terms of the Spirit. It is the Spirit of God in the Old Testament who guides the prophets, who guides Jesus in His ministry, and who empowers the earliest witnesses of the Resurrection. This enables Paul to adopt something of a definitive approach when he proclaims that as many as are led by the Spirit of God they are the children of God. So the doctrine of the Church and the doctrine of the Spirit in the Bible seem to be inseparable; and the New Testament proclaims that wherever the Spirit of the Lord is, there is freedom. Now that freedom is either unconditional and Spirit-filled or else it is not freedom at all. Just as God in Christ broke Himself free from the shackles of Judaism, so too does the Spirit of God keep His children free from ecclesiasticism. "Churchianity" is totally invalid.

Our historic Christian tradition has enabled us to affirm in our liturgies that we believe in One, Holy, Catholic, and Apostolic Church. These four terms are usually referred to as the "marks" of the Church. For purposes of our reflections here, we will assume that the first two marks, One and Holy, are indicative of our understanding of the origin of the Church. They have their origins in the character of God as He has disclosed himself to us chiefly in the experience of Israel and in the Christ Event. There is only one God, who is the sovereign Lord of creation, and He is the God and Father of our Lord Jesus Christ. That God is characterized by holiness. The people of God within the framework of the Church are expected to reflect that character of the God who has called them into being. So the Church is One and Holy, chiefly because of its experience from the beginning of that One God who is Holy. We acknowledge that these marks of unity and holiness for the Church involve much more than is being suggested here, but we simply wish to register this elemental understanding in order to move on to the other two marks, Catholic and Apostolic, which appear to be areas of grave contention and division, and areas from which our understanding of the meaning of mission, as it relates to the Church, can go in several different directions.

The notion of the Church's catholicity has created untold pain and anguish among Christians who have problems with virtually nothing else. Some actually renounce the recitation of any of the traditional creeds of the Church because this one word "Catholic" becomes for them something of a stumbling block. Catholicity seems to spell out for them everything that they are opposed to in the name of their faith. So they prefer the word "Universal" or "Christian," or they drop it entirely. It represents for them the element of protest in Protestantism that must never be allowed to die or to wax thin for lack of meaning. I wish to suggest, however, that if we were to understand catholicity not in terms of historical or denominational traditionalism, but rather in terms of the demands of the whole Gospel to which every Christian must affirm allegiance through baptism, we might well be on the way to setting ourselves free to deal with a much bigger problem for mission that should concern us as Christians, regardless of our denominational affiliation. This problem has to do with the meaning of catholicity as it relates to those who consider themselves to be Christian but who remain outside the Church. What is our basic understanding of the challenge from those who claim to be Christians but have nothing more to do with the Church? Put another way, how do we relate to the increasing phenomenon of churchless Christianity in the world? A closely related issue is that of our relationship to those who are Christians no more—the "no-more Christians." We shall have to deal with that later on.

The German theologian Wolfhart Pannenberg has helped us to think through the meaning and the nature of this problem of churchless Christianity in his book *The Church*. Our forefathers and foremothers have often reminded us that "nearer to church farther from God," and they claim that if one wishes to see God's face one should stay far away from the church. I have heard eminent church leaders admit that they have experienced much more of the forgiving love of God and the meaning of true peace and wholeness amongst people who have nothing at all to do with the Church. The falling away of church membership in parts of the Western world is not entirely due to the loss of faith in God, but rather to the loss of a vision of God in the Church. No one can deny that every denominational quarrel and conflict, either within denominations or between denominations, has served to weaken the credibility of Christianity as proclaimed by the Church. But some people's faith in God and in the power of the Gospel has been strengthened as a result of these tensions; however, they have opted for the maintenance of a Christianity that is external to the "church-like" pattern.

Pannenberg claims that "Christians who have reservations about the life of the church are often more open and less pretentious about what it means to be a Christian than active church members are."[5] He also suggests that with the increase in denominational division and the autonomy of economic, political, and social life, over against religion, and with religious allegiance rapidly becoming a private matter, the nature of Christianity began to change. For example, the churches in their separate state lost their claims to universality; religion (Christianity) still continued to permeate society and culture; there was much more emphasis on Christian freedom and tolerance, and general civil liberty; and the basic issue of human rights resulting from the idea of Christian freedom gave strength to the acceptance of freedom from sin through faith in Christ and not religious allegiance. Pannenberg states:

> The development of the idea that this had general applicability to all humanity as the foundation of a new, nonsectarian, common basis for life in society was itself dependent at the start of the modern period on legitimation in terms of the principles of the Christian tradition.[6]

No denomination of the Christian Church possessed the capacity to express within itself this struggle for Christian freedom, and so churchless Christians emerged. It is a modern form of Christianity that we all have to take very seriously whether we actually affirm it or not. Somewhere along the line, the rebuke of Jesus of Nazareth to his exclusivist friends seems to stick like a lump in our denominational throats: "He who does not gather with me scatters." Pannenberg comments:

> It is the misfortune of this modern form of Christianity—open, tolerant, freedom-loving—that it has found no institutional form of its own but, must depend for its survival on denominational churches.[7]

What we are dealing with here is a certain degree of ambivalence that the churchless Christian must experience, since there is no question about whether the Christian faith can exist without a community of faith on which to draw. But what happens to the universality of the Gospel and the faith when the average member of that community is overwhelmingly constrained by a denominational consciousness? His theology is denominational—so are his liturgy, his spirituality, his priorities for witness and service, even his concept of God. For although they do not actually say it, many Christians infer that God is absolutely the highest member of their denomination and that God can only be adequately worshiped in their style. But do we not need to experience and express at the same time the universality of Christianity and the wholeness of the Gospel? And is not the Christian outside of the Church better able to demonstrate the true meaning of catholicity than the church member who so actively confuses the whole truth of the Gospel with the narrow denominational outlook? What should church members do—should they leave the Church in an attempt to be more authentic Christians? Is this really possible? The fact is that the Christians are outside the Church because we who are insiders have by our separated state and self-centeredness urged them to leave. We are therefore faced with a major task of reconciliation at a number of levels if we are to become the major sign and symbol of the unity of mankind that is inherent in our belief in God as the Lord of history. This can come about when our understanding of the Church as community is not only proclaimed but practiced at all levels. Let us therefore identify briefly the characteristics of this community called church before we examine the meaning of mission as that integrating focus of the Church.

First, since the days of Karl Barth, renewed emphasis has been placed on the meaning of the word "church" in terms of the Greek word ἐκκλησία ("ecclesia"). The stress was-placed on the call: the Church was the community of those who were called together, out of the world, up to the life of God through the Word in the Bible. Perhaps the time has come for us to make a shift of emphasis away from the call as such, since this has always characterized God's activity and since there are so many ways in which God calls even those who are not within the fold of the visible Church. We might well be on a better track if we were to think of the Church more in terms of a community of response, a community that has accepted a new and special relationship with God through Christ, as a result of that responsive relationship that Christ experienced through his own volition in the first place. The notion of response does indeed presuppose a call, but it places more emphasis on the fact that the call could have been ignored, just as Jesus could have done. For if Jesus was not free to ignore the call of His Father, then everything goes wrong with the nature of His obedience "even unto death." The responsive community does not take the initiative away from God, what it does is to affirm continuously that ours is a decisive response to what has been offered to us through Christ. It also means that the nature of the call is just as continuous as the nature of the response.

Second, the Church is eminently the community of the Risen Christ, for there can be no Christian faith without faith in the fact that God raised Jesus from the dead. It is the life of the Risen Christ that permeates the life of the Church. Our understanding of the life of the Spirit of God is vacuous if we attempt to isolate the meaning of the Resurrection either from the meaning of the Holy Spirit or from the essential nature of the Church.

Third, the Church is the community of forgiveness. This cardinal aspect of the nature of the Church is very often missed because we are tempted to gloss over the reality of sin in our modern world. The people of ancient Israel grappled continuously with what sin meant to the relationship that ought to exist between themselves and their God. They accustomed themselves to the use of the sacrificial system, which did for them something of a patchwork job, but it never removed the guilt or the scar that sin engendered. So total forgiveness was always impossible to experience. In the life and death of Christ, Christians have come to an acknowledgment of that something more, which the sacrificial system of the Jews never permitted. So they are the ones who know what it is to say that their sins have been forgiven by God, and they also know what it is to be responsible for the proclamation and practice of the Gospel of forgiveness. Forgiveness means restoration. Wherever there is brokenness, there also must exist the possibility for restoration of relationships and structures. We must never forget that the first command that the Risen Christ gave to the Church in the Upper Room was to forgive the sins of others. This was the direct result of the Peace, the *Shalom,* which He breathed into their presence. In the final analysis it is only those who truly know what it means to have been forgiven by God who can share in the ministry of forgiveness of others; this is the inescapable duty of the Christian fellowship. Furthermore, where there are modern manifestations of sin, there too must be activated the Church's witness in modern manifestations of forgiveness from God.

Fourth, the Church is the community of transformation. No other aspect of human existence receives as much prominence in the message of the New Testament as the reality of God's transforming activity in Jesus Christ. Christ, as the New Adam, or even as the New Moses, represents the radically new beginning that God has ushered into the affairs of men. Love becomes transforming love, and truth becomes transforming truth, and the Kingdom of God comes with power not in the overthrow of secular authority but in the transformation of the real meaning of power. So Jesus makes bold to remind Pilate that He could have no power at all except that He had derived it "from above." The Church then as the community of transformation is both the transformed community as well as the transforming community. Within it, the ordinary terms of reference are changed, and human life itself becomes sacred.

Fifth, the nature of community itself provides the Church with a basic understanding of what its prior obligations are to its own.

A community is an order of sharing, a common order, an arrangement of mutuality, a fellowship of interaccountability. A Christian is by definition one who shares, for the true value of the many
blessings he has received from God cannot be affirmed unless he
shares what God has given to him. The love of God means nothing
to us unless we are actively engaged in giving it away. The reality
of sharing, then, is crucial to our witness as Christians; for although Christianity is a personal religion, it is not to be an individualistic religion, but a religion of the person. It is impossible to
overstress how important this virtue of sharing is for the Church
of today, when there are so many variations on the theme of
collective individualism within denominations, which have in no
small way exacerbated the problems involved in the search for
Christian unity. These words of Philip Potter are very hard but
very true:

> There is far too little sharing within and between the churches
> themselves—the sharing not only of material and technical resources
> which so much dominate our thinking, but all the gifts of grace that
> we have received. What we have learned in the ecumenical movement
> is that our disunity as churches is in large measure due to our inca-
> pacity to display this genuine sharing of gifts in love with one an-
> other. We tend too much to hang on to the inherited selfish forms
> of power and prestige, and above all the petrifying habit of self-
> sufficiency and obsequious begging.[8]

Sixth, we need to recognize all the time that the Church is a
community in pilgrimage; it is a band of people on the way. The
fundamental aspect of the Church as a movement creates innumerable difficulties for the proper understanding of what is our
real obligation as missionaries, for we find ourselves unable to
overcome the feeling that we are bound by an institution called
"church." Whenever we allow the static feeling of the institution
to overwhelm the dynamic consciousness of the movement or pilgrimage, things seem to go wrong: the prophet in us turns into the
priest of the establishment, the fresh charism from God becomes
the office, love becomes routine, and all our spirit-filled creden-
tials are deflated by preoccupations with the politics of preservation. While we can in no way pretend that we are living in New
Testament times with all the pioneering fervor we sense from the
literature, we still need to acknowledge that the Church cannot be
true to itself if it is bound by anything other than the Kingdom of
God. As a community in pilgrimage, the Church is to be much
less a sanctuary of tradition and much more a sign of the Kingdom. This means that it is marked by provisionality at every point

rather than by a sense of worldly permanence. It means that it is a society of anticipation, working and waiting for that which is still to come. There is so much of a not-yet-ness about the Church that we should always be encountering great difficulty in determining what should be safely regarded as being fixed, except the loving presence of God, which is His grace. We are beings who live toward God's future.

Finally, what about the apostolicity of the Church? Is this to do with the origins of the Church, especially where we seek to underline the apostolic tradition? Does the claim to be apostolic mean that we stand in line with what the first Apostles believed and practiced? Is it the affirmation of a pristine nature, or even the exercise of apostolic authority—whatever they mean? Apostolicity seems to me to have everything to do with why and how we have become Christians in the first place. In his book *The Church in the Power of the Spirit* Jürgen Moltmann makes the claim that the four marks of the Church—one, holy, catholic, apostolic—are not only statements of faith and hope, but they are also statements of action. He identifies unity in freedom, catholicity in partisanship for the oppressed, and holiness in poverty. With respect to catholicity as universalism, Moltmann explains the Christian option for the oppressed with these words:

> The rich and the mighty are not rejected out of revenge but in order to save them. Masters are rejected because of their oppression, so that they may experience the fullness of common humanity, of which they are depriving themselves and others. Christian universalism will therefore be realized in particular conflict situations in a partisanship of this kind; otherwise it is still in danger of being abstract and of dissolving the community itself.[9]

He speaks of apostolicity as "the church's special historical designation" and calls it a "designation of the kingdom." He says that the term "apostolic" denotes both the Church's foundation and its commission.

Moltmann thus calls on the Church not so much to seek legitimation in its apostolic identity, but to do the equivalent of what the first apostolate was about—namely, to be oriented toward the future, the future of Christ. He says that the real apostolic Church will leap forward to what is new and surprising, because it will seek to fulfill Christ's apostolic mission in its own historical situation. Moltmann therefore perceives apostolicity in the light of the crucified and Risen Christ and suggests that participation in the mission of Christ leads inescapably into tribulation, contradiction and suffering. The apostolate is carried out in the weakness and the poverty of Christ, not through force or the strategies of force. Reserved and withdrawn men and women and closed societies are opened through the witness of apostolic suffering, and can only through this be converted to the future of the kingdom.[10]

Pannenberg also places his thoughts on the eschatological grid when he states thus:

> The apostolic doctrine is not expressed through traditional formulations as such, but only through the proclamation of the finality of the message and work of Jesus, proclamation always related to the present day and always casting light on the present experience, as it sets forth the message and work of Jesus as the truth that brings this unfulfilled world towards fulfillment. When it does this, the universal mission of the church is in one way or another a part of the apostolicity of the church.[11]

Both of these theologians are obviously right in their attempt to lift apostolicity into the vision of the future. But, nevertheless, there seems to me to be something special about the apostolic community called "church," which takes into account many other things: the compelling witness to the Risen Christ in the faith of the whole Church, the transforming power of the whole Gospel, the nature of the hope of the poor in Christ, the relentless surge of deep joy from those who seek to realize God's reconciling and healing love. All this seems to me to be also involved in apostolicity, not as an afterthought or secondary effect but as fundamental reality. Time and again those who go forward because they are on a mission that is Christ-related experience joy and depth of transformation as they actually go. The lepers: "As they went they were cleansed." The disciples: "We saw Satan fall like lightening from heaven." The Emmaus companions: "Did not our hearts burn within us?" Peter: "I perceive that God is no respecter of persons." So apostolicity seems to me to spell out not only the foundations of the Church and its commission toward the future, but also that unspeakable depth of being that the community alone can experience when it is actually on the mission road. The apostolic nature of the Church is both mystical and missionary, and we would therefore do well to discuss the integration of mission and church in this light.

The Integration of Mission and Church

If all that we have been saying so far about mission and church is to be taken into account, what happens to the so-called mission of the Church? Is the Church a part of the mission or the chief executing agency of that mission? Or is the mission a much broader and deeper issue than the Church as a community could ever seek to contain? We need to bear in mind certain factors of ambivalence that characterize our religious perspectives. First, God is active in history, in the world's history, outside of the Church; and yet, the Church sees itself as having a primary obligation to the world in God's name. Second, there is the continuing tension in the Church between the sense of that which already is and that which is not yet. Third, the Church as community feels the need for order, arrangement, and establishment; and yet none of this actually bears out the essentials of what it is called to do. Fourth, although we are conscious of the abiding presence of God, we still need always to be free from the assumption that God will always be on our side whatever we do. Fifth, because of human limitation and sin, the Church is at one and the same time the sign of the Kingdom and also a signal of what the Kingdom is not. Finally, whether as individuals or as groups we find ourselves constantly caught within the tension of our legitimate quest for survival and prosperity (enjoying the good things that we say that God has provided for our use) and our need to travel lightly, because we have here no abiding city. Is the mission of God, then, concerned with us, or is it concerned with others? I would safely say that it is primarily concerned with the otherness of ourselves, and this is why, and how, mission and church can be integrated.

This focus on the otherness of ourselves will always be based on the realization that the only reality that we possess is our utter and complete dependence on God, who is the sovereign Lord of history. So that mission would have very little to do with either church growth or denominational spread. The struggle of the Christians to grow in grace is radically different from this struggle of any group of Christians to grow fatter. Indeed, the one is antithetical to the other. The mission of God provides the stimulus for the Church not in going out to seek more members, but in keeping it actively engaged in the unfinished task of witnessing to the Kingdom of God. It is that which sustains the Church in the value of hope in things not seen, rather than holding on to the many things that are seen but are not worth hoping for. If only we could see mission as the focal point of God's involvement in history, then the Church would always be recognized as being the chief agency offering faith, hope, and love to the world, not on its own account, but God's, and witnessing through faithful hope-in-action in loyal response to what God has already done in the world. J. G. Davies is correct when he suggests that "the true goal of mission is not just to add a religious dimension to natural life, but to enable natural life to be its true self as communion with God."[12] David Bosch adds yet another dimension to our understanding when he states thus:

> Mission takes place where the Church, in her total involvement with the world and the comprehensiveness of her message, bears her testimony in word and deed in the form of a servant, with reference to unbelief, exploitation, discrimination and violence, but also with reference to salvation, healing, liberation, reconciliation and righteousness.[13]

We need also to keep before our minds the centrality of the Cross as the axis for mission. It was not for little, or for nothing, that Paul held firmly to his slogan: "We preach Jesus Christ and Him crucified." The writer of the letter to the Hebrews would further remind us that Jesus was crucified "outside the gate," so that our testimony to the crucified One must always be borne in the process of going out and away from our accustomed selves. The meaning of mission is very closely bound up with all of this, and we would do well to underline these words of Simon Barrington-Ward:

> Once the church participates more fully in the death and risen life of its Head, that whole work of witness, in word, deed and being, which is mission, becomes, as in the New Testament church, more of a gift exchange, set in a context of friendship and genuine caring. Then it can be seen that Christ on his cross indeed grapples with the issues confronting all human beings and societies and their shifting faiths and cultures now as then. The truest exponents of mission are people in the Spirit committed, with Christ, to this grappling, people profoundly grasped by his divinely sharp yet wounded love which is fully "in the world" but yet never "of it."[14]

Bosch states quite profoundly: "Mission never takes place in self-confidence but in the knowledge of our own weakness, where danger and opportunity meet."[15]

The integration of mission and church, then, is only possible in the living witness of the people of God, who seek to resolve the inevitable tension between the world order and the Church's self-understanding, in the light of the faith that God raised Jesus from the dead and that new life in Christ summons all to constant renewal and to fullness of life. Several implications follow from this.

First, the integration of mission and church involves both a concern for outreach as well as for inreach. The "outreach" denotes not merely affirmation of the otherness of ourselves as Christians, but also the conscious provisionality that the responsive nature of our community demands. "Inreach" then is not to be seen as antithetical to outreach, but rather as the gradual realization of what we are called to do and to become. We find our true selves in Christ and His world as we reach out in faithful response to what God has already done in Christ.

Second, we need to recognize the Church less and less in terms of organization, or order, or establishment, and more in terms of its sacramental origin and nature. It is not that the Church is a member of us and functions in service of our dreams and human aspirations, however legitimate they might happen to be, but rather that we are fully members of the Church that is a mystical community and that we bear in our lives sacramental dimensions both visible and invisible. It is James White who has recently pointed us to the significance of the sacramental life as "persistence" and continuity. Because the Christian is constantly surrounded by the realities of injustice, the struggle for justice is never an optional extra in Christian witness; it remains central. White writes:

> Because Christians experience God's self-giving in the sacraments, they can give themselves for others. The Church's contribution to social justice derives largely from its power of making God's love visible in the world through the sacraments. That visibility is a constant need for any Christian's lifelong growth, shaped and transformed by God's acts. Persistence is essential for efforts for justice . . . the powers of evil are too strong, the rewards for wrong too lucrative to readily concede to single setbacks. Injustice is persistent, too, and only yields to greater persistence. The sacraments provide strong rations to enable Christians to "hang in there" in the combat with evil.[16]

Even if we would perhaps recoil from speaking of the sacraments in terms of "rations," we would, however, agree with White in respect of God's self-giving love and the meaning of persistence through the sacramentality of the Christian life. Church, mission, and sacrament seem to me to coincide within the framework of God's gift to us. They draw heavily on each other for their meaning and significance.

Third, White says that "sacraments set us free from obsession with self so we can give of ourselves."[17] This is particularly true of baptism and the Eucharist, the two sacraments that must be understood in terms of mission and that are at the same time central to the life of the Church. By baptism we are included in the obedience of Christ and His mission, and in the Eucharist our commitment to God and to His mission is renewed. White has more to say about the Eucharist. He says it is

> both a source of power for the Christian to change society and a condemnation of false confidence in any existing society inasmuch as it falls short of that Kingdom God wills to bring about. The eucharist promises a much more radical vision for humanity than any social reformer has hoped to bring about through the dictatorship of the proletariat, laissez-faire capitalism, or any other purely human panacea.[18]

In this connection we must not be unmindful of the divine ascendancy of the power of love over the human propensity for the love of power. The Eucharist plays no part in the latter. Mission itself is to bear testimony to the former.

Fourth, there is undoubtedly an integral connection between mission and worship. But what is this connection? Some Christians readily make clear what they consider the distinction to be—namely, that mission is anthropocentric and emphasizes the horizontal dimension of the Church's witness, while worship is theocentric and emphasizes the vertical dimension of that witness. While there is some value in such a distinction, there would seem to be greater value in affirming the meaning of mission and worship in terms of God's activity and human response. Mission and worship would, therefore, be acknowledged as interdependent functions or aspects of a single divine-human activity—the enlisting of the human response by God to God's approach to man. Worship is thus offered to God on behalf of the whole human order, and engagement in the missionary enterprise is essentially the existential discovery of what baptism as faith-response really means and entails.

Contemporary missiologists are given to underlining the significance of the Church's missionary intention. The thought behind this is that the expansionist design of particular Christian bodies need not, in this age of contextualization, be confused with or programmed into the inherent characteristics of the Church's witness. Whether the "intention" can be pursued, the "dimension" still needs to be promoted. Perhaps the promotion of worship as mission and mission as worship might be the most appropriate means of liberating our attitudes from the dilemma of dimension versus intention. The overriding intention of responding to God, in all and through all that we can see God to be, renders the Church's dimension of mission and worship neither separable nor incomplete.

Fifth, Christian witness to the world is always conditioned by Christian witness in the world. No historical study of Christian missionary enterprise could dare ignore the fact that those who "carried the Gospel" to far-off lands often confused those who were to be "converted" because they were in such bitter competition with their missionary counterparts. For example, the darker side of the emergence and growth of the Church of South India, or of the Church of North India, would betray the uncomfortable answer to the question of why there were so many different Christian churches in India—it has its origins in the basic human failure in Christians to strive to give expression to that unity which the Spirit has already given.

The Christian's mission to others, as Christians, is no less important than that to non-Christians. It is difficult to perceive of a more effective sign of the meaning of Christian unity than that of experiencing the mutuality of affirmation and responsibility among Christians themselves.

A very strange corollary to this thought exists in the patent reluctance of North American and British Anglicans to extend genuinely warm and open fellowship to black and colored Anglicans from the Third World, while nurturing a strong and proud delight in their provision of money and manpower for missionary enterprise in the Third World. Third World Anglicans often exclaim: "These people prefer to see us in pictures than to see us in person!" Is there a way out of this phenomenon, so strange and yet so true? Can mission and church be integrated on this point?

Sixth, like all other religions, Christianity is concerned with the relentless search for meaning in the world of human experience. The particularly Christian search is shaped by an unfolding understanding of the Gospel of Jesus Christ. The search is both intellectual and spiritual. While theologians and church leaders do much to promote the intellectual search, the obvious needs of, and for, the spiritual search often seem to be neglected. Why is the Christian witness in South Africa, or Poland, or Latin America spoken of today with such fervor and admiration? The answer seems to lie in the fact that the Christians there have been forced to integrate the meaning of mission and church through the experience of a common responsive and interpretive spirituality. Black South African Christians know what it means to practice the "spirituality of liberation," in the face of the most powerful regime in postwar history. Constitutional racism plus Western support at all levels in Pretoria ranks second to none in terms of effective control. Even American presidents are forced to resign under the pressure of "national pride," but that same "pride" ensures the viability of the South African regime. God provides His own with an appropriate spirituality in the context of this and every other situation. Such a spirituality offers a provisional answer to the persistent question: Whose side is God on?

One must not ignore the difficulties involved in discovering what are the divinely authentic elements of an interpretive spirituality. The South African regime is itself based on one which its proponents believe to have been made in heaven. Pannenberg calls for a renewed connection between sanctification and politics. He writes:

> The political impact of a Christian theory of justice will depend upon the renewal of the theocratic idea; and a spiritual theocracy can be effective only through a theory of justice that uses the theocratic framework in redefining social reality.[19]

There is much in this statement with which one would, on the face of it, be forced to disagree. Nevertheless, the need for an interpretive spirituality is important for the cause of "redefining social reality." Let it also be said that the Christian is preoccupied with meaning and faithful response rather than with social reconstruction.

Seventh, the Lutheran theologian Carl E. Braaten, in his book *The Flaming Center,* has called for the exorcism of some contemporary demons in order to make way for the universal gospel. Braaten lists the demons as follows: (a) a retreat to an "a-historical" mysticism in religion; (b) subjective experience as the norm of theology; (c) the retrenchment of church in society, seeking its own security behind a wall of separation; (d) a relapse into legalism in morality, the placing of a precedence on law over the course of freedom; and (e) a resurgence of nationalism in world affairs.[20] Now, if one were to ask a Desmond Tutu, or an Allan Kirton (general secretary of the Caribbean Conference of Churches), or a Philip Potter to list what they consider to be five contemporary "demons," one imagines that the list would differ in each case. It mainly depends on where you are and the quality of vision you bring to your concerns. The cultural matrix is indispensable.

Braaten offers us a very curious piece of proclamation, and we need to refer to it in the light of our concern that the integration of mission and Church should also take place in our identification of the demonic in our experience. He contends that the greatness of the Christian mission, despite its overwhelming attachment to Western culture, is that it has successfully started new churches in non-Western cultures. This is the best proof of the transcendent origins and universal validity of the Christian message.[21]

The greatness and transcendence of the Gospel seems to me to lie entirely in the opposite direction, in its freedom from the demonic manipulation of, and "attachment" to, any culture, starting with the Jewish, and in its universal capacity to shed quite easily the trappings by which it moves from one place to another. So that on the whole there is great theological merit in seeking to promote the intercultural over the cultural mode of communicating the Gospel; there is the inherent duty of the Christian to witness against the demonic absolutizing of the Gospel in any culture or superculture. The Kingdom of God is supracultural.

Eighth, we often speak of the prophetic mission of the Church; and by that we seem to imply the obligation on the part of the few to be aggressive, outspoken, daring, confrontational, or even eccentric. All of these attitudes may indeed have their place and exemplars. But what does being prophetic mean in the light of the ministry and mission of Jesus of Nazareth? To what extent is the proclamation of the Gospel bound up with the response to a prophetic vocation? Who shares in that vocation, and who does not? To whom is the prophet sent? By whom? When does the particular prophetic role cease? Is it institutional? Or, indeed, can it ever be an institutional role? Could Saul be truly leader of Israel, and prophet in Israel at the same time? Or is prophecy an inherent dimension of religious leadership? The concept of Christian prophecy is fraught with some grave difficulties, and it is no wonder that the early Church seemed eager to usher such an office into early insignificance. The office goes but the vocation still remains, however vague and indeterminate.

The Church is called to be in itself a prophetic minority to the world on God's behalf. It is called to take the risk of proffering and living in critical reflection and response to the world in the light of the unfolding Word of God. It is associated with "bad news" when it fails to respond faithfully to the cross-bearing demands of the Gospel of Jesus Christ. Its motivation is God's revelation, God's self-disclosure. Its medium is Christological—the proclamation and practice of the Lordship of Christ in history, over against the Lordship of Christ of history. The implications of this distinction are enormous, but would carry us far beyond the scope of this study. Its message is to be found in the proleptic interpretations of history—every time is God's time, and the future is there already in the present, but it is still on the way. The prophetic integration of mission and church lies in the dynamic conjunction of ultimate concern with present reality. There is no alternative.

Ninth, the question of an appropriate Christian ethic is always a difficult one to propose, since the meaning of "appropriate" is directly related to the particular situation. Be that as it may, we should still be able to posit a general ethical framework that ought to inform the Christian conscience toward right conduct. Ethicists are not always clear on what are the elemental constructs of virtue, or on what method of coidentification should be applied to the so-called cardinal virtues and the Christian virtues. It would seem incumbent on the Christian, however, that the virtue of love should be accorded a pivotal place in our understanding of right conduct. Love carries with it some basic characteristics in the light of the Gospel and the revealed character of God. It not only signifies radical renewal in the human experience, but it also denotes a process of sanctification in which the agency of God takes hold of the activity of man, as a result of a radical renewal or regeneration.

This has implications for the question of ordinary human integrity. Human integrity is not necessarily Christian integrity—Jesus of Nazareth often alluded to this in His preaching. Something more always seemed to be required of the Christian. It is here too that mission and church must be seen to be integrated. The Church must not merely stand for something, it should most certainly be seen to stand for something more. The ethic of ambivalence and vacillation is roundly condemned by Jesus. The ethic of sanctification knows nothing of two masters, or double-mindedness, or uncertain sounds. The vacillation is evident when Christians are merely church-oriented, rather than mission-controlled. The former keep "God" in their hands and pockets; the latter worship God in their hearts, at the center of their lives. The ethic of sanctification and Christian integrity has its ramifications in the Church's response to questions such as the sanctity of human life, nuclear weaponry and global peace, social justice, racism, sexism, and imperialism. They are not easily resolved, but they should not be readily evaded either.

Finally, there is still the issue of the relationship with those who "follow not with us." How does the integration of mission and church affect such a relationship? Who are these people anyway, and what are the priorities of their concerns? To what extent do they really differ from the church-member Christians? Some were born and reared in other religious traditions. Some were regular church-member Christians, but they have since chosen to become churchless Christians to pursue their own distinctive spirituality. Some were once Christians but are now Christians no more; yet they have not acquired for themselves any new labels. Some have never had any religious training or discipline at all and have been reared in a totally secularist environment. What is the Christian attitude to such classes of people, many of whom may be our associates, colleagues, clients, or relatives? Many of them present an embarrassing contrast to the regular Christians by reason of their witness against human depravity and social sin.

Do we not need to pose the question from the standpoint of God's probable relationship with them? How does God view their Christ-like actions, although they are not Christians? David Bosch contends:

> God looks more kindly on the indignation of those who rebel against injustice, hunger, exploitation and suffering than on those religious hucksters who preach a gospel of individualistic and hedonistic faith which shuns all controversy.[22]

While it may not be possible to speak with certainty about God's comparative assessment, Bosch's comment is to be understood as an affirmation of the divine disfavor of social injustice and human discomfort. But are we ascribing to God's judgment what we consider to be unacceptable to ourselves? Do we call pain and sufferings evil simply because they are uncomfortable? Is pain evil in the sight of God? This is an ongoing philosophical and theological debate, but it is related to our present concern about God's approval of those persons and things of whom we as regular Christians would rather disapprove.

Mission and church integrate here at the point where we make the conscious decision not to "play God." As servants of the Kingdom, we give ourselves in obedience to that vocation, we witness with fervor and love to what we have received from God, and we testify in loving and sanctifying relationships with others—however different in faith or style—that God is able to relate to them in God's own way. Thus, our attitude to mission is that we will always be ready to proclaim, while being always ready to learn. Ours is the responsibility to enlist ourselves with others in the cause of human rights and social justice, so long as our faith assures us that this is in faithful response to the Gospel. "Not-yet-Christians" and "no-more-Christians" may well be active participants in God's total mission in a way that is not readily clear to us. It is more dangerous for God's mission and the Church if we opt for cautious withdrawal rather than risk positive engagement. After all, what do we wish for ourselves that we would not wish for them? The fatherhood of God may not spell the brotherhood of man, but it certainly spells for us brotherhood in Christ. We need to struggle to become who we are.

Conclusion

Can mission and church be integrated? The times are urgent, the days are evil, and the powers of man are ignoring the rights of man. Can mission and church be integrated? Can they afford not to be? If indeed the mission is understood to be solely that of God—the Author, the Giver of life—then the Church, as the community of response, must also be understood to be a gift from that same Source. It is only as we relax our hold on the Church as the amorphous body over which we so jealously preside, and recognize it as that mystical communion given to the world by the God who gave life to the world, that we really begin to live in the light of that mysterious integration of mission and church. Missiology and ecclesiology are not identical, but they cannot be authentically pursued apart from the axis of Christology. The meaning of Christ as the Word and Sacrament of God gives life to our common witness, and in that witness we respond in faith to God's call to mission.

Injustice, poverty, militarism, nuclear threat, ecological decay, social disintegration—all threaten the world. The call to guard and enhance God's good gift of life is the universal obligation of Anglicans everywhere. The search for peace is synonymous with the struggle for justice, for "the true peace has justice for its roots."[23] May it never be that Anglicans anywhere become so oblivious to the meaning of justice in the call to mission by hiding within the walls of the Church for the sake of peace. Mission and church will always be integrated wherever the Cross of Christ constitutes the unmistaken symbol of paradox, contradiction, and confrontation between a world redeemed already and that which is yet to be redeemed. As a viable participant in the fellowship of the Body of Christ *Ecclesia Anglicana* must continue to reflect in its own life and witness the pain and the possibility of becoming what it already is in the Crucified and Risen Christ.

NOTES

1. See *International Review of Mission*, vol. 73, no. 289 (January 1984), p. 67.
2. See Gerald H. Anderson and Thomas F. Stransky, eds., *Mission Trends No. 1* (New Jersey: Paulist Press, 1974), p. 56.
3. *Your Kingdom Come: Mission Perspectives—Report of the World Conference on Mission and Evangelism, Melbourne, Australia, 12–25 May, 1980* (Geneva: CWME, World Council of Churches, 1980), p. 176.
4. Cited in J. G. Davies, *Worship and Mission* (New York: Association Press, 1967), p. 98.
5. Wolfhart Pannenberg, *The Church* (Philadelphia: The Westminster Press, 1983), p. 10.
6. *Ibid.*, p. 11.
7. *Ibid.*, p. 13.
8. See *International Review of Mission*, vol. 72, no. 288 (October 1983), p. 577.
9. Jürgen Moltmann, *The Church in the Power of the Spirit* (London: SCM Press, 1977), p. 352.
10. *Ibid.*, p. 361.
11. Pannenberg, *op. cit.*, p. 53.
12. Davies, *op. cit.*, p. 36.
13. David J. Bosch, *Witness to the World* (Atlanta: John Knox Press, 1980), p. 18.
14. See Alan Richardson and John Bowden, eds., *The Westminister Dictionary of Christian Theology* (Philadelphia: The Westminster Press, 1983), p. 374.
15. See *International Review of Mission*, vol. 73, no. 289 (January 1984), p. 32.
16. James F. White, *Sacraments as God's Self-Giving* (Nashville: Abingdon, 1983), p. 109.
17. *Ibid.*, p. 110.
18. *Ibid.*
19. Wolfhart Pannenberg, *Christian Spirituality* (Philadelphia: The Westminster Press, 1983), p. 70.
20. Carl E. Braaten, *The Flaming Center* (Philadelphia: Fortress Press, 1977), ch. 1.
21. *Ibid.*, p. 34.
22. Bosch, *op. cit.*, p. 507.
23. See *International Review of Mission*, vol. 72, no. 288 (October 1983), pp. 664–665.

Toward a Latin American
Understanding of Mission

The Reverend Doctor Jaci C. Maraschin

In order to speak on theology of mission, we need first to speak on the mission of theology. For behind any attempt to understand the expression "theology of mission" there is a theological presupposition that is methodological in its roots. This theological question vested in methodological dress comes from the vagueness of the concept "theology of mission." One can rightly ask: "Of what theology are we talking?" Still, more complex: "Of what mission?" Or: "Is there a mission?" After, of course, deciding and agreeing on the meaning of the concept of "mission."

This would be an easy task if we had appeal to an infallible, recognizable authority. If no one is entitled to tell us the meaning of "theology of mission," and if we still insist on trying to uncover its meaning, we have to follow a path built from tradition through consensus and illuminated by hermeneutics. This is why the methodological question comes in the first place. And, curiously, it is at the same time also the theological question. What I am saying is that theology is a process of construction and that the way in which we build it is already the phenomenological disclosure of the results we are seeking. Theology, which looks for the truth, is a way of looking at the truth and is not truth itself.

In the second fortnight of March 1984 there appeared in *30 Giorni*, an Italian monthly dedicated to Roman Catholic thinking, an article by Joseph Cardinal Ratzinger, the Vatican's top theologian, on the dangers of the movement known as "theology of liberation." *Time* and other important journals and magazines all over the world reported the cardinal's intervention as somehow reflecting the Pope's thinking on the matter as "the toughest theological attack yet mounted from the top level of the Church" against this theological current. This has to be seen as the reaction of the official Roman Catholic Church, which employs a particular methodology when confronted by another methodology, new and "dangerous" to its own tradition and, therefore, to its own preservation.

Let us take from the Ratzinger text some examples to show how the methodological question lies behind any attempt for theological expression. According to Ratzinger, theology of liberation represents a danger to the faith of the Church because it contains error under the appearance of truth. That is why it is so appealing today. Ratzinger, naturally, thinks that classical theology has expressed truth without any doubts, that truth is attainable in conceptual form, and, therefore, that concepts are immutable and eternal—that is, similar in a way to the real thing to which they point.

Secondly, in the theology of liberation, Ratzinger sees a new hermeneutics of the Christian faith changing all forms of ecclesial life. The interpretation of Christianity as a praxis of liberation in the socioeconomic and political realms is taken as a deviation from the true faith, even when it does not change the contents of faith. Theology of liberation sees the contents of the faith from the perspective of the poor and oppressed and of their struggle for liberation. It, then, takes sides.

Third, the importance given to praxis is fundamental. This is also linked with the question of truth. Truth is not a metaphysical entity. For Ratzinger this means the transformation of spiritual concepts into political ones. For classical theology the concept of orthodoxy comes first. For theology of liberation, orthopraxis. Orthopraxis means the action of the Christian faith in the contemporary world for the liberation of the poor and oppressed.

Behind the questioning of Ratzinger lies the enmity—traditional among many Christians—between the Church and Marxism, as though any dialogue would always protect Marxism and endanger Christianity. In the methodology of the contemporary Church, we see a decisive struggle between Ratzinger's way of doing theology on the one side, and the theology of liberation on the other. They are, in general, caricatured to serve particular purposes. For instance, to say that theology of liberation represents a reduction of the faith (as *depositum fidei*) is methodologically to treat the theology of liberation as if it were classical theology, asking from liberationists the production of a system that is not in their imagination to achieve. Leonardo Boff, a Brazilian, Roman Catholic theologian, says, "the affirmations of theology of liberation are purely assertives and not exclusives."[1]

It is not surprising that the theology of liberation started in Third World countries is strongly marked by poverty and suffering. For Ratzinger there were three important factors behind the appearance of this type of theology: the new theological situation created by Vatican II; the new historical-spiritual situation of the world after World War II, where the promises of Marxism and neo-Marxism represented a new moral impulse strongly appealing to youth; and the moral challenge of poverty and oppression in the same moment in which Europe and the United States were reaching an opulence never before known. Third World countries—in Asia, Africa, and Latin America—were asking the question of the mission of the Christian Church in the face of the new division of the world—the First and the Third. This division of the world is reflected in Latin America in a very dramatic way. As a member of the Standing Committee of Faith and Order of the World Council of Churches, my question has been the following: "How can the oppressors and the oppressed confess the Christian faith in common?"[2]

It was in Latin America that this type of theological expression came to be enormously influential in society in general. It caught the attention of not only churchgoers but of politicians, the military, as well as the common people. A year ago when the Pope was visiting Central America, he came up against the movement, especially in Nicaragua. It is worthwhile considering the alleged reason for his condemnation at that time. The Pope was concerned about the division of Roman Catholics between a "hierarchic church" (the official church) and the "people's church," blaming the theology of liberation for that threatened schism. This also demonstrated a question of methodology. The Pope started from above, from the perspective of the curia. He could not see that the emergence of a "people's church" was the result of socioeconomic and political factors and not particularly of some metaphysical thinking responsible for the creation of the theology of liberation. Indeed, liberation theology was only the result of the underlying praxis behind the many forces of struggle during those days in Nicaragua.

As it is practiced today in Latin America, the theology of liberation has to be seen as a fresh contribution to contemporary theological debate, going on not only in Third World countries but in the Christian world at large. It has deserved a place, for good or for bad, in theological dialogue even in the best theological centers of First World countries. This is why Anglicans should pay attention to this kind of theological practice—not only because Anglicans do theology, but chiefly because the Anglican Communion is represented in many Third World countries and participates in the life of these countries where the theological debate is alive and fruitful.

The importance of the theology of liberation for Anglicans, then, should be seen in at least three basic points. In the first place, it tells us something about the nature of theology itself. In other words, the theology of liberation is a reflection on theology itself to the extent that "liberation" is seen first of all as "liberation of theology." This means that theology, as a church activity, is and always has been a human activity open to criticism and change. This also means that when related to particular topics, as for instance, "mission," it has to start from the analysis of its own mission and then proceed to the understanding of what would be a theology of mission. In the second place, and deeply related to the first point, the theology of liberation has to be studied in relationship to other disciplines—not as disciplines, but as results of human activities in our time and in certain particular places. This means that we may, in a determined period, avoid philosophical questions (and descriptions) in favor, let us say, of sociological or political questions. It is not because sociology or politics are better than philosophy as such. It is because in this particular moment of our human history the questions that are more important are better raised by sociology and politics and not particularly by philosophy. Our philosophical questions are left in brackets for the time being. In the third place, the theology of liberation faces the question of ideology and, through it, the importance of hermeneutics for our Christian discourse in contemporary life. So, the question of social, political and economical interests is related to the question of ecclesial and theological choices. What is in question here is that which lies behind the establishment of our theological agenda. In other words, what are the interests commanding our decisions?

The theology of liberation raises again the question of the nature of theology. What is theology and what is its mission? Gustavo Gutierrez understands theology as a "reflection, a critical attitude." For him, "theology *follows;* is the second step."[3] This means that theology is not the starting point for Christian life but something of a secondary character. Important, then, is what comes first. And what comes first is life in all its dimensions. For Gutierrez, "it is—at least ought to be—real charity, action, and commitment to the service of men." So, theology has to do with the interpretation of this "service of men" in the light of the Gospel of Jesus Christ. Theology has a mission. It has a task to perform, and this task is always related to what is happening in human society. We could say that theology is always missionary theology, apt because of its own missionary experience, to be also a theology of mission. It is done in the way. In order to be this kind of theology, in the way, it has to be freed from all types of dogmatism. In order to have a theology of liberation, we need in the first place to liberate theology from the bondage of academic and dogmatic theology.

This is not to minimize the mission of theology. A "second step" is a very important step. It by no means signifies any sort of anti-intellectualism. Liberation theology looks for epistemology other than the classical one. It is not against epistemology. Liberation epistemology means that theology is not a set of universal declarations coming from Revelation and established by ecclesiastical authority. If it were so, theology should be a well-balanced system embracing the whole of the Christian faith and trying to relate its many different parts. The theology of liberation tries to liberate theology from this anxiety. It understands that many good and traditional questions (valid in themselves) have to be left unanswered for the time being. The theology of liberation means a liberation of theology from the enormous burden usually required of theologians—namely, the discussion of all questions raised through the long history of the Church.

The theology of liberation is a process. For instance, liberation theologians in Brazil are now asking themselves questions not yet raised in the beginning of the movement—such as the place of spirituality among Christians, the understanding of tenderness in human relationships, the importance of the individual against the sociological vision of struggles and the transformation of structures, and the relationship of the human body to the sacramental life of the Church.

The question of the mission of theology is also related to the question of the form of theology. The Association of Theological Schools of Brazil recently sponsored a Brazilian Congress of Theology to discuss "Theology in Brazil: Theory and Practice."[4] On that occasion a great amount of time and interest was given to the question of the form of theological thinking. We suspect in Brazil that there is something evil in the noncritical reception of, let us say, the German way of making theology or the Roman way of doing it. We do not have a theological tradition like the Germans or the English. On the other side, we do not think that Christians in this part of the world are unable to do theology. So theological creation in Brazil as in many other Latin American countries has been developed on lines completely different from those of Europe or North America. The majority of our theological thinking has circulated among the people in the form of little popular songs, poems, small mimeographed meditations, editorials in newspapers, articles in journals or books, and proclamations written in a collegiate way. The best theological works produced in Brazil are the statements and documents issued by the National Conference of Brazilian Bishops of the Roman Catholic Church.

It is true that theological schools and diocesan seminaries still believe in traditional textbooks in order to teach students the "right" content of what used to be called the "theological corpus." In many places the most conservative Christians still spend a lot of money and effort in producing and spreading what they call "theological education by extension," based on a methodology of passing on information (data) without critical training or opportunity for debating the issues of contemporary life. The merit of publishing books on the theology of liberation is to show to the defenders of the erudite theology of the academies that, as Juan Luis Segundo points out, "liberation theology is not provincial or fundamentalist, whatever else one might think about it."[5]

Through the centuries theology has been in dialogue with culture. We could even say that it has been part of culture. For many centuries the privileged partner in this dialogue was philosophy. In more recent days other disciplines have been called to enter the dialogue—for instance, psychology, linguistics, and sociology. Following Gutierrez, when he says that theology is the "second step," we also should say that sociology, economics, or politics are also second steps in relation to reality, which is always "the first step." If the theology of liberation is the thinking "in the way," not yet the systematization of that thinking, it has to be related to the realities of that way. It would be too easy to understand the theology of liberation as a kind of theological elaboration about liberation. Writers who produce from their offices or academies a lot of articles and books about liberation are, in truth, speaking on "liberty" and not on "liberation."

In Latin America Christians are becoming aware of the social mechanisms at work behind the mere appearance of reality. We are Christians in a context. In general, such mechanisms are not evident at first sight. As Juan Luis Segundo has pointed out, "for certain reasons of convenience the mechanisms of social reality normally remain hidden from human awareness even though they are operative and determinative." What then is important for the theologian is not a discipline called sociology for its own sake, but the "operative and determinative" mechanisms in action in society. Of course sociology can be called upon as a tool to help us to understand social reality. But social reality is "the first step." Things get a little bit complicated when we get to know that tools are not neutral and that it is impossible to work with them without presuppositions. It is not enough to think sociologically, but to perceive what kind of sociology lies behind the usual schemes used officially for the interpretation of social reality. What I am saying is that there is not a single discipline called sociology, but many different and divergent "sociologies," the positivist being the dominant one in our countries (in general under the sponsorship of the United States of America). That is why theology cannot simply be the result of a dialogue in the traditional way with a discipline called "sociology."

Sociology is not only the organization of society, say, internally. It is also an interweaving of many other factors, politics and the economy being the chief ones. Politics and ecomomics are, as sociology, particular disciplines with a proper history and tradition. It is, however, different to be living the daily politics in El Salvador—with the constant threat coming over the border—and a situation in which political experiences are not so crucial as there. The kind of permanent state of guerrilla warfare now going on in Central American countries affects the experience of economics and transforms the concept of poverty into a tremendous reality capable of destroying human lives.

So, a theologian in countries like this is forced to think from the living reality where he is, and will, inevitably, interpret the Bible, the Christian sacraments, and the proclamation of the Gospel, with the living tools of his political, economic, and social experience. The mission of theology in such places differs greatly from what would be the mission of theology in a university setting in Switzerland, let us say. This is why it is very difficult for a person in another context to be sympathetic to the theology of liberation. Europeans and North Americans tend to assess the whole thing by its academic results. Academic results, on the other hand, are not neutral. They are related to particular interests and can be analyzed. Sociology, politics, and economics also are not neutral sciences. They depend on a specific philosophy. The enemy in Latin America is the First World. Our suffering comes from the imperial domination exercised now by multinational enterprises and militarist governments.

Multinational enterprises and militarist governments are supported by European and North American countries. These countries have economic and political interests in our part of the world and do not hesitate to exploit and oppress us. Latin Americans are growing more aware of the world situation and are very critical of it. It goes without saying, also, that dictatorships in Latin America have been immoral and ineffective almost to the point of selling our countries to foreign interests. What is the mission of theology in such a situation? Would it be a reflection on the faith as stated in the Nicene Creed or an attempt to interpret that same faith in relation to the realities of our daily living in our part of the world?

A theology of mission cannot start from another point. It asks the question: What intellectual tools has the theologian to analyze such a situation? Certainly not the behaviorist tendencies so strong in America. Nor the so attractive existentialism of some years ago. Nor even the new waves of mysticism, Oriental meditation, and hyper-spiritualization of the many Pentecostalisms sprouting all around. In Latin America our best theologians have turned to Marxism as a scientific tool in order to understand the state of domination in which we live. This attitude has been responsible for the enormous distrust that the theology of liberation has acquired among some theologians of First World countries. Rightly so. Marx, however, is not the father of our theology of liberation.

At this point we should try to understand the place of Marxism in the liberation theology movement. Leonardo Boff thinks that "theology of liberation always understood that Marxism was a mediation, an intellectual tool, for social analysis." This, however, has been considered "dangerous" by classical theologians. Boff argues that "this is so, Marxism is really dangerous, but is very helpful for the understanding of a social reality especially in relation to poverty and to the superation of it." Besides, "it is not because a tool may be dangerous that we are not going to use it, especially when we need such a tool and cannot find any other better."[6] Marxism has been able to unveil the mechanisms of domination and has helped many Latin Americans to perceive reality in a completely new way. I do not pretend to offer an explanation of Marxist philosophy in this short paper as it is easily taken for granted that my readers are familiar with it and may even know better about it than I do. But let me point to some principles that may help us to understand what is of interest for our theme at this moment.

First, theologians of liberation make a distinction between Marxism as partisanship and Marxism as a scientific instrument for interpreting reality. Even if among some notorious liberation theologians we may find people uncritical of some particular Marxist regimes, this is not the rule. Liberation theologians tend to be critical of Marxist regimes through the *via* of their prophetic understanding of Christian faith.

Second, theologians of liberation tend to accept the Marxist critique of religion as an important instrument for understanding the usage of religion made by the powerful capitalist world. In other words, theology of liberation is not atheistic.

Third, theologians of liberation tend to accept the idea that "all the superstructures, including religion, can play a determining role in furthering or retarding any possible social change within the existing economic framework," meaning, of course, that the economy is not the only factor determining the march of history.[7]

Fourth, theologians of liberation believe that Christians could and, on some occasions, should make alliances with other people fighting for liberation without compromising their biblical faith. In fact, these alliances would be made in the name of that same biblical faith.

One of the chief aims of theology is the disclosure of its own ideological structure and, of course, of theology as a whole. This also should be seen as part of its mission. In other words, any theology worthy of that name starts with the humble recognition of the ideological element in its own interior. This recognition is part of a self-imposed discipline prior to any attempt to interpret the Christian faith for our world. This is, indeed, a new feature not found in serious theological thinking in the past. Even the Roman Catholic theologian Edward Schillebeeckx, quoted by J. L. Segundo, thinks that theology never can be ideological "because it is nothing but the application of the divine word to present day reality." For Segundo, "he seems to hold the naive belief that the Word of God is applied to human realities inside some antiseptic laboratory that is totally immune to the ideological tendencies and struggles of the present day."[8] The task of theological hermeneutics in Latin America has been devoted to the clarification of this ideological element in theological work in First World countries as in countries also of the Third World.

The most disturbing element in the theology of liberation is, as Ratzinger has pointed out, the fact that it is not similar to any heresy. Theology of liberation is not interested in creating a new theological corpus. What disturbs is the suspicion that every theological affirmation, by its own nature, expresses some ideological posture, consciously or not. And "ideology," here, means, in short, the presence of an element of interest, of passion, of belonging to some particular space and time, of justification of its own position in the face of others, which leads inevitably to distortion and domination, as Marx stresses. In discussing the question of ideology, Paul Ricoeur tries to go beyond Marx, to whom only the ruling classes are ideological, and thinks that ideological elements are present in any group or class.[9] The function of domination is related to the existing systems of authority in any social group. We do not need to remind ourselves how this function has been present in the history of the Christian Church since its beginning. The function of distortion tries to justify inverted processes in society. Religion can be seen as the first and most important inversion. Christian faith, then, subject to the interpretation of historical groups, has been through the centuries and in many places kept in bondage by the ideology of the ruling classes sustaining the powerful and the rich (through a symbolic system of constant dissimulations) and distorting the vision of reality in those cases. Popular religion also has been subjected to ideological manipulation.

The recent book published by the World Council of Churches, *Towards a Church of the Poor*, indicates at least four negative uses of popular religions: (a) "Structures of power have used the elements of popular religion to preserve their privileges and the mechanisms which maintain them." (b) "The control of the means of socialization of dominant groups has made it possible to introduce into popular culture the ideological elements of their class." (c) "With the infiltration and domination of the capitalist system, principally by the western world in underdeveloped countries, all the elements of society came to be seen as objects of consumption and profit. . . . In Latin America, religious leaders enriched themselves through the 'industry' of religious healing: industries were set up to produce and sell objects of popular piety, pilgrimages were organized, and religious festivals and ceremonies were used for tourist and economic purposes." (d) "In recent years, especially in African countries, the colonizing nations or their representatives have very often used the values of popular culture as a means of sowing division among people."[10]

It is, then, impossible to think of a particular "theology of mission" without understanding the hermeneutical question. We could perhaps say that hermeneutics is the new name of theology—such is the importance of this undertaking in contemporary thinking. Hermeneutics teaches us that any given message moves between two poles. We have what we suppose to be the original form of the message brought to us by a culture, a religion, a society, or any other group. This process is what we understand by the concept of tradition. The particular message has to be interpreted for each new generation and culture. Hermeneutics tries to establish the link between the two poles. This can be applied to the Gospel message. The Church preserves the original Gospel and also interprets it. These two poles, however, are uneven. We have a text—brought to us through the process known as tradition—permanently preserved by a nonpermanent Church. We have a changing Church as the bearer of an unchanging text. Hermeneutics has to do with this—permanence in the context of change. Then there is the question: How can we reach the original meaning of the text through the different ways of the history of the interpretation of the same text? All of us are aware that the *magisterium* of the Church has tried to hide this dramatic disproportion, establishing arbitrary rules of interpretation or creating infallible authorities to speak in the name of the Holy Spirit of God. But this has proved to be a failure.

The fundamental issue there present would be the establishment of an arbitrary authority as final judge and the loss of different historical readings of the text in relation to diverse historical contexts and needs. The question of the possibility of a single (unique) authorized interpretation presupposes the possibility of discovering the original meaning or, as Schleiermacher would say, the possibility of a "historical and divinatory reconstruction, objective and subjective of a given speech."[11]

In contemporary philosophy it was Heidegger who developed the notion of "hermeneutic circle," saying that "any interpretation never is the apprehension of something arrived at without a supposition." Still more than that, "any interpretation that seeks understanding has to have already understood that which is going to interpret."[12] This means that we work (and think) inside a world vision already given, through which reality manifests itself as such. Heidegger speaks also of the need of a "pre-comprehension" that can be understood as our possibility for understanding—rooted, on one side, in our own rational potentialities, and, on the other, in our historical conditions of existence. So, it is impossible to arrive at a *univoque* interpretation of any given message or text. Interpretation, then, is dependent on the place where we are and on the interests we have. And this is precisely what we mean by ideology.

Let us turn now to an attempt to analyze the concept of mission in relation to our ministry, which could be understood as one way, among others, of actualizing mission. In our common language "mission" means the effort realized for the accomplishment of a given aim. It aims at actualization. It has to do with praxis. It expresses itself in the dimension of doing more than of thinking. It is a type of action, however, that creates thinking and requires some sort of relation between action and contemplation. It engenders new reflection from that action in such a way that new forms of action may appear. It is not a mechanical action, out of life, tending merely at the preservation of the things already achieved. It is not similar to the work of restoration in which restoration substitutes for creation. The work of the mission, even in its popular understanding, is always an interfering work. In order to fulfill a mission, we have to interfere in a given segment of reality in order to modify it, having in view some determined aim. The fulfillment of a mission, being an interference, changes the old reality into a new reality. Mission, then, is a transforming practice. The transformation envisaged may be constructive or destructive.

For Christians, mission is a positive action, aiming at construction. However, being also an interfering action, turned to the creation of the new, by its own nature it is also negative—it denounces and destroys the old. It is not, then, something peaceful and easy. It is like a battle. The Bible is rich in examples of that kind. The biblical witness about the mission of the people of God shows an epic nature. We read of swords, fights, wars, blood, and death. Nothing happens as though we were already in heaven. The scenery of that epic is a particular land, and the persons involved are real human beings. Epic is history. And history is human. In the New Testament the scheme is not much different. "Think not that I am come to send peace on earth: I came not to send peace, but a sword. For I am come to set a man at variance against his father, and the daughter against her mother, and the daughter-in-law against her mother-in-law" (Matthew 1:34–35). Jesus calls the attention of the disciples to the difficulties of the mission. "Behold, I send you out as sheep in the midst of wolves. . . . And ye shall be brought before governors and kings for my sake. . . . And ye shall be hated of all men for my name's sake" (Matthew 10:16, 18, and 22). Jesus' own ministry was not peaceful. He met opposition, distrust, and the Cross. During the time of His earthly ministry, things were not easier. "The Son of Man has nowhere to lay his head" (Matthew 8:20).

Mission can be linked to creation as the beginnings of its understanding. When we seek to interpret the nature and function of mission today, it may be helpful to remind ourselves of how the biblical testimony speaks about the action of God and the ways of his manifestation in the world. The Bible starts with creation as the fundament of history. In that beginning we can see already the end. God creates. In other words, God acts. God creates, so interferes. He takes possession of the dominion of nothingness and in creating fills with His glory the emptiness of all indistinctions and abysses. His Word establishes the world and initiates our history in this world.

Frederick Denison Maurice thought that the two narratives of creation in Genesis, *J* and *P*, were retained in the sacred text to demonstrate the double aspect of creation itself—in the mind of God and in its temporal expression, in process through the history of the world.[13] Perhaps to relate the old writings to the Epistle to the Ephesians: "Even as he chose us in him before the foundation of the world, that we should be holy and blameless before him. He destined us in love to be his sons through Jesus Christ, according to the purpose of his will" (1:4 and 5). It was understood that God Himself thinks of His creation as a mission. He gives to Himself a mission. He wishes to actualize that which He chooses. The Bible, then, can be interpreted as the disclosure of that mission. In the book of Genesis, that which is complete (the vision of the end) in the first chapter is historic in the second. The development of history only will be meaningful if seen from the perspective of the mission of God finally to be fulfilled in the Apocalypses. The final purpose was the day of rest, the life in God, the realization of humanity.

It then would be possible to speak of the mission of God—of God as the starter of any missionary enterprise. According to the biblical witness, the mission of God had to face in the realm of history innumerable obstacles, reduced in the traditional theological understanding to the concept of sin. This is why in the theological reflection on the divine mission, the *J* narrative of creation is much more important than the *P* narrative. In the *J* narrative the obstacles to the mission are part of the drama of love and liberty inaugurated by God. It describes what is still happening today in our historical development. Sin is represented by disobedience. Human beings wanted to become independent, affirming themselves not with God but against God. Curiously, this became also an affirmation against their fellow human beings. Sin was interpreted in the Bible as a disorder made possible by God's decision to create a free and responsible human being. Inside that possibility of freedom and responsibility resides its contrary— namely, the possibility of servitude and irresponsibility. The *J* narrative speaks of creation not as finished, but as the proper continuous mission of God in the direction of the "new heaven" and the "new earth," which is the rest on the seventh day.

God established human history as place and time for His creative activity, which, in the face of sin, becomes also saving activity. It is in history that God will reveal Himself as savior through the instruments He establishes, movements He coordinates, institutions He inspires, and human beings He calls. Israel's history is typical of that mission. Its many institutions are destined for salvation. The most important movements of that history—for instance, Exodus—are movements of liberation. The great leaders of the nation—some kings, all the prophets, judges, and poets, among many others—proclaim the never-ending salvific will and activity of God and offer themselves to that service.

To Christians God's salvation comes through Jesus Christ. As it is a historical salvation and not a metaphysical one, Jesus, known as the Christ, is before anything else a human being born in a particular time and place, completely immersed in His own history and aware of the peculiar traditions of His world. In Him Christians sense the presence of the same God of Creation and see in Him the continuation of the same mission of God disclosed already in the witness of the Old Testament. His life, passion, and death transcend the local environment and acquire universal meaning. Jesus of Nazareth, errant and poor, is also the cosmic Christ, the future *Rex Gloriae,* in whom we want to live and whom we desire to follow.

How did Jesus see Himself in the interior of that *missio Dei?* We read in Luke 4 the interpretation He gave to Isaiah 61:1–2 and 58:6. After reading this text, in the house of prayer of His native town, He said to His astonished hearers: "Today this scripture has been fulfilled in your hearing" (Luke 4:21). What the people heard was the following summary of His own mission: (a) the Spirit of the Lord is upon me, (b) He has anointed me, (c) to preach good news to the poor, (d) to preach deliverance to the captives, (e) recovering of sight to the blind, (f) to set at liberty those who are oppressed, and (g) to proclaim the acceptable year of the Lord (Luke 18 and 19).

In that manner Jesus was making present the mission of God in an historical and concrete way in the midst of the people. Bringing the text of Isaiah into the context of His ministry, Jesus placed Himself as part of that history piercing the centuries. But He did not understand Himself as an event of the past. On the contrary, His links with the past were only in terms of the promise. His ministry was turned to the future of the Kingdom of God. His presence and teaching questioned the external religiosity, the absence of practical justice, and the empty morality. For that reason "all in the synagogue were filled with wrath" (Luke 28) and "thrust him out of the city" (Luke 29). His mission already was disturbing the people. Why should it be seen so intolerable? Why should the proclamation of "good news to the poor" and "liberation to the oppressed" be so dangerous? Perhaps because the listeners were themselves the oppressors, the keepers of the prisoners, or the persons in charge of darkening the vision of the people. According to the witness of Scripture, the mission of God is a mission of liberation. In many instances the Gospels are binaries; they move in a dialectical way. Against the powers of evil, sin, and death, they announce the victory of the powers of good, grace, and life.

The mission of God fights against sin. The fundamental question in a place like Latin America is related to the interpretation of that word. The concept of sin has become worn out, not only in First World countries but also in our more peripheric situations. The mass media have created in popular imagination connotations far away from the teachings of Jesus and of our catholic and apostolic tradition. Especially in our Latin cultures, for instance, sin means everything related to sex or, at least, to our human body in its personal dimension. We could explore many aspects of such a deviation, but for our purpose it is sufficient, perhaps, to indicate the reduction that it signifies and the fact that it has been used (ideologically) to mask other dimensions of sin much deeper and destructive than the sexual one. In our contemporary cities we are experiencing an ontology of destruction and violence never thought in other periods of human history. Of course sex and the human body are also entangled in this process of deterioration, but, as far as I can see, not as its cause but as consequence of something worse and extremely dangerous. Human beings, created for love, by the same God of love, have developed ferocious capacities visible in armed conflicts among nations or political parties inside of a nation; also, they have developed extremely sophisticated expressions of sadism to serve political regimes in favor of the rich, the powerful, and the ruling classes of society.

The manifest impassibility of many Christians in the face of such terrible forms of sin is the outcome of a certain commitment to ideological factors to which they are slaves, consciously or not, in which the vision of sin is advantageously limited to some small lapses in their personal lives, innocuous and inoffensive, compared to the atrocities dominant in organized society.

The primordial mission of God is His mission. He is the author and force of that mission. He creates the world; and after the fall, he sends His son to save His world through the liberation of human beings from the bondage of sin. He sends, also, the Holy Spirit to remain with us until the end of time. God sends all the prophets. Israel became conscious of this God of mission. The book of Jeremiah, among others, discloses clearly that conscience: "Since the day that your fathers came forth out of the land of Egypt unto this day, I have even sent unto you all my servants the prophets, daily rising up early and sending them" (7:25; compare also 26:5, 29:19, 35:15, and 44:4).

This concern with mission acquires more intensity with the prophets of Israel and prepares the way for the character and missionary work of Jesus Christ. Assuming entirely the mission of God, Jesus also behaves as the one who, having been sent, now also sends. "And he went up into the hills, and called to him those whom he desired; and they came to him. And he appointed twelve, to be with him, and to be sent out to preach and have authority to cast out demons" (Mark 3:13–15). "After this the Lord appointed seventy others, and sent them on ahead of him, two by two, into every town and place where he himself was about to come" (Luke 10:1).

Mission is never a mere retrospect. It is not the establishment in the present of some eternal pattern that would be mysteriously given to us in the past. The mission of God has the intention of implanting His Kingdom once for all, in the future. The Kingdom

of God and also His redemption were already given to us as foretaste and anticipation. We still have to hope for its fullness. For
that reason we have to be aware that our mission oscillates between an "already" and a "not yet."

In the Bible the final fulfillment of the mission is described
through futuristic images. It speaks in terms of promise. God is
even the God of the promise. An extraterrestrial language has
sometimes misled many good people into escaping from earthly
reality.

Eschatology returns to the theological debate nowadays. Mission and missionary activity have to be understood in relation to
this eschatological emphasis. Von Rad demonstrates how the
great prophets of Israel understood that eschatology is at the advent of completely new realities. The basis of salvation is considered an act of God in the future.[14] This act, however, is inserted in
the present time as it is historical and will be historical precisely
because it is an act of God. The hope of the people in relation to
this coming act of God has to do with the living experience of a
present time of infidelity, oppression, and suffering. In connection with this, Gustavo Gutierrez denounces the attempts made by
some Christians to "espiritualize" the eschatological words of the
prophets, weakening the concrete and historical element in them.
For him, as for many other Latin American theologians, "the
prophets announce a new world of peace," supposing justice, defense of the human rights of the poor, punishment of the oppressors, and liberation of the oppressed. Gutierrez points out the
danger of transforming Christianity into a religion of the soul,
disincarnated, in which "peace, justice, love and freedom" would
be only intimate realities. However, they are not so. They are
social realities related to a historical liberation.[15]

The intentionality of the Gospel is also futuristic. Jesus is the
sign of that new world of the future. In the penultimate chapter of
the book of Revelation, verse 5, the one sitting on the throne
defines his mission in the following way: "Behold, I make all
things new." Then, an intense fervor of praying accompanies this
affirmation expressing our human desires that these "things new"
may come to happen without delay. "Behold, I come quickly,"
Jesus says. "Surely I am coming soon." And John and the entire
Church repeat, "Amen, Come, Lord Jesus." (Revelations 22:7,
12, 20.) The Book of Revelation ends with the "grace of the Lord
Jesus" as the realization of the promises of God to everyone.

The members of the Commission on Faith and Order of the

World Council of Churches, meeting in Bangalore, India, in 1978, issued "A Common Account of Hope," deeply related to the mission of the Church and its ministry. This document denounces the existence of many obstacles to our common hope in the contemporary world. I quote:

> Our common hope is threatened by *increasing and already excessive concentrations of power with their threats of exploitation and poverty.* [The refusal to use the powers of science and technology responsibly] threatens us with environmental collapse, biological catastrophies and nuclear destruction. . . . The most alarming concentration of power in our time is the *seemingly uncontrollable growth of armaments.* . . . *There are pressures and forces everywhere which threaten to disintegrate the human community.* [Also, we are threatened by] *assaults on human dignity,* [expressed in discriminations of all types, the arbitrary arrests, and] the increasingly systematic use of torture as an ordinary method of exercising power. [Our hope is also] eroded by *meaninglessness and absurdity.* [The conference, notwithstanding, affirmed Christian hope in the face of these obstacles. So,] to live in hope is to risk *struggle . . . the use of power . . . affirming the new and reaffirming the old . . . self-criticism and the channel of renewal . . . dialogue . . . cooperation with those from whom we differ . . . new forms of community between women and men . . . scorn . . . death for the sake of that hope.*[16]

The beautiful document from Bangalore is, after all, political. And it is political because it is theological. And more. Because in the very proclamation of the eschatological hope is present the criticism of the Gospel to the structures of society where the Gospel is being preached. The mission is, therefore, fundamentally political—but not in the sense in which religion and political parties could be mixed up (as in the case of the abominable Christian democrat parties or Christian socialist parties) but, on the contrary, in the sense in which they cannot in any way be mixed. "To Caesar the things that are Caesar's."

The Church is, then, the mission-privileged place. It is, indeed, the only human institution able to criticize society from the standpoint of the Gospel. The same Gustavo Gutierrez understands that this "critical mission of the church will be defined as a service to the liberation of man,"[17] which, of course, supposes a new Church.

In this way the function and the character of theology are changed. Theology will never more intend to be immobile. It will strive to express the Church reflected in the face of concrete situations, dated, accepting flexibility as a value and pluralism as its outcome. Theology will understand itself as "in the way," therefore provisional instead of pretending to be essentialist or idealistic.

The mission of God cannot be parochial. It is an historical mission. It is even cosmic. It is inserted in the total movement of God's activity in the world and transcends even the realm of the Christian Church. The Christian Church is the institution that heard the voice of God and decided to live by the power of that Word. By the grace of God the Church can be constantly accepted by Him as His privileged space for mission. For that reason the Church cannot be understood as the limit of God's action. God cannot be understood inside the limits of our poor hermeneutic. The Spirit of God blows where He wants, and Jesus Himself recognized the existence of other factors working for the realization of the infinite purposes of God for the world.

John said to Him, "Master, we saw a man casting out demons in your name, and we forbade him, because he was not following us." But Jesus said, "Do not forbid him; for no one who does a mighty work in my name will be able soon after to speak evil of me. For he that is not against us is for us" (Mark 9:38–40).

These things were not said to weaken our responsibility in the face of mission. They only reveal to us the privilege given to us of knowing that we are at the service of the same Lord who is the creator of the world and the sovereign of the Kingdom without end. It is in that consciousness of mission that all our ministries have meaning.

Let me briefly indicate some consequences of this "theology of mission" for our pastoral ministry. In the first epistle to Timothy we read that God "will have all men to be saved, and to come unto the knowledge of the truth. For there is one God, and one mediator between God and men, the man Christ Jesus; who gave himself a ransom for all, to be testified in due time" (2:4–6). Werner Schollgen affirms that "in virtue of this universal promise of salvation, no one is *a priori* lost; on the contrary, every man is a brother to whom the salvation was promised."[18] Our pastoral ministry, after that, has to be seen in the broader perspective of the mission of God. According to this vision, God does not limit His action to men but aims at the restoration of all things (His creatures) for joy and freedom. Pastoral ministry is an instrument of that mission. It is related to that mission of God seeing God as the pastor of the world through the mediation of Jesus, His Church, and its structures.

The Episcopal Church in Brazil and, as far as I know, in some other countries in Latin America, has developed a pastoral ministry limited to a narrow vision of mission and captive to foreign structures and ideologies. This may also be applied to other churches in Latin America. However, faithful to the line I am trying to develop in this paper, I shall limit my comments to my own experience in Brazil and, perhaps, Latin America.

I am selecting four elements as examples of the application of the concept of mission to the pastoral ministry of the Church today. The first one is the pastoral activity known as "cure of souls." As it has been practiced in most of our churches, it faces the risk of becoming a subjective activity mounting to a dimension hardly found in the Gospels. The expression *cura animarum* is related to some aspects of Platonic philosophy and, of course, to the influence it exercised in the first centuries of Christian history. It is very hard to find a place for the image of the sheep in that subjectivist-theological, pastoral plane. The expression "cure of souls" in my country is related to an individualistic type of mission, of bourgeois nature, greatly appreciated by the middle class people of our big cities. The emphasis in this type of ministry corresponds to a certain capitulation of the Christian Church in the face of the most crucial problems confronting men in contemporary society. This type of ministry reduces the mission of the Church to a private affair of private "souls." It turns out to be very agreeable to the maintenance of the *status quo*.

My second example is related to the local parish. I could call it the *"parishcentric"* missionary point of view. It believes that man is a religious being, destined to live with God in eternity, through the mediation of certain instruments—for instance, prayer, contemplation, liturgy, sacraments, Bible reading, and so on. For that purpose local communities have to be centers of "retreading." Mission is bringing people to that local community in order to save them. The danger of this simplification is the reduction of mission to certain uncritical denial of the world. The parish may become, in that way, "opium for the people."

My third example has to do with behavior—personal behavior, certainly. Conversion means the establishment of a catalog of vices and virtues and the decision to follow the virtues and deny the vices. The list of prohibitions is larger than the list of the positive recommendations. They are all related to personal affairs. It is very difficult to find any socially related virtue or vice. They also belong to the sphere of the individual.

The last example has to do with the growing of the Church.

This concept of mission understands that parishes or dioceses are the only instruments the good God has to save His world. The practical consequences of this kind of pastoral theology is the enforcement of the ideology of the group and the development of dogmatic attitudes. In the churches of the Anglican tradition, the defenders of this type of pastoral theology do not like self-criticism and delight themselves in announcing the "incomparable wonders" of this "bridge Church," with its "liturgical treasures" embodied in the unique *Book of Common Prayer*.

Of course it is possible to look at the four examples and see them also as instruments for the liberation of the people. After all, the Church has to develop its mission in relation to persons. In order to be catholic, the Church has to be local. The Church has to express itself, its struggle for liberation, through the public worship, the sacraments, the Bible readings, the singing of Christian hopes. Christians have to behave as Christians. Our conversion means also a change of life. This cannot be limited, however, to personal and subjective desires. It has a social and political dimension. In our part of the world, theology of liberation is calling the attention of the churches for that inversion of the missionary reality. Individuals are part of a whole. Personal piety has to do with social justice. The worship of the Christians is a moment of engagement in the face of the problems Christians are living in their daily lives in society. Anglicans do not exist for the sake of Anglicans. They can only justify their presence in Latin America for the sake of the liberation of the poor and oppressed millions of people in that part of the world.

With our eyes open to social, political, and economic reality, and to the way the Christian Church (and the Anglican in particular) has related to it, in the past, in Latin America, we have a right to be suspicious of an ideological intrusion. Should we, Anglicans, in Third World countries reflect rather the spirit of establishment and avoid this ideological reading of our history and experience? If so, why? Would it not be by virtue of some ideological preference or submission? In Latin America we may ask ourselves if we should not apply to the *Book of Common Prayer* and the English and American hymnals the ideological test. Should we not start looking at them with suspicion? We have been taught to read the Bible in the English way of reading it, even if we read the Bible in Portuguese. Are we able to read the Bible in our Latin American context, and, doing so, start a new way of doing exegesis and biblical hermeneutics? Finally, we should ask in what way we, Anglicans, could read our Christian faith and express it, as liberation theology?"

All these questions are missionary questions. They are raised in a missionary situation and are related to the two basic issues discussed in this paper, the mission of theology on one side, and the theology of mission on the other. I will finish this paper by offering four glimpses into this basic question.

Our theologies of mission are always forms of reading the original texts. They depend on the hermeneutics behind the readings. Hermeneutical reading can be made inside closed hermeneutical circles and stay inside of such a protective element. The theology of liberation is asking the Church to invert that situation. It is asking the Church for a rereading of our texts no longer inside closed hermeneutic circles but according to a vision of horizons, always where they appear and where they are actually read.[19] As a consequence, we would free ourselves from the tyranical, authoritarian interpretation (always thought of as infallible) and would be able to perceive that different horizons are possible and can be interwoven. The proposal of the liberation of poor and oppressed people is not original with the prophets or Jesus. It comes from the original intention of the creation of the world and expresses itself through the wind of the Holy Spirit from the depths of the times.

Texts are material elements. They are given not only to the reason but also to the senses. We see them. They can be touched. In the second place, conscious that we always read our text from our place and time, we should make clear that we understand that fact. Ricoeur points out that we always belong in a history, a social class, a nation, a culture, one or more traditions. Recognizing this may be a help in our perception that we need a sort of distance from our time and place in order to criticize our "belonging" and, therefore, our own ideology. Of course this has enormous consequence for our Anglican churches in Latin America. Our first missionaries tried very hard to teach us to read our texts as though we were in the United States or in England. They were not aware of what could be called in the same way they used to teach us, the "Brazilian ethos." In order to read the texts of our faith, we had to travel long distances to read them where they really belonged, in some academic setting of the First World. Place and time are conditions of ideology. And the choice of time and place for any reading at all is related to ideological preferences.

Texts are related to messages. Are texts equal to the messages they intend to preserve? Writing recently on the Lambeth-Chicago Quadrilateral, I raised a suspicion about its adequacy to the intended purpose of its adoption. It seems to me that the problem is not the acceptance of the Bible but the way in which the Bible is accepted.[20] It seems to me that Christians, in general, have no problems about accepting the Bible, the creeds, and some amount of liturgical practice. We do accept them according to our own traditions. Of course, being historical animals, we cannot ignore tradition. Tradition has formed us. The question, then, should go as follows: To what extent do these texts and ceremonies represent, in the scenery of Third World countries, a real proclamation of good news? Are they passive to translation? How can the Bible and the liturgy—say, the *Book of Common Prayer*—be translated for our suffering people in Latin America? Translation means interpretation. At least, the persons engaged in that work should be aware of the difficulties present in that task.

Lastly, we have to be aware that the theology of liberation is not a magical program, above the most common imperfections of our human condition. We call this manner of translation and, therefore of interpreting the Gospel, ideologic precisely because it is only one of the many possible ways of doing this interpretation. But we believe that in contemporary Third World countries, especially in Latin America, this is the most faithful answer we can give to the call of God for participation in His mission today. We are used to thinking in Greek, rational terms. We want clear-cut answers. Descartes is our father in modern times. This is why we find it so difficult to understand the vinculation of our Christian faith to ideology. Perhaps the difficulty comes from another source—the naive belief that Christian faith does not belong to history and descends from heaven directly to our souls. Christian faith, however, is faith of human beings, lived by human beings by the grace of God. And, as such, Christian faith participates in the categories by which human beings express themselves.

Christian faith rests on the basis of the humble acknowledgment that we do not have absolute truth. Christian faith and absolute truth are not similar. We have only reflected images as in a mirror. Our faith, because it is precisely a faith, comes always mixed with doubt. It is much more a practice than a theory. Christian faith is incarnated in every historical moment. And it can be at the service of the powerful oppressors or at the service of the poor and oppressed in their struggle for liberation. In the context of our liberation practice, we Christians experience our own humanity under the illumination of the practice of Jesus; and as human beings (therefore ideologically) we walk to that fullness announced by the prophets and promised by our Lord.

NOTES

1. Leonardo Boff, "O grito da pobreza a partir de fé," in *Folha de São Paulo* (March 24, 1984), p. 3.
2. See *Towards Visible Unity*, vol. II, Faith and Order Paper no. 113, (Geneva: World Council of Churches, 1982), pp. 24–27.
3. Gustavo Gutierrez, *A Theology of Liberation* (Maryknoll, N.Y.: Orbis Books, 1972), p. 11.
4. The Congress took place in São Bernardo do Campo, São Paulo, in September 1983.
5. *The Liberation of Theology* (Maryknoll, N.Y.: Orbis, 1979), p. 5.
6. *Op. cit.*
7. Juan Luis Segundo, *op. cit.*, p. 60.
8. *Op. cit.*, p. 7.
9. *Interpretação e Ideologias* (Rio de Janeiro: Francisco Alves, 1977), pp. 67–77.
10. Julio de Santa Ana, ed. (Geneva: World Council of Churches, 1979), pp. 52–54.
11. Friedrich Schleiermacher, *Hermeneutik* (Heidelberg: Carl Winter, Universitätsverlag, 1959), p. 31 *ff.*
12. See *Sein und Zeit* (Halle: Niemeyer, 1927). Reference from 7th ed. (Tübingen: Niemeyer, 1963), p. 32.
13. See *Patriarchs and Lawgivers of the Old Testament* (London: J. W. Parker, 1855), Sermon 1, on Creation.
14. See *Theologie des Alten Testaments* (Christian Kaiser Verlag, 1957), esp. 2nd vol., G, on the "eschatology of the profets."
15. *Op. cit.*
16. *Sharing in One Hope* (Geneva: World Council of Churches, Commission on Faith and Order, 1978), pp. 6–11.
17. *Teologia de la liberación* (Lima, Peru: CEP, 1971), pp. 211–215.
18. *Sacramentum Mundi: Enciclopedia Teológica* (Barcelona: Editorial Herder, 1972–1976). Quotation from vol. V, p. 266.
19. See Hans-Georg Gadamer, *Truth and Method* (London: Sheed & Ward, 1975), esp. 2nd and 3rd pts.
20. *The Chicago-Lambeth Quadrilateral* (London: Anglican Consultative Council, 1984).

Mission Theology: A Hong Kong Chinese Understanding

The Reverend Canon Doctor Alan Chan

Contemporary Missiological Insights

This presentation is written with certain insights from contemporary missiological thinking. First, mission can no longer be confined to missionary agencies, whether national, regional, or global. Bishop Lesslie Newbigin has put the process of change very nicely.

> The great missionary movement of the non-Roman churches grew up at a time when these churches were largely blind to the missionary implications of churchmanship. There was no way in which those who were obedient to the Great Commission could express their obedience except by forming separate organizations for the purpose. It was thus that "Mission" came to mean something different from "Church". Much has changed during the succeeding decades.
>
> There was clear justification, in the historical circumstances, for the creation of missionary organizations separate from the church. There was much less justification for the perpetuation of this dichotomy among the converts of the missions. . . . The separation of these two things which God has joined together must be judged one of the great calamities of missionary history, and the healing of this division one of the great tasks of our time. It is a matter for thankfulness that in so many places healing is taking place.[1]

Bishop Newbigin wrote this in 1958 for a special purpose—looking forward to the merging of the International Missionary Council and the World Council of Churches (WCC), and trying to assess the opportunities of the possible merger. Now his insight has gained increasing recognition. When missionary agencies and their whole band of professional, though dedicated, Christian expatriates are no longer the sole agent of mission, the question of "Who else?" naturally comes up and a wide range of new possibilities emerge.

As a matter of fact, there have been various suggestions and responses—both in theory and in act—to the question "Who does mission?" After the merging of the International Missionary Council into the WCC in 1961, the predominant response has been the "Church." But more and more questions are coming up as to what "Church" means. Does it mean the institutional church? The community of believers? The basic community composed of both Christians and non-Christians committed to struggle with the oppressed for justice, the dominant feature of the Kingdom of God?

Second, mission is no longer conceived just as a one-way track heading always from West to East and from North to South. The era during which Africa, Asia, and Latin America were the targets of missionary activities from Europe and North America has gradually passed away. This is specially clear if we look at mission from the point of view of the worldwide Church instead of that of the European or North American churches. Where is the home base? It is everywhere—wherever the Church is, we are commissioned to preach the Gospel to the end of the earth. But where is the end? From the point of view of Hartford, Connecticut, Hong Kong may be the end. Yet from the point of view of Hong Kong, Hartford may be the end.

This insight has been vividly expressed by the title of the records of the meeting of the Commission on World Mission and Evangelism of the WCC, held in Mexico City in 1963—*Witness in Six Continents.*² So it was written:

> The main shift of emphasis illustrated at the World Council's Division of World Mission and Evangelism meeting in Mexico City (1963) carried with it a new insight into the nature of the church's missionary task. *Mission to Six Continents* was the title of the published report. The assumption that the western world itself no longer needed to be evangelized was radically challenged. All Continents need to receive the Gospel anew and to come to terms with its demands and promises.³

This is a liberating and challenging insight to Third World churches, formerly missions of the Western world. It has opened the eyes of Third World churches in that they realize that mission is also their task; that they are not always the object of Western mission, always at the receiving end; and that theology of mission can be conceived out of their own encounter with God and their fellow men.

Also important is the reevaluation of the role and need of Western missionaries in the Third World countries. A brief statement written by Federico Pagura, a poet, author, hymn writer, and a bishop of the United Methodist Church of Panama and Costa Rica (1968–1972), serves well to illustrate my point:

Missionary, go home. Or stay.

If you are not able to separate the eternal Word of the Gospel from the cultural molds in which you carried it to these lands and taught it with genuine abnegation: Missionary, go home.

If you are not able to identify with the events, anxieties, and aspirations of those peoples prematurely aged by an unequal struggle which seems to have neither termination nor hope: Missionary, go home.

If your allegiance and fidelity to your nation of origin are stronger than loyalty and obedience to Jesus Christ who came "to put down the mighty and lift up the lowly" (Lk 1:52): Missionary, go home.

If you are not able to love and respect as equals those whom once you came to evangelize as the "lost": Missionary, go home.

If you are not able to rejoice at the entry of new peoples and churches upon a new stage of maturity, independence, and responsibility, even at the price of committing errors like those which you and your compatriots committed also in the past: Missionary, go home.

For it is time to go home.

But if you are ready to bear the risks and pains of this hour of birth, which our American peoples are experiencing, even denying yourself, if you begin to celebrate with them the happiness of sensing that the Gospel is not only proclamation and affirmation of a distant hope but of a hope and liberation which are already transforming history, if you are ready to give more of your time, your values, your life in the service of these peoples who are awakening, then:

Stay! There is much to do: hands and blood are lacking for an undertaking so immense in which Christ is the protagonist and pioneer.[4]

This experience may be looked upon as a necessary result of the breaking down of Western Christendom, but it can also be taken as a liberating opportunity for the growth and maturation of Third World churches—an opportunity of experiencing Jesus Christ directly in their own cultures and contexts and not in Western ones, an opportunity of formulating mission theology out of such an experience, and an opportunity of planning missionary strategy to meet the contextual demand of a particular locality and to fulfill, relevantly and effectively, the missionary command of our Lord Jesus Christ.

Third, mission is no longer a taken-for-granted synonym for evangelizing. To begin with, may I quote the Reverend John Stott: "The older and traditional view has been to equate mission and evangelism, missionaries and evangelist, missions and evangelistic programmes: Even the Commission on World Mission and Evangelism did not distinguish in its constitution between 'mission' and 'evangelism.'"[5]

But "mission" is properly a comprehensive word, embracing everything God in Jesus Christ sends His people to do, through the Holy Spirit. Therefore consciously, people would not confine mission merely to the work of evangelizing, which normally means preaching the Good News and making converts. But unconsciously, quite a number of Christian thinkers do so. In talking about the priority of evangelism in mission work, John Stott cited statements of a number of people to support his view. But from what he quoted, it is easily seen that unconsciously mission for them is almost synonymous with evangelization. For example, John R. Mott, in his book, *The Decisive Hour of Christian Missions,* referred to the millions of non-Christian people in the world, saying, "It is the church's duty to see that this long-standing reproach is completely removed. Its plan of work, to be adequate, must provide for the evangelization of the whole of this multitude." Bishop Stephen Neill, in his book, *The Church's Witness to God's Design,* said: "The problem of the church's mission is the crisis of the ecumenical movement. If an ecumenical movement is not primarily a strategy of worldwide evangelism, then it is nothing but an interesting academic exercise."[6]

The slogan through which John R. Mott had given inspiration to the World's Student Christian Federation in the 1880's and 1890's and had attracted tremendous support even at Edinburgh in 1910 was "The Evangelization of the World in this Generation." Although in Mott's mind "the slogan was based on an unexceptionable theological principle—that each generation of Christians bears responsibility for the contemporary generation of non-Christians in the world, and that it is the business of each such generation of Christians to see to it, as far as lies within its power, that the Gospel is clearly preached to every single non-Christian in this same generation."[7] Yet the fact that quite a number of critics thought that it was naive to suppose that the whole world could be made Christian in thirty years showed that somewhere in their mind they confused evangelism with conversion. Even though these people might not admit that evangelization was a synonym of mission, the place of evangelization was so high in their priority list of missionary work and so central that one cannot help thinking that mission for them was almost, if not totally, synonymous with evangelization, which primarily aimed at conversion. It is true that even for the traditionalist, education and medical work were considered part of mission; but they were primarily regarded as useful adjuncts to evangelistic work. How-

ever, as time went by, things began to change. One very important clarification was made on the term "evangelize." *Euangel-
izomai* is "to bring" or "to announce" the *euangelion*. The Apostles
just went about evangelizing the word (Acts 8:4) to the people in
towns and villages (Acts 8:25, 40), and there was no mention
whether the word was believed or whether the people were converted. That is to say, "to evangelize is not to preach so that
something happens. Of course the objective is that something will
happen, namely that people will respond and believe. Nevertheless, biblically speaking, to evangelize is to proclaim the
Gospel, whether anything happens or not."[8] This clarification has
set evangelism free from the bondage of conversion. Evangelism
need not mean gaining people for God or His Church; so does
mission.

In the light of such understanding, a whole range of key words
connected with new concepts of mission have emerged: witness,
presence, dialogue, development, humanization, liberation; and
quite a number of mission concepts have come out. Mission could
mean evangelization and the planting of the Church among the yet
unreached; it could mean the venture of witnessing to Jesus Christ
in the time between His first and second coming with the aim of
gathering people to be the children of the Kingdom so that they
could escape the coming destruction; it could mean the transformation of the latent church, in its hiddenness under the forms of
paganism, Judaism, humanism, . . . into its manifestation; it
could mean participation in God's mission to gather up all things
in Christ and to set up signs of the shalom of God in this world.[9]
Or it could even go so far as to mean the calling of the people of
God into God's happenings that take place everywhere, inside or
outside the institutional churches or missionary agencies, to the
point and in the sense that God can "create a body of Christ with
honest politicians for saints, seekers after truth as priests, writers
and artists and film-makers as preachers, and flower-children,
civil rights marchers and crackpot advocates of total disarmament
and world government as martyrs."[10]

With these insights at the back of my mind, I shall try to show
the kind of struggles that have been going on in the churches in
Hong Kong and China.

Struggling for a Unified Understanding of Mission
The ecumenical movement was borne out of the missionary movement because disunity would discredit witnessing and evange-

lizing in mission, while unity would strengthen it. As we look at the achievements of the ecumenical movement at various levels, we find that not all of them are satisfactory. On the one hand, we rejoice at the founding of the World Council of Churches; various regional, national, and local councils; the founding of the Church of South India, the Church of North India, and of many national, united, or uniting churches. But, on the other hand, we feel sad to see the splitting of mission into liberal and conservative or ecumenical and evangelical camps, resulting in animosity and division among churches and Christians all over the world. Walter Freytag put it well when he said, "Formerly mission had problems; to-day it has itself become a problem."

There are many attempts to understand and to describe the different emphases of the two views of mission. Dr. W. A. Visser t'Hooft described one view as the vertical interpretation of the Gospel essentially concerned with God's saving action in the life of individuals; and the other as the horizontal interpretation of it, mainly concerned with human relationships in the world.[11] Noting the importance of seeking to embrace the truth of the Gospel in its fullness, he said:

> A Christianity which has lost its vertical dimension has lost its salt and is not only insipid in itself, but useless for the world. But a Christianity which would use the vertical preoccupation as a means to escape from its responsibility for and in the common life of man is a denial of the incarnation, of God's love for the world manifested in Christ.[12]

The Reverend John Stott described the extreme conservative camp as taking mission to consist "exclusively of evangelism also concentrated on verbal proclamation."[13] Other forms of mission, such as education and medical work, might be done, but were understood only in terms of evangelism. "Man's only hope lies in being born again. Only then might society conceivably be reborn. But it is too late now even for that."[14] Stott characterized it as unbiblically world-denying pessimism failing to recognize God as both Creator and Judge.

As for the other camp, John Stott observes that it began as early as the middle of the 1960's in the preparatory work for the WCC Uppsala Assembly. This camp asserts that

> God is at work in the historical process, that the purpose of his mission, of the MISSIO DEI, is the establishment of SHALOM in the sense of social harmony and that this SHALOM (which it was suggested is identical with the kingdom of God) is exemplified in the "emancipation of colored races, the concern for the humanization of

industrial relations, various attempts at rural developments, the quest for business and professional ethics, the concern for intellectual honesty and integrity" (WCC, "The Church for Others," p. 15).[15]

John Stott acknowledged social concern arising out of Jesus' command to love our neighbor as an important part of mission. Yet at the same time he maintained that evangelism arising out of God's commission to preach the Gospel is primary:

> Anything which undermines human dignity should be an offence to us. But is anything so destructive of human dignity as alienation from God through ignorance or rejection of the Gospel? And how can we seriously maintain that political and economic liberation is just as important as eternal salvation?[16]

A third description is found in the writing of Father William Frazier. On examining the new concept of church as "sign," which was proposed in Vatican II, he thought that the word "sanctuary" might represent the Church's self-image prior to Vatican II. In his understanding:

> A sanctuary is a place of refuge situated in a hostile environment, which justifies its existence by bringing men into its premises in order to protect and nourish them. . . . The mission of this church was to extend its unique riches to all men by labouring to contain all men . . . . [a] sign is a term and a concept which runs counter to the major premises of sanctuary thinking. . . . Unlike a sanctuary, a sign is meant to point beyond itself and to have its impact outside itself, . . . a sign is not an enclosure, but a disclosure. A sign performs its function not by containing, but by communicating; not by annexation, but by representation.[17]

And William Frazier succinctly pointed out:

> A sanctuary-church, by its very definition, is obliged to look upon conversion as a maximum priority. Among the most important signs of its vitality will be its size and its rate of expansion. A sanctuary-church is essentially a converting church. . . . The church as sign is interested primarily in perfecting its loving service of men, not as a kind of bait offered to lead unbelievers to baptism, but simply as a testimony to the presence of God's saving love in the world. . . . So conceived, the church will not be content to take care of itself, but will actively shoulder the whole range of human problems in testimony to the saving concern of God. Aware that a disincarnate Gospel will not reach the ears of men, the Church will strive to proclaim the good news first and foremost in the idiom of action.[18]

As William Frazier took seriously the secular reality of the world and the men come of age, he demanded that "the church become thoroughly rooted in the human condition and obedient to the demands of development, peace and unity in the world," [19] and that the new mission of the Church "be a mission of sharing and exchange with all peoples and cultures, an ecumenical venture in the broadest sense of the term. Dialogue must be the ruling theme rather than unilateral imposition."[20] And as the grace of Christ always precedes the Christian mission, "accordingly, the church is sent to the nations not only to enrich, but to be enriched."[21] To put it more simply, such a view as represented by William Frazier favors social concern more than evangelism.

What is common in all these three descriptions is that they all recognize the two different emphases in mission: evangelism and social concern. This may be expressed in different ways: to evangelize, to convert and to lead to personal salvation or to dialogue, to serve, and to liberate, leading to witnessing of the presence of the Kingdom of God. There may have been various responses to this phenomenon, but almost all have their worry that it may split the Church and want to do something about it.

In the persons that we have quoted, we see that Dr. Visser t'Hooft, with the ecumenical movement in mind, appealed to embrace the two emphases in mission into a full gospel. Father Frazier, taking the coming of secular reality seriously, was in favor of social concern. Mr. Stott, seeing the importance of the two arising respectively out of God's commission to preach and His commandment to love, took both as actions of a responsible Christian, even though deep down in his heart he thought that evangelism was primary. No matter what, the desire to settle the competition of evangelism and social concern in mission was obvious.

This has been true in Hong Kong churches. Apart from worship as a form of Christian manifestations, the churches have been doing a lot in both evangelism and social service. With regard to evangelism, Hong Kong churches have sponsored two Billy Graham crusades; have held numerous evangelistic meetings (although doing less now); have had strong, school-campus evangelism, using the method of personal evangelism and small group Bible studies; and have experimented on new forms of evangelism: labor evangelism, evangelistic drama, and Christian television programs. Recently an effort has been made to coordinate overseas Chinese Christians and to start a worldwide Chinese missionary movement. So the dynamism is undoubtedly there.

With regard to social concern, the churches are very much committed to providing social service. They provide about one-third of all primary and secondary school places, and a significant percentage of medical care and other services to the young, the old, the family, and the community. Also recently, out of the question of whether what the churches have been doing has become a buffer between the government and the people, thus perpetuating the status quo with all its dynamism and social injustice, a number of Christian pressure groups have emerged, achieving a high degree of radical action and community credibility.

All look fine and good. But when we examine all these carefully, we observe:

1. Evangelism is done mostly and wholeheartedly by conservative, sectarian churches or their members, while social concern is mainly expressed by established denominations and traditional Christian service organizations. At one time the divergence almost developed into division.
2. Evangelism has been done enthusiastically, but the message is very traditional and Western-oriented. What churches in Hong Kong have done is to give it a good wrapping for "market" purposes. Indigenous efforts or results are still very much on the peripheral. Social concern is no better. Except for a desire to serve, there has been little attempt to articulate the rationale of the involvement; and, therefore, there is a lack in the theological and strategic dimension of the services.

As a whole we can see that the mission question facing Hong Kong concerns not only a unified understanding of mission, but also the content of the missionary message itself. We are in search of a mission theology that is comprehensive enough to embrace the current demands of evangelism and social concern, and is rooted in depth in the experience of the Chinese people in the Hong Kong situation.

In the search we agree with John Stott that social action should not be regarded as a "means to evangelism" because:

> In its most blatant form this makes social work (whether food, medicine or education), the sugar on the pill, the bait on the hook, while in its best form it gives to the Gospel a credibility it would otherwise lack. In either case the smell of hypocrisy hangs round our philanthropy. A frankly ulterior motive impels us to engage in it. And the result of making our social programme the means to another end is what we breed so-called "rice-Christians."[22]

As to the view that social action be regarded as "a manifestation of evangelism," John Stott felt uneasy because manifestation is a natural one from a man of evangelism. Yet as such, the manifestation would have an evangelizing effect and would be regarded as part of evangelism or a subdivision of evangelism. Gradually people will be lead to think that to do social action is to engage themselves in evangelism. We understand his uneasy feeling.

As mentioned earlier, John Stott would like to see that social action become "a partner of evangelism." He said:

> As partner, the two belong to each other and yet are independent of each other. Each stands on its own feet in its own right along-side the other. Neither is a means to the other, or even a manifestation of the other. For each is an end in itself. Both are expressions of unfeigned love.[23]

This seems to be a very clear-cut way of showing the proper relationship between both evangelism and social action, and to give due respect to each of them. It is alright to think along this line, but the difficulty lies in backward thinking—that is, social concern is to meet people's physical need while evangelism will lead people to eternal life. My reading of Matthew 25:31–46 does not agree with John Stott's understanding. There the social actions of feeding the hungry, quenching the thirsty, caring for the homeless and the prisoner are directly connected with eternal life. Doers of these will be given eternal life, and failing to do them will end up in eternal punishment. The story of the Good Samaritan is also an answer to the question of who is the neighbor whom one should love. This is a story Jesus gave to answer the scribe's question on eternal life and not on good works. So it is too simple to say that evangelism and social concern are partners independent of one another, and unbiblical to say that only evangelism leads to salvation and eternal life and social concern does not.

Up to now, it seems that we have come up to a point where both evangelism and social concern are related to mission and are connected with the Gospel and eternal life. But as to how they are related, we have not found a form of articulation satisfactory to both conservatives and liberals, or evangelicals and ecumenicals. Bishop John V. Taylor did write of a three-stranded presentation of the Gospel, by which he meant that Christians were called to "articulate the Gospel . . . through what they say (proclamation), what they are (witness) and what they do (service)."[24] It is well said, but it is only a call to articulation, not an articulation itself. As to how proclamation, witness, and service can be linked together, there is a long way to go.

In the Bangkok Salvation Today Conference of 1973, sponsored by the Commission on World Mission and Evangelism of the World Council of Churches, the mission of God is conceived as the total liberation of the world through the struggles for economic justice, political freedom, and cultural renewal. No salvation is true if it is not totally concerned with this mission of God. Therefore, to engage in evangelism is to engage in the struggles for economic justice against the exploitation of people by people, in the struggle for human dignity against political oppression of human beings by their fellowmen, in the struggle for solidarity against the alienation of person from person, and in the struggle of hope against despair in personal life.[25] What the conference managed to say was that these four dimensions must be related even though there can be a priority of one over the others in a particular situation. It has succeeded in giving a comprehensive content of mission, but not yet a unifying one.

In Hong Kong, in view of the divergence of mission gradually heading toward division among churches and Christian organizations and groups, and also in view of the formation of the Chinese missionary movement, the search for a unifying concept of mission becomes very urgent. Out of the many unsuccessful attempts of articulation, one seems to emerge with promise. That is the articulation by Raymond Fung, formerly the director of the Hong Kong Christian Industrial Mission (HKCIC), now the secretary for evangelism in the WCC. His articulation comes out of an eleven-year involvement in industrial mission in Hong Kong, and he himself is a firm believer in the evangelistic component of mission. So while he was doing industrial mission, he had evangelism in his mind. He described his experience of evangelism in detail.

> When I began involvement in Urban Industrial Mission some fourteen years ago, much as I had hoped, I could not engage in evangelism during the first five years. First, there was no audience. Factory workers were not interested in hearing about Jesus. Second, I did not know how to do it in a way which could do full justice to the Scriptures and to the working class. I was afraid I might be preaching opium rather than Gospel, in the process, violating both the Scriptures and the people. My experience is not unique.
>
> There has simply been too much evangelism which blesses sinful powers and forces and subdues the poor and the oppressed. Too much evangelism which divides the people among themselves instead of creating solidarity. Too much evangelism which preaches a middle class consumer Gospel instead of the Gospel of the cross. Too much evangelism which prostitutes the name of Jesus and His Good News.[26]

With all this in mind, he began to reflect on the Urban Industrial Mission experience in terms of evangelism.

1. In dealing with the reality of the poor and oppressed, we discovered that people are not only wilful violators of God's will but are also the violated. They are both sinners and the sinned-against. Therefore, the Gospel must come to them offering not only forgiveness of sins, but, also power to resist forces which sin against them.

The gospel must demand not only humility before God, but, also defiance before exploiters. Much of the evangelism in our churches ignores the latter reality and therefore proclaims only half truth, which is falsity. A genuine evangelistic message must take sin seriously, all of its horror on human lives, and empower us to resist sin "to the extent of shedding our blood." With this understanding, the evangelistic and prophetic are one ministry.

2. The perception of human sinned-againstness provides a basis for solidarity with the poor and the oppressed. Community does not have to depend on common religious commitment. No religious preconditions are laid down for community. In the common struggle against evil forces, Christians work hand in hand with others, regardless of their attitude towards Jesus Christ. In this context of struggle, evangelism is much more effective because communication takes place within, among equals, in trust, and in a state of heightened awareness of sinful forces. In most of our churches however, we always start with preaching and then community. We proclaim, and if the people respond well and become Christians, then we say we are in community. If they do not respond, then we say good-bye. No wonder the people do not give a hoot about our evangelism. Evangelism must take place in solidarity. Proclamation in the context of community.

3. The community of the sinned, struggling against the forces of sin is an evangelising community. In this context, one soon comes face to face with the reality of personal sin. The poor exploit the poor. The oppressed trample on their fellow oppressed. The leader wants the biggest slice. In the context where the poor have their rightful place, and participating in shaping their own destiny the poor are responsible human beings. They cannot shrug their sins away, saying "so what?" They must deal with the reality of their own sinfulness. There they come face to face with the personal God, and must decide to seek or not to seek forgiveness.

4. Evangelism's first call is the call to repentance. To repent is to change life's direction. For the sinned against to repent is to turn from self contempt to self respect, from existing among the tombs, to living in community, from hopelessness to hopefulness. To the poor, the leper, the widow and the demon-possessed, Jesus said: "You come and follow me" or he cured them, drove out the demons, and asked them to return in dignity to their own people. Jesus never said to the sinned against, "you are a sinner." . . . To the poor, the gospel comes first as affirmation of their human worth. To the rich, the gospel comes as judgement. Both must repent, in different ways from their different references points.

5. What is the Good News to the poor and the oppressed? The

Good News is that God hears their cries for justice and dignity, and responds by calling them to discipleship "take up your cross and follow me." In other words, God affirms their value as human beings, and invites them into community. And so, community is not only the medium of communicating the Good News. It is in itself, the Good News. A Christian is one who follows Jesus Christ. Following Jesus, action-oriented, and a process of coming to take Jesus seriously, is a more preferable formulation than the Pauline formulation of "believe in the Lord Jesus." The latter suggests a definite step in intellectual consent, with a marked demarcation line between belief and unbelief. The other case has a blurred distinction which is advantageously suited for community and solidarity.[27]

Personally, I like this articulation of evangelism, which provides mission theology with fresh air:

1. The whole articulation, though coming out from Urban Industrial Mission, goes beyond it and is useful in other human situations.

2. The whole articulation takes seriously the reality of personal sin, which is the key concern of the evangelist; and at the same time it takes seriously the reality of the "sinned against"—the oppressed and the poor who are in the mind of those who are keen on social concern. Yet the sinner and the sinned-against are not independent from one another, but are closely related. The sinner is the cause of the sinned-against, who in turn understands the terrible consequence of sin and therefore is keener about keeping oneself from sin.

3. The whole articulation gives a full picture, not a half one, of the total human reality; and the Gospel is seen in its fullness dealing with sin in its total reality, not just experienced by one who sins, but also by one who is sinned against.

4. This whole articulation helps Christians to cooperate with those outside the faith yet does not lose sight of the Christian insight of the sinfulness of both the individual and the world. It helps the Church form functional communities with those outside its wall, yet keeps the Church alive through a new vision gained in the process.

This concept of mission and evangelism, although arising from the context in Hong Kong, is now exposed globally both in the CWME Melbourne Conference on "Thy Kingdom Come," and in many occasions is also presented as a significant part of the new mission thrust in the name of Gospel for the poor. This is a new attempt to formulate a mission theology that aims at unifying the divergent concerns for evangelism and social concern in mission, and the new formulation definitely brings new light to the concept of mission.

Mission and Identity

National identity has long been a sensitive issue in the history of mission in China. Before the nineteenth century, the national identity of China was expressed through cultural heritage, mainly Confucianism. Dr. Lee Ming Ng rightly observed that "China's cultural heritage, or for all practical purposes, Confucianism, was what really held the people together. . . . Culturally speaking, Confucianism was China."[28]

Any foreign religions coming from outside must be in some ways related to Confucianism. The Nestorian Bishop Alopen came to China in A.D. 635; and in 638, with the help of Chinese associates, completed the first Christian book in Chinese, *The Sutra of Jesus the Messiah*. In it Alopen expressly showed that Christianity contained nothing subversive to China's ancient traditions. He pointed out that loyalty to the state and filial piety to one's parents were not contrary to Christian teaching. But, unfortunately, he and his later successors, on account of their limitation, too freely had borrowed Buddhist and Taoist terms to express Christian doctrine to a point that Chinese Nestorian writings were increasingly becoming syncretic in nature, resulting in the disappearance of distinctive Christian elements. Nor was it any more closely related to Confucianism. So when Buddhism lost the favor of the Royal Court and was persecuted, Nestorianism was wiped out along with it.[29]

For the causes of the fall of Nestorianism in China, the Reverend Lee Shiu Keung, a Chinese church historian, remarked: "The fact remains that Nestorianism in China was largely a foreign church, without deep roots in Chinese soil. It had not entered the hearts of the people and really made itself at home."[30]

The second missionary movement into China was begun by Mateo Ricci. To him Confucianism rather than Buddhism was the proper manifestation of Chinese culture. Lee Shiu Keung again observed:

> To Ricci it became increasingly clear that the best Hope of spreading Christianity was to ally himself with the Confucians. Here in China the Western Church was confronted with an ancient civilization. She must recognize and tolerate all that was best in China and introduce only her essential message, her reflection and theology. She

must consider western philosophy and ritual as unessential or, at best, secondary.[31]

So here came Ricci's theology of accommodation.

> In him, to be a Christian was not to break the continuity of culture of one's own country. Ricci and some of the Jesuits pointed out that certain Confucian ceremonies such as the veneration of ancestors were not incompatible with Christian practice. Ricci concluded that rites to ancestors and Confucius were pious, not superstitious, ceremonies and could therefore be tolerated.[32]

The attitude of Mateo Ricci, with his deep understanding of Confucianism and his scientific knowledge, contributed greatly to his success in converting a number of notable mandarins, including the eminent scholars Hsu Kwang-chi and Li Chih-tsao. To them Ricci not only taught hydraulics, geometry, and astronomy, but also Christian doctrines. Hsu later was not only able to help De Ursis to write *Western Water Hydraulics* (1612), but Hsu also wrote the momentous study, *Complete Works on Agricultural Administration* (1612–1628), which covers a vast field, from sericulture and horticulture to hydraulics. Hsu was not only Ricci's student in science, but also in faith, both in theory and in action. When Ricci and the Jesuits were attacked for inducing people to follow the way of the foreign barbarian and for introducing pernicious doctrine that gradually infiltrated into the heart of the common people and the literati, Hsu stood up and made courageous defenses.

> They are not only in deportment and in heart wholly free from aught which can excite suspicion, but they are indeed worthies and sages: their doctrines are most correct; their manner of life most strict; their learning most extensive; their hearts most true, their views most steady.[33]

Not only was Hsu able to testify unreservedly to the integrity of the Jesuit missionaries, but also to write to his Chinese colleague concerning the Christian faith in Chinese understanding.

> Tien Chu (Lord of Heaven) is the same as Shangti (Sovereign King above) in the Confucian classics. Once we believe in His existence, we must observe His commandments and obey His doctrines as a son obeys his father or a subject obeys his sovereign. This is true in China as in foreign lands. Now in a country, the sovereign can be seen only by the Courtiers and the ministers in the Imperial Capital. His subjects living by the seashore or in the wilderness have no opportunity of seeing him. Although the sovereign is not seen, his subjects must believe in his existence. If they infringe upon his laws and regulations, they will suffer penalty in the judicial courts. . . . The essence of Christianity lies in repentance and newness of life. Even in the last

moments of one's life, one can still repent and avoid eternal damnation. . . . As you are good enough to ask me questions, I consider this to be a golden opportunity. To discuss this fully with you will enable us to save not only you but through you many others.[34]

By respecting the culture of the Chinese and by introducing science (something useful to the country), Ricci and his group were not only able to introduce Christianity to the Chinese literati and mandarin, but also able to survive many persecutions and slanderings, such as political subversion, unsound Christology,[35] and contempt for China.[36] The threat to Ricci's mission—namely, the Rites controversy—came not so much from outside as from inside. Lee Shiu Keung observed that "It was not only a question of rites and terminology. On a deeper level it was also a question of adherence to Western traditions or adaptation to Chinese ways of life and assimilation of the indigenous culture."[37]

Ricci himself believed that Tien Chu (Lord of Heaven) or Shangti (Sovereign King above) were adequate expressions for God, but others—especially Longobardi, the office of superior since 1610—did not agree and held out instead for a phoneticized form of the Latin term *Deus*.

Also with the question of rites, the Jesuits allowed their Chinese converts to participate in the ancestral rites on condition that the burning of paper money should not be allowed; nor should Christians direct any prayer to the dead. In 1693 Charles Maigrot, the French vicar apostolic, ordered that the customary rites for the dead were to be banned because he did not agree that Confucian rituals to the spirits were more cultural than religious.

In spite of the explanation given by the Emperor K'ang Hsi upon the Jesuits' request that Chinese people keep their ancestral tablets to express their sense of gratitude for parental care and upbringing, the Congregation for the Propagation of the Faith and the Holy Office issued a decree in 1704 to ban all Confucian or ancestral rites. In the following years, Pope Clement XI in the bull Ex Illa Die reaffirmed the prohibition in more solemn form. In December 1720, when K'ang Hsi had occasion to read the Chinese translation of the bull, he added his own rescript:

> In reading this document, one can only say that the little men of Western countries are in no position to discuss the great way of China. Alas, no Westerner can master the Chinese classics. Their conversation and their opinion often provoke laughter. Now as I read this foreign subject's declaration, it is indeed very much akin to the heresy and sectarianism of the Buddhist monks and Taoist priests. There is no more striking example of sheer ignorance. Henceforth,

no Westerner shall preach in the Middle Kingdom. We shall prohibit them in order to avoid further trouble.[38]

That ended the Roman Catholic mission in China before the nineteenth century.

To conclude, the failure of this mission was due to disrespect of Chinese national identity, which, as suggested by Dr. Lee Ming Ng earlier, was expressed through Confucianism. When the missionaries did not respect Confucianism, the Chinese national identity was also not taken seriously. This hurt the Chinese people and the natural outcome was: "Missionary, go home." China became an almost closed empire for about one hundred years (1740–1840). Then the whole scene changed.

The Opium Wars (1839–1842) shook China out of her complacency. Western powers succeeded in shaking down the wall of culturalism as expressed in Confucianism. The Western powers invaded the country and divided it into spheres of influence, and Confucianism seemed helpless in facing the crisis. Under such circumstances, a new expression of nationalism emerged. It was advocated by the new intellectuals and the vast number of students coming out from the new school system. Their aims were two-fold: to save the country from humiliation imposed by the powers and to make China strong. The first aim brought about anti-Western sentiment; and the second aim led to the attack on Confucianism and the introduction of democracy and science, which were considered elements that could produce strong nations. It was unfortunate at this time that the third entry of Christian mission into China was accompanied by unequal treaties and that religions in China were considered to be dogmatic, superstitious, and unscientific. It was natural for the new intellectuals and students to be suspicious of Christianity and picked it out as the target of fire. And from 1922 to 1927 an anti-Christian movement blasted off with a series of organized attacks on Christianity in China. The week between December 22–27 was designated annually as "Non-Christian Week," and students "demonstrated in the streets, gave out pamphlets, made speeches, and created disturbances in the churches."[39]

With regard to Christian schools, the Young China Association at its fifth annual conference resolved: "That we strongly oppose Christian education which destroys the national spirit of our people and carries on a cultural program in order to undermine Chinese Civilization."[40] Pressures were put on government to remove all foreigners from control of schools in China and to forbid religious education in the schools.

Dr. Yu-tang Lin commented strongly that during his early childhood, when he was reared in a Christian family, he often had heard the story of the fall of Jericho, but had never heard of the famous Chinese folk story of Lady Meng weeping over the Great Wall. He felt that he was deprived of his right to national and cultural inheritance.

All this might explain why, with so much effort, Christianity had never taken root in China. It was an imposition from outside, it was a cultural imperialism, it had no respect for the people's identity as Chinese. It is no wonder that Bertrand Russell remarked in *The Problem of China* (1922) that "education in mission schools . . . tends to become denationalized and have a slavish attitude toward foreign civilization . . . and of course their whole influence, unavoidably if involuntarily, militates against national-respect in those whom they teach."[41]

The response of the majority of the leaders of the Chinese church tended to look at the anti-Christian movement in a positive light, and they embarked on a positive course of action, both institutionally and theologically. Theologically, the work of indigenization became one of the major undertakings of the Chinese church in the twentieth century. Institutionally, the three-self principles—namely, self-government, self-support, self-propagation—were made an urgent task. K. S. Latourette remarked: "The growing nationalism of younger Chinese expressed itself in the slogan, 'China for the Chinese', and here and there Chinese-Christians began to ask for a larger share in the control of the church."[42]

It was sad that most efforts in indigenization and in the three-self movement were far from being adequately actualized as expected. On the one hand, people questioned the work of indigenization. Wu Lei Chuen, the first Chinese president of Yenching, University, rightly said: "Chinese culture itself is now seeking a new direction of development. It is therefore only futile for Christianity to identify itself with traditional Chinese culture."[43] On the other hand, quite a number of missionaries were unwilling to give up their control. "Missionaries feared that if the Chinese assumed control, they would make the church something scarcely recognizable to western eyes."[44] Dr. Lee Ming Ng observed that there were elements of distrust and arrogance that were seldom recognized as they were under argument to preserve the purity of the Christian faith.[45]

Indigenization and three-self principles were meant to make the mission and evangelism of the Church more easily understood, trusted, and hopefully accepted by the Chinese people. But for the reasons just stated, both did not go very far. Then with the pressure of foreign encroachments mounting each day, by the 1930's the Chinese people were less concerned with maintenance of their country as a sovereign political entity. "National salvation," or "national reconstruction," was all that mattered. Patriotic Christians were ready to take "national reconstruction" as the important thrust of Christian mission. Some participated in rural reconstruction, and some took whatever models were available, even opting for the Communist theoretical model.

All these—indigenization, three-self principles, national reconstruction in whatever models—showed that mission of the Church in China were very much related to nationalism expressed in forms either related to old Confucian culturalism or to new national reconstruction. That is to say, mission—if it was to be meaningful to the Chinese—must take national identity seriously.

With this background, it is perhaps easier to understand the three-self and patriotic emphases of the Chinese church today.

Bishop K. H. Ting said, "For the church in China to be Chinese is a pre-requisite for communication."[46] He also added:

> In order to insure the emergence and growth of a church in China that is just as Chinese as churches in England are English, we have to raise a protective wall against an "internationalism" which does not give due respect to rightful national aspirations.[47]

In order to push even one step further from national selfhood to national success, Bishop Ting stressed the importance of the identification of Christian mission with national success, and the possibility of loving God and loving one's nation should be explored and made the important part of the mission of the Church.

> We do not think the success of Christian evangelism depends on the failure of the socialist experiment in transforming the country and the people. Indeed our success depends to a large extent on the identification of ourselves with the people in the experiment.[48]

And so,

> There are situations in which the church has to tell the inquirer: "go and sin no more." But quite often the church's message is to encourage the people to carry on their valuable work, but to see it from a higher point of reference and to relate it to the loving purpose of God in all His work of creation, redemption and sanctification, and thus to gain a new and fuller sense of its value.[49]

In other words, the Church's mission should not aim at taking the people out of their own national identity nor at setting them against their own rootage, but it should awake them to their origin and should be in solidarity with them in their common struggle for a stronger nation and a better world. The Right Reverend R. O. Hall, the former bishop of Hong Kong and Macao, once said, "Nation and family are two classrooms provided by God for the training of His people." Instead of making conversion its sole aim, mission and evangelism should be taken as a long-range, overall, ongoing, cultural process. "The church is to be a leaven. The functions of the leaven is to transform the whole mass of dough into bread, not into leaven."[50]

That is to say, Christians should not regard those outside the Church as objects of evangelism, for by so doing, there will be mutual opposition between belief and unbelief and the automatic assumption between moral inferiority of the unbelievers. Such an attitude will result in Christians isolating themselves in the tiny world of the Church. Rather Christians should go among the broad masses of the people; merge with them simply as neighbors, fellow workers, and peasants; and let witness take place naturally and spontaneously.

Actually when we look at the Gospel, we find that God takes human identity so seriously that He became a human being Himself and dwelt among people, full of grace and truth (John 1:14). In Jesus Christ the identity of human beings was not disregarded, trampled down, nor destroyed; but was restored, uplifted, and brought to the height equivalent to that of the children of God as originally intended. So among Christians, there should be room to call some British Christians, U.S. Christians, Canadian Christians, Malaysian Christians, Hong Kong Chinese Christians. Then the verse "all the members of the body, though many, are one body" (1 Corinthians 12:12) would surely take on a richer and broader understanding.

Mission and Urbanization

In the last thirty years Hong Kong has undergone a rapid process of urbanization. For example, Shatin, a village-town that ten years ago had a population of 50,000, now has become a satellite city of 300,000 people; and it is estimated that by 1990 the population will increase to 800,000. These figures serve to show the high speed of social change taking place everyday in Hong Kong.

Sociologists have indicated that urbanization does not just mean change from rural life to city life. It is a complete change of life-style. Competition, efficiency, planning, well-defined bureaucratic structure, differentiation, and specialization are all key words in describing such a life-style.

In such a process human beings live for the system rather than the system for them. Their worth is defined by what they do and not what they are. Even what they do is not really what they like to do but what they are assigned to do. The concept of individual worth becomes less and less significant. Relativism and pluralism dominate day-to-day life, resulting in some kind of aimless or meaningless pursuit of material reward or sense of success or achievement. Fewer and fewer people find any motivation for total involvement and commitment to something of "high" or "eternal" value. In a highly differentiated and specialized society, many will become maladjusted, will be pushed to the periphery of life, and will become the marginalized and the outcast of society. Indifference, alienation, and helplessness will constitute the dominating mood.

It has taken some time for the Church to realize that responsibility of mission is its own and not that of the missionary agencies. But now, in front of this urbanized situation, it is confronted with the following difficulties in discharging its missionary responsibility effectively:

1. The urban world speaks and acts in terms of professionalism while the Church, in terms of voluntary amateurism.
2. The urban world is changing quickly and is forward looking, but the Church is static and very much burdened by the past.
3. The urban world comes up with a whole bundle of new problems, which the Church has not faced before.
4. The urban world is full of numerous specialized groups of people while the Church is still very slow in developing its specialized ministries.
5. Looking at the Church as an association for the religious minority, the urban world does not expect the Church to be involved in secular business and so finds it hard to accept and to support the social involvement of the Church.
6. The business-like style of the urban society is still foreign to the working style of the Church.

No matter how big the voice from the concerned faithful that the Church is by nature not an institution, the face remains that existing churches are institutions and they are looked upon by the urban world as such. It is both a crisis of identity and a crisis of relevance for the Church. In order to find a way for the Church to discharge its missionary responsibility, something new has emerged from the urban situation in Hong Kong. That is the springing-up of numerous Christian groups. They exist parallel to the Church, but do not belong to any particular church or denomination. Most of the these groups are financially independent and self-governed and have independent structures. Their appearance is a response to the Church's crisis of relevance and also a phenomenon that is threatening the identity of the institutional Church. The ratio of these groups compared to local churches is alarming: more than 120 groups out of about 670 local churches—that is, 1:5.6. The fields of work that they cover are so vast that tidy classification is very difficult. But roughly we can at least identify the following:

1. Groups with purely evangelical outreach to special groups of people, mostly students and workers.
2. Groups with prophetic concern—both in voice and in action—for the welfare of the workers, the underprivileged, and the marginalized.
3. Groups with pastoral and evangelistic concern for sustaining people working in professions or in specialized fields.
4. Groups exploring new frontiers in and new media for missions. They play the role of pioneers, especially in the fields of art and drama.
5. Groups with miscellaneous concerns not included in the items above—for example, contextual theology study groups and ad hoc groups to study the meaning of religious freedom and church action before 1997.

Quite a number of keen lay people join these groups and find in the life and work there, more opportunities to use their talents and specialties, more contacts where their new social consciousness and growing involvement can be expressed, and more situations where they can render direct person-to-person help, thus giving more authentic witness to the Christian faith. Compared to the institutionalized Church, these groups are definitely more at home with the urbanized world and can give more effective service to the people. Since they are more communal in nature, they are more capable of caring for their own members, new and old. Quite a number of nonbelievers are also challenged by the tasks performed by these groups and by the meaning they offer.

All these descriptions show that although the Church has been entrusted with the responsibility of mission, it now finds that such a responsibility is borne by the concerned groups of lay persons, with one or two concerned ministers serving in individual capacity as their consultants.

With all the good intentions from both the Church and other groups, there still exist certain tensions. In an editorial of a special issue on parachurch organization of the *Chinese Church Today*, published by the Chinese Co-ordination Centre of World Evangelism, it was emphasized that all of the work of the parachurch groups should be church-centered and should play the role of servants to serve the Church. The rationale for this was that the work of the parachurch groups is time-bound and specialized while the work of the churches is permanent and wholistic. In spite of the willingness of the groups to be so and the effort to do so, the tension is still there. Analyzing the situation, Ms. Pui-lan Kwok gives the following reason:

> If these groups remain passive, playing a supportive role, and the church dictates what sort of "commodity" to buy, one wonders whether this is good for church development as a whole. If the experience and the challenges and problems faced by the para-church groups are not brought back to the church and help to shape the life of the church, the existence of these groups will just help to perpetuate the institutionalized and static character of the church. And at the end, the church has not faced up to the challenge of the society which leads to the emergence of the para-church groups.[51]

In other words, the kind of reaching-out done by the groups just cannot be done by churches. As a result, the kind of new converts resulting from the work of these groups also cannot fit in with the present structure and life-style of the institutionalized Church. The consequence is obvious—either a new and more comprehensive ecclesiology can be found or a new type of "church" will come into existence. One church of this type has just opened as a result of mission among the workers. It is marked with distinctive activities and worship. Their activities include labor education, a labor-law advising service, a counseling service for labor disputes, theological education for workers, and visitation of those injured in industrial accidents. Their worship life bears the distinctive mark of industrial life. It may be interesting to cite the call to worship as an example:

Leader: We who assemble to-day come from the factories.
People: Some of us are garment workers; some work in elec-

tronic factories; some weave; some work in metallic factories.

Leader: Though we have different jobs, we have one thing in common: we use our hands to serve the Lord.

People: Work is part of human life.
God creates men to be workers.

Leader: Through one's work, one becomes a member of society. We assemble together to-day, let us strengthen our faith and encourage each other.

People: Let us strengthen our trust in fellowship, prepare ourselves to be united and to co-operate with the workers.

We can see that it is not easy for this type of activity and worship to be taken in by the normal church every week. But such groups fit well with urban life. They enjoy the feeling of togetherness with people of the same profession or trade. They are familiar with the problems and anxieties arising from their own profession and are able to react quickly to them, not just individually but corporately. They can face their own people as insiders, not outsiders—thus making it comparatively easy to lead to mutual acceptance. They can behave in a very business-like and professional way in tackling problems yet very congenially in their communal-like way of life together. In performing the task of mission, there are great advantages for these groups:

1. Christian mission to other people comes in the context of the common mission of the Christians and non-Christians to change the unjust or the unconcerned world. Certain community life comes before evangelism in order to enable evangelism to take place; and does not come after evangelism, when there is bound to be a great divisive distinction of believer and nonbeliever.

2. There is no room for Christian self-righteousness, for both Christians and non-Christians have to struggle against evil social forces on equal footings. But if they persist in faith, love, and hope in the difficult process of struggling for social justice, there is room for credibility on the side of the Christians. Actually it is only on such credibility that Christians can speak and would be listened to.

3. There is a mutual and spontaneous sharing going on within the groups all the time, with both success and failure, happy and sad moments, sense of achievement, and feelings of frustration. Out of sharing comes friendship, and out of friendship hopefully comes fellowship, which means mu-

tual support and mutual edifying. Such a fellowship in depth surely will lead to the sharing of convictions in depth—not in an atmosphere of competitory beating-down of the other, but of an atmosphere of offering one's best with the concern that it may be of help to another fellow human being.

Although it is attuned to an urban style of life and is effective in attracting people to faith, such a model of mission nevertheless presents a great problem to the institutional Church. It creates a dilemma: either the institutional Church must go on its own way with no regard and no support to these groups, heading most probably toward the periphery of society; or it has to review its ecclesiology so that these groups can function legitimately and properly within the more comprehensive concepts of the Church, and the Church can be brought back in the midst of the urban life again. How the Church will face this situation is outside the scope of this paper. But the problem of mission, I hope, is made clear here—church in mission or Christian groups in mission?

Concluding Remarks

In the previous discussions of mission we can see that mission theology has to be formulated and understood contextually. In the Hong Kong–China context, certain insights have emerged.

1. Although it is initiated by God in Jesus Christ through the Holy Spirit, Christian mission must not divorce itself from the total need of the people. Actually, in the life and ministry of our Lord Jesus Christ, He never sent needy people away by just forgiving their sins without meeting their needs.

2. The traditional emphases in mission on sinners only is not a full Gospel unless it takes into consideration the sinned-against, caused by our sin and the sinful structural power of society.

3. The aim of mission is not to replace a racial, national cultural or professional identity with so-called Christian identity, but rather to seek ways so that true Christian identity can be expressed through our various identities.

4. Mission has to take the world seriously, to the point that we do not impose our demand on it, but rather see that the world may live life to its fullness even with the risk that those engaging in mission may have to undergo changes themselves.

5. It is not the missionary agencies nor the institutional

churches to be in mission, but the whole people of God in groups of which they are part.

It is not easy to say whether Anglicanism is helping mission or hindering mission. But on account of all the new insights on mission as previously highlighted, one thing is clear— when Anglicanism is understood only as the distinctive mark of Christians in the Anglo-Saxon world, thus allowing other distinctive marks to be equally valid and respectable in other contexts as a result of mission, then Anglicanism is a liberating symbol and is helpful. But when Anglicanism is absolutized and made the binding criteria of what Christian churches or Anglican churches all over the world should be like, it will suffocate the initiative of mission, strangle indigenous effort, and become a hindrance to mission.

NOTES

1. Lesslie Newbigin, *One Body, One Gospel, One World*, pp. 25–26.
2. Edited by R. K. Orchard.
3. *What in the World Is the World Council of Churches?*, p. 26.
4. Gerald H. Anderson and Thomas F. Stransky, eds., *Mission Trends*, no. 1, pp. 115–116. This essay is taken from *The Christian Century*, (April 11, 1973).
5. John R. W. Stott, *Christian Mission in the Modern World*, p. 15.
6. *Ibid.*, p. 36.
7. Stephen Neill, *A History of Christian Missions*, p. 394.
8. John R. W. Stott, "The Bible Basis of Evangelism," in Anderson and Stromsky, eds., *Mission Trends*, no. 2, p. 10.
9. Hans Jochen Margull, "Mission '70'—More a Venture Than Ever," in Anderson and Stromsky, eds., *Mission Trends*, no. 1, pp. 50–51.
10. Collin Morris, "Include Me Out," quoted from Johannes Aagaard, "Mission After Uppsala, 1968," in *Mission Trends*, no. 1, p. 19.
11. Norman Goodall, ed., *The Uppsala 68 Report*, pp. 317–318.
12. *Ibid.*
13. John R. W. Stott, *Christian Mission in the Modern World*, p. 15.
14. *Ibid.*, p. 16.
15. *Ibid.*, p. 17.
16. *Ibid.*, p. 35.
17. William Frazier, "Guidelines for a New Theology of Mission," in *Mission Trends*, no. 1, p. 27.
18. *Ibid.*, p. 30.
19. *Ibid.*
20. *Ibid.*, p. 31.
21. *Ibid.*

22. John R. W. Stott, *Christian Mission in the Modern World*, p. 26.
23. *Ibid.*, p. 27.
24. John V. Taylor, *For All the World*, p. 40.
25. Material taken from *International Review of Mission* (April 1973).
26. Raymond Fung, "Good News to the Poor—A Case for a Missionary Movement," in CCA-URM Discussion Series, *Proclaiming Christ in Solidarity With the Poor*, p. 6.
27. *Ibid.*, pp. 8–11.
28. Lee Ming Ng, "Christianity and Nationalism in China," in *East Asia Journal of Theology*, vol. 1, no. 1 (1983), p. 72.
29. Lee Shiu Keung, *The Cross and the Lotus*, pp. 21–23.
30. *Ibid.*, p. 23.
31. *Ibid.*, p. 56.
32. *Ibid.*
33. Translated by Dr. Lee Shiu Keung in his book, *The Cross and the Lotus*, pp. 60–61.
34. Translated by Lee Shiu Keung in his book, *The Cross and the Lotus*, pp. 61–62.
35. In regard to *A Summary Record of the Early Worship of God*, written by the Chinese-Catholic convert Li Tsu Pol, Yang Kwang-hsien (1597–1669) remarked, "How could a criminal in his own country, once his teaching came to China, be hailed as the sage who created Heaven?"
36. Yang Kwang-hsien wrote: "According to Li's book, our China is nothing but an offshoot of Judea; our ancient rulers, sages and teachers were but the descendants of a heterodox sect, and our doctrines no more than the remnant of a heretical religion. Is there no limit to foolishness?"
37. Lee Shiu Keung, *op. cit.*, p. 71.
38. Translation from Lee Shiu Keung, *op. cit.*, p. 76.
39. N. Z. Zier, "The Anti-Christian Movement," in *China Christian Year Book* (1925), p. 22.
40. K. S. Latourette, *A History of Christian Missions in China*, p. 697.
41. Carl T. Smith, "The Chinese Church in a Colonial Setting: Hong Kong," p. 55.
42. K. S. Latourette, *op. cit.*, p. 607.
43. Wu Lei Chuen, "Christianity and Chinese Culture," p. 18. Translation from Dr. Lee Ming Ng, "Christianity and Nationalism in China," in *East Asia Journal of Theology*, p. 84.
44. Paul Varg, *Missionaries, Chinese and Diplomats*, p. 101.
45. Lee Ming Ng, *op. cit.*, p. 83.
46. K. H. Ting, "The Church in China," in *A Monthly Letter on Evangelism*, no. 3 (March 1983), p. 3.
47. *Ibid.*
48. *Ibid.*, p. 4.
49. *Ibid.*, p. 5.
50. *Ibid.*, p. 6.
51. Pui Lan Kwok, "Ecclesiological Issues Emerging From the Experience on Para-Church and Action Groups," in *Tradition and Innovation*, pp. 62–63.

184 *Alan Chan*

Anderson, Gerald H., and Stransky, Thomas F., eds. *Mission Trends, no. 1 and no. 2* (New York–Paramus–Toronto: Paulist Press, 1974 and 1975).

China Christian Year Book. 1925.

Christian Conference of Asia (CCA) and Urban Rural Mission (URM) Discussion Series. *Proclaiming Christ in Solidarity With the Poor*. Hong Kong: Urban Rural Mission, Christian Conference of Asia, 1983.

Commission on Theological Concern (CTC) and CCA, eds. *Tradition and Innovation—A Search for a Relevant Ecclesiology in Asia*. Singapore: Christian Conference of Asia, 1983.

Goodall, Norman, ed. *The Uppsala 68 Report*. Geneva: World Council of Churches, 1968.

International Review of Mission. Geneva: WCC, April 1973.

Latourette, K. S. *A History of Christian Missions in China*. New York: Macmillan, 1929.

Lee Shiu Keung. *The Cross and the Lotus*. Hong Kong: The Christian Study Centre of Chinese Religion and Culture, 1971.

Neill, Stephen. *A History of Christian Missions*. London: Hodder & Stoughton, 1964.

Newbigin, Lesslie. *One Body, One Gospel, One World*. New York: Friendship Press, 1958.

Orchard, R. K., ed. *Witness in Six Continents*. London: Edinburgh House Press, 1964.

Stott, John R. W. *Christian Mission in the Modern World*. London: Church Pastoral Aid Society, 1975.

Taylor, John V. *For All the World*. London: Hodder & Stoughton, 1966.

Ting, K. H. *The Church in China* ("A Monthly Letter on Evangelism"). Geneva: Council on World Mission and Evangelism and World Council of Churches, March 1983.

Varg, Paul. *Missionaries, Chinese and Diplomats*. Princeton, N.J.: Princeton University Press, 1958.

What in the World Is the World Council of Churches? rev. ed. Geneva: W.C.C., 1981.

Yeow Choo Lak, ed. *East Asia Journal of Theology*. vol. 1, no. 1. Singapore: Singapore Association for Theological Education in South East Asia, 1983.

Mission and the Common Life
of the Church

Mission and Establishment

The Right Reverend Colin Buchanan

It is my practice to begin my presentations with a note outlining personal disqualifications. This paper is the work of an individual rather than that of a representative, and establishing the point enables the author from this moment onward to be unashamedly himself. If the paper does not draw upon vast numbers of other authors and actually overlooks important studies, then that is inherent in the limitations of the author.

The Mission of Christ's Church

Simply and seriously, I hold that the mission of the Church is to bring all things under the rule of Christ, to work to bring in His Kingdom. This includes and indeed spotlights the proclamation of the Gospel to the individual, but it also includes the striving to reform the injustices of this world, whether they hurt the individual, or classes of peoples, or nations, or regions. All that is signified in the Incarnation is, I take it, included in the commission "As the Father has sent me, so send I you." There is a tension in this concerning the priorities to be observed by individuals, by congregations, and by dioceses and provinces; and that tension is not relaxed in the analysis that follows. Rather, we see the Church of England in transition from one kind of tension to another.

The Inheritance of the Church of England

The Church of England can easily give an impression of enormous strength. It has been warp and woof of English society since the sixth century of the Christian era, with antecedents going back to Roman times. It has been in the forefront of the national life, and it has also lodged deeply in the corporate subconscious. It has a dominance in the folklore or "implicit religion" to be found in the land, although it must be added that some glimpses of pre-Christian paganism, druidism, satanism, and witchcraft are still to be found; and also new folklores of ethnic minorities are burgeoning all the time. The Church of England covers the land, with a building (as like as not a medieval building) in the tiniest hamlets as well as in every corner of the towns. Between 10,000 and 11,000 parochial clergy (let alone lay workers of various sorts) are to be found in a tiny compact geographical area no larger than a single diocese in many other parts of the Anglican Communion, and hardly larger than parishes are in some more remote places. Ancient parish boundaries still allocate this street to one parish, that street to another, and the whole population of England is to be found living in one or another carefully marked Church of England parish with a Church of England clergyman in charge. In the parish in South Manchester, where I was an assistant curate twenty years ago, the parish boundary was a brook, now largely underground and running through pipes and culverts, which had been the "natural" boundary in the eighth or ninth century when the first church building had stood on a high point in a field that gently sloped down to this brook. And although boundaries have often been unresponsive to social and demographic change, the Church of England remains in principle a "territorial" church, at whatever cost of keeping a building open and a semblance of ministry going in every part of the land, even if the folk of the area have virtually wholly deserted her. In this she contrasts with those "free churches" that only exist in places where the worshipers can in effect maintain their own buildings and ministry.

This actual existence on the ground testifies to the historical role the Church of England has fulfilled. It is England's church—yes, the state, or established, church. It had a life of its own, distinct from that of the state, prior to the Reformation, in that the clergy, its officers, owed allegiance to Rome and in the last analysis—as, for instance, when undergoing trial for misdeeds—acknowledged the sovereignty of Rome, as they were enabled to take appeals there. From this point of view the English reformation was a struggle about sovereignty; and although it became much more than that, it was at no point any less than that. Rome was the the headquarters of a transnational corporation, which was, in its English branch, nationalized by Henry VIII. All the corporation's servants had now to promise loyalty to the sovereign of their own land and settle down to working as a department of the state. The state in turn took action to ensure that an office of this national religious welfare organization existed in every part of the land. And thus the parishes, parish churches, and structures of the Church of England testify not only to the vast antiquity of the organization, but also to its close involvement with the national and political life of English society. There are vast strengths here for the Church of England's mission; the difficulty is in interpreting aright just what those strengths are.

To this day the Church of England has its diocesan bishops appointed by the monarch. To this day, the General Synod of the Church of England is subject to the authority of Parliament, not just in the general way in which any corporation in any country has its activities bounded by the law of the land, but also in the specific sense that the powers of Synod derive not from a voluntary compacting together of an association of like-minded persons, but rather from devolution of such powers from Parliament and at various points Synod itself. If it will reform the life and organization of the Church of England, Synod must return to Parliament to ask for a change in the laws of the land to enable this to happen. We are a department of the state still—in some ways a very privileged one, nevertheless, a department of the state. There is a theological question here about whether Christianity ought to have an established place in Britian today, but also a consequential question about whether the Church of England is not wrongly favored—and also, curiously correspondingly hampered—by its inherited integration with the fabric of the state.

Out in the parishes the "folklore" corresponds to the establishment. The Church of England is deemed to be the church from which the average nonchurchgoer is abstaining. But the Church of England is also thought to be the provider of certain benefits—such as "rites of passage"—which should be available whenever they are sought. This folklore is logically distinct from the establishment of the Church of England; for technically the folklore could die but the establishment continue, or the establishment could cease—as, for instance, it did in Wales in 1920—but the folklore expectations run on. For the moment, though, there is a broad correspondence between these two features of the Church of England, and the correspondence is enough to make many think that the folklore factor justifies the establishment factor. Personally, I do not.

The inheritance of the Church of England is more than its buildings, its state links, and its role in popular religious folklore.

For instance, there is a considerable sum of hard cash. The ancient glebe and other benefice endowments once provided clergy without costing the parish or diocese any allocations of money from today's givers and today's collections of money. In the last twenty years that has ceased. Everywhere now the clergy are paid in large part from today's giving. Yet the ancient endowments remain either centralized in the church commissioners or, in the case of glebe, placed in diocesan trusteeship. These funds pay for the episcopate, pay for all retirement pensions, and pay a proportion (between 25 and 50 percent, varying from diocese to diocese) of the stipends of the parish clergy. Each year the "living church" takes on a larger proportion, groaning under the weight, yet still just raising the necessary cash. In the process the Church of England worshiper has had to be weaned from that "Sunday school penny" on which our grandmothers were brought up and has had to learn to give in proportion to his or her earnings, thus giving by banker's order and possibly tax-free covenant. It is good for the Church of England to learn this lesson. It is arguable that it has been supporting stipendiary ministers out of proportion to its willingness to pay for them. Yet it is also true that the commissioners' millions, inherited from the past, are by most reckonings an asset, not a liability, and an asset without which we would have been in a sorry state.

A cognate feature of our inheritance is the Church of England's clericalism. In part this is an unsurprising bequest of the pre-Reformation era, when the clergy became the chief possessors of learning and literacy and the sole possessors of the responsibilities of leadership in the Church. The established character of the Church of England left the clergy without directly evangelistic tasks to fulfill, but rather endowed them with the role of being spiritual fathers to all their parishioners. With the growth of the slum towns of the Industrial Revolution, the theory of clericalism was never dented, although it quickly lost touch with realities; and even when parochial church councils came into being in 1920, they were simply charged with assisting the clergy in their work— it still being assumed that the clergy in essence do the work of the Church, but that "because that work has become mountainous" the clergy may need exceptional help from elected laity. I am tempted to say that the "Catholic Revival" of the nineteenth century has assisted the lingering of clericalism, as the "magnifying of the office" of the priesthood inevitably sets low ceilings for the nature of lay ministry. At the evangelical end of the church, however, where the laity are in theory being given a much fuller ministry, clericalism has often been, in fact, as bad as among those who at least had a doctrinal excuse for it. The upshot is that until the day before yesterday, the Church of England has functioned with a very passive laity and the fantasy of an omnicompetent clergy.

We thus have a parish system in the towns, where ten, twenty, or even thirty thousand people may live in one ecclesiastical parish, all of them still, in establishment theory, the "sheep" of the one ordained "shepherd." In fact only between one and five percent of them attend Anglican worship, and the vast majority are probably practical atheists. So the ancient theory of the parish has to be revamped to be credible. The best that can be done is to allow that the attenders are the Church, that the nonattenders really are not, and that the congregation as a whole has a corporate responsibility for evangelism to the rest. The establishment theory not only does the wrong thing and gives the wrong message about the role of the incumbent, but it also blunts the apparent need for evangelism and paralyzes the lay Christian in his duty.

There is a vigor in the Church of England that much of the above account would obsure. It is not only that many, many congregations have come independently to the conclusion that those who voluntarily gather on Sundays are the Church and have reappraised their role and calling accordingly; that in many, many parishes full development of lay Christians into leaders, pastors, teachers, and evangelists has gone ahead full steam; but it is also that there is a vigor in the Church springing from outside its formal structures. This is the vigor of the voluntary societies. The Church of England has so often seemed to be vast and torpid (like one of those prehistoric monsters that is said to have faded from the earth because if its tail were wounded its brain only registered the fact a fortnight later) that men and women of action have worked through voluntary societies. The overseas missionary societies are one example, the Bible Society another. The theological colleges of the Church of England, out of the heart of one of which I now write, are similar—the product of impatient men who wanted the clergy grounded in doctrine and pastoral skills in generations when the official structures made no provision for this. The religious communities (as in Rome) come in the same category. So does the Mothers' Union, so does much of the youth work, and so does most Christian publishing (including the two main Church of England weekly journals and the more serious bimonthly and thrice-a-year ones).

Finally in this section, I look at the organization of the Church

of England. There is a big strain upon the nature of episcopacy in
the Church of England. It takes the following forms. Each diocese
has an average of around 250 parish clergy, plus lay ministers of
various sorts. The bishop may try with great energy to know them
all and be known by them all. He may alternatively take the view
that the parish clergy work best without interference and thus
justify his throwing his own weight into other tasks, including the
many national tasks of the Church of England, such as chairing
boards or commissions of the General Synod. In either case he
will have to provide what has been called an "ambulance service"
to the clergy as troubles arise and the bishop is summoned to solve
them. He will have to be abreast of a host of diocesan committees
and relate them to his own staff and to his personal pastoral care of
the clergy. He will have—with present initiation patterns—to go
round the parishes on Sundays, and on midweek occasions, taking
confirmations and preaching relatively fresh sermons for these
inevitably similar events. He runs the terrible risk of never thinking a new thought, never breaking fresh ground, only running a
maintenance ministry. This will be all the sadder if the best parishes in his diocese have broken beyond that "maintenance" concept and are actually evangelizing.

The Church of England has met this problem quite inadequately and done so by two routes. From 1836 to 1927 there was a
considerable increase in the number of dioceses. For legal reasons
this division of territory is easier to achieve nowadays, but in fact
has not happened since 1927. There are many factors behind this
institutional inertia, including financial ones and the reluctance
sometimes of a diocesan bishop, in spite of all the pressures on
him, to let his territory be reduced. This need not necessarily be
due to unworthy motives; it is also true that keeping the territory
large gives maximum flexibility in terms of appointments and of
movement of the clergy. There is a recent tendency instead toward "area schemes," whereby a diocese is subdivided internally
and an "area bishop" has a responsibility under the diocesan for
each area.

The other route by which the Church of England has striven to
reduce pressure on its bishops is by the appointment of suffragan
bishops. In the last analysis these are "episcopal curates." They
are appointed by the diocesan alone, and they fulfill such tasks as
the diocesan may assign to them. In particular, of course, they
join the round of doing confirmations and of general pastoral
contact with the ministers and people of the diocese. But they lack

any theological rationale, as most attempts to expound episcopacy relate to powers and responsibilities inherent in the episcopate itself, not to those handed out by some kind of contract in a manner that is logically subsequent to the appointment and consecration of a man as a bishop. Second-century episcopacy and twentieth-century episcopacy alike are monepiscopal, or their rationale collapses. The suffragan may be a good friend, but he is a theological anomaly.

The episcopate is by definition conservative. It is not only that the pressure is upon bishops to run a maintenance ministry; but it is that they are themselves at the upper end of the age bracket of the serving clergy, and they inevitably are supremely sensitive to the dangers of rocking the boat. In fast-changing times they may reflect the ethos of yesterday, and under heavy administrative and other pressures they may fail to do the reappraisal that is necessary.

The doctrine of the Trinity may be attacked at intervals by Church of England writers. The Incarnation may be expounded in ways contrary to the creeds. But whatever else it sees at stake, the Church of England is not going to negotiate about episcopacy and shows little sign that it is going to vary much in its practice of episcopacy. We are in urgent need of new models and provocative argument on this issue.

Our round-up of the organization of the Church of England would not be complete without reference to the General Synod, the central governing body of the Church. Because of its historic integration in the machinery of the state, the Church of England is viewed as plausible both as a single national unit subdivided into dioceses (and then again into parishes) and as a federal structure built up by the affiliation of dioceses to each other, in the way that many overseas provinces have come to be. Because of its strong central character, the General Synod meets three times a year. And because of the tight geographical character of England, travel for 550 Synod members is no great hardship. Indeed, because virtually all members of the General Synod can get up to London and back home in a single day by a return ticket on the train, quite a large number of them discover themselves doing just that in order to run the committees and boards and councils of the General Synod. These functions of the General Synod require a multi-story church house for their servicing and a noble (and they are noble) quasi-bureaucratic staff of around 150 persons to keep it all going. To be a member of General Synod, as I am, is to have the

Durham, Professor David Jenkins of Leeds University—have recently attacked the General Synod as "unrepresentative." I think there are problems in getting "working" men and women into a synod that meets so frequently, but I yield to no one in my conviction that the synod is as representative as any Church of England body that could actually be had.

The Mission of the Church

Such then are some of the distinctive strengths and weaknesses of the Church of England. How, over the years, has it defined its mission and addressed itself to the corresponding task?

In terms of evangelism, it has been slow to acknowledge that the country of England is a place for mission at all. Until the day before yesterday "mission" meant overseas mission work—the "mission field." The assumption remained that the people of England basically "belonged" to the parish churches, even though they were casual about coming. In the early and mid-nineteenth century the great concern was with church-building—the fear being that if the people "out there" actually came, there would be no pews to seat them. How many there were who did not actually come was exposed first of all by the religious question in the census of 1851, and the answer was that the land of England fell into roughly three groups, each with between five and six million members on that day: those who attended Church of England services, those who attended other religious services (largely nonconformist), and those who did not attend worship at all. The Industrial Revolution was proceeding, and the new towns (particularly in the north of England) were being spawned without the slum-dwellers in them having any idea of Christianity and with particular abstinence from the Church of England. The clergy might baptize, marry, and bury, but people virtually unchurched were in vast tracts of new housing. It is astonishing to report that the notion of all parishioners "belonging" to their parish churches has survived to the present day when, since 1851, the total population of England has multiplied by two and a half, and the churchgoing population has declined to perhaps one-fifth of what it was then. Congregations of 100–200 in parishes with 10,000 or more inhabitants are viewed as thriving, and with more than 200 worshipers they are exceptionally good. Yet they may be less than two percent of the parishioners. The evidence is that the formal acceptance of all Englishmen as "Church of England" has not had any positive effect in public worship.

In 1945 there was a famous report, *Towards the Conversion of England*, which was subtitled *A Plan Dedicated to the Memory of Archbishop William Temple*. Temple had inspired it, and it was decades ahead of its time. Copies are much sought after to this day. But the point of note in this paper lies in the very title; the country needed a "conversion." I recall in my own undergraduate days in the mid-1950's that "conversion" was still a dirty word associated with firebrand evangelicals, such as, I suppose, I was. But the word had some faint respectability through its use in the title of this report. There was just a dawning possibility that conversion might become part of the agenda of the Church of England—a possibility strongly assisted in the mid-1950's by the coming of Billy Graham to Britain, with his unashamed message of conversion to Christ. The main avenue of evangelism, however, was still in those days assumed to be religious meetings, preaching meetings, to which unbelievers were invited on the assumption that there was enough Christianity in their background and their bones for them to be relatively at home in such meetings. No doubt there was such a penumbra to the Church, and in many areas there still is; but, equally, there were then and are now vast tracts of urban England where the people generally have absolutely no connection with the Church whatsoever, no instinct for the God whom we preach, no experience of Christian worship, and no desire for any of that at all—except possibly that they expect the undertaker to provide a clergyman to take a funeral service at the local crematorium when someone in the family dies.

If we put together the general Anglican presuppositions of the postwar years, we may arrive at the following uncomfortable list:

1. The people of England naturally belong to the Church of England, although they do not come every Sunday.
2. They can be drawn in a little closer by the clergyman's preaching on the one hand, and, on the other, by his ministrations to them at times of baptisms, marriages, and funerals.
3. The laity themselves should perhaps smile a little more at strangers at the church door, which will help to cement their notion that they "belong."

Of these, the first presupposition is, on the strength of the above analysis, palpably false. The second has never been believed by many in the first part—least of all by the Anglican clergy who have generally thought their sermons were valued principally in inverse proportion to their length—and, although widely believed in its second part, it has never yielded actual growth of any significance. It lays far too much weight on the role of the clergyman, and is exposed to its own counterthrust—that as many people leave church because of the clergyman as begin to come, and the more so when there has been a change of clergymen. The Church is being identified with the clergy, a view wholly in line with the inherited clericalism of Anglican clergy and laity, but wholly out of line with the New Testament or the needs of the times.

The third presupposition fixes the expectations placed upon the laity as low as those placed upon the clergy are high. The Church of England hitherto has had no notion, or at least very little notion, that the lay people are capable of articulate Christian action. The traditional program of Sunday worship has left them literally speechless; nowhere in the average Sunday has any individual spoken from his own experience or his own heart either to God in the presence of others or about God to others. If the clergy have taken evangelism seriously, they may have encouraged the laity to witness to Christ to their neighbors; but it is more likely that they have seen this witness in simply being good neighbors. If they have wanted Anglican Christians to speak about Christ, then their church program has done nothing to equip them to do so, and the laity have been correspondingly dumb about the Gospel when they have been with their unbelieving neighbors. The external partners in the Partners in Mission Consultation (1981) listed among the impediments to the proclamation of the Gospel "lack of knowledge of scripture and inability to share it" (*To a Rebellious House?* page 34); and as the list of impediments also included "contemporary apathy" and "English reserve," it is clear this is near the heart of the problem. But it is not generally seen that the problem relates to what Christians do when they are together. If they do not become articulate then, they will then not be articulate in the world.

For this we are unashamedly looking at what happens on Sundays, not at the nature of more specialist midweek meetings. If the people of God do not shed their corporate anonymity in Sunday worship, then not only do they remain infantile in relation to the speaking of the Gospel, but they also fail to relate to each other in such a way as to form a loving Christian community. The liturgical movement, and its characteristic Church of England expression of it, the parish communion, have emphasized the corporateness of the Church and built into our liturgical forms much mention of being "the body of Christ." The clergy have gone out of their way to insist on the point from the pulpit. The coffee gatherings after Sunday communion have tried to express the same truth. But the heart of it is still generally missing. The laity are left passive and inarticulate at the center of Sundays, and it is only the enthusiastic few who come to informal meetings during the week who start to articulate their faith. The average Sunday attender is left secure in the impression that he is there to receive gentle feeding or comfort and not at all to be trained as part of a Gospel fellowship. Thus the outsider has difficulty sensing that there is a loving fellowship. The most he will so often encounter is friendly groups having coffee, whose conversation is about anything but the Gospel, or alternatively an actual grasping of the hand during the Peace at the Eucharist, with an inarticulate mumble to accompany it.

In the New Testament evangelism was conducted through the power of the word of God ministered outside of formal church contexts and by the impact on unbelievers made by the actual persons of a Christian fellowship—an impact that came with the word proclaimed. The Church of England not only seems to have few starting points toward such a pattern of evangelism, but it is also hampered by presuppositions that run on from an establishment past and deter it from even seeking those starting points.

Of course, however, evangelism is only part of the mission of the Church and it cannot be conducted in a social vacuum. The Gospel must relate to the unemployed man, the abandoned wife, the trades union on strike, the ethnic minority, and so on. If the Church exists to seek to usher in the rule of Christ, then it must protest on behalf of those under injustice. Traditionally, this has often taken the form of church-operated charities, alleviating distress and tempering winds to shorn lambs, although the abolition of slavery and industrial legislation in the nineteenth century should not be forgotten. The charities were very often, although not always, administered by the clergy. But nowadays, not only has the welfare state taken over many of the charitable tasks done earlier in the Church, but it has also become clear that the "charity" outlook is wholly marginal to the actual needs of society. As David Sheppard, bishop of Liverpool, put it in his recent Dimbleby Lecture (April 17, 1984), we now have a "comfortable Britain" and alongside it a much-less-comfortable one. Although the Church of England, as shown above, has a presence of sorts in every area of every town in the land, it is yet visibly identified with "comfortable Britain." Numbers at public worship stay relatively high in such areas, giving of money can be sustained and increased, lay leaders may be discovered, weekends or longer periods at conference centers can be afforded, and the Christianity stays nicely within the middle-class family. Resources, human and material, which would be tremendously valued in the more working-class or even deprived area down the road go neglected in the "comfortable" congregation. And the Church of England generally can shut its eyes to the national scene. The central clergy appointment advisor has, within a few days of my writing this, drawn attention to the fact that the majority of the clergy wish to minister in the "comfortable" areas—no doubt for good reasons connected with which schools their children should attend, what jobs their wives can do, what success they can expect in communicating the Gospel, what intellectual rapport with their parishioners they can expect.

The main point, however, that I wish to make here is that on the national scene the social conditions are part of the concerns we have in the Church of England's mission. And here the question of establishment reenters the picture. It must not be misunderstood. The established position of the Church of England does not mean it becomes the lackey of this or that political party. It does not mean that the General Synod should not or does not criticize government policy; the synod can and does criticize, and has done so recently in respect of nuclear bombs, abortion, the British Nationality Act, and a host of other issues. But establishment does mean that the synod can appeal to certain broad moral, if not actually Christian, principles in addressing the state and must also watch lest its own stance on, for instance, divorce and second marriage, becomes so far distant from the law of the land that the Church of England clergy can no longer operate as national marriage registrars with good conscience. On social and political issues there is an advantage apparent in establishment, but it can easily turn into a disadvantage.

The Church of England is not afraid to address the state on such issues. But it has the greater difficulty of knowing how to address the state. A genuine Christian compassion leads easily to a left-of-center political position. A conscience in respect of being the "comfortable Britain" leads easily to a blow for the underdog, although it can look terribly paternalistic. But actual programs for political reform are always open to secular, political, and economic critiques; and neither the Church of England nor the British Council of Churches can expound a Christian political philosophy in such a way that is both ideologically well based and internally consistent and actually related to the political situation on the ground. A church that is in a minority in a nation must also beware lest it is indulging in an unwanted paternalism in telling a nation what is "good" for it, even if the nation is not wanting to go down that path. And the temptation then becomes all the stronger to take firm moral stances on, say, the political situation in South Africa or the foreign policy of Israel rather than on social ills nearer to home.

Perhaps the outstanding problem is one that is common to all Christians. It is the problem of integrating an evangelistic program with a political program. We are not lacking voices telling us to stick to men's spiritual well-being (even one recently that suggested that the clergy should "give up politics for Lent"), and there is a radical wing that at times seems to have forgotten God, and the Incarnation, and the "life of the world to come" altogether. I assume that other parts of the Anglican Communion—just like successive Assemblies of the World Council of Churches—are feeling the same tension.

What Should the Church of England Do?

When it comes to a practical program, the old "mother Church" has much to learn from her independent children. Indeed, it is not so long ago that Archbishop Ted Scott of Canada, when addressing our General Synod, remarked that there are those who wonder when the Church of England is going to "rejoin the Anglican Communion." By this he meant that at a whole series of points the Church of England is unlike the rest, and that the future lies with the rest rather than with the Church of England. And the sooner we realize it the better. As a Canadian he had in view our current nonrecognition of ordained women from Canada, which is felt as a serious breach of fellowship by those churches and provinces that have ordained women. But as a pan-Anglican he had in view our state connection, the incredibility of which seems to be apparent to everybody but English Anglicans. Theologically, establishment is virtually indefensible. At one time it could be expounded as the proper expression of sovereignty in a sovereign Christian nation. But now that it is recognized that the nation is not Christian and is arguably secular and possibly pluralist, the case for Parliament running the Church is absurd. Indeed, it is felt to be so by many parliamentarians themselves. But no action for disestablishing has been begun in Parliament, and the onus for making the case and initiating the action lies on the Church of England itself. In general the Church of England has been content to see that progress toward total independence of the Church from the state was occurring, without worrying too much about the speed at which the progress was being made. And this makes for virtual inertia.

Apart from the indefensibility in theory of establishment, many practical problems flow from it. Notable among these are the following:

First we do not choose our own bishops, although we now do have a very strong advisory say in their appointment. We are not free, as I would advocate, to have open election of bishops by, for instance, an electoral college. We are simply not free.

Second, we find ourselves with a curious ministry to the thousands of English people beyond the plausible boundaries of the worshiping Church. This could be sheer gain if the laity at large could exercise it and did not involve our conniving with the "world" as though it were the Church. It is arguably a terrible loss if the burden falls upon the clergy, as tradition and, up to a point, the law make it do.

Third, we are subject to the occasional humiliating exercise, like the one I attended in the House of Lord's gallery a fortnight ago (April 11, 1984) when there was debate about a private member's bill that would have taken back to Parliament powers already devolved upon the Synod—that is, the powers in relation to the parochial choices between ancient and modern language services. The bill would have enabled 20 percent of the electoral roll of a parish to force the use of the 1662 prayer book upon an incumbent once a month. The debate proceeded in large part upon the premise "we own the Church of England," and the defense of the bishops present was to say "things are not as bad as you are saying" rather than "this House ought to give up any pretense at these powers." To be fair, there were episcopal speeches to the effect that the House would be unwise to attempt to legislate for the Church of England, and these voices helped lead to the point at which the bill was withdrawn. In July 1984 the House of Commons acted similarly when it rejected a measure (of a largely cosmetic sort) passed overwhelmingly in the Synod.

Fourth, on some fronts it is not clear whether the Church of England is asserting some doctrinal nonnegotiability about establishment. I am peculiarly conscious of this in relation to Roman Catholic dialogue. My friend Julian Charley, a member of both the old and the new Anglican-Roman Catholic International Commission (ARCIC), tells me how establishment puzzles Roman Catholics. The Church of England owes it to international Anglicanism to make it clear that it is not an article of faith, and, insofar as it is an accident of history, it is up for reform.

Fifth, the Church of England cannot unite with any other church. To my mind it is astonishing that a Christian body with all the brave talk about being a "bridge church" and "ecumenical movement in one denomination," both "catholic and reformed," should in fact cling to old-fashioned privileges of a sort that forbid true integration with other ecclesiastical bodies. The Anglican-Methodist scheme of the years 1956 to 1972 and the Convenant for Unity of the years 1974 to 1982 were both affected by this fatal flaw—that the Church of England could not and would not unite with any other body and could only talk about changing the pattern of relationships with others, largely by episcopalianizing them. The end result was that an apparently costless scheme was drawn up in each case, and this was lost because opponents could raise the enthusiasm to find flaws (and there were plenty); whereas, proponents had so little actual ecumenical progress to offer. It was not even institutional joinery; it was mere institutional juxtaposition.

At the time of writing I am on a working party on "local ecumenical development," which involves drafting considerable legislation, ultimately intended to go to Parliament, to give the faintest of permission for Anglican and nonepiscopal clergy to share the ministry in ecumenical congregations.

In sum, the establishment of the Church of England tends to define the Church as the clergy (or sometimes as the synod) because there is no "body of the faithful" at all. As Schmemann says about Justinian, so we can say of the present establishment—that it unites church and state by simply abolishing the Church. The Church is only reidentified as the pilgrim people of God as it strives to shake free of the state, and to live its own life, answerable only to its Lord.

The point came home to me the more strongly when I found myself in debate with Professor Martin about the use of the 1662 prayer book. He was the chief rallying point of those who wished to keep the old book in regular use and were claiming (as they still claim) that the wicked clergy were bamboozling an innocent laity into using the Alternative Service Book and other modern services, contrary to their own desires and certainly contrary to their souls' health. In the argument, I began to detect that a wholly different understanding of the role of the Church of England underlay our differences about the language of worship. He conceived of the Church as a national, spiritual welfare agency, with its local officer (the clergyman) functioning in his local office (the parish church) in order to provide a standard welfare benefit (a prayer book service) to all those who come. In his view the benefit could be no more changed by local voting than could the antidote for snakebite. The mere fact that most of the citizens most of the time were not availing themselves of a benefit for which they felt no great need had no implications whatsoever for the character of the benefit that should be on offer and available when the needy do show up.

My own opposed view may help move us on from the traps of the establishment question. There is a people of God, expressed in local congregations but united in a catholic fellowship; and they are separate from the world in principle and have a message for the world and a mission to the world. Establishment not only abolishes the Church; by the same action it abolishes the world. It is no accident that the 1662 prayer book, of a nation assumed in that age to be wholly conformist and "C of E," has no concept of mission at all. Let the boundaries be drawn too tightly or too loosely (and mistakes can certainly be made), and there may be problems. But let no boundaries be drawn, and there is catastrophe. The Church of England shows some signs of "converted" life today because the Gospel has thrust through the "establishment" encrustation and is by its own God-given vigor setting up a half-discerned alternative to it. The future lies with this alternative.

This is not to suggest that the only change the Church of England needs to make in its life is in the area of its formal links to the state. There are many needed reforms that can only follow on from the ending of establishment, but there are many that need not wait. I have already dropped broad hints about a trained, informed, and witnessing laity. The sense that baptism is the commissioning of lay people to be soldiers and servants (witnesses and missionaries) of the Lord Christ needs urgent recovery. The creation of a loving fellowship, a company of Christ, unashamed of Him in every parish, can be the aim immediately. There are tremendous implications in this for Sunday worship, not least in what it implies for the restructuring of many of our Victorian buildings. There may also be midweek implications, particularly if unemployment can be handled creatively, as releasing many voluntary energies for the work of Christ, as well as defensively as a great social problem. But there are also implications for the work of the ordained ministry.

At first glance the answer is simple: The clergy are there to teach and train the laity. But there are many nuanced statements of this sort around, and the main statement itself evades large contemporary questions. Is the minister, for instance, to be a jack of all trades, or a specialist, or even a kind of holy man wholly other than the laity he is to train? And, of course, can "he" be "she"? Does it make any difference that a bishop's hands were laid on an Anglican minister's head, but only presbyters' hands on a Presbyterian or Methodist minister's head? Some of the doctrinal questions here are before our churches in both the ARCIC report and also the Lima statement *Baptism, Eucharist and Ministry*. The practical ones constantly get *a posteriori* answers in England—for instance, through the coming of the nonstipendiary ministry and then through the "local nonstipendiary ministry." Each of these involves ordination to a kind of "tent-making" ministry (in total breach of the terms of the 1662 Ordinal), and each has appeared on the scene before the ideological questions have been properly handled. And still the selection conferences of the Church of England propel upward of 300 candidates per annum into college or part-time course training with a view to their being ordained to fulfill between now and 2024 a ministry of a character that is quite undetermined. We receive them gladly; we train them for we know not what.

The Church of England has, interestingly, had a go recently at defining a "Strategy for Ministry." This is the title of the major report by the Advisory Council on Church's Ministry (ACCM) written by the chief secretary, Canon John Tiller, and published in September 1983. He envisages the end of the pocket-hand-kerchief-sized independent parish served by its own minister and even to the present day still appointed by any one of a number of heterogeneous "patrons" or "trustees." Instead, the "local church" would be a unit comprising several congregations (perhaps like a Methodist circuit), with a ministry of mixed character that is leading, serving, and servicing it. The "mix" would include lay and ordained, men and women, stipendiary and nonstipendiary, and "diocesan" and local. A fairly traditional-looking bishop would have oversight of the many "local churches" in his diocese, but—through the existence of the (slightly undefined) diocesan clergy—would have more scope for reinforcing the ministry in different places than he currently has.

In my own publishing capacity, I have recently published

Whose Hand on the Tiller? a Grove booklet responding to the Tiller report. Here four contributors offer alternative ways forward, with a greater conserving of the existing parish structure. They press more strongly than Tiller himself does for the total mobilization of the laity, the full use of the gifts that exist among them, and a proper oversight of such ministry by the ordained pastors. They call for "resource-parishes," which, being strong themselves, can send flying or temporary help to the weak to get established. While the general desire to make the inert Church of England adaptable to fast-changing times is still there, the differences of perspective from Tiller partly reflect their parochial standpoint (for his, by his office, is more of a bird's eye view) and partly reflect the character of the Tiller report that it is presented to the Church of England for the stimulation of debate with a view to clarifying the strategy needed for the future. Sadly, it looks as though General Synod's handling of the Tiller report in November 1983 and February 1984 is such as to kill it with faint praise. Perhaps the initiatives have to come from unexpected places (as so often in the past), and central planning may have difficulties in getting the strategy right.

But above all, the Church of England needs faith in God. All its liturgical life, all its role in the life of society, all its responsibility for burying the dead and touching the penumbra of the Church, all its prestige (if such there be) in the Anglican Communion, all its inherited wealth, all its voluntary institutions—all are nothing if they are not the outward expression of a true inward grasp on Jesus Christ, with the vigor needed in this day to make Him known. It is His life in our life that will "send" us on His mission in the world.

Mission and Church Identity

The Most Reverend Paul A. Reeves

The search for a relevant ecclesiology and identity for the Church in New Zealand is not a process of discarding the foreign and inherited as opposed to what may be authentically New Zealand. There is a flow of church history; so much of our New Zealand church history has its antecedents in "Western" church history. The continuing task, however, must be seen as a search for and an exploration of our identity in the contemporary New Zealand situation. The universal expresses itself in the particular. The demand is not so much to maintain the "universal characteristics of the Church," but to be authentic manifestations of the Church in a particular context.

Incarnation is the opposite of foreignness. The Church is not to be foreign to its community and its historical context. The two primary contexts that the New Zealand church has to grapple with and relate to one another are the biblical context on the one hand and the New Zealand context and its setting in the modern world on the other.

In the New Zealand context the following issues are very important:

The Issue of Wealth
There was a time when New Zealand was comparatively egalitarian in its distribution of wealth and opportunities and when its geographical isolation meant that national wealth was not brought into awkward juxtaposition with world poverty. That time has passed. The quest for social and economic security provided for free education, and health service, labor legislation, and provision for old-age and children's allowances. But now the gap between rich and poor in New Zealand is widening. Symptomatic of this is the growing incidence of unemployment in New Zealand society. The gap between rich and poor nations is widening, and New Zealand remains identified with the rich of the First World.

The Issue of Race

The proportion of Maoris and Polynesians from the Pacific in New Zealand's population is growing. These same people have migrated to the cities where they are to be found substantially among the urban poor. Relationships between races is being severely tested in New Zealand over issues such as the distribution of land, adequacy of health services, provision of housing, opportunities for employment, and the administration of the law. Within the geographical area of the diocese of Auckland, Maoris and Polynesians have a disproportionately high percentage of their number among the low income earners. Some believe that the industrialized New Zealand society requires a controlled low income work force. If that is so, Maori communities in particular will continue to bear the brunt of this economic policy. How can the Church best minister the Gospel of reconciliation to a fragmenting society whose several cultural roots are eroding and whose dividing lines are drawn more and more on issues of wealth and color?

The Issue of Pluralism

Consensus on the fundamentals of religion, morals, justice, and education does not exist. Christianity is but one element in this pluralism. In 1926, 4.9% of the New Zealand population either had no religious adherence or refused to declare it. The figures rose steadily over subsequent years: 1966, 10.0%; 1971, 10.6%; then rapidly, 1976, 17.2%; 1981, 23.5%. Over the same period (1926–1981), Anglican adherents declined from 40.9% of the population to 25.6%, with the most significant indicator being the accelerating rate of decline. Compared with the 2.1% drop from 1971 to 1976, the 1976–1981 figure was 3.5%, which is a decrease in membership from 915,202 in 1976 to 807,132 in 1981.

The Issue of Family Life and Human Relations

There is widespread concern about the family unit, some of it based more on emotion than on evidence and sometimes in terms of a very narrow view of what constitutes a family. But clearly, family life is both changing and undergoing strain. New social norms for sexual behavior; the changing role of women and men in the family, society, and the Church; smaller families and the erosion of local community by shifts in population—these are some of the factors that, for better or for worse, affect family life.

The Issue of Authority

There is a widespread change in leadership patterns, especially as this is experienced by many children in schools and families and by people in business management. The change is from a hierarchical to a more democratic participatory style. This is in marked contrast to a growing distrust and alienation of many people from the institutions of civil government, which are perceived increasingly in terms of mere power rather than legitimate authority. It is also in marked contrast to the trend to authoritarianism evident among those threatened by social change.

The End of Isolation

Those who left England in the 1840's were either ready to sacrifice their cultural roots or mistaken in supposing that they would transplant easily in New Zealand. They unloaded their pianos from the sailing ships and tuned them again in wooden houses filled with mementos from home, but the old songs never did sound the same again. In fact traditional links with Britian have been weakening since the days of the first European settlement. Rex Fairburn, a noted man of letters writing in the 1930's, said: "I have an increasing conviction that I shan't be able to stay away from New Zealand indefinitely. Men are not free. They are bound by fate to certain things and lose their souls in escaping. This natural scene in England is lovely but I have no sympathy with it. I had rather be beside a smelly New Zealand creek." The weakening of these links has precipitated a far-reaching reevaluation of New Zealand's position in the world. The nation has had to find new trading partners (Russia, Iran, Japan) and to decide what strategy of military alignment (or nonalignment) best suits its economic and social interests.

This list of issues is not exhaustive. A church, however, whose orientation and manner of operation meant that it was ignoring these issues would run the risk of irrelevance and isolation from many people in New Zealand society. Specifically, can the Church of the Province of New Zealand evolve into a genuine "church of the people," in which ministry is not limited by the availability of money and stipendiary clergy? If so, it will be the people in low income areas who will shape the direction and content of the ministry of the Church. Or will the Church resist such a movement and become increasingly tied to the wealthier sections of New Zealand society because of a combination of financial con-

208 Paul A. Reeves

straint and a clericalist model of ministry that is theologically
indefensible?

There are three particular matters concerning the polity of the
Church that bring the issues I have cited into focus and that
provide as well a way of giving expression to the nature of the
Church's mission in New Zealand. The issues are the nature of
episcopacy, the nature of ministry, and the nature and place of
authority in the Anglican Communion.

THE CHURCH, THE TREATY, AND THE BISHOPRIC OF AOTEAROA

Let us look first at the nature of episcopacy and its relation in the
New Zealand context to mission. I shall make this investigation
by tracing the development of the office of bishop in New Zealand. The story begins over a hundred years ago.

For the first forty years of the nineteenth century, the British
Government had done its level best to stay out of the affairs of the
European settlement in New Zealand. Nevertheless the growing
European population and the prodding of the Church Missionary
Society forced it to act. On February 6, 1840, a treaty was signed
between the representative of the British Crown and various Maori
chiefs. But ever since then, the meaning of what was actually
transacted has been the subject of debate and argument. It has not
been helped by the fact that "the Treaty of Waitangi was hastily
and inexpertly drawn up, ambiguous and contradictory in context, chaotic in execution."[1] No wonder, if as an historian says,
colonial office policy in 1840 was to "obtain sovereignty, incur no
avoidable expense, see what happens."[2] The English text of the
treaty (which is always quoted) differs significantly in meaning
from the Maori text, which is what the Maori chiefs at that time
signed.

Yet through 140 years of uneasy history since 1840 lies the hope
that the Treaty of Waitangi can be the basis for a social contract in
New Zealand. It provides the foundation for a partnership concerned with the Maori's ability to maintain and develop their
culture and institutions in the same way that *Pakehas* ("white
people") are able to maintain and develop theirs and to use the
resources of the state to achieve these ends.

The Anglican Church played an important part when the Treaty
of Waitangi was signed. Beyond question, the missionaries "held
the confidence of the Maoris. . . . It was upon this missionary

body that Hobson (the Crown representative) had been instructed to place his chief reliance and it was to this group that the Crown owed that peaceful transfer of sovereignty which was shortly to take place."[3] I believe that the Anglican Church in New Zealand has the responsibility to ensure that the treaty that it actively supported in 1840 can still be the basis for a social contract or living partnership today.

That partnership at present has an uncomfortable uncertainty about it. In my estimation, democracy safeguards the rights of individuals but does not readily safeguard the rights of a group, especially if it is in a minority. Maori language, Maori institutions, and Maori values are group possessions that have been denied real substance. Maori land is also a group possession. The alienation and sale of this land as a result of warfare, confiscation, and social disintegration is a continuing source of frustration and resentment.

The annual ceremony to commemorate the Treaty of Waitangi has increasingly become a focus for Maori discontent. This year a group of people, which swelled from a couple of hundred to two thousand strong, walked in a peaceful and disciplined manner from an initial assembly point to Waitangi in the Bay of Islands, a distance of three hundred miles. The bishop of Aotearoa and I joined the head of the column, or *hikoi*, as it neared Waitangi. We came to a narrow bridge, and it was here that the *hikoi* was stopped by the police. The sun was beating down, some of the older marchers were beginning to be affected, and as the negotiations dragged on tension mounted. The leaders were determined that what had been an entirely peaceful operation should not descend into confusion and violence. Prayers were said—some of them traditional, some of them Christian, but all of them fervent. We moved on to the bridge but were stopped again. Eventually the police allowed the *hikoi* to cross the bridge and assemble on an open space on the other side. The intention to present a petition to the representative of the British Crown, the governor-general, was frustrated because the police insisted that only one hundred people should go forward to meet Sir David Beattie. The *hikoi*, which was walking under the banner of the Kotahitanga (Unity) movement, decided that such a restrictive condition was unacceptable. Time ran out before anything else could be negotiated.

From that experience, three things stay with me that are vital for the Church's understanding of its mission in New Zealand. First, there is what I call a theology of the land. When one thinks

of life one thinks of one's mother. A Maori viewpoint is that
the land is *Papa-tua-nuku,* our "earth mother." We love her as a
mother is loved. It is through her, the portal of *Hine-ahu-one*
("earth-formed maid") that we entered this world. We will return
to the bosom of *Papa-tua-nuku* through the portal of *Hine-nui-te-
po* ("maiden of darkness"). When someone says, "land is my
mother," it means that in the land they dig down to the deep and
basic things about life. They are in tune with the rhythm and the
movement of life—the tilling, the sowing, the growing, the reap-
ing, and so on. And as they work the land they are engaged in the
sacred act of bringing life to birth. To rob people who believe this
about land is to rob them of life. Land is their right to life, to
power, and to eternity. It is not something to be given up easily.
We are part of God's creation—His world—and to be redeemed
people means that we approach creation with a care and a reverence and with a sense of responsibility.

The second is a theology of hope. This century has seen a mood
of buoyant hope turned into a common mood of deep anxiety.
People have learned to distrust themselves. There is great activity
but little hope. Hope points to possibilities that presently lie beyond our situation, which for many Maoris is a situation of deprivation and grievance. Hope starts with the belief that this is God's
world; and since He made it, it remains His world—a world in
which God's purposes will ultimately be brought to pass. There is
a deep hope born of the conviction that God is at work in the
world identifying with those who are humiliated, suffering with
those who are alienated, and constantly seeking ways to heal and
bring wholeness. This hope that the new creation is on its way
sustains the little flock that seeks to cooperate with God's redemptive activity.

First Timothy 4:10 says, "the point of all our toiling and battling is that we have put our trust in the living God and he is the
savior of the whole human race but particularly of all believers."
Christ is the Savior, particularly of all believers. Christian hope is
expressed in a committed fellowship of sisterhood and brotherhood. God's mission of hope calls forth a concrete human
agency, the people of hope, the Church. But Christ is also the
Savior of the whole human race, and so the special nature of the
Church does not mean an exclusive privilege or even monopoly of
hope. The Church and Christians have no rights or ownership but
only the privilege of mission. Mission points beyond the boundaries of the Church. The hope of Israel becomes the hope of all

nations. There is a wideness and breadth about hope. The Church may be the cradle of hope but certainly not its prison. Hope searches both for the unity of the Church and the unity of humankind.

The third is a spirituality for struggle. The increasing tensions, conflicts, and frustrations that people experience as they get involved in struggles for justice demand their price. Prayer, worship, and reflection remain at the heart of any spirituality for struggle needed to sustain a long and costly commitment. We will need to explore deeply Christian modes of resistance to the powers of oppression and death. What does the *kenosis* of Christ imply for Christians in situations of violence and counterviolence? There must be a stronger emphasis on genuine communities of faith whose members share a common hope and offer each other support as they struggle for justice and reflect on their experience in the light of the Bible. There must be a stronger sense of God the Holy Spirit at work in the world. We suffer from a narrow and ecclesiastical understanding of the Spirit who is frequently spoken of as a kind of possession of the Church. Contemporary renewal movements in "rediscovering" the Spirit have too often trivialized Him. Alongside the New Testament's emphasis on the Spirit of the Church and the lives of individual Christians, we need to set the Old Testament's witness to the power of the Spirit in creation and in the unfolding of human history. We need to see ourselves as part of a renewal movement that is as profound as God's purpose for His world.

In the bishopric of Aotearoa, the Church of the Province of New Zealand has a vital means of encouraging a Maori identity and exploring a Maori/non-Maori partnership. It has as well an opportunity to give expression to the importance for Maoris of the land, to speak a word of hope, and to develop a spirituality for struggle. Significant legislation was enacted in 1978. The intention was to give more freedom and authority to the office of the bishop of Aotearoa by associating the office with the primate rather than with a diocesan bishop. The bishop of Aotearoa was provided with a council elected by Maoris, and the council acts as a synod for the support of the bishop. If the bishop of Aotearoa believes that a priest proposed by a diocesan bishop for work among the Maori people is suitably trained and adequately equipped, he issues his letters of authority. This provision now gives the bishop of Aotearoa a direct influence, by right, over the staffing of Maori work. It means that the bishop of Aotearoa is able to define his clerical team precisely, and it helps to clarify the meaning of the partnership between the bishop of Aotearoa and the diocesan bishops created by the General Synod of 1978. The diocesan bishop still licenses the priest and can revoke the license. Quite obviously to act in this way without the support of the bishop of Aotearoa would be a serious and perhaps intolerable situation.

When the Archbishop of Canterbury visited New Zealand in 1983, he was presented with a collection of essays written by members of the bishopric of Aotearoa. In one of those essays Chief Judge Durie wrote:

> As with most partnerships it is important that the partners be equal if the partnership is not to founder in unwarranted suspicions. Our Church laws have been carefully drafted to ensure that the Bishop of Aotearoa is as an equal Bishop and that his Council operates on parity with equivalent bodies within the Church. This is important for me as a Maori. "Standing" is the basis for my culture and the standing of the Bishop as my Father, determines also where I stand in relation to my Church. I consider the equality of the Bishop of Aotearoa to be important, not just for me and mine, but for the whole Church. The Bishopric symbolises the equality of all people.[4]

In a fundamental way the bishopric of Aotearoa legislation invites us to do for the Church what the Treaty of Waitangi desires for the life of the nation. In the end Christianity is not an institution but truths and propositions about life. If we can understand what partnership between Maori and Pakeha means in the life of the Church, then we can also look to our national life and discover what true partnership between Maori and Pakeha means in education, health services, judicial processes, employment opportunities, housing policy, land resources, and so on. That is a process that has its tensions as we adjust to changes in decision making and the sharing of resources within the life of the Church. It is significant that the council of the bishopric of Aotearoa put the following motion to the General Synod in May 1983:

> That whereas the Treaty of Waitangi has significance in our nation's history and a continuing prominence in the affairs of our nation. . . Now therefore General Synod hereby resolves to establish a bicultural Commission;
> —to study the Treaty of Waitangi and to consider whether any principles of partnership and bicultural development are implied and the nature of any such principles that may serve as indicators for further growth and development;
> —to consult with Maori and non-Maori people thereon at such marae and other venues as may be appropriate;

—to advise General Synod on any ways and means to embody the principles of the Treaty in the legislation, institutions and general life of the Church of the Province of New Zealand:
and
appoint six persons to be now nominated and elected by the General Synod to constitute that Commission with one of the persons to be named as convener;
and
notes that the Bishopric of Aotearoa is prepared to fund from its own resources or elsewhere $10,000 for this purpose, and resolves to provide $10,000.

In 1981 the Primates' Conference made a guarded response to a presentation on the bishopric of Aotearoa. For African bishops, tribal divisions are real political issues. They saw the bishopric as a divisive rather than a unifying factor. Archbishop Burnett of Cape Town was even more forthright in his diocesan paper of June 1981. "As a son of God in Christ I still wear some cultural clothes, however, and the way I express my sonship may be coloured by them, but essentially sonship is expressed by the obedience of faith which is expected of one who is baptised into the death and resurrection of Christ. That death includes divesting myself of my cultural clothing in order to allow the lord of life to determine how much of that is consistent with the life of a son and how much I need to retain." One is uncomfortably reminded of a saying repeated by Bishop Ting of China: "One more Christian one less Chinese." We must acknowledge that Christ speaks to culture, speaks from within a culture, and remains a stumbling block to all cultures. But culture is certainly not something that you take off and put on like an overcoat. Culture is the way in which people do things together. It is the life force that holds those people together over a period of time. Culture tends to be what white people identify in others. They have great difficulty in identifying the signs and symbols of their own culture.

It is very noticeable that minority groups in other parts of the world are taking a great interest in the bishopric of Aotearoa. They have been subjected to the same experience of powerlessness within the life of the Church. Rarely to any significant extent are they represented in the episcopate of a national church. Colonial exploitation, land rights, loss of language, and culture form a common agenda. We can expect a strengthening of links between the bishopric of Aotearoa, native Canadians and Americans, Hawaiians, Australian aborigines, and so on. The precious gift that minority groups offer is the realization that the unity of the Church can contain pluralities of structures, theologies, and spiritualities. Where the tensions between unity and diversity are experienced, the Church is likely to be alive and adventurous.

The bishopric of Aotearoa is part of a religiocultural search that is going on under various guises. There are stirrings among the Torres Strait Islanders of Northern Queensland for their own bishop. The Order of Ethiopia, within the Church of the Province of South Africa, has its own bishop, clergy, and parishes, mainly for Xhosa-speaking people. In 1982, while visiting Canada, I was given the following note:

> In the civil Province of Quebec there are two Dioceses (Montreal, Quebec) and four others with some of their territory in the Province. . . . Francophone congregations are scattered in the Province but there should be a common mission body/Francophone jurisdiction that can cross diocesan boundaries. However some Diocesan authorities, afraid of encroachment on territory, block common Francophone endeavours. Francophones feel crushed by Anglophone imperialism. It is worsened when the Church, being mostly Anglophone, does the same. Can Francophones feel comfortable in an Anglophone Church? The cry of Quebec, vis-a-vis the rest of Canada, is that we want to be "maitre de chez nous" (masters in our own house). Can they be maitre de leur eglise (masters in their own Church)? Or do Francophones have to become Anglophones to be Anglicans?

I can respond to those questions from Canada with great sympathy. Perhaps Maoris and Pakehas in New Zealand and native peoples, Francophones, and Anglophones in Canada are involved in a common struggle as they seek to understand unity and diversity.

MINISTRY, LAY AND ORDAINED

A second issue that brings into focus the mission of the Church in New Zealand is the pattern of ministry, lay and ordained, it ought to develop. In New Zealand, the Church's dominant model for ordained ministry is the parish priest. It is this model with which lay people are both familiar and comfortable. Lay people sometimes fail, therefore, to understand or value the ministry of a priest whose focus and creation of ministry is outside the gathered and settled congregation. This institutional view of the ordained ministry poses particular difficulties because over the past fifteen years a group of people have been ordained deacon or priest with an original vision of fulfilling a priestly role in which they might exercise that vocation in partnership with their other vocation or paid employment, parenting, or voluntary community work. Even where such employment was with a church agency, the distinctive work of the ministry was its bivocational nature.

The nonstipendiary ministry as we began to call it contained many sharp challenges to current church thinking and practice. Vocation had become an individualistic matter between a person and God. Most bishops have had the unhappy experience of being pursued by some individual who wants to be ordained because God had called him, but is not open to the possibility that this may not be what God is saying. We began to see that vocation is really the calling of the Church expressed in individuals but shared by all. It was a viewpoint that encouraged us to visit local communities and ask them to put forward the one they believed could be a priest. We came to see that ministry depends on vocation and not on training. Certainly training should nurture vocation, but it can never replace vocation. Theological colleges seemed to be following a model of academic excellence and as institutions never related completely or successfully to the context of ministry. As a consequence several dioceses began to develop schemes of training people within their local context.

The original vision stressed the workplace rather than the residential parish and the evangelistic rather than the pastoral role of the priest. What has happened is that, to a greater or lesser degree, the dominant, parochially-based structure of the Church has eroded this vision. The task of reconciling or even acknowledging the respective worth of two different models of ministry—the parish-based ministry and the ministry that revolves around a priest's secular employment—has not been achieved. For too long we have been struggling with an inadequate understanding of priesthood as leading and doing things on behalf of other people. The task is still to understand priesthood, in a parish or at the workplace, as serving and enabling others to be fulfilled and obedient to the call of God.

The task is easier to state than to accomplish. Nonstipendiary clergy judge their acceptance by the congregations to be high, and this appears to be the case. Mostly this is because they have had a high profile in the parish before ordination. In those instances where nonstipendiary clergy are choosing to interpret their priesthood in the workplace or away from the parish they are less certain of the support and understanding of the congregations. Someone said that theological colleges prepare people to exercise leadership in communities where there is already leadership. One of the difficulties of nonstipendiary ministry is that it may place people of initiative and leadership within a set of relationships and expectations that effectively stifle their gifts.

Quite obviously a system of licensing clergy that presupposes parish ministry and little else no longer fits our evolving situation. Random geographical features, such as where a person lives or worships, should not necessarily determine where and to whom that nonstipendiary priest is licensed. If the issue is considered from the standpoint of a question such as "Who is the person best equipped to support the ministry of this particular priest?" the answer may be the bishop or some other person of appropriate standing. For some of our nonstipendiary clergy, their license will emphasize their diocesan rather than parochial role. Our licenses are presently being examined by a commission of the General Synod.

Another area of concern is that some of our nonstipendiary priests are experiencing the pressure of having too much to do and not enough time in which to do it. Availability is a problem for those who focus their ministry in the parish and hold down full-time employment at the same time or have heavy family commitments. Women priests are reporting stress. Theirs seems to be a double role of being both a woman and also a priest in the life of the Church. Conversely some of our most creative work is being done by these same women who exhibit a strong feminine spirituality and whose efforts to "re-image" God are already affecting our liturgies and who understand what oppression means in society because they have been victims of the same oppressive forces.

Between 1968 and 1983 thirty-five men and fourteen women were ordained to a nonstipendiary priesthood within the diocese of Auckland. Nearly all of them state that their ordination has created new openings for ministry and new relationships. It remains a challenge for the Church to ensure that this enrichment is used to its fullest potential. So there is hope for the nonstipendiary ministry. The frustration is that the original vision of a ministry carried out among the people with whom the priest lives and works, a ministry in which both priest and laity are freed from unhelpful understandings of authority and restrictive relationships, has not completely materialized.

What are some of the dangers in this development of ministry? Specifically, the nonstipendiary ministry can perpetuate the clericalism that is alive and well in the Church of the Province of New Zealand and needs no further encouragement to reduce the great questions about ministry to questions about the Ordained Ministry. Clericalism is about the misuse of power to the deprivation of some and the advantage of others with a myriad of control mechanisms which lock us into an unjust system. In the end, there is little difference between the language and assumptions of clericalism, racism, sexism, or classism.

In the Church of the Province of New Zealand a disproportionate amount of time, creative effort, and money is devoted to training people for ordination, compared with the task of supporting and encouraging those who want to exercise their ministry as lay men or women. This is partly due to the very rich endowments of the Provincial Theological College in Auckland. Likewise, the Church is missing out on its contact with low income communities through its commitment to a model of a church-centered ministry requiring a high level of maintenance because of paid clergy, high-cost buildings, administrative and training structures. At some point the laity have to decide to be the Church, be about their ministry, and stop waiting to be authorized by the clergy. One very interesting and potent model for doing just that is the program called Development Education, offered by the Ecumenical Secretariat on Development (ESOD), an agency sponsored by the Roman Catholic Church and the National Council of Churches of New Zealand. The program drew on two approaches that had their origins in action for justice. One was the action-reflection-action model of "conscientization" as developed by the Brazilian educator Paulo Freire. The model enables people to accept responsibility for their own lives, renounce dehumanizing structures and influences, and construct their own vision of a just society. The other approach was that of Community Organization pioneered by Saul Alinsky and others, which offers strategies of mobilizing people and assists them to establish and achieve realistic goals that lead to a redistribution of power in the community.

ESOD realized that development education serves two distinct constituencies, the advantaged and the disadvantaged in society. It is the middle class community who fill the pews and pay the bills. The same people are to be found on church committees. What must be dealt with is not simply their commitment to the Gospel but their comprehension of what that Gospel is and what it requires of them. On the other hand, some low income groups— such as health groups, work trusts, preschool groups—are using methods of analysis and group process to design their own reflective processes out of which theology and ministry are born. The two constituencies were effectively brought together within a program called "Education for Social Change" or "Structural Analysis." The program enables groups of oppressed people to analyze their situation and groups of Christians to determine those points at which they can most effectively assist the struggles of the poor for justice, dignity, and liberation. The Gospel for the economically oppressed speaks of liberation from the shackles of slavery to other people's greed; it speaks of a worker being worthy of his or her hire; of the last being first; and the mighty and the proud being overthrown. The Gospel for the economically powerful speaks of shedding power in order to pass through the needle's eye; of a vine owner paying his workers equally; of the evil of usury; and the sorrow of the rich man unable to divest himself of his wealth. Quite obviously there are spiritual dangers in seeking to act for justice and peace. Under the guise of doing things for others, it is possible for someone to communicate personal obsession, aggressiveness, and prejudice. I observe people for whom structural analysis is important also working on a spirituality, nurtured by Word and Sacrament, which will sustain them in their witness and ministry. "The personal is political" is an oft-repeated phrase. The life and writings of Thomas Merton, whose father was a New Zealander, speak to them. In Henri Nouwen's words, "Perhaps Merton's most important discovery was the discovery of his fellow man at the depths of his own solitude. . . . Through purification and solitude 'God alone' became 'together with all men.' In silence Merton discovered that being a monk is preeminently a social calling."[5] One of my priests wrote to me, "There needs to be an alliance between the empty parts of ourselves and the pains of the poor." She added, "If we are made in the image of God, who we are becoming may point towards who God is."

The relationship of this program with the institutional churches is uneasy. Development education has never been slow to point out that while the Church's language is concerned for the liberation and redemption of humankind, the Church's institutional behavior has more often than not led to its identification as one of the oppressive agents in society. The middle class fears chaos within its own systems. It is uncomfortable with the knowledge that people once denied access to the radical faith of Christ might now decide to use their new-found faith to turn the tables of middle class contentedness. Each year, ESOD promotes Christian Action Week. In 1983, when the theme was "Homelessness," a group of homeless "street kids" squatted in a house owned by an Anglican social welfare agency and highlighted the fact that the Church owns much real estate and with several notable exceptions uses it for purposes that have little to do with the poor. New Zealand is a society where status is gained from the value placed on material possessions and on numbers. The Church reinforces those values that contain and restrict the poor instead of evangelizing and liberating society from these structures and ways of thinking.

ESOD completed its mandate in September 1984, but plans are already afoot to replace it. Persons influenced by agencies such as this do not sit comfortably within the institutional Church that they may now perceive in very different ways from what used to be the case. Some sit loosely on a denominational attachment, but a substantial number are to be found somewhere in the institutional Church. Their hope is to set the poor free to express their wisdom and power and also to free the middle class to change and receive the Good News the poor may bring. We are not good at handling conflict either within the fellowship of the Church or with society. The reality is that building the Kingdom often means conflict. The deep conflicts opened up in New Zealand by the visit of a South African rugby team in 1981 are still with us in the form of divisions and of tacit understandings to avoid certain topics in conversation. Some conflicts must be managed, but others must be won. When a crisis strikes, Christians are faced with a range of impulses to be prophetic, pastoral, and to search for common ground with an erstwhile opponent. To most that is a puzzling and unreal task. We are still searching for ways to live with diversity and pluralism.

AUTHORITY AND TRUST WITHIN THE ANGLICAN COMMUNION

Finally, we must look briefly at the nature of authority in the Anglican Communion and the relation of that authority to the mission of the Church in New Zealand. Describing the spirit of Anglicanism, Paul Elmer More speaks of

> the pragmatic argument from effect to cause which permeates the theology of Anglicanism. Not only in the seventeenth century but from the time of Henry VIII to the present day, if there is any outstanding note of the English temper it is a humility of awe before the divine mysteries of faith and a recognition of the incompetence of language to define the ultimate paradox of experience. It is a pragmatism not of the lips only, as with the scholastics of the past or the

present, but from a deep conviction that the rationalisation of the supernatural is always in danger of pushing on to a formula which magnifies one half of the truth to an absolute by excluding the other half.[6]

To a New Zealander with roots in Maoridom, that is a curious statement. It is more concerned with cultural traits than with the outline of a theological method. The key phrases seem to be "humility of awe," "a recognition of the incompetence of language," "pragmatism." If you have been nurtured in a culture that emphasizes, say, decisive insight and leadership, where do these fit into any spirit of Anglicanism? More commends, as part of the spirit of Anglicanism, a certain "pliancy of mind," which is concerned not so much with finality as with direction. Unfortunately the nineteenth-century missionaries who came from England to New Zealand displayed not pliancy but certainty. Perhaps in a strange, hostile environment certainty serves you best, but the English missionary showed little recognition or interest in the fact that he was dealing with indigenous people with their own integrity, own history, own value system, own hopes and spirituality. In a way things have not changed.

The 1968 Lambeth Conference report in the section "The Renewal of the Church in Unity" set out the aims of Anglicanism:

1. To welcome, encourage and be ready to give counsel in the merging of Anglican Churches in united national or regional Churches.
2. To enter into full communion with all such united Churches, even while certain anomalies remain.
3. To maintain support of such united Churches, as well as to support one another, Church and Church in the Anglican Communion, as need and opportunity arise, with spiritual, intellectual and material assistance; and to take common counsel.
4. To preserve and enrich our special insights, and to contribute them to the whole Christian Church and to the world.[7]

Ten years later the mood of the 1978 Lambeth Conference was very different. The failure of all manner of church-union schemes and proposals made the commitment to organic and visible union with the Christians among whom we live much more muted. In New Zealand we had tussled with a Plan for Union, which, if accepted, would have produced a United Church. We failed because our negotiations were largely a matter of doctrinal give-and-take rather than a matter of responding to the social, political, and religious context in which this union would take place. With hindsight it would have been more productive to focus on practical, shared goals and let any Plan for Union rise to help bring them about.

Rightly understood, the process of union is concerned with the renewal of the Church in a particular context. Union then becomes an act of trust between churches coming together rather than a matter of doctrinal precision. What we longed for during our negotiations and deliberations over the Plan for Union and what we still long for in New Zealand is an open-ended ecclesiology, where the major issues of church life, worship, and witness are not necessarily solved beforehand but are worked out in the process of becoming a church in the New Zealand context. Will the Anglican Communion help us in New Zealand to do that or do we face the possibility of being part of a more self-conscious world body moving from being a World Communion to being a World Church in which the issue of authority is now of great importance?

The Constitution of the Church of the Province of New Zealand came about in 1857, not because of British or colonial legislation but because of a "voluntary compact" made by its members. The two essential things about the constitution were that there was no intention to depart from the doctrine and ritual of the Church of England and the consent of the three orders of bishop, clergy, and laity in the synod would be required for all acts binding upon the church at large. Authority was to be shared.

George Augustus Selwyn, the first bishop of New Zealand and subsequently bishop of Lichfield, was the motivating spirit behind the Constitution of the Church of the Province of New Zealand. He supported the initiatives from the American church and the colonial churches of Canada and South Africa that ultimately led to the first Lambeth Conference. The Lambeth Conference of 1867, however, was regarded with a good deal of suspicion by the Church of England and indeed no bishop from the province of York attended. Archbishop Longley had been persuaded to call a conference of bishops, but such a conference was something less than the real objective of those who worked hard for its calling. They wanted a synod of bishops, clergy, and laity from the whole Communion and a voluntary appellate tribunal. Such was not to be, and by the fourth Lambeth Conference of 1897 it had been firmly established that the purposes of such gatherings were to be mutual consultation and the giving of advice. In fact a report of the 1867 conference accurately described the position: "Decisions could only possess the authority which might be derived from the moral weight of such united counsels and judgments, and from the voluntary acceptance of its conclusions by any of the Churches there represented."

The Lambeth Conferences continued, and it was not until the conference of 1978 that the issue of authority came to the fore again. The reason for this was the question of the ordination of women to the priesthood and the way in which this was handled between the Lambeth Conference and the Anglican Consultative Council. Quite clearly Lambeth 1968 abdicated its responsibility to the ACC over this issue; ACC carried out the task assigned to it; and then Lambeth 1978, or a section of the conference, dissatisfied with what had happened, tried to assert for itself the kind of authority that earlier Lambeth conferences had refused to accept. There is some irony in the fact that it seems to have been largely the Church of England that has been most upset at the ordination of women to the priesthood, and yet it was the Church of England that at the early Lambeth conferences was unreceptive to the proposal for a synod representative of the whole communion, and for a central appellate tribunal.

Lambeth 1978 asked for an examination of authority. The primates' meeting in 1981 had the benefit of prepared material, including a paper by New Zealander Philip Thomas, in which he said:

> At the conclusion of my study, I had come—somewhat unexpectedly—to the conviction that the Anglican Communion was held together by a coherent ecclesiological framework, not just by a series of historical accidents and a sense of personal affection. The framework can be related to what a Lambeth Conference (1948) called the theory of "dispersed authority," the idea that Christian authority is derived from a variety of sources, and exercised by means of a number of offices. It is an authority which is based on moral and spiritual insight, and is quite different from that of the "great men" of whom Jesus spoke, whose authority was expressed legalistically and as of right and, by means of bureaucracy, coercion and the raw manipulation of power. If this is so then the proper place for a shared Anglican history and mutual Anglican trust and regard comes into its own. It is out of the authentic life of local Churches, nourished and stimulated by a continual process of consultation and prophetic leadership, that the consensus fidelium is disclosed afresh to the Church. And it is out of this process that the People of God come to share in that authority which is marked by the service of mankind, the Cross of Christ and the Kingdom of God (Matthew 20:20–28).

What we need to concentrate on is the mutual Anglican trust and regard Philip Thomas talks about and discover how it can serve the authentic life of local churches. Take the issue of full communion. The report of the Preparatory Group on Ecumenical Affairs, entitled "Steps Towards Unity," reminds us that Anglicans use the term in three ways: for an advanced state of unity between two hitherto separated churches; for the relationship between Anglican provinces and the united churches of the Indian subcontinent; and for the relationship between Anglican provinces themselves.The report asks the question, "What is the proper balance between autonomy and interdependence?" and goes on to state:

> The decision of some Provinces to ordain women and the decision of some other Provinces not only not to ordain women, but also not to allow the women lawfully ordained in other Provinces to exercise their full ministry in their own Province—these decisions have put a strain on relationships within the Anglican Communion. ACC-1 and Lambeth 1978 affirmed that the ordination of women was not a "communion-dividing issue. However some have claimed that full communion no longer exists since there is not a full interchangeability of ministries."[8]

When I visit Australia or England, I certainly feel our churches are in a relationship that is less than full communion. In the eyes of my sister churches, the priests in New Zealand are divided into those who are acceptable and those who are unacceptable, and this division is strictly on male and female lines. I do not perceive my clergy in this way and consequently I share some of the confusion and pain that the same clergy feel, especially the women. For me the choice is whether I preserve my own unrestricted and full communion with a body such as the Church of England or whether I accept for myself the restrictions that are placed on those women ordained to the priesthood within the Church of the Province of New Zealand. At this time I have chosen the former course of action in order to keep communication open and in the hope that the Spirit of God will help us all through this difficulty.

The issue was thrown up in sharp relief when the Archbishop of Canterbury visited New Zealand in 1983. There was a reported statement that when abroad the archbishop abided by the practices of his own province. While in New Zealand, the archbishop said, "There are difficulties about this issue in England, however, and it would not be honest for me to preside jointly at a communion service with women priests. This would not reflect the situation that actually exists in our Communion worldwide and the Archbishop of Canterbury has some responsibility not only to act according to his personal whims, but also to listen to the views of other parts of the Anglican world, including his own Church."

In actual fact, the archbishop was being asked to act not according to his personal whims but according to the Constitution of the

Church of the Province of New Zealand. One is conscious of the pressures upon the archbishop, and one had to be sure that the invitation for him to preside jointly at a communion service with women priests was motivated not by some political considerations but by a desire to share a genuine celebration of Word and Sacrament. We were saddened, however, by the decision he made. It raises questions about the archbishop's regular visits to various parts of the Anglican Communion. If one of the main reasons for visiting an autonomous province is to support it in what it has carefully and responsibly decided to do, then I believe he cannot affirm some aspects of its life and practice and decline to participate in other aspects. If he does that he brings a division into our local situation that we do not acknowledge and makes it hard for us to understand how he can be a focal point of unity for us New Zealanders who are part of the Anglican Communion. Hopefully we are in a transition period, and I would want to acknowledge the graciousness and genuine goodwill that the archbishop showed when we shared a meal with a group of women priests in New Zealand.

I believe that the future of the Anglican Communion depends upon our ability to encompass unity and diversity, autonomy and interdependence.

NOTES

1. Ruth M. Ross, "Te Tiriti o Waitangi: Text and Translations," in *New Zealand Journal of History* (October 1972), pp. 129–157.
2. Ian Wards, *The Shadow of the Land: A Study of British Policy and Racial Conflict in New Zealand, 1832–1852* (Wellington: Historical Publications Branch of the Department of Internal Affairs, 1968), p. 28.
3. *Ibid.*, p. 40.
4. John Paterson, ed., *He Toenga Whatiwhatinga* (Bishopric of Aotearoa, 1983), p. 33.
5. Henri Nouwen, *Pray to Live. Thomas Merton: Comtemplative Critic* (Notre Dame, Indiana: Fides/Claretian, 1972), p. 5.
6. Paul Elmer More and Frank Leslie Cross, eds., *Anglicanism: The Thought and Practice of the Church of England Illustrated From the Religious Literature of the Seventeenth Century* (London: S.P.C.K., 1935), p. xxxvii.
7. *The Lambeth Conference 1968: Resolutions and Reports* (London–New York: S.P.C.K. and The Seabury Press), p. 142.
8. "Steps Towards Unity," p. 23.

The Mission of Christ in Urban America

The Right Reverend A. Theodore Eastman

A Biblical Metaphor

In all times, places and circumstances it is the mission of the church to attest in word and act to what God has made known and accomplished in the life, death and resurrection of Jesus and to pray that, through the Holy Spirit, all people will come to know and love God as he in truth is.

The worship of the church, its holy scriptures and sacraments, creeds and preaching, the pattern of its common life and practice, all attest to a fundamental belief. God and no other is the creator, redeemer and sanctifier of the world. God is the source of all things and only in God will both nature and history find their fulfillment.

It is the mission of the church to testify . . . to its belief that it is God in and through Christ who speaks the first and last word in the great drama of history of which the present age is a part, and that it is God's presence, his speaking and acting, that move the course of events toward their fulfillment. In a real sense, all mission is God's.

The church is sent to give testimony to all who will hear that God is the world's creator, redeemer and sanctifier and that in this work he never speaks or acts in a way contrary to the way in which he has spoken and acted in the life, death and resurrection of Jesus. In Christ, God has spoken the definitive word about himself and about human destiny and in so doing he has also made known who he is. God has at the same time overcome the forces which separate us from himself and which place us in conflict with him and with one another. In Christ, therefore, God is manifest as one who can be trusted, followed and obeyed. He has made himself known as one whose love, power and justice are such that no matter what the circumstances may be, we may give our lives over to his care and guidance. It is this self-revelation in Christ that makes known God's way to himself, which points the way to our fulfillment and so gives birth to faith, hope, love, joy and peace. God's way to himself and so to the destiny appointed for all people is through Christ and it is this way which leads in fact to the health and fulfillment for which all people seek.[1]

These words from a 1982 statement of the Episcopal Church's Joint Standing Commission on World Mission describe succinctly the nature and purpose of the Christian mission. The mission is from God, about God, fulfilled by God. The Christian Church is that body of people who are called apart, formed, and sent forth by God to witness to the whole truth of God revealed in Jesus Christ. Christians are a people commissioned with a purpose. The marching orders are clear: "Go . . . and make disciples of all nations" (Matthew 28:19a).

Both the vision and the reality of being chosen and sent are highly charged. They have propelled Christians into all the world with tremendous power for two millennia. But the notion of the Church as a people sent is full of pitfalls. These traps include pride, isolation, competitiveness, imperialism, triumphalism, and despair.

Those who are sent may be tempted with feelings of self-importance. (We have it; they do not.) Those who are sent may feel alone and overwhelmed. (A sense of isolation can quickly develop when home base is seen to be left behind.) Those who are sent may fall prey to rivalry. (Who will get through with the conquest? Now we can color our part of the map blue! Here's another scalp for my belt!) Those who are sent and fail to meet worldly standards of success may feel despondent. (What did we do wrong?)

Seeing the people of God as chosen and sent is not the only metaphor for mission. Another potent figure is suggested by the statement of the Standing Commission: "In Christ . . . God is manifested as one who can be trusted, followed and obeyed." This idea, which is rooted in the New Testament, may be helpful to us today.

From the outset of His public ministry Jesus challenged people to follow Him. The Twelve were recruited in this way. The Gospels portray an energetic Christ, who is continually moving on ahead of His disciples, spiritually as well as physically, bidding them to follow in faith. The image of the leading Christ, the compelling Christ, imparts a sense of purpose, determination, and expectancy, precisely the qualities that a church engaged in God's mission is meant to have.

Woven in and around and through the Resurrection appearances of our Lord, there is a cluster of images that clarifies this alternative metaphor of mission. They are "the traveling Christ," "the waiting Christ," and, above all, "the beckoning Christ." The traveling Christ joined two disciples on the road to Emmaus (Luke 24:13–35). The waiting Christ stood on the shore of Lake Tiberius until a few of His followers joined Him for breakfast (John 21:1–13). The beckoning Christ instructed the disciples to meet Him in Galilee (Matthew 28:10). The point of these events is that the risen, living Christ is always moving on ahead of His disciples, ready to meet us when we arrive on the scene. He invites us to come and join Him on the road, the beach, the mountain top.

When two bar magnets are arranged with like poles close together, iron filings are propelled away from the space between even as they are drawn toward the magnets at other points. The risen Christ is like that magnetic phenomenon. He is the One who sends. At the same time He is the One who draws His disciples and, indeed, all humanity to Himself. We are familiar with the Christ who sends. It may be that a renewal of mission will occur as we become better acquainted with the Lord who attracts.

If we grasp the reality that the risen Christ invites as well as sends, it is possible for us to be released from our tendencies toward self-dependence, competitiveness, imperiousness, and hopelessness. We go forth, but we go forth to meet the Lord who is already present in every situation; and there we engage the world, not for Him but with Him. As we greet Him on the road, He opens our eyes to new ways of seeing God's truth. As we find Him on the beach, He shows us where the fish are to be gathered. As we meet Him on the mountain top, He shows how broad our calling is. As we go out to discover Him we find that He is present to welcome, guide, and sustain us.

The vision of Christ's mission as a beckoning mission promises exhilaration because the journey is transformed from a delivery route into an exploration of unknown territory. No precise road map is at hand. What is at hand is a crudely drawn sketch that identifies only the most obvious landmarks. Missionaries—by which I mean all Christians—are called to be explorers, searchers, discoverers, learners who are being drawn by their Lord into the unknown. Anxiety is modified by joy because faithful explorers know that Christ is with them along the way and awaits them at the end.

Mission in Context

The Gospel accounts of Jesus' public ministry contain a powerful underlying current. Beneath the flashing white caps of His teachings and healings there is a deep ground swell that moves Jesus inexorably toward Jerusalem. It was to that pivotal city that God drew Jesus and Jesus beckoned the disciples. They went along reluctantly, for the most part, only vaguely understanding what he knew full well: It would be in the city that His ministry of servanthood would reach its climax.

After Pentecost the seeds of the Church were scattered by the wind of the Spirit to the lands of the eastern Mediterranean. It was in the cities of these lands that the germs of the faith first took hold and put down roots. As the young Church organized itself, the episcopal office emerged as the focus of leadership. Bishops almost always resided in major cities. Cities, therefore, became the wellsprings of mission. In time certain cities were recognized as primary sees: Rome, Alexandria, Antioch, Constantinople, and, of course, Jerusalem.

From the beginning, then, cities have had a central place in the life and mission of the Church. God seems to use them in a special way. We do well to understand what that is all about.

In the American *Book of Common Prayer* there is a collect for the mission of the Church that is now one of two alternative prayers mandated for use every time Morning Prayer is read. Variations of this collect appear in other Anglican prayer books around the world.

> O God, you have made of one blood all the peoples of the earth, and sent your blessed Son to preach peace to those who are far off and to those who are near: Grant that people everywhere may seek after you and find you; bring the nations into your fold; pour out your Spirit upon all flesh; and hasten the coming of your kingdom; through Jesus Christ our Lord. Amen.[2]

I grew up in the Church thinking that this collect was primarily, if not exclusively, related to foreign mission. This was the form that we always used when we prayed for the evangelization of "those people over there." The images in my mind—shaped by current hymnody—were of people traversing the dangerous slopes of Greenland's icy mountains, strolling on the pleasant beaches of India's coral strand, or splashing playfully in Africa's sunny fountains.[3] Interestingly enough, the prayer does have a connection with India. It was written by George Cotton, who 120 years ago was bishop of Calcutta, a diocese containing one of the largest and most depressing cities in the world.

Bishop Cotton's prayer has to do with Christ's universal mission, of course, which is addressed to those who are "here," as well as to those who are "there," the far-off and the nearby. It is also an urban prayer, rooted in the city, not just Calcutta, but London and Baltimore as well.

I am an urban American living in one of the major cities of my country. Of the two bishops in my diocese, I am responsible for seeing that an urban mission strategy is developed and that the Church's ministry addresses not only individual human needs but also the structural defects of the social order. I find that George Cotton's collect, with its urban linkage and its universal application, serves as a useful matrix to help me sort out my thinking about the Church's task in an increasingly urbanized culture.

What are the unique characteristics of the city as the context of mission? While there are undoubtedly many others, four characteristics are suggested by the bishop of Calcutta's prayer.

First, everyone and everything is gathered in the city. It is a microcosm. The entire world resides there, at least symbolically. The city is the world writ small. Because all of the forces, all of the pressures, all of the richness of the world come together in a compact geographical area, there is not only excitement in the city but also confusion and danger. Bishop Cotton understood this and said so in his prayer. In a city one cannot separate those who are far-off from those who are near. The exotic stranger from some place else is a next door neighbor in the city. In the urban context international and intercultural accord is a constant concern.

Second, because "everyone" lives in the city, problems are compacted. Needs and interests are in fierce competition with one another. Sin in the city is compounded. Seeing ourselves at the center of God's world places us at odds with our neighbors, who also see themselves at the center. Ethnocentrism abounds. So does pollution. I am not thinking only of noxious gases in the atmosphere, garbage in the streets, or sounds that are deafening. I am thinking of spiritual pollution as well. As our diocesan manifesto on urban mission puts it: "Hopelessness, isolation, lack of vision, and destruction of the spirit are the faith issues that underlie the worldly dilemmas of helplessness, hunger, unemployment, inadequate housing, lack of education, and crime that touch every community . . . but stagger life in the city."[4]

Third, because "everyone" resides in the city, exhilaration and excitement abound. There are not only ethnic tensions, there is also ethnic vivacity. As the best-selling book *Megatrends* points out, the cities of America (and the world) can no longer be thought of as giant melting pots.[5] The standard urban concoction is more like stew than fondue, with large, delicious, unassimilated chunks of various ingredients still intact to delight the palate. Baltimore, the city in which I live, takes pride in its neighborhoods and its ethnic diversity. In a summer-long series of festivals, it celebrates the rich and varied background from which its people come. Differences become pluses rather than threatening minuses. The contributions of many can inform and animate everyone.

Fourth, one of the reasons that "everyone" congregates in the city is that so many have come as seekers. Even those in the second, third, and fourth generations stand in the tradition of their forbears who came questing to the city. People come to the city seeking their fortunes because the city is seen to be the source of jobs. People come to the city seeking education because the city is the center of learning. People come to the city seeking health because the city is the site of great medical centers.

When we pray, as Cotton's collect leads us to do, that the people of our urban world may seek after God and find Him, we Christians articulate what people who are drawn to the city really want. Those who come to the city are searching for God. If George Gallup were to poll people on what they seek as they gravitate to urban centers, not many would acknowledge a quest for God. Yet at the heart of our striving for security, knowledge, and health is a yearning for God, who is the source of all.

Seeking, of course, is not the whole story; finding completes the equation. People come to the city seeking God, and God can be found there, although the competition is heavy. There are multitudinous temples of religion—and irreligion—in the city.

A perceptive urban priest stresses this point as she writes about the city where she lives and works:

> There is every conceivable option in the city, everything. Every time you think you've heard it all, there is another wrinkle in it. . . . People are really searching and searching and searching. . . . You can't go up many streets in New York without running into a "botanica." . . . It comes from Latin America and . . . it's a place to buy herbs [and] all kinds of potions to mix together. You go to the botanica to learn how to put a curse on somebody who's really bothering you. . . . At a different social level the city seems to produce people who realize that they have achieved everything—they've got their careers put together, the right kind of family, the right kind of education—yet they haven't achieved anything. There's a great spiritual hunger in the city. You can feel it and see it.[6]

St. Paul faced a situation similar to ours in first-century Athens.

Seekers were attracted to the cultural hub of the empire. Much time was spent in philosophical disputation. New ideas were always of interest. Because of his preaching, Paul was summoned to the Areopagus to give an account of his strange beliefs to a group of puzzled, if not resistant, Greek leaders. He spoke directly to the heart of the urban situation, then as now:

> I see that in everything that concerns religion you are uncommonly scrupulous. For as I was going around looking at the objects of your worship, I noticed among other things an altar bearing the inscription "To an unknown God." What you worship but do not know—this is what I now proclaim.[7]

In the city where everything is concentrated and where the quest for God is intensified, it is the task of the missionary church to discover how the beckoning Spirit of Christ is already present in the confused strivings of men and women and to proclaim that Presence in bold and winsome ways. As with Paul in Athens, some—but not all—will hear and respond.

Mission in Action

How does the Church of Jesus Christ work faithfully in an urban context? Cotton's prayer for mission suggests four areas of major concern.

Reconciliation. As was acknowledged at the beginning of this paper, our mission is nothing if it is not the mission of Christ. He came "to preach peace to those who are far off and to those who are near." We who are His followers are called to join with Him, where He is already present, in preaching peace to the incredibly diverse concentration of humanity in the global city.

The scriptural reference in Cotton's prayer to the preaching of peace comes from the second chapter of Ephesians, which in turn echos the fifty-seventh chapter of Isaiah. The proclamation of peace is rooted in *shalom*, the Hebrew word so richly laden with meaning. *Shalom* is not only the absence of conflict, enmity or hostility, although it is that in part; it is the promise of complete well-being. *Shalom* involves bringing an entire people to spiritual and physical wholeness, so that everything works together for good under the providence of God.[8]

Shalom is God's free gift to us. As Walter Brueggemann writes in *Living Toward a Vision:*

> *Shalom* is not what we have to do; it is a gift from the intruding transformer and the certifying maintainer. Israel can say both, "He comes," and "Underneath are the everlasting arms." They are both

statements about the one who is as father and mother to us—as father who intrudes, as mother who embraces. And we are recipients of the gift of *shalom.*[9]

Shalom, or "peace" as the New Testament has it, is possible precisely because Jesus Christ has broken down forever the walls of separation that divide human beings into camps. This is God's supreme gift. In his own person, Jesus, the Divine Intruder, has closed the breach between God and recalcitrant humanity. He has bridged the gap, and men and women may traverse the chasm as they put their whole trust in Him. As our relationship with God is restored, our relationships with others are restored as well. A reverse dynamic may also work: When we strive to break barriers between ourselves and others, we may find ourselves, much to our surprise, standing face to face with God. No matter how the road is traveled, when people are at one with God and neighbor, then peace reigns.

Enduring peace, of course, is an eschatological matter. Ultimate peace will endure only as God's Kingdom is fully realized at the end of time. Nevertheless, a top priority for Christians is to find ways for peace to reign here and now, however imperfectly, however provisionally. This means working to create an atmosphere of reconciliation within the Christian household itself. We have little to offer the world if the world cannot observe our life and exclaim, "See how those Christians love one another!" Conversion, spiritual formation, and renewal must be a continuing process within the Church, not as an end in itself but so that our worldly witness may be grounded in and point toward the One whose mission it is.

A ministry of reconciliation, rooted in a reconciled community, may be done in many ways in a variety of arenas. Some Christians, for example, will be drawn together to work for nuclear disarmament and the easing of international tensions. Within that endeavor there will be honest disagreement about methods used to achieve agreed-upon goals. What is essential in this kind of peacemaking is openness to one another and to the One who is the Prince of Peace. Christians may also come together to represent the needs of the poor of our cities against structures and systems that overlook or disregard the interests of those without power. Others may be working conscientiously to humanize the same structures and systems from within. How can these two aspects of Christian social concern keep in touch with one another to serve the common good and to create an atmosphere of *shalom?*

Sometimes small efforts at meeting human need produce surprising results. A year or so ago, a handful of church people began a soup kitchen on the premises of a struggling parish in the Pigtown area of southwest Baltimore. The effort was a compassionate response by people who lived in the suburbs to the stark reality of hunger and undernourishment among the urban poor. With a minimum of organization, more than enough volunteers signed up to help, and adequate food and cash began to flow in. Episcopal Social Ministries, the social action arm of the diocese of Maryland, offered to help with management and support services. First a seminarian and then a deacon were hired to provide oversight and cohesion to a venture that expanded to six days a week and involved volunteers from eight or ten suburban parishes. A spin-off of the feeding program is a shelter project on the same site that provides overnight housing for a dozen street people, again under the nightly supervision of volunteers from the suburbs.

Aside from the obvious benefit to the hungry and the homeless, two encouraging things have happened to the helpers and to the segment of urban culture from which they come.

First, the volunteers testify to the spiritual renewal they receive as they work in solidarity with the needy poor with whom they now have direct personal relationships. Many volunteers say that they wouldn't miss their day at Paul's Place for anything. These contemporary disciples have discovered Christ afresh as they have moved forward to meet Him already at work in, of all places, a soup kitchen. They have found the existential meaning of Matthew 25:40, and it is changing their lives.[10]

Second, a study made of urban mission in the dioceses of Newark, New Jersey, and Atlanta, Georgia, came to this sobering conclusion:

> If a thing is true of both Newark and Atlanta, it is very likely true of every city in America. The very term *urban,* means, more than any one thing, poverty and oppression pocketed in the middle of and in outrageous juxtaposition to indifferent affluence. To be the Church in urban America means to engage in the travail of penetrating that pocket in love and service.[11]

The hopeful thing about the Baltimore project called Paul's Place is that the comfortable and the poor participate in an enterprise in which each group has a different but equally important stake. As they work together in mutual—although perhaps not fully acknowledged—support, they are breaking stereotypes about poverty in America and the indifference of establishment institutions like the Church. As stereotypes are smashed, walls of separation are dismantled and *shalom* is established for a time in one place.

Comprehensiveness. When we pray that God will bring the nations into his fold, we imply that His mission is universal in more than a geographical sense. His mission is universal in that it embraces all people. Our participation in His mission, therefore, must reflect inclusiveness and openness to all. Everyone in global urban culture is subject to our care and concern—not just some groups, not just certain people, not just "our type." Prudence is obviously called for; it would be foolish for Christians, who are increasingly in the minority, to spread themselves too thin. Still the point needs to be made that no part of the population is beyond the concern of the Church.

Again, in my own diocese we have struggled with this issue. We are geographically, racially, socially, and culturally diverse. We are urban/industrial, suburban-exurban/commutational, rural/agricultural, rural/recreational. We are largely black or white, with a smattering of Oriental and other racial strains represented. Most of our congregations are either all white or all black; a few strive for balanced integration. Many of our people fall in the category labeled "blue collar workers"; a large number would be described as "white collar workers"; a significant number are in the professions, such as law and medicine. An increasing number are retired.

Keeping all of this diversity in creative harmony is a challenge. Most of the time it just seems to happen, doubtless by the grace of God, for we don't often work at it with intentionality. The introduction of a new element into the mix can be unsettling. We are just beginning to experience that now, with the inauguration of an Hispanic mission directed to the 6,000 Spanish-speaking people in the Baltimore area. Although we have raised up an Hispanic candidate for ordination, researched the need for a Spanish-speaking ministry, found ample start-up money, and received the blessing of the appropriate diocesan authorities, there is nagging doubt about our starting something new when we have not fully met older and continuing needs.

I have urged us onward, not only because the need is authentic but because it is important that each generation in the Church take measured and thoughtful initiatives to demonstrate the comprehensiveness of the Gospel. In Maryland in 1984 an Hispanic mission is the opportunity that presents itself.

Diversity. When we ask God to pour out His Spirit on all flesh, we make several assumptions. We reinforce the universal nature of the Gospel. We also unfold the possibility that there is more than one way to perceive and respond to the promptings of the Spirit. People that come from different cultural backgrounds are likely to hear and appropriate the Good News in different ways. God can handle that. The question for us is: Are we big enough to handle it? I am, of course, raising the ecumenical issue.

The Christian mission to the variety of the city clearly requires that diversity of the several Christian traditions. Even with un-limited funds and personnel, no one body could ever do it all. We Anglicans may be particularly aware of ecumenical opportunities because we struggle with the question of unity within diversity all the time. We know that our strength is grounded somehow in that strange roominess of ours. Yet we may have to agree with the note of realism sounded by William Yon:

> The idea of unity-in-diversity is prized by Anglicanism and so compelling in its promise that it obscures the real and practical prob-lems that confront parishes aspiring to it. "How much heterogeneity can we take?" is not necessarily the defensive question of bigots. It may come from the frustration of trying to decide whether the right thing for the parish is to have a Spanish language service at 9, an English service at 11, and a Gospel service in the afternoon—or to alternate them at the same hour in the morning—or to combine ele-ments from all three at every service.[12]

The positive and negative aspects of our Anglican experience lead us to make an essential, further ecumenical leap. That expe-rience enables us to say, "Sure, we understand how God works through us Episcopalians in an amazing variety of ways, so we can see how God also works among our Christian brothers and sisters in an amazing variety of ways." Two courses of action logically proceed from such a conviction.

First, we need to continue with all seriousness the theological-ecclesiological conversations that are occurring between the other traditions and our own. The hope is that we will one day be able to recognize each other as authentic manifestations of the Church of Jesus Christ and permit full access and exchange. This kind of activity must take place at the highest national and international levels.

Second, we need to train ourselves to look for opportunities to put the Lund principle into operation—that is, to do nothing by ourselves that can better be done ecumenically. Much of our past effort in this direction has been through councils of churches. But the conciliar movement has only had limited success in the United States.

Lukewarm cooperation may be a result of our existing in a nation where the churches are not as yet threatened by an unsympathetic or hostile culture. It may also be related to the underlying nature of a pluralistic society, which so often pulls groups apart rather than together. In such circumstances it is likely that ecumenical cooperation will work best at the local level, in a town or in a neighborhood or in a section of a city.

A simple opportunity may look something like this. Two nearby congregations—one Lutheran, the other Episcopal—have been struggling to maintain large and aging plants, full-time clergy, and responsible programs that involve internal ministry and outward mission in the face of a changing neighborhood and declining membership. The two clergy know and respect one another. Their two churches nationally have entered into a new relationship that involves interim eucharistic sharing and suggestions about cooperation on educational ventures and social concerns. One physical plant is in better shape than the other and could easily accommodate cooperative programming. Worship could take place jointly on certain stated days throughout the year, according to guidelines already worked out by the parent bodies. Routinely, worship would proceed at separate hours for each denominational group. The less-viable redundant plant could be sold with the proceeds going to improve the other facility and enable new missionary ventures to be launched. What a natural ecumenical opportunity this is! And how easily we let our traditional ways of thinking divert us from seizing it in faith.

Urgency and Restraint. What do we mean when we urge God to hasten the coming of His Kingdom? We are, first of all, remaking the fundamental assertion with which we began these musings: God is totally in control of His mission and He will conclude it in His own time with the full and complete inauguration of His Kingdom. All to the good. But there are several subsidiary issues that if not in direct conflict with one another are at least paradoxically related. We do well to renounce the conflict and lovingly embrace the paradox.

Bishop Cotton's choice of the word "hasten" clearly expresses a sense of urgency about the Christian mission. Why is that? After all, God has as much time as there is to accomplish what must be done. Can't we relax and let God do what God will do when God wants to do it? In one sense we can; and that is gloriously liberating, if we don't let it lull us into undue quietism.

On the other hand, there is too much confusion and suffering among our brothers and sisters to permit us to be idle. We must get on with attending to human need and proclaiming with clarity the Good News of the age that is dawning. The coming of the Kingdom in no way depends upon our efforts; still God has chosen us to point to the signs of the Kingdom that is arriving— signs of hope that remind us and show others the sublime promise of *shalom.*

After the 1964 riots in the inner city ghetto of Atlanta, the diocese of Atlanta resolved to become directly involved with the city's poor people. The bishop of the diocese chose the white rector of an affluent, suburban, Anglo-Catholic parish "to lead the Episcopal Church on its plunge back into the decaying center of the New Atlanta." The bachelor priest found two suitable houses in an area called "People's Town" and moved in along with a Mennonite student and a Roman Catholic nun. From the beginning the priest maintained his usual Anglo-Catholic patterns of daily and weekly worship, but wanted to avoid old patterns and keep his options open. "The last thing we had in mind was starting a parish," he said years later. "There were already plenty of black churches in the area, and we didn't want to compete with them." That is the way Emmaus House got started as "a place to be present, to listen, to learn, and if possible, to find a way of serving."[13]

In time, distinctive ways of serving became apparent. Emmaus House became a center for a local welfare-rights organization, was instrumental in confronting several forms of social oppression, developed means for defending the legal rights of the poor, and, in the process, earned the scorn of some and the gratitude of many.

The thing to note about this story is that while there was an urgency for the Church to be involved with the poor in a strife-torn city, considerable restraint was exercised at the outset in order to allow the Spirit of Christ to lead this community of faith into ministries that are signs of the Kingdom.

Anglican Peculiarities

Because of our particular heritage, Anglicans in the United States have certain peculiarities that shape the way we engage in the mission of Christ in the world of our day. While these traits could be separated into categories labeled "advantages" and "disadvantages," such sorting seems not only artificial but misleading; for every advantage appears to have a disadvantageous angle to it, and each disadvantage somehow proves helpful in unexpected ways. It would be better to sift our peculiarities into four somewhat leaky but neutral bins that successively contain characteristics related to sociology, theology, polity, and methodology.

Sociological Issues. As indicated in the previous section of the paper, American Anglicans place a high value on diversity. We not only tolerate but relish the fact that our single household can contain conservative evangelicals, charismatics of various stripes, liberals, middle-of-the-roaders, various shadings of Anglo-Catholics, and a large group that resists being tagged with any label. And, of course, there are various combinations of these elements as, say, in a charismatic Anglo-Catholic. Our diversity helps us relate to a highly diverse culture. That is an advantage. On the other hand, our diversity sometimes prevents us from speaking or acting with unity, certainty, and strength.

Despite our diversity, some see powerful traces of our Anglo-Saxon heritage still at work in the American Episcopal Church. We are individualistic, independent, self-reliant, reluctant to make corporate commitments or to take collective action, reticent to articulate either our needs or our convictions. It is fascinating to see Americans who come from other national, racial, and cultural backgrounds take on these traits as they grow up in or move over into the Episcopal Church.

Although we Americans don't think of ourselves as class-conscious, the Episcopal Church retains vestiges of "classism" that have their roots in the Church of England. In a perceptive paper delivered earlier this year, Professor Robert W. Carlson of Seabury-Western Theological Seminary discusses the low esteem with which working-class people and parishes are held in the American church. He gives a painful example:

> Our seminaries and our diocesan commissions on ministry do a good (or bad) job of training seminarians to give up working class ways. One of my woman advisees from a working class background was forced by her diocese . . . to delay ordination and spend a year in a Chicago North Shore parish, because she foolishly did her Field Education (with my advice) in a small working class parish. They felt that she hadn't sufficiently learned the "Anglican ethos!"[14]

In general, Episcopalians tend to be well educated. This opens doorways to high-paying jobs, to positions in the professions, and to places of power and prestige in society. Although they may be persons of influence and wealth, not many Episcopalians see a clear connection between their secular status and the obligations of their religion. Studies have shown, for example, that Episcopalians are among the largest givers to the financial need of universities, schools, hospitals, and other institutions in the United States—but not to their churches. Because many American Anglicans are persons of power and prestige, they tend to identify themselves with the establishment and are therefore naturally resistant to any changes in the status quo. When the pressure for change does occur in the Church and there is openness to it, even among prosperous, well-educated individuals, there is always a strong, reflexive, countervailing force. This creates situations of serious conflict within the Church, which is further evidence of the price paid for diversity and comprehensiveness. The Episcopal Church has experienced considerable conflict of this sort in the last twenty years.

High levels of education and a certain amount of latent wealth make the Episcopal Church a natural instrument for an apologetic mission to the sophisticated in American society. There is a place for the clear articulation of the Gospel in reasonable and intellectually respectable ways in contemporary American culture. Unfortunately, there are only rare signs that the Church even considers pressing home this advantage.

Because many Episcopalians are both urbane (in the root meaning of that word) and well-to-do, they have the luxury of living outside of the city and the ability to commute back to it for work, cultural sustenance, and spiritual nurture. In Baltimore the strength of a number of inner-city parishes is the prosperous people who drive many miles (past several other churches) to worship and study in town. An advantage of this sociological phenomenon is that the wealth is spread around instead of being concentrated in suburbia or exurbia, enabling the Church to have a few viable downtown ministries. A disadvantage is difficulty of generating deep commitment to an inner city neighborhood when most of the communicants do not live there.

A Theological Issue. Diversity is as evident in the area of theology as it is elsewhere in the Church. There is no longer, if there ever was, one distinctive Anglican theology, especially in the United States, which is continually swayed by the winds of pluralism. In the main, however, Episcopalians seem still to be anchored by the venerable four-fold balance among Scripture, tradition, reason, and experience—all weighed, understood, and quickened in the power of the Holy Spirit. This single and secure anchor allows us to be open and flexible in the face of historical changes and the promptings of God's Spirit. It enables a tolerant, measured response to almost any situation. The very moderation of this stance, however, leads us too easily into lukewarmness or compromise, which are further reinforced by the Anglo-Saxon trait that makes us uneasy with enthusiasm and passion.

Issues of Polity. The American Episcopal Church has worked out a distribution of institutional power and authority that is so balanced that paralysis sometimes seems endemic. Almost nothing can disturb the complacent autonomy of the parish church as long as it is financially solvent. Systemic parochialism is compounded by the Anglo-Saxon strain of fierce independence, which still lingers among us. Bishops have opportunities for moral suasion that, when coupled with character, can be potent. But they have very little direct power to shape missionary strategy or deploy missionary resources. This may be all to the good, for it drives us back to the basic biblical principle of action based on covenant. Everything must be negotiated. All parties must claim ownership of plans made and steps taken. Responsibility is shared all around. What advantage is lost in the slow pace of decision-making may well be gained in broad popular support.

Issues of Methodology. Many believe that Anglicanism's greatest evangelistic tool in America is our liturgy. Although the revision of *The Book of Common Prayer* has been somewhat devisive, time is proving the changes to be sound in almost every instance and absolutely exciting in many cases. For example, the revised rite of Holy Baptism promises to do more than any other single initiative to awaken the corporate mind of the Church to the centrality and urgency of mission. As the Baptismal Covenant is rehearsed repeatedly in frequent public baptisms and at every confirmation, Christian consciences are being formed. Few will be able to avoid knowing that it is every lay person's responsibility to "proclaim by word and example the Good News of God in Christ," to "seek and serve Christ in all persons," to "strive for justice and peace among all people and respect the dignity of every human being."[15]

Large numbers of current Episcopalians testify that they found their way into the Church initially by being captivated by the power and beauty of liturgical worship. There is no reason why that phenomenon should not continue. The new prayer book, in fact, enlarges the possibilities, for here again the hopeful note of diversity is struck. With its variety of services the prayer book enables us to craft worship to meet almost any need. Because liturgical revision has forced Episcopalians to study, interpret, and discuss the substance of the prayer book, we have developed a new generation of church people who are liturgically literate and sophisticated. At the persistent urging of the rubrics, many more lay persons than ever before are participating in the leadership of worship. The liturgy truly belongs to the people in deeply transforming ways. How this will manifest itself evangelistically, however, remains to be seen; but the converting power of the liturgy must not be overlooked or taken for granted.

One of the most fascinating and perhaps troublesome facets of Anglicanism in the United States is reflected in our apparent hierarchy of evangelistic energy and effectiveness. We do poorly in assisting people to convert from paganism or secular atheism to faith in Jesus Christ. We do fairly well in ministering to our own people and in forming or renewing a reasonable share of each succeeding generation we produce. We are at our best in helping people move from other traditions into the Anglican form of Catholic Christianity. Very often these "converts" have lapsed from the church of their beginnings. Many Protestants are attracted by our sacramental and liturgical life. Many Roman Catholics are attracted by the democratic and reformed aspects of our Catholicism.

While our evangelistic inclinations are not exactly parasitical, they do tend to remove us a step or two from the difficult but renewing enterprise of primary evangelism. It may be that the surging forces of conservative evangelicalism and the charismatic movement, which are strongly felt in the Episcopal Church today, will reshape our propensities and priorities. An even more interesting prospect to ponder is the effect that the experience of primary evangelism among Third World Anglicans could have on the American church, if we can be open to it.

Conclusion

God in Christ beckons us Anglican Christians to join Him in His mission as He moves into the unfolding future. As we participate in that mission we need to do three things: remain open to the promptings of God's Spirit; assess our environment realistically and take it seriously; and recognize, appreciate, and utilize our

God-given strengths and talents wisely. For American Episcopalians, the environment will be increasingly urban; we cannot wish
it otherwise; our part of God's mission must take that into account. As American Christians with Anglican roots, we need to
accept ourselves as we are, with all of our sociological, theological, political, and methodological peculiarities, and permit
ourselves to be used as creatively as possible to the glory of God
and the proclamation of God's Kingdom.

NOTES

1. The Standing Commission on World Mission, *Mission in Global Perspective* (Cincinnati, Ohio: Forward Movement Publications, 1982),
   pp. 14–15.
2. *The Book of Common Prayer* (1979), p. 100.
3. *The Hymnal 1940*, Hymn 154.
4. *Journal of the Convention of the Diocese of Maryland* (September 1982),
   p. 109.
5. John Naisbett, *Megatrends* (New York: Warner, 1982), esp. ch. 5.
6. Carol Anderson, "Ministry in the Inner City," in *Mission and Ministry*, vol. I, no. 2 (Lent 1983).
7. Acts 17:22–23.
8. For a helpful exposition of *shalom* as distinguished from *pax*, see
   Allan M. Parrent, "Making Distinctions About Peace," in *The Virginia Seminary Journal*, vol. 35, no. 2 (December 1983).
9. Walter Brueggemann, *Living Toward a Vision: Biblical Reflections on
   Shalom* (Philadelphia: United Church Press, 1976), p. 36.
10. "Truly, I say to you, as you did it to one of the least of these my
    brethren, you did it to me."
11. William A. Yon, in the Introduction to *To Build the City . . . Too
    Long a Dream: Studies of Urban Churches* (Washington, D.C.: The
    Alban Institute, Inc., 1982), p. 4.
12. *Ibid.*, p. 63.
13. *Ibid.*, p. 35.
14. Robert W. Carlson, "The Working Class Ministry of the Episcopal
    Church," a paper delivered at a conference sponsored by Appalachian
    People's Service Organization in Louisville, Ky., March 2–4, 1984
    (mimeographed), p. 2.
15. *The Book of Common Prayer* (1979), p. 305.

The Mission of the Church and the Culture of a Nation

The Most Reverend Edward W. Scott

The Mission of the Church

The mission of the Church starts with God and His action in creation. In creation, human beings, male and female, made in the image of God, have a very distinct role. They stand within the created order as "decision makers," "choosers," "initiators." They are given freedom by God—freedom to seek, to know, and to do the will of God and so to become co-creators with God. The same freedom, however, allows them to set themselves over against God, and it is this use of human freedom that constitutes sin. The biblical affirmation is that all human beings are both made in the image of God and are also sinful. Jesus' life, death, and Resurrection must be understood in relation to both creation and fall. He entered history at a particular time and in a particular place and historical context. In that context He called people to turn about, to affirm the reality of God, to acknowledge His rule, and to make Him the central focus of their living. His life and teaching were centered on God and God's will and purpose. In claiming that He was "the way, the truth, and life," Jesus was expressing concern about method, truth, and relationships. We need to be concerned about each of these three as we consider the mission of the Church because this mission flows from the life, teaching, death, and Resurrection of Jesus Christ.

Contemporary Reflections on Mission. The eternal mission of the Church is to give expression by word, attitude, action, and quality of life to the breaking into history, in every age and place, of the rule of God in Jesus Christ. The Church, the people of God, are called to reflect the reality of the love of God in all their relationships—their relationships with God, with each other and all human beings, and with the created order. Christians are also called to reflect God's love in their recognition of their own worth and value as persons made in the image of God and loved by God. The context in which this must be done is very different from the context of the New Testament times. Today this must be undertaken in the context of an urban, industrial, technological culture that dominates many parts of the world and that deeply influences the parts it does not dominate. This means that it is necessary to reflect upon appropriate ways to be "in mission"; on appropriate ways of helping people to be aware of the ways in which God, in Jesus Christ, is breaking into history in our day in a way that is Good News. Much thinking and reflection has been taking place about this, and in this decade an Ecumenical Affirmation about Mission and Evangelism has been produced by the Joint Working Group of the World Council of Churches and the Secretariat for Promoting Christian Unity of the Roman Catholic Church. The following are a number of quotations from the statement:

> The Church is sent into the world to call people and nations to repentance, to announce forgiveness of sin and a new beginning in relations with God and with neighbours through Jesus Christ. This evangelistic calling has a new urgency today.

> There is a growing awareness among the churches today of the inextricable relationship between Christian unity and missionary calling, between ecumenism and evangelization. "Evangelization is the test of our ecumenical vocation."

> Based on their testimony which is preserved in the New Testament and in the life of the Church, the Church has as one constitutive mark its being apostolic, its being sent into the world.

> The starting point of our proclamation is Christ and Christ crucified.

> The call to conversion, as a call to repentance and obedience, should also be addressed to nations, groups and families.

> Thus, the call to conversion should begin with the repentance of those who do the calling, who issue the invitation.

> The experience of conversion gives meaning to people in all stages of life, endurance to resist oppression, and assurance that even death has no final power over human life because God in Christ has already taken our life with him, a life that is "hidden with Christ in God."

> The teaching of Jesus on the kingdom of God is a clear reference to God's loving lordship over all human history. We cannot limit our

witness to a supposedly private area of life. The lordship of Christ is to be proclaimed to all realms of life. Thus, Christian mission is the action of the body of Christ in history of humankind—a continuation of Pentecost. Those who through conversion and baptism accept the Gospel of Jesus, partake in the life of the body of Christ and participate in an historical tradition.

"As the Father has sent me, even so I send you" (John 20:21). The self-emptying of the servant who lived among the people, sharing in their hopes and sufferings, giving his life on the cross for all human-ity—this was Christ's way of proclaiming the Good News, and as disciples we are summoned to follow the same way. "A servant is not greater than his master; nor is he who is sent greater than he who sent him" (John 13:16).

Churches are free to choose the ways they consider best to an-nounce the Gospel to different people in different circumstances. But these options are never neutral. Every methodology illustrates or betrays the Gospel we announce. In all communications of the Gos-pel, power must be subordinate to love.

John Howe, former secretary general of the Anglican Con-sultative Council, in a yet-unpublished manuscript entitled "Highways and Hedges," prepared for the council, summarizes his reflections on mission in these words:

Mission is not something the Church *does*, it is part of being one, holy, catholic and apostolic. Mission is about being sent. So, too, in its Greek origin is apostle. At once we are involved in a "mark" of the apostolic Church and of its ministry, and behind that, and towering over it, is Christ the Redeemer Himself and his words "As the Father sent me even so I send you." The death which was for the whole world and its generations was died in loneliness on a certain day. The outreach to the whole world, and to all the individual lives of which it is composed, is the mission laid upon the Church.

Verna Dozier, in an extremely important booklet, *The Authority of the Laity*, expresses her understanding of the mission of the Church in a very short statement that is packed with implications.

God came into history (in Jesus Christ) to create a people who would change the world, who would make the world a place where every person knew that he or she was loved, was valued, had a contri-bution to make and as much right to the riches of the world as every other person.

As we reflect upon these quotations, and on the biblical insights upon which they are based, we can see mission involving a call to repentance of persons and groups to personal refocussing of val-ues and loyalty, and also involving a movement toward systemic changes in every area of life. In the more complex situations of today, values that are centered upon the life and teaching of Jesus—integrity, justice, and righteousness—become increasingly important. To illustrate: If integrity is lacking in a simple societal pattern a limited number of people are affected. If it is lacking at the head of a complex human system, it permeates and affects far more people and does so in ways that are much more difficult to respond to and to correct. There is also very great need to keep the issue of personal faith alive in the midst of the pressures of corporate involvements if the latter are to be responded to effectively. One of the most unkind and destructive things that the Church has often done is to call upon people to be involved in concrete expressions of Christian mission without helping them to become and grow as Christian persons in supportive Christian communities. This is to call them to do Christian things without having the resources that are necessary to enable them to struggle to respond as Christians involved in the pilgrimage that is ours. To relate this to Verna Dozier's statement, it is only when people have learned in Jesus Christ that they are loved, valued, and have a contribution to make and a right to share responsibly in the resources of creation that they are really able to help others come to those awarenesses on a personal level and so to become involved in the changing of the world so it acknowledges the rule of God.

Early I made reference to the fact that Jesus was concerned about method, about truth, and about relationships. This is made clear in His claim to be "the way, the truth, and the life." The methods we use for mission must surely be the methods used by Jesus. These are revealed as assuming the role of a servant and choosing the road of love, which involved suffering of incredible depth. It was not the road of pomp and power. All too often Christians and the Church have forgotten this central fact. In claiming that He was the "truth," Jesus made "truth" something that transcended abstract verbal statements. Truth is always something more than can be expressed in a creedal statement, although such statements have an important role in the lives of people. Even as none of us totally understands ourselves or the person we love most, so none of us totally understands Jesus, the Word made flesh. We are called to the pilgrimage of seeking an ever-deeper understanding of Jesus, ever-deeper understanding of truth. We commit a very subtle and dangerous idolatry when we limit Jesus to our understanding of Him, when we absolutize our understanding of truth. When Jesus claims to be the "life," we come to recognize life as real relationships. We cannot begin to understand His life without seeing it as a matter of internal integration arising from His relationships with God, with other human beings, and with the created order. These relationships are characterized by such words as integrity, love, justice, mercy, righteousness, reverence, and respect. The mission of the Church in any and every age must take what we learn from Jesus about method, about truth, and about life, seriously.

In the carrying out of the mission of the Church, it has always been necessary both to disturb and to comfort, even as Jesus did. He disturbs us when we become too self-satisfied and self-centered. He comforts us, surrounds us with strength, when we are struggling to be faithful amidst the ambiguities, injustices, and destructiveness of a world in which sin is real and very powerful.

Church and the Social Order

In commenting upon my perceptions relating to this question, I want to start with another comment from Verna Dozier's book: "A strange thing happened on the way to the Kingdom! The Church—the people of God—became the Church, the institution."

I would say, more accurately I believe, "the Churches, the institutions." The Church in Canada, as elsewhere in its institutional forms, is not unified; and one of the seeming realities about institutions, including church institutions, is that they tend to become more concerned about maintenance and survival than about mission and purpose. In Canada there are many institutional forms that all claim to be the Church, and within nearly all of the major forms there is considerable diversity. In addition to the diversity within the church institutions, both in structure and theological insights, there is the diversity of Canada itself. This diversity is partly the result of historical events, but is also, in part, the result of conscious decisions. As a nation, Canada opted to reject a "melting pot" concept of development and chose to try to become a cultural and ethnic mosaic. This has resulted in a very complex, pluralistic social order. Even when the social order is viewed in terms of government structures—and it is always much more than this—we have a very complex and developing pattern of governmental structures involving now at least four levels of government: federal, provincial, regional, and municipal. Nongovernmental institutions cannot escape the interplay between those levels, and both affect and are affected by them. I believe it is possible, however, to make some general comments about the relations of the churches and the structures, particularly the Anglican Communion, to the social order.

Even though the Anglican Communion was never the established Church of Canada in practice, many of the clergy and laity, even after confederation, continued to act as though it were established. The bishops and clergy took for granted many of the privileges that they had enjoyed under the establishment and saw them as rights, not privileges. Church leaders were in close contact with the upper middle class, the decision makers, and wielded great influence, very often through personal contacts rather than through structural relationships or formal power.

As the country developed—and this development included both an increasingly diverse pattern of immigration and also the gradual but steady development of an urban, industrial, technological culture—the situation began to change, and the rate of change has increased in the last four decades. Political power and wealth came to be more and more concentrated in the hands of those who possessed or could purchase knowledge and technological skill, and the decision-making groups became smaller and more interlocked. During this period, the Anglican Church of Canada, which had close contacts with the upper middle class, tended to become more and more domesticated to the values of the culture. The Church became more of a social institution and less and less of a "community of faith" with a mission to perform. The realm of religion became privatized, and the proclamation of the rule of God over the whole of life was muted. The Anglican Church of Canada was more and more both "in the world" and "of the world" and tended to foresake its calling to be leaven, salt, and light. There was a failure to examine the cultural values, and there was a gradual loss of any real sense of accountability to the transcendent God who had acted in history in Jesus Christ.

There were always the prophetic voices that spoke out, but they were few. With the growing awareness of the seriousness of the human situation that has come to develop during the last three decades, a very distinct change has been taking place. As people become aware of the negative aspects as well as the positive ones of scientific, technological developments, much deeper questions begin to be asked and the voices of the prophets began to be heard. This has been a tumultuous and disturbing period, but I believe the churches, including the Anglican, once again are becoming more and more faith communities that are both helping people to find a new sense of their value and worth and also a new sense of mission, and are once again in a much more vigorous way beginning to examine the culture in which they are set and to work to change the world. They have not always done this in the best way, using the methods of Jesus as well as His truth and pattern of relationships, but a new and much more creative relationship both with governments and with other aspects of the social order is coming into being in a slow and, sometimes, very painful process.

Common Life and Mission

It is much easier to outline some of the changes that would enable the Church to carry out its mission more effectively than it is to say how these changes can be achieved. I will make my comments a combination of the two.

The first great requirement is for a new vision and a deeper faith. The vision in Canada is cloudy, and we have many clergy and laity who are tired and, in a number of cases, depressed. A new sense of the reality and power of God is much needed, and a new sense of the calling of the whole people of God as providing the locus for the expression of the power of God would make a tremendous difference. Here a number of practical possibilities lie before us. The invitation to all the institutional churches to become involved in a study, on an ecumenical basis when possible, of the document on baptism, Eucharist, and ministry, the *Final Report* of the Anglican–Roman Catholic International Commission, and the Ecumenical Affirmation on Mission and Evangelism could provide the possibility and create the vision for a great forward step. If this is to happen, there needs to be more real work done to improve the morale and outlook of many denominational leaders. People in authority have an incredible and often unrealized power to block. What is needed is a new realization of a power to liberate, to set people free to dream and to experiment.

Related to the above is the very great need for some hard analysis of the needs confronting us in the churches and in the world and of the resources that are available with which we can respond to these needs. Our resources are much more than material resources. They are spiritual and liturgical. They are the resources of mind and imagination that are so much more important than material resources that are always focused by the human resources. We need to work for an ecumenical sharing of resources.

The growing common recognition of the reality and complexity of the issues that confront the world today provides a living opportunity for the churches to invite a wide range of people to meet and reflect together about possible responses. The easy optimism and the assumption that answers are immediately available are both dying, if not dead; and a new possibility of people reasoning together in community, searching for more adequate insights, and, in the process, developing deeper faith and experiencing mutually supportive community can lead to growth and creative action.

Another area of concern is the affirmation of the local parish as the place where Christian people live and move and have their being and are nurtured in the faith and equipped for ministry. In some cases this means a change of focus for the parish and even more often for the parish clergy. One vital question that ordained people have to face is where to find their basic sense of identity. Is it in the baptized community or is it in their order? I am convinced that it should be in the former and that those of us who are ordained should see ourselves as called to special ministries within the baptized community, the community to which ministry is committed. A parish priest who finds his Christian identity within the baptized community and knows that he or she is called to a specialized ministry of Word, Sacrament, and pastoral care is able to help people grow, develop, and set them free for mission and ministry and not to build dependency or to establish control mechanisms. In such parishes mission takes place and people are equipped for a wider mission beyond the borders of the parish. They are also enabled to share their insights and learnings from being involved in the wider ministry back in the parish community, which enriches the parish for all concerned.

The central thread running through all these comments is the need to be more concerned about the growth and development of people and community for service and much less concerned about institutional glorification or self-preservation. The two stem from the same limitation. They make the institutional form an end rather than a means. The aim comes to be to facilitate the growth of committed Christians and not to be content with loyal churchmen.

Mission and the Anglican Heritage

I want now to ask if the heritage of Anglicanism is a help or hindrance for the work that lies ahead. I have already dealt with some of the ways in which it has been a hindrance. These include the ease with which it becomes a noncritical part of the social fabric, a social institution rather than a community of faith; the ease with which it becomes domesticated by culture. A second hindrance is the way in which it has become so identified with the middle class and usually the upper middle class. In so doing, it tends to sanction rather than challenge the cultural values and practices making it difficult for the prophetic word to be heard or responded to by others. In this way, parishes often tend to become exclusive clubs rather than accepting, redemptive communities.

More could be said about the hindrances, but I prefer to give attention to the ways it has helped as I believe these are becoming more obvious. One of the more obvious and so often overlooked ways is the biblical base of its liturgical life. The way in which the story of creation, Incarnation, redemption, and salvation are constantly being repeated provides an ever-present foundation for renewal that can be built upon when new vision comes, sometimes from the most unlikely sources or events. A further way in which it has been a help is in the Anglican view of authority as resting upon Scripture, tradition and conscience enlightened by reason, and upon the Anglican refusal to try to describe precisely all details of faith. This has made it possible for Anglicans to be more open to respond to new insights from new knowledge in many fields. I believe that because of this Anglicans have had an influence out of proportion to their numbers.

A further great help has been the Anglican conception of dispersed authority, which is expressed, in part, by the Anglican Church being both episcopal and synodical. This leads to an internal tension that can be, and often is, creative. It provides a realm for continuity of leadership focused in persons who exercise canonical authority. In this exercise of dispersed authority, the challenge of and response from people in leadership positions is an essential element; and this is coming to be accepted more and more in Canada.

One of the issues that the Anglican Communion in Canada and in its worldwide manifestation must grapple with very seriously relates to how we use our time, energy, and resources in relation to mission. A very destructive pattern of pan-Anglicanism can easily develop. What we need for mission is that kind of security in the baptized community so that we can participate far more freely in the ecumenical sharing of resources. In Canada this has been expressed through the development of many ecumenical coalitions that make human and financial resources available in response to need. In such coalitions there should be a constant pressure to clarify the theological insights from which action flows. There is also the need for those personally involved to recognize the importance of being accountable to their own church and to make sure that the insights they gain are examined and reflected upon by the wider church community. Here again, the fact that responsibility is assigned to persons and accountability flows through persons is a real help and strength.

Summary

Anglicans are constantly involved in mission in Canada. Since the Anglican Congress in Toronto in 1963, developments have deepened the sense of mission that is expressed in part through the concept of "mutual responsibility and interdependence in the body of Christ." Gradually, in practice as well as in theory, the body of Christ is seen to be "the people of God, the baptized community," a much wider and more extensive group than the Anglican Communion alone. As this sense grows, as the need for mutual responsibility and interdependence becomes more recognized, then we are more truly the Church, more truly "in mission." Symposiums like this symposium on "Theology of Mission" are important events in enabling this to happen.

The Mission of the Church in an Islamic Country

The Reverend Clement H. Janda

Introduction

The presence of the Church of Christ throughout our created earth has come about as a result of many, sometimes contradictory, factors. Some of the churches have grown out of a deliberate effort on the part of some Christians from other parts sending missionaries afield to evangelize the unevangelized, while other churches have come about as a by-product of other operations. Whatever our origin, the Church Universal today is able to bring together peoples from various backgrounds and nationalities (*ethnos*) to worship, celebrate, and reflect together. It is even possible for a worldwide group of Christians to come together, claiming a common heritage, history notwithstanding, such as the Anglican Communion. Hence the gathering of several dozen Anglicans from the "five regions" of the world to celebrate the two hundredth anniversary of the consecration of Samuel Seabury as America's first native-born bishop (and frontiersman of the Anglican Communion) must be considered more than just a mere celebration. It is a clear manifestation of the reality of the worldwide Anglican Communion working in partnership.

While leaving the writing of the historical perspective of Bishop Samuel Seabury and the growth of the Church in America to the presenters from North America, I would like to indicate that it has great significance for parts of the Church from which I come. Although I shall not be able to bring about the relevant point of that history for the Sudan until I hear more about it, the present work of this church, however, has a direct effect on our mission in the Sudan because of the partnership we have developed.

A Brief History of the Church in the Sudan

If you read the history of the early Church you will discover that, technically, the Sudan was one of the earliest parts of our planet to receive the Good News. Even as early as the days of Prophet Isaiah, contacts between the Sudan and the Judaic tradition were already there (Isaiah 18).

According to the customs of Merowie, the Ethiopian Enuch from Queen Candace, who was baptized by Philip (Acts 9), was from the present Sudan. The great kingdoms of Egypt, Merowie (which extended up to Kabushiya, north of Khartoum), Axum, and Ethiopia received the Christian faith quite early. Christianity has held out against all the pressures of traditional religions and Islam in both Egypt and Ethiopia, up to the present. But the great Merowie temples are only historical monuments that can only be observed in the national museum of modern-day Sudan.

The Coptic Orthodox Church often sent its members from Egypt to work in the Sudan. This trend continued even after the disappearance of Christianity in Nubia. The Copts were engaged in trade or served the kings of Sennar, up the Blue Nile, as secretaries and accountants. They were generally called *Mu'allim* ("teacher, learned man"). With the coming of the Turks (1820–1881), the Copts increased their presence to the point they could build a church in Khartoum; and later, by 1879, the see of Nubia and Khartoum was established. Today the Coptic Church has two dioceses in the Sudan.

The Roman Catholic Church was started in 1842 by Father Luigi Montouri, who had fled to Khartoum from Ethiopia, where the Orthodox Abuna Salama had stirred up a persecution against Catholic priests. By 1846 Sudan was included in the Holy See's Vicarate Apostolic of Central Africa. The aims of setting up this vast mission were the proclamation of the Christian message to Africans, assistance to Christians residing in these regions, and the fight against the slave trade.

The arrival of Father Daniel Comboni in 1857 boosted the mission work. By 1864 he drew up a new project that he called "Plan for the Regeneration of Africa by Means of Africans." Since Europeans could not work for a long time in the interior of Africa, and since Africans could not resist the cold climate of Europe, both the Africans and Europeans could survive and work in the coastal towns. Therefore, in the "plan" it was suggested that Africans be trained in several fields of learning, including Christian religion, and then be sent back to their own countrymen, under the guidance of experienced directors, to raise the social level of their people. The novelty of this plan was that Father Comboni already envisaged the possibility of Africans running their own affairs in every field. This became a reality to the extent that today the Roman Catholic Church in the Sudan is led by eight native bishops and is the largest single denomination in the Sudan that has its presence throughout the country.

The beginning of the Anglican Church in the Sudan dates from 1899 with the arrival of a Welsh Christian, Llewellyn Henry Gwynne, in Omdurman. "He intended to open a mission in the Sudan, but Sirdar Kitchner refused him permission because of the lack of security in those remote regions. So Gwynne stayed in Khartoum for five years, looking after the religious needs of the foreigners there." It is important to note here that Gwynne was not allowed to evangelize Arabs or those who were either converted to Islam or lived as though they were part of that faith. This is because the imperial government suspected that discord and violence might break out, especially since the British and the Egyptians had learned the lesson of the Mahdist Ansar resistance movement in the 1880's. This decision to prevent Christians from preaching to Muslims later proved to be a dogma—a feeling among latter-day Christians that Muslims were not to be preached to. In 1905 Pastor Gwynne and three fellow priests set off by boat up the Nile to evangelize the "animist" Africans. But even there the British governor, who placed political convenience above spiritual or religious sentiments, made a great deal of "palaver" before allowing these three priests to start their mission south of Bor. Here they were visited by the village chief, and Pastor Gwynne recorded these words of their encounter:

> They wanted to know whether we were government men? No. Soldiers? No. Merchants? No. What were we? Servants of God sent by Him to tell them of how His Son was born into the world to reveal to mankind that the Great God Almighty, who had made heaven and earth and all men, was the Father of us all and loved all His Children of whatever colour or tribe or language. And would like to call them to worship Him "in spirit and truth."

Father Giovanni Vantini adds: "The village people were not convinced. Later on, thank God, they did see, and not only they, but the whole of the Southern Sudan."

This short account of the history of the beginning of mission work in the Sudan gives a brief perspective of the concept of this movement—"mission" in the Sudan today. We have to underline the following facts. First, the Sudan, lying between the two oldest churches in the world—the Coptic Orthodox Church (of Egypt) and the Ethiopian Orthodox Church—was not evangelized until after the early Church was choked off by the Muslim advent during the ninth to sixteenth centuries. The two churches have developed into state churches, with hardly any desire for outreach. The presence of the Coptics in the Sudan throughout history did not produce any missionary spirit.

Second, the beginning of the modern missionary work in the Sudan was limited by the colonial government to certain areas only: The Southern Sudan was open to evangelization by Christian missionaries; whereas, Christian missionaries were prevented by colonial administrators (most of them Christians) from evangelizing greater parts of the Northern Sudan. Thus two regions were created in the Sudan—the African South that was open to Christian influence and the Arab North that was closed to all except Islamic influence, with Christians mainly performing chaplaincies in Northern urban centers.

Third, the Church started in an area with so many ethnic groups (sometimes called tribes) who had never been involved in any proselytizing among themselves. Each ethnic group always knew its own religion and passed it from generation to generation without any difficulty. Each member of the society then belonged naturally to the religion of the clan. This new idea of a God, who considered all people His children and, therefore, called them to a unitary approach to Him, was and remains by and large a new idea. Furthermore, the idea that members from some ethnic groups could go to other ethnic groups to propagate the new idea of religion was equally new. But the new had started.

What Is the Mission of Christ's Church Today?

At this point the reader may already have deduced what the mission of the Church is, as I see it. I have mentioned the fact that the presence of the Christian Church (in its present form) in the Sudan is about one century old. Most of us are either first or second generation Christians. Hence, the first answer to the question about mission could still be what Pastor Gwynne told the Bor villagers in 1905—that is, "it is an enterprise of those servants of God sent by Him (in spite of their human frailty) to tell others of how God's Son was born into the world to reveal to humankind that the Great God Almighty, who had made heaven and earth and all humankind, was the father of us all and loved all His Children and of whatever colour and creed or tribe or language, and would like to call them to worship him 'in spirit and truth'" (John 4).

If this seems archaic it is simply because some parts of the Anglican Church, such as ours, are still living very near to the New Testament period. This must have some qualification. After the Great Commission, the disciples did not start off in a grand way because their world was limited in many ways. They did not have the fast ships or boats that we have today, nor did they have any engine-propelled means of transportation, be they cars, trains, airplanes, or rockets; they walked for long distances and occasionally, like our Lord Himself, rode on donkeys, horses. And, of course, St. Paul traveled by ships that are now better found in museums. The early missionaries did not travel with great funds stuck in their purses, nor did they necessarily come with fantastic new skills and ideas about civilization. They simply traveled to tell of the "new kingdom of God," where the lives of those who "received" Him were transformed. They did not settle to build empires for themselves, although the Coptic Orthodox Church claimed that St. Mark settled to establish the See of St. Mark in Alexandria, and the Indians attributed their origin to the work of Doubting Thomas. As the book of Acts will remind us, the message, the *kerygma,* was simple: "God who spoke to us in the past through the prophets has revealed Himself to us through His Son Jesus Christ, and has invited humankind to respond and come to him in repentance." Baptism was immediately administered to those who acknowledged the validity of this message, and teaching and nurturing of the new converts continued thereafter.

After eighty years or so, this is still the simple mission being carried out in the Sudan. In spite of the modern technological advancements in other parts of the world, most of our evangelists are still persons of no high learning, first generation Christians (here I mean people like myself who came to Christ after listening to the preaching of others, made up their minds to join this faith, and got baptized as an adult). They use canoes or walk for long distances with a copy of the Bible—sometimes portions of the Bible that have been translated into the local language—a hymn book, and a prayer book. There is no commentary or lectionary of any kind. The most "sophisticated" evangelists use bicycles to pedal long distances in order to reach some villages and preach the Word, baptize, and carry on the teaching of the newly converted. Sometimes it takes a year for an evangelist to complete

a single round. A year ago it was discovered that some archdea-
conries had not witnessed any confirmation by their bishop for
about two years. This was due to difficulties of communication
and transportation.

The evangelists and pastors go on for months without receiving
any stipend; and when they eventually get some money, it is not
enough to get them the basic requirements for life. So they must
supplement their living by cultivating in their fields for a great
part of the year. All these conditions lead to the problem of sustained ministry; preaching and teaching are rendered inadequate.
Converts are left to fend for themselves for many weeks, and one
can expect how easy it can be for heresies to develop unchecked.

It is worth noting that, like the early Church, the matter of
elaborate meetings that have to deal with Church structure, financial management, administration, canon laws, and many of the
concerns that I read about in the rest of our communion are significantly absent. Instead there are too many evangelistic conventions, where much time, in fact too much time, is devoted to
preaching and singing.

What has the above to do with the mission of Christ today? In a
nutshell, it is still what the early evangelists preached. And what
did the early evangelists preach—that we would get heaven on
earth? By no means. St. Mark starts his Gospel by telling us about
the in-breaking of God's Kingdom in time. "The right time has
come," he said, "and the Kingdom of God is near! Turn away
from your sins and believe the Good News!" (Mark 1:15). But this
is (even during the early Church) the proclamation of the Word.
There is the doing of the Word—the making of the Word incarnate in the daily life of every ordinary human being. In the Gospels we read of the works of Jesus Christ after his proclamation
and teaching. Sometimes the proclamation was dramatized by a
deed, a miracle, an event. In the midst of our proclamation we
discover that humankind needs more than just to "hear these
words."

In the Sudan, as in other parts of the world, the proclamation of
the Word was supplemented or complemented by deeds, such as
the provision of basic education to the converts. So missionaries
had to open schools. They felt the need for the healing ministry
and opened health centers and hospitals. Those were the early
mission days. The situation has changed dramatically. The mission schools and hospitals were nationalized twenty five years ago,
and for a brief while it seemed like the Church was left with the

proclamation of the Word only by preaching. But no sooner was the Church deprived of mission through provision of education and healing than new opportunities and dilemmas presented themselves. First, there was the state of civil war (1955–1972). The Church was called upon to be a mediator between the warring factions. The Church had to be involved in the ministry of reconciliation. During the civil war, every Sudanese family lost at least one member. Thus the amount of animosity that developed between families was quite great. A serious teaching on forgiveness and reconciliation was launched by all the churches. This teaching produced something positive during the period from 1972 to 1982. But no sooner did the Church embark on the ministry of reconciliation and forgiveness for its own Sudanese members than it was confronted with a new situation—an influx of refugees from our neighbors, Uganda and Ethiopia.

The Sudan experienced the first wave of refugees in the early 1960's. The first to come were Belgians and other foreigners who escaped from the Congo soon after independence, fearing reprisals from the new native rulers. This number, however, was nothing compared to the next wave four years later, when natives started to rebel against their own rulers. Not less than ten thousand Congolese refugees ran to the Sudan for shelter. On the eastern side, thousands of Eritreans and, later on, Ethiopians of other nationalities (such as the Tigray and Oromo) started streaming into the Sudan. Today there are about a half million Eritrean/Ethiopian refugees in the Sudan.

After Idi Amin took over the government from Obote in 1971, about five thousand Acholi and Langi also made their way to the Sudan for refuge. When Idi Amin himself was overthrown, the five thousand or so returned to Uganda; but they were replaced by another thirty thousand or so pro-Amin refugees. This was not all. Since Obote regained power, more Ugandans have fled for refuge to the Sudan—so many that there are not less than one hundred and sixty-five thousand Ugandan refugees in the Sudan.

To the west we have the Chadian refugees. Although the number is not known exactly, rough estimates place it at about twenty thousand. This imposes a burden of about seven hundred thousand refugees on the Sudanese situation.

Although the biggest country in Africa, with about one million square miles of land, the Sudan is sparsely populated and therefore the population cannot afford to develop an adequate infrastructure. Thus it can happen that one part of the country has a crop boom while another is suffering from drought. Between the two parts are eight hundred miles with no roads of any type, so food cannot be moved from one part to the other. The churches have identified these areas as priorities for mission service.

While the churches and the total community are trying hard to minister in the midst of these problems—reconciliation at home, hunger caused by drought and refugee problems—the Sudanese government has introduced new measures that have again produced another cycle of violence. The new situation threatens the country more than the seventeen-year civil war (1955–1972). This is because there is a high probability of dragging in a superpower confrontation. Once again, the Church will be called to exercise its ministry of reconciliation and moderation. In order to be able to carry out such a mission, the Church needs a conducive atmosphere at home. But how can one operate effectively in a situation where Militant Islam is on the upsurge?

It is common knowledge that Militant Islam is a force shaping the world today, especially affecting North Africa and the Suhelan belt, Southeast Asia, with the center being the Middle East itself. It is true that within that force are tensions and contradictions that could break it apart. But using its newly acquired oil wealth, Islam is struggling to assert itself within the modern world order. The attempts for a return to a pure Islamic state of affairs in Iran, Pakistan, and, lately, Sudan have created new challenges for the Church. Questions that remain unanswered are: How can the Church minister in a situation where the legal system describes it as a "tolerated institution"? How can a dialogue be instituted unless there is some semblance of parity? This is the dilemma in which the Church in the Sudan will continue to find itself under a Sharia system.

To sum up this section, it is important to note that the mission of the Church in the Sudan continues to concern itself with proclamation of the Word to the unreached, ministering to the divided people of the country through reconciliation, service to refugees, service to the hungry and the unemployed, and, most of all, a concerted teaching about the love of God in Jesus Christ among people who are threatened with religious intolerance because of Militant Islam.

Church and Social Order

The Democratic Republic of the Sudan is about one million square miles of land with a population of about twenty two million people, sixty percent of whom are young people under twenty one years of age. Since 1898 the country has been divided into two parts. One part, the Northern Sudan, is about two thirds of the country both in land area and population. It is inhabited by people of Afro-Arab descent. But the predominant culture is Arab, with Arabic being the common language of trade and office work. Islam is the main religion. The Southern Sudan is mainly African—populated by tropical and savannah blacks, sometimes called the negroes. The dominant culture is the traditional African way of life. And many African languages are spoken: Bantu, Nilotic, and Sudanic groups. Since the creation of the modern Sudan and the penetration of the Southern Sudan by Christian missionaries, there has been a sizable number of Christians among almost every ethnic group; and many cultures have acquired some aspects of Christianity as the latter has also taken on local forms, especially in forms of prayer, singing, and even the theological interpretation of certain social issues.

Into this divided Sudan, the Church introduces its own structure. The Roman Catholic Church, which has its presence in almost all parts of the Sudan, has responded by having two archdioceses, one for the Northern Sudan and and the other for the Southern Sudan. Likewise, the Episcopal Church has evolved similar structures. It has three dioceses in the Southern Sudan and one in the Northern Sudan. While one can find Christians of both regions anywhere in the country, the jurisdictional boundaries have kept faithfulness to the political boundary.

Other smaller churches are either found in some parts of the North only—for example, the Sudanese Church of Christ in the Nuba mountains and in the three towns; or in the South only—such as the Presbyterian Church in the Sudan and the African Inland Church.

These divisions have naturally lent themselves to the easy labels one tends to hear in common places. The North, which is predominantly Arab and Muslim, is also the better developed part of the country. The South—with its many African groups of various African religious expressions, but with a sizable number of influential Christians—is still considered relatively backward and underdeveloped. Ironically, however, Southern Sudanese are considered to be more westernized than Northern Sudanese, who consider themselves part of the Middle East Arabs.

With these easy labels, moments of strife, such as the period of the civil war in the South (1955–1972), tend to polarize even

Christians into North-South positions. Although much has not been apparent in public discussions about the polarization of North and South in the Church, it is important to underscore its presence, even in a very silent way. Proof of this could be adduced in the debate before the formation of the Province of the Episcopal Church of the Sudan. Episcopalians from Northern Sudan argued that the See of the Archbishop of the Sudan should be in Khartoum, in the Northern Sudan; while the majority of the Episcopalians who happened to be Southerners argued that the see ought to be in Juba in the Southern Sudan. Similarly, until a year ago the structure of the Sudan Council of Churches tended to perpetuate the same divisions. Churches that had a presence in both North and South, such as the Roman Catholic Church and the Episcopal Church, sent delegates to Council meetings in a manner that reflected the North-South tension. It was only a year ago that this system was abolished in favor of national representation by each church instead of fielding the representatives by regions. Still, further voices continue to be heard by the majority of the Christians who happen to be Southerners calling for the head office of the Sudan Council of Churches to be moved to the Southern Sudan. The only problem at the moment is that the status of the South as a unit is being dismantled. Otherwise one might not be surprised to see a vote at the next assembly of the Sudan Council of Churches asking for an amendment in the Constitution to provide for the head office to be based in Juba in the Southern Sudan.

Common Life of the Church

I have already noted the physical divisions that have affected the structure of the Church and its common life. Because of the vastness of the country, most mission boards could not field missionaries throughout the country, even if that were allowed. Therefore, as early as the end of World War I, mission boards of all denominations worked out some formulas in which some boards operated in certain zones and left other areas to other boards. This zoning has resulted in many areas being left entirely to one mission board for quite some time. It was quite late when some boards of the Roman Catholic and Anglican churches started to extend their work to areas that had hitherto been left to other mission boards. In several cases mission boards had handed over their work to missionaries of another board because they could not cope with keeping their station open.

The implications of this zoning system for the work in the

Sudan is that on the one hand polarization on a theological basis is downplayed because this tension was not exhibited at the earliest stages of church formation. This is reflected further in the sense that there are no deep-level theological discussions among Christian denominations. People easily say, "We are all Christians, and that is what counts." This factor is behind the easy formation of the Christian Council, in which all the Christian traditions are present: Catholic, Protestant, and Orthodox. On the other hand, the zoning has led to whole ethnic groups being identified with one or the other denomination. This sounds like the conversion of whole kingdoms into one faith or denomination. Many ethnic groups have never known that Christians are beset with so many unhappy divisions. Members of those ethnic groups who are brought up in a monodenominational society often get the shock of their lives when they come to discover in town centers, such as Khartoum, the multiplicity of Christian churches under the labels of Catholic, Protestant, and Orthodox. Most of them will not even try to understand why.

In all these, greater issues common to all churches have often lifted the churches to express their life together. In 1929, faced with the multiplicity of Southern languages, the various mission boards, representing various denominations, came together at Rejaf, near Juba, and tried to group Southern languages to make it easy for translation of the Scriptures. This action concerned both Catholic and Protestant groups. The vastness of the country occasions an opportunity for the mission groups to settle for some common strategy of mission, as has already been mentioned.

Later in their work, when the state threatened to nationalize mission schools and hospitals in 1957, the churches came together in the negotiations for the takeover. Furthermore, from 1960, when the state threatened to curtail the operations of the churches in preparation for an Islamization program, the churches banded together to meet this threat. It was this particular event that led the Roman Catholic Church, the Episcopal Church, the Evangelical Church, and the Presbyterian Church to push forward for the formation of a National Christian Council in 1967. This council became instrumental in the negotiation for a peaceful settlement of the Southern Sudan civil war and, later, in undertaking the huge job of resettlement, rehabilitation, and reconstruction in 1972.

The new introduction of Islamic law (*Sharia*) in the Sudan in 1983 has given the Church yet another opportunity for common expression of the faith. Christians in the Sudan are more united today than at any other point in their history. Most Christians are seen carrying their crosses on their chests and collars. Even Christians from denominations that one would not associate with carrying crucifixes because of Low Church evangelical emphasis elsewhere are seen carrying them in the Sudan. Christians do not find it difficult anymore to enter the nearest church available in any station for worship. This must be one of the healthiest things I have ever seen in my whole life.

The Anglican Heritage and Mission

In this section one would have to look at the work of the Anglican Church through its local constituent member, the Episcopal Church of the Sudan. First the Sudanese Anglicans are a result of the Low Church, evangelical line as it is practiced by members of the Church Missionary Society of England. Churchmanship is quite simple—liturgy and the Word, with the Sacraments being given a low rating. Pomp and rituals are downplayed, sometimes eliminated entirely. The rich Anglican fellowship can enrich the Sudanese worship and learn from its simplicity also.

Secondly, on discipline, the leadership is too rigid. Everyone must conform to all aspects of social standards. Deviation of any kind, whether justified or not, is unacceptable. There is too much intolerance of the sinful. One fails to see the grace of God in some cases. The studies being undertaken elsewhere within the Anglican Communion could benefit Episcopalians in the Sudan.

Thirdly, the ministry of bishops, priests, deacons, and laity, orderly as it is, has become too rigidly monarchical. The rule of the Episcopate vibrates from echelon to echelon to the extent that free discourse and discussion of issues is discouraged. A challenge to the bishops, priests, deacons, or lay elders is almost tantamount to challenging the Lord of the vineyard Himself. This leads to submissiveness, and "majestic rule" becomes the order of the day. Creativity is killed, and people tend to be conservative.

Whether intentional or due to the need of their time, the early evangelists were jacks-of-all-trades—though, as usual, they were masters of none. This image has been passed down to the first-generation, national leadership who believes in knowing and doing all things in the name of the Lord. All evidence is that the time has changed sufficiently for the Episcopal hierarchy to realize that it can no longer be expected to do all things—that the society is full of faithful persons who are knowledgeable and therefore can do certain things better for the "company of Christ's flock." There is need to delegate responsibilities to people within the flock.

Mission in Partnership

There are Christians from other communions at the local level. These include the Roman Catholics, the Presbyterians, the Orthodox, and a few Congregationalists. Oftentimes the approach to these Christians is too simplistic: "You are ok, we are ok." There is no attempt to engage in meaningful dialogues on issues of doctrine and/or practice. Acceptance of "the other" just as a Christian without dealing openly with points of conflict or disagreement can lead to false "peace." Worse still, it can lead the flock to bewilderment and confusion because there is no attempt to explain issues rationally. Even in situations where there are other faiths like Islam, there is hardly any consistent attempt to create a real awareness of what Islam stands for. A program of the Sudan Council of Churches on dialogue with other faiths does not receive the active participation of the Episcopal leadership. In fact, in the first half of this century it was included in the Anglican catechism that Islam was a pagan faith that no church or Christian should have anything at all to do with. Similar to the prevention of early evangelists from preaching to Muslims, present-day Episcopalians have no program to reach the Muslims.

On the international level, partnership is understood as receiving only, not giving, even when it is apparent that the Episcopal Church could give of its own experience with traditional religions—for example, its interaction with Islam, its experience with conflict or civil-war situations, its work among refugees. These are very valuable experiences for other parts of the communion. So far, there is a great process of receiving only from other partners, to the extent that the experiences of Sudanese Episcopalians in the areas I have identified above will get lost as time passes. Because there is so much to do and so few workers, there is hardly any writing of the experiences into books. Although an independent province, our church still considers itself a mission field for work originating from other parts of the Anglican Communion.

This comes about from the poor teaching of stewardship that has been passed down since 1905. To date there has yet to be developed in all parts of our province a system where the faithful can respond to the total issues of mission in a systematic manner. Occasionally some congregations know how to deal with one aspect of mission better than others, even where the same problems exist throughout the country. The ease with which problems are addressed to external partners is quite disturbing. It has created a feeling that "our partners out there will always provide. They know that we are too poor to meet these needs." And yet one immediately notices the contradictory extravagance exhibited at feasts when the local churches host visitors. The cost is unimaginable. When one looks at expenditures incurred to organize big conventions that are held three or four times in a year in each diocese, one realizes what I mean when I talk about the faulty teaching of stewardship.

One feeling that seems to be permeating the relationship between our "young" province and its external partners is an awareness that the external partners know of the inadequate work that they have done in the past. Therefore, their guilt ought to be exploited so that they can "help us keep on doing the work they left undone."

This is a situation that must be dealt with frankly and honestly by partners of the Sudan. These are issues within the Anglican Communion that must receive serious attention. It is too late to spend too much time criticizing the faulty teaching or practice of stewardship by mission personnel, but there is room to investigate the present practice and put it on a right footing.

Conclusion

In conclusion it needs to be said that the Church must not consider itself outside mission. The Church is the result of mission— God's mission to humankind through the Incarnation of Jesus Christ. The Church that considers mission as just another of its many faculties has lost mission. For there should be no such thing as a mission of a church, but a Church of Mission, a Church that is born of and lives for no other purpose than mission.

The Anglican Communion in Latin America

The Right Reverend Adrián D. Cáceres

The Mission of Christ's Church

The Mission of Christ's Church is the dialectic process of God's initiative and man's response, in which all Christians (clergy and laity) are at the same time objects of God's love and part of this offering of love to others. All men are part of this incarnate life and proclaimed process. This is God's will since the beginning and is our vocation and responsibility from baptism to the Judgment. If God is at the heart of the world and is the Lord of the world, Christ came to the center of the world and from that center calls His disciples to fulfill the mission with Him and to form the communion of the citizens of the Kingdom. The Church and its people should carry this job out within the same demands that Christ, the Great Missionary, had, and within the same framework that He laid out for this action. The following characteristics constitute the basic elements of the mission:

Mission Is Love. "God loved the world in such a way" that He has given the mission to His Son, and His Son to His disciples. This missionary love is defined in the thirteenth chapter of 1 Corinthians and in the letters of John, the "beloved disciple." Christ's mission was love; He died for love on the Cross and there created the love for the Christian mission.

Mission Is Incarnation. Incarnation is deliberate, not accidental; total, not partial; insertion, not incursion. When the Indians made incursions against their enemies, they carried off as trophies the scalps they had taken. Incarnation does not deal with the religious emotions of a sort of external triumphalism, but with the total man.

Christ is not a kind of "religious varnish" like the icing on the cake, nor a religious colony like a single raisin in the cake. Christians are yeast, salt, and light. The mission wants and looks for the total man—the total society—and that is why His Incarnation must be total, in a context, indigenous, and identifiable.

Mission Is Service. This is the general mobilization of everyone for all men and everywhere. "The Son of Man has not come to be served, but to serve" (Matthew 20:28), said Christ, the Missionary. And in His Church there are none who are served, but only servants with ministries to the believer and nonbeliever—to the individual and to society, in their spiritual and temporal needs, in their body and soul, in the home and on the street. If every baptized person is a minister, then all are missionaries, not just the foreigners that come from "outside," but, even more, the "missionaries" from among us.

Mission Is Passion. Love is engendered out of suffering; salvation out of crucifixion; the apostolate out of martyrdom. "He who wants to follow me, must take his cross and follow me." "Truly, you will drink from my cup." Mission is to be the Simon of Cyrene, carrying the Savior's Cross. St. Paul said: "Who now rejoice in my sufferings for you, and fill up that which is behind of the afflictions of Christ in my flesh for his body's sake, which is the church" (Colossians 1:24). Mission is to walk shoulder-to-shoulder with the suffering, to give one's human life for the eternal life of others.

Mission Is Living the Holy Spirit. An essential element for the validity and strength of the mission is: "You will receive power." The Holy Spirit is the Missionary that makes missions; the soul that gives life; the dynamic that moves; the tongue that proclaims.

Mission Is Testimony. The efficiency of mission, more than in the "go" of Matthew 28, is in "and ye shall be witnesses" of Acts 1:8. When the Lord sent His disciples out two by two, it was precisely to give credibility and legal proof in trials. The word "witnesses" compasses all that the Apostles had to do—what they received from the Lord, what they lived with Him, and what He died for.

Mission Is Discipline. If mission is to "make disciples," the discipleship is the quality of following the "discipline"—that is, the doctrine or the teaching of the Teacher. The discipline of the Gospel is obedience and humility, prayer and study, commitment and loyalty. The mission's discipline is to evanesce yourself in some way when faced with the tremendous reality of a God of revelation, for whom no one has a monopoly. The poet Antonio Machado said: "Your truth? No, the Truth. And come with me to look for it. Yours, keep it for yourself." That is why the mission is one, not sectarian; it is ecumenical, not denominational; it is ecclesial, not ecclesiastical; it is not Roman nor Protestant, but catholic, in a continous "purification" and "semper reformanda." That is why the discipline of mission has a condition: "That they may be one in us, so that the world will believe that you sent me" (John 17:21).

These elements constitute, at the same time, the requisites for the missionaries of the Church's Great Divine Mission.

How Is the Church's Mission Carried Out?

The catechism gives the answer: "The Church pursues its mission as it prays and worships, proclaims the Gospel, and promotes justice, peace, and love" (*Book of Common Prayer*, p. 855).

In 1982 the General Convention of ECUSA approved "The Next Step in Mission" in terms of service, worship, evangelism, education, and pastoral care. Implied, as well, is the evaluation by every congregation of its potential for ministering more effectively in all of these areas. Since 1971 the diocese of Ecuador has planned its program based upon the seven following areas of mission:

Kerygma or Proclamation. To be, to do, and to make do the Gospel; to be God's agents and bearers of His Word; to confirm it in those who have heard it; to bring to perfection those who have received it; and to prophesy to those who resist it or have received it imperfectly.

Before the real situation that Latin America is "sacramentalized" but not "evangelized," our first responsibility is to "evangelize" and "reevangelize," with emphasis on the Indian mission in Quechua, university mission, family pastoral, community pastoral, and ecclesial or contextual ministry.

Didaché or Teaching. The enabling of God's people to learn and teach Word and Action of God, the word and action of man. "Practice what you have learned and received, and have seen and heard from me, and the God of peace will be with you" (Philippians 4:9). The people are tired of hearing; what they need is to see the Gospel. Against the religious illiteracy and egotism of the baptized, we have to give the confirmation of the baptismal vows and the ordination of layministry—the enabling of the ordained diocesan and "local" ministry. More than classrooms for theologization, the seminaries must be Upper Rooms for apostolization. It is to teach the pure doctrine of God, not the culture of one nation, nor some pastor's idea, nor the ideology of some group, but the Bible, and only the Bible, interpreted by Church tradition and applied with reason.

Liturgy. Personal and community worship, a particular and official prayer; renewed and united, lived out and native, sacramental, and ecumenical.

Stewardship. To create, guide, and practice men's sacrificial offering with all their gifts, talents, goods, time, and total life.

Diakonia or Service. To the people in the spiritual and temporal areas; to be within the people, commit oneself to the people, and to be the voice and support of the ones who lack them.

Koinonia or Christian Brotherhood. With "our own" (*koinonia*) and with those "outside" (ecumenism). To be a family, a community, and citizens of this kingdom. "The Church that lives for itself, by itself will die."

Autonomy. Since the first missionary day, to teach and guide toward the concept of adulthood, as much in the local community as in the national or regional community. There can be no autonomy without *autoctony* ("indigeousness"). There can be no "interdependence in the body of Christ" unless there is independence of dependence. Dependence, maintained indefinitely, institutionalizes religious colonialism and contributes to an underdeveloped status. Foreign missionaries, international agencies, and the mother churches are responsible for creating churches that are always either "children" or "old maids" who have never let go of their mother's skirts. St. Paul's missions were autonomous from the beginning, and that is why they quickly matured and engendered others.

Autonomy begins in Sunday school, is practiced through stewardship, is carried out in the parish, and is consummated in the autonomous province. The mission schedule and missionary planning ought to indicate precisely the process by which autonomy is reached.

This is the concept of mission that we have conceived for Ec-

uador and, in general, for the mission of the Anglican Communion in Latin America.

The Historical Religious Vision of Latin America

Using the language of the world calender within the Christian
context, I could say that 1492 delineates a dividing line between
"before Christ" and "after Christ," for the Aztecs, the Mayas, the
Chibchas, and the Incas, "discovered" in their own world.

Theologically speaking, the Indian was not Christian, but he
was religious. He had his gods, his cults, his liturgical year, his
rituals, his morality, and his priests. He believed in "things heavenly" and in things of the nether world; in spirits; in rewards and
punishments. The Mayan *Popol-Vuh,* the chronicles of the colonial writers, and the survival of indigenous cultural traditions
are witnesses to this.

In the moral area the Incas had three commandments: *Amasua,
Amallulla,* and *Amakella:* Don't steal; don't lie; and don't be lazy.
True, they are negative commandments; but they comprehend
honesty, sincerity, loyalty, respect, justice, work—fundamental
bases for personal and family life, for progress, and for social
peace. In respect to the gods there were no commandments to
keep simply because they had no concept of the nonreligious man,
but rather the practicing believer in the area of the personal and
the communal, or because their gods were for them less explicit
and more tolerant.

The Christians arrived, and at the point of the sword and har-
quebus surprised them, killed their chiefs; invaded their territories; and took possession of their lands, their treasures, and their
women. Once this was accomplished, and in order to justify it all
to their authorities and their "Christian consciences," they converted the Indians to Christianity and baptized them with Christian names. By means of this sacrament, the process of invasion,
looting, and servitude was sealed.

Thus began the Christian era in the Inca's empire, and so it was
with the other invasions, whether Spanish, Portuguese, French,
English, or Dutch. The only difference was that some killed all
the Indians and established the colonial system among themselves, and the others took over everything but left the Indians
their lives, only to put the men into a slave work force and the
women into sexual "mestization." The Church's mission was that
of a "transport" and a "transplant" from the mother Church, with
an experiential dualism. On the one hand, the laws for the Indies

and the laws of the Church hierarchy set forth laws and pastoral letters of such evangelical value that they are a real theology of mission. On the other hand, the colonists not only did not obey the laws but, to the contrary, used and abused the Church and its ministers for the purpose of subjugating the Indians in such a way that they would continue to be Indian, as it is even today. Actually, they were not civilized, but contrariwise. Their culture was killed, their systems and governments were taken away, and those of the colonists were imposed. Churches were built on the ruins of their temples, and the Church remained established with all the power of the colonial sovereignty and with a total monopoly of religion, morality, and ministry.

We understand that the coming-into-being of new people is always dramatic, involving them in light and darkness. Evangelization as a human task is always subject to historical vicissitudes, but in spite of sin is always looking to transfigure with the fire of the Spirit, on Christ's road, the center and meaning of all history. In spite of the frustrations of those founding times (in Latin America), that early Christian labor is one of the most relevant chapters in the history of the Church. There are the saints Toribio de Mogroviejo, Martín de Porres, Pedro Claver, Luis Beltrán, and so many others who, overcoming the human weaknesses that surrounded them, sowed sanctity in this land. Others like Antonio de Montecinos, Bartolomé de Las Casas, Juan de Zumárraga, Vasco de Quiroga, Juan del Valle, and Julián Garcés defended the Indians against the colonists and "encomenderos," even to the death—as with Bishop Antonio Valdivieso—defending the dignity and liberty of the Latin American.

John Paul II does well to refer to the religious who came "to proclaim Christ the Savior, to defend the Indian's humanity, to announce and claim their inviolable rights, to encourage their integration into society, to inculcate the brotherhood of all as people and sons of the same Lord and Father."

The Religious Situation Today
After the years of absolute religious triumphalism during colonial times and the first years of independence, Christianity today finds itself struggling with laicism and secularism. Liberalism has taken away the former absolute ownership and control of universities, schools, hospitals, and corporations and has left Christianity off in a corner with its churches. The crosses on the buildings, the religious medals on the chests, the processions on the streets, and

the Masses at civic festivals are the only signs that remain from a triumphant and glorious past, which appears today only in a superficial tradition of the people, while secularism continues digging deeper into people and societies. God is not spoken of in the universities; the labor unions forget about the Lord; He is left out of public offices; and He has been put aside in the laws and processes of change. The Church has conformed to its defeat, has lost its zeal and enthusiasm, and left Latin America to its own devices.

The situation today is that the people are sacramentalized, but not evangelized; baptized, but not "confirmed." This same Church, conscious of this reality, did not balk at calling Latin America "a mission field"; and its first Latin American bishops' conference (CELAM, in 1955) said that the Church has four main enemies: "Communism, Protestantism, Laicism, and Masonry." It began to fight against them. The result is that the "enemies" are advancing, winning new frontiers and establishing themselves among the masses, and Christianity as an institution continues losing its place in the hearts and in the institutions of men. The Roman Catholic Church, the majority church of Latin American Christianity, seems to accept this religious crisis, thanks to the new light of Vatican II. Beginning with Medellín and continuing on through Puebla, it began to examine the signs of the times; and it seems disposed to contribute to the building of a new Latin American society—more just, more evangelical, and more Christian. Puebla states: "Inspired by yesterday's great mission, we want to come close, with pastoral and Christian eyes and hearts, to the reality of today's Latin American man, in order to understand and interpret him, so that we can analyze our pastoral mission arising out of that reality."

Vision of the Sociocultural Reality of Latin America
The profound economic crisis to which our contemporary world is handed over—accentuated in the Third World countries, like ours, by the generally poor development of the means of production and the deforming of their structures—has direct repercussions in the dramatic situation in which people live at their various personal, family, social, cultural, and spiritual levels.

Since the Gospel gives us a Jesus Christ doing good (Acts 10:38) and loving everyone without distinction, with that vision of faith and a commitment to mission we put ourselves into the realities of the Latin American. This faith and this commitment lead us to

discern the callings of God in the signs of the times and to announce and put forward the evangelical values of justice, peace,
love, and social communion, denouncing everything that is
against the liberation and promotion of man.

The Church tries to help man make less human situations into
more human ones. It calls for a continual individual and social
conversion. It calls all who believe themselves to be, and call
themselves, Christians, to collaborate in the changing of unjust
structures, to communicate Christian values to the global culture
in which they live, becoming a voice—"the voice of him who
cannot speak, or of him who is silenced."

The Church speaks with the voices of the millions of "mortgaged" people with all its energies in the fight to overcome whatever condemns them to live on the margins of life—hunger,
chronic sickness, ignorance, illiteracy, impoverishment, injustice
in international relations (especially in the world of commerce),
and neocolonial economic and cultural situations, at times as cruel
as the political ones.

As Christian people, we see as a scandal and a contradiction,
the growing breach between rich and poor. The luxury of the few
is converted into an insult against the misery of the great masses—
a situation of social sin, even worse when seen in countries and
people that call themselves Christians and have the capacity to
change.

We take as the most devastating and humiliating epidemic the
situation of inhuman poverty in which millions of Latin Americans live, expressed, for example, in infant mortality, a lack of
adequate housing, health problems, hunger-level income, unemployment and underemployment, malnutrition, employment in-
stability, and helpless and forced massive migrations. These and
other situations find their roots in mechanisms shot through, not
with an authentic humanism, but with a materialism that assures,
on the international level, the rich getting richer at the expense of
the poor getting poorer.

We see countries where there is no respect for fundamental
human rights—such as life, health, education, housing, work,
family, rest, religion—in a situation of permanent violation of the
dignity of personhood. A flagrant and unpardonable violation that
cries for vengeance to Heaven is the violation of religious liberty
and the respect that the individual with his faith deserves, trampled upon by the Roman Catholic Church and the fanatic and
intolerant sects. We know that no one has the monopoly of re-

ligion. From Atahualpa, murdered for the "crime" of ignoring the missal, through the martyrs of the Inquisition, to the sacrificed believers, whether evangelicals or of other churches, who came to Latin America, these deeds cry out for religious justice, religious liberty, religious reform, religious commitment, and respect for man as man, and for the Christian as Christian. There has been enough of the religious power brought by Spain, used by the colonists, taken advantage of by the politicians of the republics, and abused by the clericalism of convents, parishes, and diocesan "chairs."

To this is added the violation of political liberty and thought, committed by the typical abuses of power by power regimes, whether military, partisan, or repressive groups. We see systematic or selective repression, accompanied by accusations, violation of privacy, unjust constraints, torture, and exile. We see the suffering in so many families caused by the disappearance of their loved ones, without so much as a word; total insecurity because of arrests and requisitions without judicial process; agonies in the face of justice repressed, tied up, or manipulated by bribery or pressure from judges. Confronted by these deeds, which unfortunately are more popular every day, the Church must make its voice heard, denouncing and condemning these sins, most especially when the responsible governments profess to be Christian.

Equally, the Church must confront the sufferings caused by guerrilla violence, the terrorism of irrational assaults, and the kidnappings carried out by extremists of whatever stripe, which compromise the guarantees of personhood and societal peace.

In many places labor legislation is applied arbitrarily or not at all; or, on the other hand, the exasperating politicization of the union leaders distorts the goals of their organizations, such as the pacific progress of their own members and of the society.

The economics of the free market, in its most rigid expression, has increased the distance between rich and poor by opposing capital to labor, the economic to the social. Marxist ideologies have spread widely among workers, students, teachers, and other milieus, with the promise of better social justice. In carrying out its strategies, many Christian, and therefore human, values have been sacrificed, and the Marxists have fallen into utopian unrealities, resulting in policies that, using force or fear as the fundamental instrument, have increased the spiral of violence, hopelessness, and loss of liberty.

Individualistic materialism that impedes solidarity, collectivist materialism that subordinates the individual to the state, and consumerism, with its uncontrolled ambition of "having more," continue drowning modern man in an immanentism that shuts him off from the evangelical virtues of disinterestedness, austerity, modesty, and humility. The deterioration of family values breaks down family stability and communion, converting it into the easy prisoner of divorce, abandonment, and the break-up of peace; the deterioration of honesty that causes either public or private immorality; hedonism, which gives impulse to vices such as drugs, alcoholism, and sexual libertinism.

In spite of advances in education and social communication, and on account of the manipulation of powerful minority groups that try to assure attainment of their interests, or inculcate their ideologies, or cover up their intentions, there exist phenomena of deformation and depersonalization.

There is a manipulation of information on the part of different power structures and groups. This appears in publicity that introduces false expectations, creating fictitious necessities. The misuse of freedom in these areas brings about the invasion of privacy of individuals, who are usually defenseless.

To sum up, without trying to determine the technical character of those bases, we see that at the heart of them there is an unrecognized sin, a loss of Christian values, a lack of the evangelical ethic, a lack of religious education and pastoral care by the churches, and inertia or sin of omission by the leaders of the Roman Catholic and other churches and religious groups. The world has the right to call us to a critical judgment, and God will inexorably demand it of us on the Day of Judgment. St. Peter advises us: "For the time is come that judgment must begin at the house of God" (1 Peter 4:17). And the interrogatory of judgment will be "For I was an hungered, and ye gave me no meat" (Matthew 25:42–46).

In order to conclude this critical review of the historical results of Christian action and of the social crises of the people of the Third World, we ask the following questions:

1. To what factors do we owe the decadence of institutional Christianity, at least in Latin America?

2. Which came first, the decay of Christianity or the social crisis, and how did the one influence the other?

3. What characteristics and "equipment" should the Church, or churches, have for the task of rebuilding the Body of Christ in Latin America? Or, in other words, what kind of church is needed in Latin America for its task here and now?

I leave the answers to each church and Latin American society in general.

From my Latin American point of view, I can say that one of the factors making for decay can be the fact that the Roman Catholic Church's believes that it is the only true church, with its consequent exclusivity and total monopoly. This has deprived Latin America of new ways of Christian experience, new theological currents, and different ways of behavior. Absolutism created a cloistered religion, prejudicing the economic, political, and social development of people. As a contrast we have the North as "First World," and the South as the "Third World." By not permitting an opening to other peoples, or persons, who had a different religion from the official one, there was a closing off of Latin America, with an attendant unilateral, or unidirectional, cultural orientation.

The evidence presented indicates clearly the needs of the Latin American people and, parallel to these, the need to develop a strong and responsible Christian action of reevangelization of all Christian people.

The Latin American people are tired of hearing the Gospel and the Mass. What they want is to see the Gospel and to do the Mass. This makes us think that our mission practically makes it into a witness that with the passage of time will be prophetic. Thus, evangelization must have one purpose—the decisive confrontation of men with Jesus Christ, and the task of the Church is to proclaim the Gospel in its specific and concrete secular sense.

We are persuaded that this humanity needs to follow a spiritual guide, a spiritual orientation, and a spiritual path. This is how the presence of countless religious sects justifies itself, since by their methods and strategies they are accepted among the people.

Characteristics and Equipment of the Church for Its Mission in Latin America, Taking Into Consideration the Advantages and Disadvantages of the Anglican Inheritance

Biblical Church. If the Anglican Communion has something of great importance for us "latinos," it is precisely that it has the Bible at the very center of its life, its thought, and its worship. Article 6 of the Articles of Religion constitutes the certification of its doctrine, the authority of its teaching, and the guarantee of its ministry. Biblical in its theology, in its morality, in its discipline, and in its worship, as well as free from the cultures of its origin and respectful of the culture of our people, it is a welcome church for these times and places, of religious frustrations, of sectarian invasions, and of the unbelief of rationalism.

Reformed Catholic Church. This church has the privilege of maintaining the difficult balance between these two basic spiritual concepts, known as "catholic" and "evangelical." We must be persuaded that Latin America will never be Protestant, but neither does it wish to stay within colonial Romanism. An apostolicly Christian and a catholicly evangelical Church—a multicolored and spontaneous Church, expressed in the simplicity of its life and in the purity of its liturgy—wants, waits, and asks. The Church will be the inheritance of our apostolic fathers, the profession of our creeds, and the voice of our councils. It will be a Church living for centuries by its Bible, but new in its context, that proclaims the Good News as though it were indeed news.

Socially Committed. By this is meant having a vision and action for, and a sensitivity to, the human condition. This "sociability" should not be limited to social programs or institutions like parish schools and clinics, but also to the better promotion of community programs in direct cooperation with those of the governments or various sectors of the community. This catalytic value should be its major effort as an authentic symbol of its cooperation with the social issues of the community. It has to redeem colonial times, extending the hand of friendship to the Indian of all countries, taking him off his reservation, raising him up from his inhuman situation, taking him out of his isolation, and encouraging his integration on a national and continental level. It has to redeem the era of the Industrial Revolution to promote prophetically "the redemption of the proletariat" with the Bible's force.

The Ministerial Church. We know that during the Reformation, reform was proclaimed in theology, worship, and the pastoral area; but it didn't reach the mission field. Today the Church finds itself in a real "Revolution of Ministry." Each Christian is part of the total ministry of the Church, with functions that have their base in God's call, the gifts received, and the recognition of the Church. It claims a return to the original situation of the primitive Church, defining the diaconate in general terms as a source of service in the area of practical ministry and the presbyterate as a source of service in the area of the ministry of the Word and Sacraments.

The attempt is being made to broaden the functions of the ordained ministry with special ministries, like evangelists, teachers, and pastors taking into account the reality of many isolated congregations and the necessity of an adequate sacramental ministry.

These tendencies need to be studied and applied with wisdom and the inspiration of the Holy Spirit. They are the values that will work for the mission to and the pastoral care of the peoples of our continent.

Missionary Church. The missionary church primarily is a pilgrim Church, poor and humble like its Teacher and the Apostles, cleansed of its self-sufficient, bourgeois, and paternalistic attitudes; and then, it is the performer of a missionary pastorate, teaching the Good News—with a novel message to the man of today that searches for transformation and changes, but also by denouncing individual and social sins, with the courage of the prophets. For this it needs to be equipped with, first, a missionary strategy, which is continually planned, controlled, and checked. The Church must consider seriously the radical changes in its approach to mission that are found in Roland Allen's provocative, and seemingly radical, works. Allen understands the "how to" of establishing and building a genuinely indigenous and autonomous Church, fully "equipped" with Bible, creeds, Sacraments, ministry, and congregational life. Second, there must be missionary personnel. If all the members are the missionaries' agents, they must receive careful training for their different levels. By the way, are foreign missionaries still necessary? Yes, but not precisely to plant the Church, but for Christian education, leadership training, and for advising the diocese. They must not expect to be bishops or directors indefinitely. Third, the missionary church needs to be equipped with a deep spirituality among the clergy and laity—that is, their life should be the voice and strength of the Holy Spirit. The seminaries must not be classrooms for theologization, but Upper Rooms for apostolization, where in prayer they nurture in the Holy Spirit in order to burst forth with the power of the Gospel.

The Anglican Presence in Latin America

Historically Anglicanism in Latin America arises from three sources, with no interrelationship between them until recently. The Anglican Church arrived in the New World primarily from England in the southern part of the South American continent. In 1825 it arrived on the Argentinian coast, brought by English immigrants who were farmers and businessmen. It established itself within those colonies of Englishmen where the colonies were established, according to their sociocultural life-style. This church was characterized by being a "chaplaincy," exclusively serving the Anglican English, as a complete transplant of the original, with its bishops and chaplains of the same blood and country, their churches built in the English style, and their church considered more a cultural center than a community of faith. The members were content to have the Anglican Church as "their Church," exclusive of the "native" population. There was no concept of the missionary role of the Church. To continue in this way means a death sentence for this church, being "buried" at the same time as the last descendent of English extraction, even though his fathers and grandfathers were born in this new world.

The second arrival, also along the southern South American coast, was brought by the missionary inspiration of Captain Allen Gardiner and his companions, who arrived in Tierra de Fuego in 1851. There the Indians forced them to take refuge in a cave, where they died from hunger. This seed of martyrdom sown in mission germinated in virgin ground; and although it did not prosper in Patagonia, it did expand slowly in the areas of Chile, Paraguay (1880), and northern Argentina (1911), thanks to the labors of SAMS (South American Missionary Society), founded by Gardiner.

As the work of an independent missionary agency, SAMS organized itself not within the context of the Church, but within the parameters of a private and extraecclesiastical missionary society, with its own doctrinal, disciplinary, and cultural structure. As such, it enclosed itself within its own "typology" and carried out a mission within its own system. Its bishops and directors are all from the same society, without the admission or the training of the native leadership. Until now, they have not had a diocesan bishop of Latin American extraction.

This type of mission is that of a private society, characterized by its development within an independent evangelical mission system, without ecclesiastical communion with any national church nor international relationship with the Anglican communion. In 1983 it became an autonomous province, thanks to the relation started with other South American dioceses through the South American Anglican Council.

The third manifestation of the Anglican presence in Latin America was from the North, through the unplanned work of the

U.S. Episcopal Church. This presence was brought in by construction companies and agricultural enterprises. The difference
between these and the immigrants of the Southern Cone is that the
American work was organized and supported by the official
Church. These missions eventually came to see themselves as
having a mission to serve the native population and, without
ignoring the expatriate Anglicans, to inspire them to mission
as well.

It should be noted, however, that even the Episcopal Church of
the United States cannot claim to have entered Latin America
because of any clear missionary vision in the beginning. It too
came into the area of the ninth province as a chaplaincy to American expatriates working with American and British firms as well
as with the Panama Canal construction and, later, its governing
authority. Had the Episcopal Church seized an absolutely unique
opportunity presented to it in the 1870's, today there would be a
large, independent, autonomous Mexican national church, in
communion with the rest of Anglicanism. Suffice it to say that the
opportunity was ignored until too late, and today's Mexican Episcopal Church is a small denomination among many, rather than a
significant national church, counting millions of members.

It was not really until 1947 that the Episcopal Church in the
United States began to see with some measure of clarity that it had
a "real" mission in Latin America—that is, a mission to the native
populations. In that year the British and Americans agreed to
transfer "jurisdiction" over Central America from the British
church to the American, and this church began planning for mission rather than chaplaincy.

Under these and similar circumstances were born the Episcopal
Church of Brazil, autonomous since 1965, and the churches of the
ninth province from Central America to El Ecuador, which are
now in the process of seeking their own autonomy. Characteristic
of this mission was the task of discovering and training native
leadership and then handing over to them the authority and administration of the Church. All the bishops and diocesan and
regional directors are Latin Americans. In spite of this vision and
strategy, the Episcopal Church on this continent, supported by
the United States, can be called "colonial."

To sum up, there are three ways the Anglican Church came to
and developed on this continent: chaplaincy, private enterprise,
and colonial expansion. I sincerely believe that none of these three
systems favor the broadest possible expansion of the Anglican

Church in Latin America, unless a restructurization is permitted that can facilitate the rapid development of an indigenous and autonomous church.

The process of this necessary indigenization and autonomy implies national identity and the division into provinces not according to the wishes of the missionaries but according to the historical, geographical, racial, and cultural cohesion and missionary strategy of the natural regions of this continent, such as Brazil, the Southern Cone, the Andean region with its five countries of the Andean Covenant (Pacto Andino), Central America with Latin Caribbean, and Mexico.

There appear to be three functional types of the Church or of its membership groups in Latin America today. The first type is the socialized church, conceived and developed within the context of a church participating in the surrounding sociopolitical problems. Its commitment leads it even to the point of involvement in political and secular revolution, putting to one side its religious mission. The second type is the conservative church, concerned with maintaining its bourgeois status by means of its traditional internal programs, behind "closed doors," without giving any incentive or reason to its clergy and laity to become concerned about the world in crisis and with no interest in taking part in the social development of the people who are living within the sound of its bells. The third type is the missionary church, fired by the Spirit and by missionary commitment, launching itself out toward all spheres of its community, not just religious, but secular as well, creating a membership that is evangelizing and promoting social action, with programs that call them to take part in the integral areas of human being in the light of the Gospel.

The Church must understand that the Latin American people are evolving rapidly and in many different ways—such as scientific/technical development—parallel to the intellectual and psychological development of the people. In this sense one of the concerns of the Church must be to move ahead parallel to the development of the people, fitting its commitment to the times.

In general, the Church has kept itself at the margin of the socioeconomic problems of this convulsed continent, at times becoming an oppressive element to its own faithful. We have churches like those in Cuba and Nicaragua that take an indirect part in the revolutionary process, while there is indifference in those countries like Guatemala and El Salvador, which are fighting for their liberation. There is repose and conformity in the more stable countries like Argentina and Venezuela, where the Church sits within its doors, waiting to evangelize those who ask to be evangelized.

Conclusion

At the Lambeth Conference of 1958 Latin America was called "the continent neglected by the Anglican Communion." Sadly, this confession is still true. I do not know if the Anglican Church has lost the missionary spirit it had in the past—or if it has no interest because its countrymen and missionaries continue returning home without much of an effective harvest, or because it is afraid to commit itself in a dangerous and challenging crusade—or perhaps (and this is an easy excuse) it has fallen into the fallacious temptation of thinking that this continent is already Christian and that it is not convenient to step on the Roman Catholic Church's private property.

It has been said, and I believe it, that the Anglican Church has been an outstanding missionary in the world. Today it has seventeen autonomous provinces, found in 165 nations, with 65 million members. Its influence is great, its prestige is enormous, its clergy prominent; it is a pioneer in a theology that is framed within biblical doctrine, guided by tradition and reflecting human reason. It has a flexible, respectful, democratic, and human discipline, without the rigidities of the convent, nor of canonical dogmatism, nor hierarchical absolutisms. It emphatically maintains the Church's global ministry, especially the ministry of the laity—the royal priesthood of the peoples of God, the pastoral "comprehension" of man, a mystical and ascetic evangelicalism, nourished in its Celtic tradition.

As a church, it is the pioneer of ecumenicism with its Lambeth Quadrilateral; its receptivity to what is happening in other churches; a respect for the historic churches; a loyalty to man as man, and to the constituted public order; a sensitivity to the social problems and sufferings of man; a zeal for evangelization and pastoral care; a concern for mission; a sacramental and historic catholicity, with evangelical reform; an awareness of interdependence in Christ's Body; an incarnate and contextualized liturgy; a loyalty to the Church without dogmatic pressures; a democratic polity in its laws and structures. Above all, it has humility, simplicity, and an adaptability, with a desire to walk with the people, and within the people, without distinction of race, class, ideology, or politics, nor even religious belief.

This is the skeleton of the Anglican Church that is offered to Latin America, and Latin America needs this kind of skeleton to flesh it out with its own flesh and culture and make it "the Latin American Catholic Church."

Its role is to be a subsidiary agency of the Church of Jesus Christ—holy, catholic, apostolic—to cooperate in the reevangelization, in the reencounter with Christ, and in the rebuilding of Christ's Body, by offering Christian reform without destroying the fundamentals that exist and by renewing the mission that the missionaries of the conquest brought. It does not come to supplant, proscribe, or persecute anybody. It does not come to curse the darkness, but to light a candle. It does not come now as a chaplaincy following along behind colonizers and immigrants; but, free from that obstacle, it comes on a missionary pilgrimage to serve the people with its total ministry.

It is true that this Church has kept itself on the edge of the Latin American reality; that its ministry has not reached out further than its altars; that its attitude has been a stumbling block to those who want to be neighbor to the wounded man, robbed and left on the roadside. In spite of this, the commitment remains, with its duty impelling it to the fulfillment of the Gospel of love that it preaches and witnesses.

It is true that the Church has committed many mistakes and sins of omission. It could have done more than it has, and it could have made less errors in what it did do. In spite of this, its sincerity and honesty redeem it through its confession and elevate it through its renewal.

In ending, I note that we are celebrating the Bicentennial of the consecration of Samuel Seabury. This event invites us to look at the past in terms of the future. The Lord said: "None of you has asked me, 'Where are you going?'" Now I ask you: My Lord, where are you going with your Church, or are you going alone? Church of mine, where are you going now, loaded with so much spiritual and institutional wealth that your Lord has given you? Where are you going decked out with so much inheritance, experience, and this wonderful mission the Lord entrusts to you?

Come to Latin America, the continent of emergency mission, and let us go together to its new conquest for the Lord. And from today on, we start to build the next centenary of the Church in America.

Notes on Contributors

THE RIGHT REVEREND COLIN BUCHANAN is the bishop of Aston in the Church of England, suffragan bishop of the diocese of Birmingham. Until July 1985 he was principal of St. John's Theological College, Nottingham, England. He is a Church of England evangelical and a specialist in liturgics and prayer book revision. He has been for many years the publisher of Grove Books, and he also has edited three volumes on Anglican liturgies from 1958 to 1985 and has coauthored *Growing Into Union* (1970).

THE RIGHT REVEREND ADRIÁN D. CÁCERES, LL.D., bishop of Ecuador since 1971, was born in Bolivia, is a citizen of Guatemala, and served as a missionary in Central America for many years. Past executive secretary of the ninth province of PECUSA, he holds degrees in theology, sociology, history, and jurisprudence. He describes his point of view as originating not from an academic theological perspective, but from the "chair" of missionary experience. His essay, "The Anglican Communion in Latin America," is the last in this collection and graphically presents the major crossroads discussed throughout this volume.

THE REVEREND CANON DOCTOR ALAN CHAN is head of the theology division of Chung Chi College, Chinese University of Hong Kong, and was a member of the Presidium of the Christian Conference of Asia (1981–1985). Educated in Hong Kong and the United States, Canon Chan has served on the central committee of the World Council of Churches and has led the Hong Kong Christian Council. He has much experience in education and youth work among the poor and has written much on pastoral care— most notably, two books: *A Pastor's Diary* and *Pastoral Care,* both in Chinese.

THE REVEREND DOCTOR KORTRIGHT DAVIS is associate professor of theology at Howard University Divinity School in Washington, D.C. Born in Antigua, he has worked extensively throughout the Caribbean and has served as the associate director of the Caribbean Conference of Churches and as vice-principal of Codrington College, Barbados. The author of *Moving into Freedom* (1977), *Mission for Caribbean Change* (1982), and *Cross and*

Crown in Barbados (1983), Doctor Davis was educated in the West Indies and England. He is currently a member of the Anglican Roman Catholic International Commission.

THE RIGHT REVEREND A. THEODORE EASTMAN, D.D., bishop coadjutor of the diocese of Maryland (U.S.A.), became diocesan bishop in January 1986. He has served in large urban parishes and has focused his energies on the mission of the Church—as executive secretary of the Overseas Mission Society and as a member of national church committees on world mission. Bishop Eastman is the author of many books, including *The Baptizing Community* (1982), *Chosen and Sent* (1977), and *Christian Responsibility in One World* (1965).

THE RIGHT REVEREND DOCTOR DAVID M. GITARI, bishop of Mt. Kenya East, was consecrated for that new and rapidly growing diocese in 1975. He is currently chairman of the National Council of Churches of Kenya and of the World Evangelical Fellow Theological Commission. Educated in Africa and England, Bishop Gitari is also the recipient of an honorary degree from Ashland College (U.S.A.). He is a former general secretary of the Pan African Fellowship of Christian Students and of the Bible Society of Kenya.

THE REVEREND CLEMENT H. JANDA, as general secretary of the Sudan Council of Churches, coordinates relations between government and international agencies concerned with refugee relief and economic development. Educated in Uganda and the United States, he previously was associate general secretary of the All Africa Conference of Churches and provincial coordinator of the Episcopal Church of the Sudan. Father Janda has written on the Nation of Islam in the United States and the Church's role in the Anyanya movement.

THE REVEREND DOCTOR JACI C. MARASCHIN, professor at the Ecumenical Institute on the Science of Religion in São Paulo, Brazil, is a theologian, composer, and musician. He holds degrees in these fields as well as in philosophy and communications from schools in Brazil, the United States, and France. Doctor Maraschin has contributed widely to theological publications and presently is compiling with Brazilian poets and musicians a hymnal, *A Native Music for a Native Church.* He is a member of the Faith and Order Commission of the World Council of Churches and of the Inter-Anglican Doctrinal and Theological Commission.

DOCTOR MARIANNE H. MICKS, professor of biblical and historical theology at Virginia Theological Seminary (U.S.A.), has devoted much of her life to the theological education of the laity. Educated in the United States, she also has worked in campus ministry and was professor of religion and dean of a college. Some of her publications include *Introduction to Theology* (1967; revised edition, 1983), *The Joy of Worship* (1982), and *Our Search for Identity* (1982). Her essay, "Mission and Prayer," begins this collection and provides an historical framework for much of the discussion.

HELEN OPPENHEIMER (LADY OPPENHEIMER) is a lay theologian of the Church of England. After reading philosophy, politics, and economics at Oxford University, she taught ethics at Cuddesdon Theological College. She has published a number of works on philosophical and moral theology; and her main works include *The Character of Christian Morality* (1965; second edition, 1974), *Incarnation and Immanence* (1973), and *The Hope of Happiness* (1983). A member of the Inter-Anglican Theological and Doctrinal Commission, she also has served on Church of England committees on marriage and divorce and on education in personal relationships.

PROFESSOR JOHN S. POBEE, currently associate director of the Program on Theological Education of the World Council of Churches, is on leave from the University of Ghana at Legon, where he is professor and head of the Department for the Study of Religions. Educated in Africa and England, he has taught in Sweden and the United States. He has published studies on St. Paul as well as several books on religion and culture in Africa, including *Toward an African Theology* (1979). He is a member of the Inter-Anglican Doctrinal Commission and the Anglican–Roman Catholic International Commission. He is vice-president of the International Association for Mission Studies and a member of the Deutsche Gesellschaft für Missionswissenschaft.

THE MOST REVEREND PAUL A. REEVES, primate and archbishop of New Zealand since 1980, was consecrated bishop of Auckland in 1979 and bishop of Waiapu in 1971. Educated in New Zealand and England, he served in parishes in Tokoroa and Okato, lectured in church history at St. John's College, Auckland, and later was director of Christian education for that same diocese. Partly Maori himself, he is a strong voice for all indigenous peoples and has worked endlessly to articulate an authentic church in New Zealand. He has served as president of the National Council of Churches in New Zealand. He recently has been appointed governor general of New Zealand.

THE REVEREND PRITAM B. SANTRAM, general secretary of the Church of North India Synod since 1980, spent the previous ten years at Bishop's College, Calcutta, first as lecturer and, later, principal. Born in 1932 in the Indian village of Ummedpur, he served in the diocese of Lucknow, where years before, his father had been a parish priest. Father Santram has written several theological articles, is editor of *The North India Churchman,* and has a particular interest in Johannine writings and the "indigenization of Christianity." He is a member of the Central Committee of the World Council of Churches and is the secretary of the Joint Council of the Church of North India, the Church of South India, and the Mar Thoma Syrian Church.

THE MOST REVEREND EDWARD W. SCOTT, primate of the Anglican Church of Canada since 1971, was consecrated bishop of the diocese of Kootenay in British Columbia in 1966. He also served as a parish priest in British Columbia and Manitoba and has had administrative posts in social service and Indian work. As a former moderator of the central committee of the World Council of Churches, Archbishop Scott has traveled to Anglican provinces throughout the world. His dedication to the value of the individual, expressed throughout his ministry, was given further recognition in 1978, when he was admitted by the Queen to the Companion of the Order of Canada, the country's outstanding humanitarian award.

THE REVEREND DOCTOR FRANK E. SUGENO is Duncalf Professor of the History and Mission of the Church at the Episcopal Theological Seminary of the Southwest (U.S.A.). He is currently chairman of the Seminary Consultation on Mission and secretary of the Church Historical Society.

THE REVEREND DOCTOR PHILIP TURNER is professor of Christian ethics at the General Theological Seminary (U.S.A.). He is a member of the Anglican/Roman Catholic Consultation (U.S.A.). From 1961 to 1971 he taught at Bishop Tucker College and at Makerere University in Uganda. He is the author of *Sex, Money and Power: An Essay in Christian Social Ethics* (1985).